The late Dr John Morris was Senior Lecturer in Ancient History at University College, London. He founded the journal *Past and Present* and among his books was the highly successful *The Age of Arthur*. The text of the present book was completed before Dr Morris's death and final revisions were made by Sarah Macready of the Institute of Archaeology, London University.

LONDINIUM

LONDON *in the* ROMAN EMPIRE

JOHN MORRIS

REVISED BY
SARAH MACREADY

PHOENIX

A PHOENIX PAPERBACK

First published in Great Britain
by Weidenfeld & Nicolson in 1982

This paperback edition published in 2005
by Phoenix Press, a division of Orion Books Ltd,
Orion House, 5 Upper St Martin's Lane,
London WC2H 9EA

A CIP catalogue record for this book
is available from the British Library.

ISBN 1 89880 162 2

Printed and bound in Great Britain by
Clays Ltd, St Ives plc

www.orionbooks.co.uk

Contents

Illustrations

Maps

Preface

Dr Morris began work on *London in the Roman Empire* in 1967, and had apparently completed the first draft by the early 1970s. He was at the time much taken up with other projects, including *The Age of Arthur* and his work on the Domesday Book, and was unable then to produce a final draft for publication. He was still rewriting and revising certain sections of the book as late as 1975, but did no further work on it before his death in June 1977. The manuscript was then virtually complete, apart from the annotation, which he had evidently intended to supply at a later date, and the maps, which were in rough sketch form. In 1977 he committed it to the care of Anthony Holbourn, a student of his, who began the task of tidying up the text and supplying the necessary documentation, but whose teaching commitments forced him to relinquish the work in 1978. I was then asked by Professor Robert Browning, Dr Morris' literary executor, to complete the task.

The text presented below is very much as Dr Morris left it, save for minor editorial corrections, and a few alterations and deletions made necessary by recently published evidence. These are mainly of an archaeological nature and are explained in the notes. The maps were based on Dr Morris' sketches, supplemented by more recent maps when available.

I am grateful to many people for their advice on points of detail, and in particular to Professor Robert Browning, Professor Sheppard Frere, Mark Hassall, Peter Marsden of the Department of Urban Archaeology (Museum of London), who supplied much help in the preparation of the maps, Mr Ralph Merrifield and Professor John Wilkes.

Sarah Macready
Institute of Archaeology
University of London

Foreword

John Morris was a man of strikingly varied talents. He was first of all a historian (he read history before the Second World War at Oxford, where his tutor was the late Sir Goronwy Edwards). After serving in the army during the war, he held a Leon Fellowship at the University of London, was for one year a Junior Fellow at the Warburg Institute, and from 1949 until his death at a sadly early age in 1977 he was Lecturer and Senior Lecturer at University College London. His own field of interest was wide. His two main areas of concentration were the study of the institutions of the Roman empire and of the people who manned them, and the investigation of what happened in the British Isles in the so-called Dark Ages, between the breakdown of direct rule by Rome and the first emergence in outline of the future nations of England, Scotland and Wales. His *Age of Arthur* offered a detailed examination and many new interpretations of a crucial period in the history of this country. The volumes of Arthurian Period Sources which he planned and in part prepared were intended to provide in readily accessible form the source material upon which *The Age of Arthur* was based, together with wide-ranging and critical discussions of the problems which they raised. Some of these volumes have been published since his death. Others are in course of preparation by younger scholars who have volunteered to continue his work.

His knowledge of the sources, archaeological as well as documentary, was astounding, his interpretation of them often original but always scrupulous. He never believed that he could reconstruct what actually happened. But he was confident that scholarship and imagination, backed by a lively understanding of how men and women, pushing and pulling in different directions in pursuit of their interests, create institutions and make them work, could bring us ever closer to a faithful account of the past. Good history books, he believed, were soon replaced by better ones; bad ones were reprinted unchanged. For him history was not an intellectual luxury for an élite, but an essential part of our insight into the world in which we live, and in which, with greater or less assurance, we make decisions about our future.

As a teacher John Morris transmitted to his students his respect for evidence and for valid argument, his understanding of the place of historical imagination, and his sense of history as being not only about the past but about the present and the future as well. His classes and tutorials always stretched and enriched the minds of his students, many of whom have now become teachers in their turn. And they were always liable to be enlivened by hilarious episodes, as when in trying to light his pipe while talking he contrived to set fire to his beard.

Unlike many scholars, he was an able and successful organiser. He could formulate a project clearly and realistically, distinguishing between what was important and what was merely interesting. He could enlist by personal persuasion – and he could be extraordinarily persuasive – the cooperation alike of world-famed scholars and of eager amateurs. He could present a case to a grant-giving body with the crispness and force of a minister defending his department in Cabinet. Once a project was under way he could keep it moving, getting the best out of others, giving confidence to the faint-hearted and gently restraining the impetuous, training the cadres he needed, sorting out personal difficulties, taking on tasks which would have daunted any of his colleagues, and all the time keeping a wary eye on budgets and deadlines.

Three enterprises in particular owe their existence largely to him. The first is the *Prosopography of the Later Roman Empire*, of which two volumes have already appeared (Cambridge, 1970, 1980). It was launched jointly by the late A.H.M. Jones and John Morris. The detailed plan was largely Morris's, as was the unremitting drive which brought in funds and collaborators. It was John Morris who conducted the delicate negotiations with the Deutsche Akademie der Wissenschaften, and John who eventually drove to East Berlin in his dilapidated old van and returned triumphantly with a vast card-index which had been begun by Theodor Mommsen.

The second is the journal *Past and Present*, which he founded in 1952 with a few colleagues, and of which the ninetieth number appeared in February 1981. It was launched in the darkest days of the Cold War, when the world-wide academic community seemed doomed to be split by ideological barriers into hostile camps, unable and unwilling to speak or to listen to one another. John Morris believed passionately that maintaining communication was the first duty of scholars and teachers on both sides of the ideological divide. His time and energy were given unstintingly to raising funds, enlisting contributors, getting together a distinguished and representative editorial board, and inaugurating a cooperative style of work which has made *Past and Present* one of the most influential historical journals of the later twentieth century. He was editor from 1952 until 1960 and chairman of the editorial board until 1972.

The third historical enterprise which he initiated was the new edition of the *Domesday Book*. This unique source for early local history was surrounded by mystique and virtually inaccessible to all but specialists. The difficult Latin text had been published twice – in 1783–1816 and in 1861–1863 (photographic facsimile) – and had long been out of print. There was no complete English translation. What John planned was an edition of the Latin with facing English translation and copious notes on matters of historical and topographical interest, published in separate volumes for each county and at a price which would make it accessible to local historians and antiquarians, school libraries, and the general reader. His single-handed and untiring efforts resulted in adequate funding – through the foresight and generosity of the Leverhulme Trust – suitable housing – thanks to University College London – and the recruiting and training of a devoted team of unpaid translators and contributors. As editor-in-chief, he gave unsparingly of his unique knowledge and experience, yet was never too busy to give his undivided attention to every problem, however trivial it might appear to be. By the time of his death about half of the planned volumes had appeared. By 1983 the project should be completed. The task will never be undertaken again. So long as there are men and women interested in the early history of England, it is to John Morris' work that they will turn.

Lastly, John Morris was a politician and a man of the left. An unsuccessful Labour candidate in the 1935 General Election, he was for a time secretary to George Strauss, MP. A founder-member of the Committee of 100 in the early days of the anti-nuclear campaign, an active participant in local political and trade union life, and the sworn enemy of bureaucracy and Bumbledom, his party affiliations changed in the course of his life. His socialist convictions did not, nor did his confidence in the ability of ordinary men and women to discern their interests and to organise and fight for them. He saw his historical work as in a sense a contribution to politics. For him history and politics were part of a seamless web.

His book on London in the Roman empire was largely written in the early seventies and put aside some years before his death as work on the *Domesday Book* became more and more demanding. In it his two main fields of interest – how the Roman empire worked and what happened in Britain when it stopped working – are brought together. That it has been possible to turn his manuscript into the present book is due to the scholarship and devotion of two young scholars, Anthony Holbourn and Sarah Macready. As John Morris' long-standing friend and literary executor I take this opportunity of expressing my warm gratitude to both, as well as to the editorial staff of Weidenfeld and Nicolson and to all who have in one way or another helped this book to appear.

Robert Browning
Birkbeck College
University of London

Introduction

AN ACCOUNT OF early London must deal chiefly with Roman London, for before Rome there was no London, while after Rome very little is known of London for many centuries. What remained was a survival from the past, unintelligible unless the past is known.

Several difficulties attend the description of these early centuries that do not trouble the understanding of later periods. The context is wholly unfamiliar except to specialists. Thanks to the particular conventions that limit the teaching of history in present-day England, most people have to begin in the middle, or later. The Tudors and the Stuarts and their successors are intelligible not only because children study them at school, but because millions learn something of them from television, novels or the stage. The Middle Ages, commonly meaning the period from the Normans to the Tudors, are quaint and remote, though still comprehensible. But earlier centuries are not only little known; simple tales told to children have filled men's minds with weird misconceptions. Most people are aware that the Tudors were Christian, Catholic or Protestant; and most would sense that something was amiss if a producer dressed Henry VII in a periwig, or George III in doublet and ruffs. But misapprehensions far more absurd, on matters less superficial, altogether confound the understanding of the Romans and the early English; and there are not a few who confound Alfred with Arthur, or are not quite sure whether the Romans came before or after the Saxons.

If early London is to be understood, much must be explained that has nothing directly to do with London, and which histories of later times may fairly take for granted. It involves accounts of many persons and places with strange names, and the exposition of circumstances that modern assumptions frequently misread. But the life of a city is without meaning unless the society in which it was placed is known; and since society changes, considerable narrative must describe these changes.

Any discussion of Roman civilization, and of the centuries immediately thereafter, must lean with equal weight upon the two main branches of historical evidence, archaeological and documentary. Their evidence commonly complements each other, but the limitations and possibilities of both must be observed and made clear; for there are many aspects of human society that material evidence cannot venture to explain, and many that the evidence of past writers wholly ignores. The archaeological evidence has recently been assembled and discussed by Ralph Merrifield, and without his *Roman City of London* no account of the city's life could be profitably undertaken. The city's structures are there meticulously catalogued and explained. Other publications list the burials, the inscriptions and the small finds, but no comparable study of Greater London is available, and the relevant information must be gathered from a multitude of scattered publications.

Texts and excavated evidence complement each other. But few texts have anything of moment to report about the citizens of Roman London. Their names are unknown, their actions have not been recorded. There is no body of evidence that in any way compares with the mass of documentation available for later times. But the lack of direct evidence is to a considerable extent compensated by indirect evidence. Roman towns, like modern towns in England, were very much alike in many important essentials, for they shared the institutions, the tastes, the conventions and the interests of a common civilization. But, in Roman or modern times, each city has its own individuality, and there are many kinds of city which differ in important respects according to their size, their location, their economic and political function, their past history and the accidents of their tradition. The archaeological evidence is sufficient to indicate what kind of Roman city was laid out at London, and the manner of its growth. Understanding of what went on in its public buildings, its streets and private houses comes not from their physical traces alone, but from the rich documentary and other evidence for the use of comparable buildings in comparable towns in comparable circumstances.

The connections between fragments of buildings and the life lived in them requires much inference. As with most useful historical study, the historian cannot often fairly assert that this or that happened for such and such reasons; all that he can properly attempt is to collect, assess and interpret evidence, as a juryman must do. Arguing from the evidence, he can only suggest that this or that conclusion is probable or improbable, in varying degrees from the near certain to the wildly improbable. But he must at all times explain his reasoning, so that the reader may judge, forming his own conclusions upon the evidence and the argument that rests upon it.

The need to enquire closely into the life of an individual city also brings into focus many questions that have not been much discussed in recent years. Sometimes the linking of the evidence to a detail of city life leads to conclusions that conflict with pleasing generalities, familiar in works that draw upon texts alone, or upon archaeology alone, or which assume too easily the operation of modern conditions in antiquity. The resolution of these difficulties requires the patient sympathy of the reader, who is often invited to explore paths that seem to lead far from the streets of London. The intention is to explain the world in which London was set; and if the reader wearies of that world, he must skim quickly back to familiar local detail. The chief aim is to set the static evidence of buildings and objects in motion, to indicate the hopes and fears of London's first citizens, and point to the changing face of the city in successive generations. If something of the change and movement be understood, this book has served its purpose.

John Morris
30 September 1971

Part One

The Making of London

Chapter 1

Before the Romans

LONDON IS A Roman town. It was deliberately founded by the Roman government for a specific purpose, on a site chosen by the government for that purpose. The choice was well made; for Rome founded many new towns, but from Roman times onward, London excelled among them.

London was from the beginning unique, a special town unlike others. The towns of Roman Britain were new in a double sense. They were built in open country, where no town or village had been before; and towns as such were new to Britain. But they all served a local purpose. They were the regional capitals of particular peoples; or they grew from forts and fortresses; or they were colonies of conquerors planted as garrisons among aliens to deter rebellion. But London was not placed among the fields of any previous people. It was built in the midst of a dark untamed forest, in a region hitherto uninhabited, save by riverside farmers, scattered thinly along the banks of the Thames and the Lea; and it was neither a fortress nor a garrison town.

The business of London was the government and administration of newly conquered lands. The site was chosen because it was the most apt for the needs of government, the most convenient centre for the natural communications of Britain; and for that reason it also became the main centre of commerce. But from the beginning its prime purpose was political rather than commercial; and so it has ever after remained. Trade followed the legions, but the legions did not fight for traders. Rome was governed in the interest of a proud aristocracy that cared little for the profit of the merchant and the manufacturer; but the purpose of government was to rule without challenge, and strong authority made commerce secure. The concerns of government required roads to service distant armies, treasury officials and administrators, and ensured that men might travel them without risk. The city was therefore built at the lowest practicable crossing point of the Thames, where the routes that link the several parts of Britain with Europe converge.

Throughout its history, London has lived as it began. Whenever the greater part of Britain has obeyed one government, then London has prospered. Whenever men have moved freely and frequently in Britain,

London has served them, and they have enriched the city. But when Britain has been divided among regional states and local armies, careless of the travelling stranger, and when men have lived their lives upon their self-sufficient acres, then London has waned. Yet even in the most dangerous ages, when floods or cut-throats have turned travel into a perilous adventure, London has remained the warehouse of whatever trade persisted, and the stronghold that any would-be sovereign must secure. Other towns thrive or fail as the fortunes of their own regions determine, but the history of London is not the history of one town, or of one region: it is the history of the government and the economy of Britain.

The origin of London explains its later history. Other Roman towns grew great in later ages: Paris, Cologne, Vienna, Belgrade and many more. London has grown larger than any of them, and has dominated the country it ruled more completely and more continuously. Of all the new towns founded by Romans, it has proved most successful in the test of time. It did not grow naturally from small beginnings. It was placed there by deliberate decision. Its long later history justifies the men who took that decision; but, like all decisions, theirs solved problems that earlier history had posed, and drew upon their own past experience. The problems and the experience emerged from the past of Britain and of Rome. The previous history of the British explains the problem that the Roman government faced; the previous history of Rome determined the solution, and explains why the founders of London built that city in that place at that time. The origins of London cannot be understood without looking back into the past of the Britain that the Romans conquered, and of the Roman Empire that conquered Britain.

Long before the Romans came, these islands and their inhabitants were known by the general name of British. They were not yet a coherent single people. They were descended from immigrants who had come at different times from different places; some had absorbed their predecessors, or been absorbed by them, others had remained distinct. Most of them left no written record. Their witness is archaeology, and archaeology chiefly observes structures that have left a mark upon the ground, or tools and ornaments made of durable materials. The evidence is necessarily imperfect, for early men made much from wood, leather, textiles and other perishable stuffs which only occasionally survive; and many men lived in lightly built homes, that left no recognizable mark.

Archaeology can only recover a part of the culture of early peoples, but it is bound to concentrate upon what it can recognize. It has therefore long been customary to name early cultures from their tools, calling them stone, bronze and iron ages, or stages, since they overlap in time and place. For many thousands of years the forests and valleys of Britain, as of Europe, supported a thin population of Old and Middle Stone Age hunters, who knew nothing of agriculture, and tamed no herds; a few of their crude tools were abandoned in the London region, as elsewhere in Britain, and many more were swept down by the melting Ice Ages.

Mankind's great leap forward was the New Stone Age. Men learnt to plant seeds deliberately to raise a crop, and to keep their meat alive in captivity until they needed to eat it. Agriculture and domestic cattle meant new tools, settled homes, and the ownership and control of land; for farmers needed to live by their crops until they ripened, and to secure the grazing of their herds. The new economy begot a new technology. Domestic sheep and cattle were bred from the agile scraggy animals of the wild; craftsmen evolved shaped axes and adzes, knives and sickles; the skills of the potter, the weaver, and other specialists evolved. The centres of the new society were the great alluvial rivers of the Near East, India and China, and in Central America. There, settled life supported cities of well-built houses, protected by stout walls; but the new techniques took several thousand years to reach the Atlantic coasts, and the harsher northern climate did not make farmers and stockmen rich enough to build cities.

The axes and pottery of the New Stone Age reached Britain some centuries before 3000 BC. The use that men made of them was determined by geology and geography. The shape of Britain has governed all its later history and has determined the part that the London region should play therein. Though the new tools reached most parts of Britain, extensive arable farming was confined to the lowlands, most of it in the south and east. The lowlands are approximately bordered by the Trent, the Dee and the Severn, and by the Exe and the Somersetshire Parrett, with a few further extensions, the largest of them the Vale of Glamorgan. Beyond lie the highlands: the moorlands of Devon and Cornwall, the mountains of Wales, and of the Pennines and the north, three separate regions (see Map 1).

These regions sharply contrast, and they have moulded the history of the people who live in them. The highlands are harder to subdue, their valleys are tenacious of conservative custom. But within the lowlands communications are easier. Men may move in all directions without encountering deep rivers or difficult hills, so that in all ages conquerors may quickly overrun the whole of the lowlands, and readily pursuade its

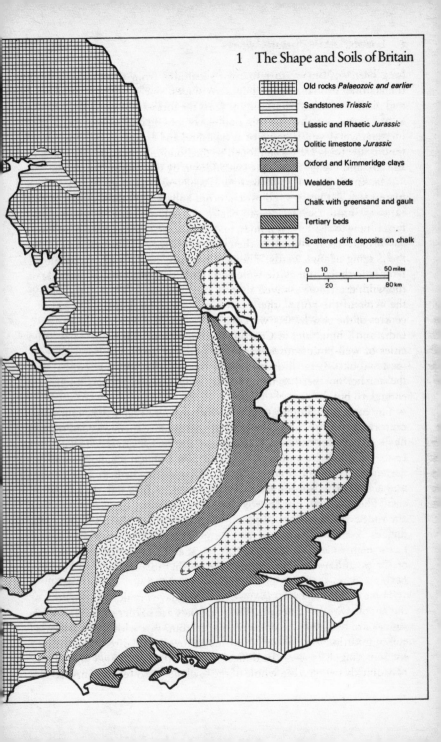

1 The Shape and Soils of Britain

Old rocks *Palaeozoic and earlier*	
Sandstones *Triassic*	
Liassic and Rhaetic *Jurassic*	
Oolitic limestone *Jurassic*	
Oxford and Kimmeridge clays	
Wealden beds	
Chalk with greensand and gault	
Tertiary beds	
Scattered drift deposits on chalk	

0   10   50 miles
0   20   80 km

people to absorb the conqueror's culture. It took the Roman armies a few months to conquer lowland Britain, but it was thirty years before they secured the highlands, and they never subdued the northern mountains beyond the Forth and Clyde. They secured their conquests by fortresses that controlled the estuaries of the Dee and Severn, whose outfall divides the three highland zones from each other. Once the three were separated, each might prolong its own resistance, but they could not unite to expel the invader and recover the lowlands. Geography forced the Roman commanders to hold these gaps, and imposed the same need upon later conquerors; the decisive battles that secured the English mastery of Britain were fought at Chester and near Gloucester, and the Norman conquerors established marcher earldoms at Gloucester and Chester. Later medieval kings discovered that these key fortresses were not wisely entrusted to the doubtful loyalty of subjects, so that even today long tradition confines the titles of Earl of Chester and Duke of Gloucester to the royal family.

The whole lowland zone constitutes a single political unit, easily conquered and controlled by one government, whose securest centre, once such a government was achieved, has always been London. But the soils and fertility of the lowland zone are not uniform. It is divided by a narrow belt of limestone that snakes northward from the neighbourhood of Lyme Regis, by way of the Cotswolds and the north-eastern midlands, to meet the sea again near Scarborough. Beyond it, heavier loamy soils are in nature more thickly forested, but to the south and east is the open chalk. North of the Thames, much of it is overlaid by clay deposits, but from the broad expanse of the Wiltshire chalk, long fingers stretch eastward. The Chilterns and the Royston Gap extend to East Anglia, and along them runs the ancient track called the Icknield Way. South of the Thames, the North Downs reach to the cliffs of Kent, narrowing to the width of a single roadway on the ridge called the Hog's Back. They, and the South Downs that run to Beachy Head, enclose the empty, unfriendly Wealden clays. But between the North Downs and the Chilterns, the Thames valley deposited thick and heavy clays that defied early agriculture, except where gravel patches and the alluvial soil of river banks offered easier tillage.

From the New Stone Age onward, farmers prospered on the chalk of the fertile lowlands. There too Roman mansions, farms and market towns were to be richer and more numerous. But the heavy soils of London deterred the early farmers. They have left abundant traces of their homes upon the North Downs, eastward and westward from

Croydon, and on the banks of the Wandle and of the Thames upstream from Wandsworth. They found fields in plenty by the lower courses of the Brent, and of the many little rivers that join the Thames higher up, and by the Lea, from Enfield northward. But the site of the city itself, and the country around it for six or eight or more miles in all directions, remained a forbidding forest, empty of men. At various times, men in all ages walked to the river bank by woodland tracks and, in crossing the river, lost weapons and other valuables. The London museums preserve a great quantity of objects of all periods, recovered from the river itself; one of the best known is the Iron-Age bronze shield found at Battersea (Plate 1). But almost all of them are memorials of passing warriors, of hunters and of fugitives who suffered mishap when they sought to cross the river;[1] downstream from Wandsworth, few are relics of settled homes by the river bank.[2]

Britain lay beyond the furthest extremity of the European mainland, far from the centres of civilization; and the site of London was a waste-land, on the edge of one of the poorer regions of Britain. The inventions of civilization took many centuries to reach these outlying borders. Before the new stone tools reached Britain, the inventive genius of the Near East had already discovered the use of metal, smelting copper and learning to alloy it with tin to make bronze. The new technology served craftsmen, but it also transformed warfare, trade and government. Workable deposits of tin and copper are found only in limited districts, and the near-eastern governments cornered the supply of metal, founding upon its control powerful centralized despotic empires. In time, travel-ling smiths brought metal tools to northern Europe and to Britain, and warriors used metal weapons. The principal monuments of the age of bronze are the round barrows that mark the tombs of innumerable local chiefs. A few are known in the London region, and some of the new bronze tools and pottery; but nearly all are found in the same area as the homes of early farmers, on the Downs, and by the banks of the Thames and its tributaries above Wandsworth. Half a dozen finds north and north-west of the future city show that a few adventurous smiths ven-tured into the woodland, where fuel was plentiful.

Greater changes followed the discovery of iron, that came into com-mon use in the centuries about 1000 BC. The new metal was plentiful, and could not be monopolized by any government. Its technique was perfected in the same centuries in which new peoples migrated, who spoke related languages called 'Indo-European'. Indians and Persians, Italians, Greeks and others moved into the countries that still bear their names. In the central and western Mediterranean, the newcomers learnt the science and technology of their Bronze Age predecessors, but escaped the need for despotic empire. In Greece and Italy, where iron tools and weapons were easily available, men were able to develop sophisticated cities, whose inhabitants governed themselves without the sovereignty of king or priest. The Atlantic lands were still too poor to support such cities, but men lived more richly than before, and in greater numbers.

Farmers with iron tools began to reach Britain in the seventh century BC, according to the dates now commonly inferred. They were the first who can with assurance be termed British. Their ornament links them with the Celtic-speaking peoples who then populated most of northern, central and Atlantic Europe. They shared their language; the variant spoken in Britain is termed Brittonic, or British, and is the ancestor of modern Welsh. Between about 500 BC and 100 BC they cultivated the greater part of Britain. In most of the highlands, and parts of the west, they lived as conquerors in heavily defended forts and homesteads; but in much of the fertile lowland of the south-east they were peaceful arable farmers, who lived in undefended homes, without weapons, with no sign of social difference, with no larger buildings or finer ornaments to suggest rulers or nobles richer or mightier than their fellows.

These farms were mainly limited to the chalk soils and subsoils, and to the river valleys. In the greater London region they are numerous and prosperous along the Chilterns by the Icknield Way, and extend down the Thames from Marlow to Chiswick, and about the middle reaches of the Lea. Men continued to live on the North Downs, but there their farms were fewer and somewhat poorer. A little Iron-Age metalwork and a few potsherds have been found in the City and in Southwark, but the finds are not enough to suggest that men lived and farmed there before the coming of the Romans. The lands between the Downs and the Middle Thames, between the Chilterns and the Lea, were still largely unpeopled. Many men lived upon the edges of the large triangle they enclose, but few within the triangle.

Shortly before 100 BC south-eastern Britain was invaded by colonists from the people of north-eastern Gaul, who were collectively known as the Belgae. Caesar and other Roman writers describe their military efficiency and the authority of their kings and nobles, whose power reduced their subjects to servility. Like many aristocratic societies, they excelled in chariot warfare, and constructed great fortresses defended by huge ditches, up to a hundred foot in width, thirty foot deep, to ward off the chariots and sling-stones of their rivals. They seized upon the nearer and richer lands, and first established themselves in Kent and Buckinghamshire; but after a generation or so the most powerful nation among them, the Catuvellauni, built a vast royal fortress at Wheathampstead on the Lea, five miles from St Albans, in the midst of the empty lands.[3]

The Belgic invaders transformed the simple economy of the southeast, and prepared it to accept Roman civilization. The Belgae of Gaul had learnt from the Romans to mint money. They brought their coins with them, and soon minted more in Britain. At first, their only coins were of gold, suitable for the great man's purchase of herds or slaves, but useless for the poor man's loaf of bread, winter cloak or cooking pot. But shortly before the time of Caesar small change was minted. Other inventions show why. Belgic craftsmen evolved the potter's wheel. Thenceforth, the potter became a specialist, able to turn out far more vessels than his family or homestead needed for their own use; he was a manufacturer, who needed to sell his wares over a wider area. The indestructible products of the potter survive, and the change in his technique argues a changing society, where wheelwrights, metalsmiths and others also needed to sell their products to individual customers. Gold coins were not versatile enough, and were supplemented by the issue of bronze coins.[4]

The spread of Belgic power is traced through the discovery of their coins and pots. Neither are easy to date, for the coins remained in circulation for centuries, and the conservative tradition of the potters maintained their styles for at least a generation after the Roman conquest, into the later first century AD. In the fortresses and large cemeteries, where both coins and pottery are found in quantity, it is possible to trace something of their growth and change; but in the open country it is usually only possible to observe the presence or absence of Belgic occupation. In time, the influence of the Belgae expanded over most of the fertile lowlands; but it never made a significant impact on the London region. The Catuvellauni of Wheathampstead evidently subdued the farmlands of the Chilterns, for there their pottery is plentiful; but they did not penetrate the London clays, and the farmsteads of the Kentish Belgae reached no nearer than Orpington and Croydon. Belgic coins and pots are plentiful down the Thames and its tributaries from Marlow to Chiswick, but rare upon the North Downs (Map 2).

The coming of the Belgae did not populate the London region, but it opened it to the movement of men. The conquerors used not only chariots, but heavy goods waggons, riding horses, and pedlars' pack trains of horses, mules or donkeys. Vehicles and animals needed paths and roads. Men travelled on occasions from Hertfordshire to Kent, from the middle Thames to Colchester, along recognized cleared roads. Caesar found them when he came, for he reported that north of the Thames the *iter*, or route, of his army followed a *via*, a road.[5] The contrast of words means that he found a roadway of some sort, cleared and used before he came; and he also sought and found a ford over the Thames, known to the natives. The layout of the later Roman roads may hint at where some of these roads were, for the first Roman roads, shown on Map 5 (p. 83), ignore the city, and were therefore in use before the city was founded. The Watling Street, from Kent to the Catuvellaunian territory, crossed the Thames in the neighbourhood of the House of Commons, and from Hyde Park Corner another road led by the line of Long Acre and Old Street to Old Ford on the Lea towards Colchester. Early coins found in the City, Southwark and Westminster, and more in the woods to the north-west, may have been lost by men who used these roads (Map 2, p. 32), although their owners may have been travellers or fighting men of a later date.

When Caesar led the first Roman invaders to Britain in 55 BC, they came to an island whose peoples shared a common language and a common religion, but who were otherwise deeply divided in their economy, their customs and their political allegiance. There is as yet no positive evidence of settled arable agriculture on any significant scale in the highland zones before the Roman conquest. Caesar and other Roman writers remarked that the interior peoples subsisted on animal products, meat and milk, horn and leather, knowing nothing of agriculture, and practised archaic customs of marriage and inheritance. Theirs was predominantly a cattle economy, where lords and kings fought each other for the mastery of greater numbers of beasts and men. In contrast, much of the lowlands had long been cultivated by arable farmers; but in the richest regions of the south-east, the isolated, self-sufficient, peaceful farmers were the resentful subjects of recent conquerors. The powerful rulers of the Belgae had begun to develop manufacture, commerce, and transport, but as yet had scarcely extended them beyond their fortified areas. The kings used their roads and chariots to fight each other, and the weaker sought help where they could. Many of the conquered were ready to welcome a deliverer, and Caesar's armies found friends as well as enemies. The immediate neighbourhood of the future city had become a crossing place for armies and pedlars, but there was as yet little traffic, and no semblance of political unity. There was no Britain to be governed, no need for a centre of government or trade, no need for London.

Chapter 2

Rome before Caesar

CAESAR INVADED AND withdrew, and nearly a hundred years passed before Roman armies came again, and stayed. But Caesar made Gaul Roman, and thereby made south-eastern Britain familiar with Roman ways. Caesar came for Roman reasons. The political crisis that brought his legions to the Atlantic swelled out of a long history. The empire of Rome combined under a single government the ancient civilizations of the eastern and western Mediterranean seaboard; conquest imposed them upon western and central Europe, to the Rhine and Danube, and upon the parts of Britain that are now called England and Wales. To the western peoples, the empire and its institutions came ready made at the beginning of their recorded history; but in its Mediterranean homeland, the empire was the last stage in a continuing Greek and Roman civilization. The rulers of Rome adapted and interpreted the Greek past, and transplanted its experience to the west.

Roman Britain was shaped at least as much by the Roman and Greek past as by its own native tradition, London much more so. Roman statesmen had studied their own history and literature at school, and so had the men who governed Britain and officered its legions. The decisions that they took in adult years were guided by what they believed about the past, whose edited record highlighted examples of proper and improper political conduct. Roman educational theory began with the Greek language, 'whence all our culture stems', and divided history into three main periods, ancient, middle, and modern. Ancient history meant the legends of early Rome and conflicts of Greek city states to the fourth century BC; the middle period was termed 'the time of the Kings', or 'of the Dynasts'; the three centuries between 330 BC and 31 BC, when Augustus founded the stable empire, the beginning of 'modern times'.

The men who founded London and moulded Roman Britain had been taught to respect standard historical judgements. The self-evident superiority of Greek and Roman civilization was rooted in freedom, in contrast with the autocratic empires of ancient Mesopotamia and the Nile. But freedom demanded obedience to the law and constituted order, and included freedom to own property, including slaves and land, the source of all wealth. After the fancies of mythology and legend, documented history began with the history of Athens. It opened about 600 BC, with the portrait of the wisdom of Solon, who 'held his stout shield as a barrier between the opposing parties' of rich and poor, conservative and revolutionary, the moderate who withstood extremists of the right and of the left.[1] Solon appeared as the father-figure and herald of Athenian democracy, which reached maturity a century later.

Like almost all Greek and Roman cities, Athens had three main political institutions: an assembly of adult male citizens, a council, and magistrates, who held office for a year. But in Athens, power lay with the Assembly, for it met weekly, and was therefore able to decide day-to-day business. The Council met daily, changing its composition monthly and its chairman daily. With two exceptions, magistrates and all officials were not elected, but were chosen by lot. To Athenians, democracy meant rule by the people, not rule by persons chosen or appointed by the people; and election, regarded as an undemocratic means of transferring power to the ambitious, the greedy, and the privileged, was confined to two offices that demanded specialized expertise, army command, and public finance. The law was deeply respected, the courts kept busy; but its operation was equally open. There were no judges. Juries of five hundred or more decided cases by majority vote; when their verdict was 'guilty', prosecutor and defendant each proposed a penalty, and the jury's vote decided which seemed more responsible.

The brief splendour of direct democracy inspired Athenians whose art and literature later men have admired, preserved, and studied. But admiration and study did not prompt men to imitate their political system. Democratic Athens was defeated in a long and bitter war by Sparta, the champion of oligarchs, in 403 BC. Greece was torn apart by wars between cities, and, though within Athens there was less political violence than in almost any later state, other cities suffered atrocious massacres by the vengeance of oligarchs and of democrats upon their opponents, as each came to power. Educated Greeks and Romans in later centuries read the critics of Athens, who pronounced that the mob was fickle and easily swayed by rhetoric, prone to foolish and hasty decisions, and that the terrible struggles between cities and between classes could only be avoided when political power was vested in men of education and wealth.

After 403, statesmen increasingly urged the Greek cities and classes to unite to seize the wealth of Persia and the Middle East. Persuasion failed, but unity was enforced when the Macedonians of the north mastered all Greece. Their King, Alexander the Great, led their combined armies to the speedy conquest of Persia, Egypt, and western India, but he died without a living heir at the age of thirty-three, in 323 BC, and his principal generals turned their commands into lasting kingdoms. He and his successors planted many dozens of new towns in conquered lands, each Greek in speech and culture, alien to the natives who knew no Greek. Like Alexander, the kings were kings of barbarians, 'leaders' of the citizens, and in the older societies of the east, where kings had always been divine, they too became gods.

Later Romans learnt from Alexander that barbarian conquests are best held by planting civilian cities rather than military garrisons in their midst. The example matched and enlarged their own experience. Rome mastered the Mediterranean a little over a century after Alexander's death. Previously, three rival civilizations had fought for supremacy in the western Mediterranean: the Carthaginians, descendants of colonists from Phoenicia, controlled its southern and western coasts, from the Ebro, through Sicily, to the borders of Libya; Greek colonies overawed the rest of Sicily and southern Italy, and the northern coast from Nice to the Ebro; but between them the Etruscans held Italy north of the Tiber. On the south bank, the city of Rome commanded the lowest practicable crossing place of the Tiber, and its position forced Rome's emergence as the bastion of the Greek south against the Etruscans. In self-defence, Rome compelled its neighbours to become obedient allies, supplying contingents to fight with the Roman army. Necessity taught the Romans to treat conquered cities more gently than the Greeks had done. Greek convention imposed heavy tribute and a garrison upon vanquished enemies, or else destroyed their city and slaughtered the population, or sold them into slavery. But Rome needed military support rather than tribute, and early learnt that the first requirement of allied contingents in battle is that they should share the interests of the allied power, and thus be less eager to desert to the enemy. The nearer allies, in the plain of Latium, received Latin citizenship, in practice citizenship without the vote, and right through the later history of the empire, long after all the inhabitants of Latium, and of all Italy, had received Roman citizenship, the term Latin citizen was reserved for second-class citizens, who were none the less citizens.

The threefold struggle in the northern Mediterranean was resolved by foreign invasion. Celtic-speaking peoples in central and western Europe expanded: westward into northern Spain, sending fresh immigrants into Britain, and crossing the Alps into Italy, where they overran Etruria and captured the city of Rome (but not its citadel, the Capitol) in 400 BC.

The Po Valley, north of the Apennines (modern Lombardy), remained permanently Gallic, known to later Romans as Gallia Cisalpina, Gaul this side of the Alps; but Roman armies cleared Etruria, south of the Apennines, and obliged its cities to become Roman allies. In the time of Alexander and of his immediate successors, Rome completed the conquest of Italy. This conquest was tested in a decisive struggle with the Carthaginians of the north African and Spanish coasts, whose climax was a Roman victory, after a long war that lasted from 218 to 203 BC.

The official history of Rome was the work of Livy, contemporary of Caesar and Augustus. He analysed and preached the causes of Roman success, stressing the interconnection between internal discords and foreign wars. From the earliest times power lay with the aristocracy and was exercised through the Council, termed the Senate. Democrats repeatedly sought power for the plebs, authority for the assemblies, but never prevailed for any length of time. Again and again, when they seemed to threaten the government, the danger from a foreign power rallied all classes to the fatherland; and in each allied state, the rulers of Rome backed aristocrats or kings, so long as they did not drive their subjects to revolt, or permit rebellion. The long war with Carthage proved the efficacy of these policies. Though the enemy occupied much of Italy for sixteen years, offering liberation from the yoke of Rome, only a small minority of the Italian cities deserted; and in Rome itself, the war discredited the radicals, for armies commanded by plebeian generals were ignominiously defeated, and the war was won by patrician generals.

To the Greek-speaking states of the eastern Mediterranean, the new Roman power looked parvenu and boorish, but not yet dangerous; for it seemed obvious that after so long a war, victor and vanquished would be equally exhausted, unlikely to recover for a generation. But Rome emerged from the war with a new and terrible energy. A ruined agriculture, and a generation of young men who had known no trade but fighting filled Italy with landless poor, a threat to the power of the wealthy, but an inexhaustible reserve of manpower. It was diverted to further conquest. Roman armies marched east, and within fifteen years they humbled two of the most powerful eastern kingdoms, Macedonia and Syria. Ptolemy of Egypt wisely heeded the advice of a Roman ambassador, and the lesser states admitted the permanent predominance of Rome in the eastern Mediterranean as well as in the west.

Rome learnt quickly from the conquered Greeks, for past experience had equipped her statesmen to absorb new subjects with discrimination.

But the speed and size of recent conquest blew apart ancient standards and conventions with the force of an explosion, and dragged Rome and her allies into a century of violence, whose bloody horrors reinforced the lessons of Greek history. Internal conflict was at first bitter, but free from open physical violence. Scipio, the conqueror of Carthage, championed the introduction of Greek arts into Rome, against the fierce opposition of Cato, who upheld a romanticized view of simple, honest, Roman virtue threatened with corruption by wily Greek intellectuals. In his lifetime, Cato prevailed. But the temporary triumph of conservative prejudice destroyed Roman prestige abroad and stable government at home. At first, Rome appeared to the Greeks as the disinterested defender of lost liberties. In defeating the Macedonians, Rome had liberated Greece from Macedonian rule and Macedonian garrisons. The sceptical Greeks wondered what the new master would be like. But Rome had no need of tribute, no wish to govern or to garrison. As in Italy, Rome wanted obedient allies, ready to fight for Rome when needed, able to govern themselves without troubling Romans. Within a few months of the defeat of Macedon, in 193 BC, the legions returned to Italy and left their allies free.

There was widespread and immediate enthusiasm for liberators who meant what they said. But it did not last, for Rome had as yet no means of controlling its citizens and officers abroad, no means of shaping or enforcing a policy of government. The institutions of city government had sufficed when Roman power was confined to Italy. Political power was confined to the Council, the Senate, whose membership was restricted to men of wealth and birth. Elected officers, or magistrates, *consuls*, *praetors* and *quaestors*, were normally sons of senators, and themselves became senators for life; and it was senators who commanded armies and went as ambassadors to allied states. The Roman citizen was subject to Roman law and the authority of a Roman magistrate, but was exempt from the laws of allied states in which he travelled or resided. Individual Romans abroad, encouraged to despise conquered Greeks, misused the natives and stimulated growing anti-Roman parties. The Senate and its envoys tightly controlled the foreign policy of the allies, brusquely vetoing decisions that it disliked, and increasingly intervened internally to demand the suppression of anti-Roman movements.

Like Athens before, and like many later imperial powers, Rome had alternative means of maintaining authority. Subject nations might be terrorized and intimidated by the exemplary, drastic punishment of selected rebels, or else by winning the support of their leading natives through gifts of wealth, privilege, and power. In each generation both philosophies of government had their committed adherents, and long experience in Italy had already taught them a prudent balance between the two, summed up in the axiom 'smash resistance, reward compliance'. But in the time of Cato, with no control over Romans abroad, there was little reward for the compliant. Rome's oldest Greek ally, the Achaean league, centred on Corinth, was driven to rebellion, and simultaneously Cato provoked the Carthaginians into a final war. Both were easily defeated and savagely punished: in the same year, 146 BC, Corinth and Carthage were both annihilated, their populations slaughtered or enslaved, their cities levelled and left unpeopled for a century, until Caesar founded new Latin-speaking colonies upon their ruins. Cities had been destroyed in the past, but the simultaneous blotting out of two of the oldest and greatest cities of the Mediterranean was an outrage never forgotten. It provoked a sullen and intense hatred of brutal Latin arrogance, and Latin confidence was henceforth shot through by fear of the resentment of the wealthy eastern Mediterranean lands. These tensions lasted as long as the Roman empire, and ultimately contributed to its fall. Brutality abroad was soon followed by violence at home. The old conventions of political conduct were uprooted and destroyed, and, when they were gone, open civil war became the only road to secure political power and political survival. It was these convulsions which brought Caesar to prominence and to the conquest of Gaul; and the invasion of Britain was a by-product of the power struggle between the magnates of Rome.

The century of bloodshed began in 133 BC. Abroad, the last king of Pergamon, in western Asia Minor, bequeathed his kingdom to the Roman people. Many of his subjects rebelled and were suppressed by a Roman army. But Rome could not find a native government able and willing to control a resentful population, and the kingdom was 'reduced to the status of a province' named Asia. A Roman garrison remained, and its commander was obliged to supervise the civilian government, ensuring that the separate cities obeyed Rome and controlled their people. During the next century nearly all the governments of the eastern allies failed, and their lands became provinces. At home, the loot of the east enriched the few, and impoverished many; the starving poor of town and country found champions in the Brothers Gracchus who pushed through a redistribution of the land and established a stable corn supply at prices fixed by the government. But, in search of wider support, they handed over the finances of the new province of Asia to uncontrolled extortion by Roman financiers, and, when the Senate refected their measures, they revived the dormant powers of the plebeian assemblies. Both brothers were murdered by gangs of young aristocrats.

The first bloodshed was the assassination of individual radical politicians, but it soon spread. The army now consisted largely of men who served for many years, and on retirement needed a gratuity; when the Senate refused to grant them land, the election of their general, Marius, as consul, in alliance with the plebeian leaders who campaigned for government food subsidies, secured their demand. The Italian allies demanded full Roman citizenship, and with it an equal share in the spoils of conquest; when the Senate refused, armed uprising won them citizenship. The exploited cities of Asia and Greece revolted, massacring all the Roman citizens they could find. The Senate appointed the conservative Sulla to the army that was to suppress the rising, but the aged Marius was appointed by the Assembly to replace him. Sulla replied by capturing Rome with his Roman army, and expelling Marius and his supporters, but as soon as he had gone, Marius' men recovered Rome, and held it until Sulla returned victorious, took Rome a second time, and enforced the cold-blooded pursuit and execution of his opponents. Since Marius' supporters controlled many of the western territories, they and their armies had to be reduced by other Roman armies. Their most eminent general was Pompey, who went on to reduce the pirates of the eastern Mediterranean to submission, and to settle the government of the east, creating new provinces and appointing new kings. On his return, the Senate refused both to ratify his settlement and to grant land to his veterans. Pompey needed allies, and found them in Crassus, the wealthiest individual Roman, and in Caesar, nephew of Marius and heir to his political tradition, who was seen as the champion of the plebs. Caesar's consulate in 60 BC secured the passage of Pompey's measures, and his allies forthwith tried to jettison him. He ended with an enormous foreign command, from the Pyrenees to the borders of command, big enough to keep him busy and out of Rome for many years, and perhaps to break his teeth.

Caesar's one source of strength was his popularity with the urban plebs and with the rank and file of the army. He was more sensitive than his rivals to the wishes of millions of ordinary Italians, and knew that above all they longed for peace. Crassus was killed in 53 BC, in a vain attempt to earn military glory, and all men sensed that peace could come only through the victory of either Pompey or Caesar; the victory of one of them, and the ending of the civil wars, mattered more than allegiance to either. Caesar understood that his survival and his chance of power depended on outstanding military success, which would both enhance his popularity, and gain him the support of small men, sick of war, and of magnates whose policy was to back the winning side. The coming struggle with Pompey was the main motive behind his conquest of Gaul, and of his invasion of Britain.

Caesar's success was instant and brilliant. In three years he annexed the upper Rhine, the land of the Belgae between the lower Rhine and the Seine, and that of the Veneti, modern Brittany. In the south-west, Aquitania surrendered without a fight. All Gaul was conquered, and the frontiers of the empire were extended to the shores of the Rhine and the Atlantic. Caesar's triumphs were splendid, but in his view not yet enough. He passed on to Britain. In the late summer of 55 BC a reconnaissance in strength spent a fortnight in Kent, and in 54 he committed two thirds of his army to a full-scale conquest of the island. The risk was appalling, for the Gauls were recovering from their stupefying defeat, and a national rising threatened. But Caesar pulled off the gamble. He marched inland, to cross the Thames eighty miles from the east Kent coast, somewhere in the region of the future London, and pursued the principal king of Belgic Britain, Cassivellaunus of the Catuvellauni, to his royal stronghold, probably Wheathampstead near St Albans. The stronghold was taken, and Cassivellaunus made a timely token surrender, which just enabled Caesar to ship his army back to Gaul before the weather broke in winter gales.

The conquest of Gaul had added a vast territory to the empire of Rome; but in Britain Caesar entered a new and unknown world, shot through with romance and magical overtones in men's minds. Greek and Roman science knew that the world was a sphere, though received opinion greatly underestimated its size. But in the common parlance of the uneducated, the world was round, like a plate; the land mass of Europe, Asia, and Africa, much foreshortened by mistaken calculation, was centred upon the Mediterranean, 'our sea', *mare nostrum*, and around it lay a wild and fearful ocean, whose monstrous waves and mythical monsters engulfed the rash traveller who ventured upon its waters. The land mass was anchored at opposite ends by two large islands, Britain and Ceylon. Ceylon was remote, but Britain was known to be the land of the dead. It lay 'beyond the end of the world'; travellers reported that at summer midnights on the coasts of the low countries empty fishing boats mysteriously sank to the gunwales, and glided on their own to Britain, returning before dawn, though the single voyage required thirty-six hours; they carried the souls of the dead to their eternal abode in Britain, for the nearest part of Britain was named Thanet, which in Greek means death, *thanatos*. Such fantasies remained a literary cliché long after the Romans conquered Britain and knew its reality; in the north poisonous vapours and venomous reptiles made human life insupportable, and in the Hebrides Saturn was confined in enchanted sleep by the hundred-handed giant Briareus. In Caesar's time Britain was still unknown, and fancy was unbounded; in conquering a land of mystic terror beyond the world's end and reducing it to plain reality, he stirred the imagination of unlettered Romans to a wonder only less than the conquest of the moon.

Caesar quickly published the plain tale of his campaigns in Gaul and Britain. It was addressed to Romans of limited literacy, and designed to win their votes for Caesar. It proved to be the most effective election propaganda in human history, and has ever since remained the classic of easy Latin. It soon rewarded its author. Caesar faced and subdued the expected revolt of the Gauls, and in 49 BC invaded Italy. The Italians rallied behind him. The armies of the Senate were beaten, and Pompey was killed. Caesar founded a monarchy. The last act of the independent aristocracy was to assassinate the tyrant; but the final civil war that followed was not fought to decide the issue between aristocratic and monarchical rule; it decided which individual should rule, and ended in 31 BC with the victory of Caesar's heir, who became the emperor Augustus.

The century of bloodshed left imprinted on the Roman mind a series of rigid assumptions about how men are best governed, based on the lessons of Greek history and of early Roman tradition. All men took it for granted that the town or city was the foundation of civil society; backward rustics were by nature subjects, to be ruled from, through, and by the town, and peoples who had as yet no towns remained unruly barbarians, a danger until they were tamed by urban rule. The history of ancient Athens and of recent Rome warned that firm government must at all costs contain civil discord and limit violence, for the conflict of parties and social classes offered no hope of permanent victory for either, only the destruction of all contestants. But recent history had taught that firm government must be firm against excess in either direction. The Assembly and the plebs must be denied effective political initiative, and dissident magnates must be prevented from making demagogic appeals for mass support against their fellows, however honourable their cause. Political power must rest with a council composed of the nobility of each state, and with elected magistrates of wealth and noble birth; but each government must curb the greed of its individual members, and ensure that its population be not driven to revolt by misgovernment.

Similar principles governed the relationship between cities. Rome ruled all, and gave final judgement on all disputes between cities. But in each province and region, greater metropolitan cities overtopped their humbler neighbours; it was the business of Roman government to guarantee that they received due respect, but did not abuse weaker towns, and to ensure that the grievances of the weak were resolved by appeal to the courts and magistrates of Rome, not by armed protest. The world must consist of a multitude of well-ordered cities, governed by their own hereditary aristocracies, obedient to Rome, at peace with one another, secured against internal disorder; and where such towns did not exist, they must be created. These were the principles of government, already formed but not yet fully realized, that Caesar's armies brought with them to the west.

Chapter 3

Belgic Britain

CAESAR SAILED AWAY, and it was almost a hundred years before a Roman army again invaded Britain. In the eyes of later Romans his expedition 'achieved nothing'; he 'revealed' Britain to Rome, but did not conquer it. Yet he had done what was needed. The most powerful state in Britain submitted, as the Gauls had submitted. Both Gauls and British soon threw off this allegiance to Rome, but the conquest had helped Caesar to win the support of Italy, and he was able to put down the rebellion in Gaul. It was the machinations of his enemies that prevented him from consolidating his success in Britain. Public opinion at first expected his heirs to complete the conquest; but the needs of other frontiers absorbed the army's strength, and loyal writers explained that Britain was not worth conquering. The Roman government left Britain alone. Yet, though Caesar's invasion of Britain had little direct consequence, his conquest of Gaul greatly changed Britain. Roman territory was henceforth literally within sight of Britain, and over the next century Gaul was slowly transformed into a quiet well-ordered Roman province. Next to nothing is known of its early years. During the dozen years of civil war, when Caesar's heirs disputed his inheritance, the Rhine frontier held, and several generals earned a formal triumph for victories in various parts of Gaul; no surviving record shows how serious was the resistance they met, but there was no widespread rising, for the rebellion that Caesar had crushed after his return from Britain had exhausted the hopes of patriots.

When Augustus' victory ended the civil wars in 31 BC, the Roman armies fought for ten years to reduce the hills of Spain, and were heavily engaged in the Balkans, but no serious fighting is recorded in Gaul until 19 BC. Then there was disaster on the lower Rhine. There is no evidence to suggest that it had significant repercussions in the interior, but in 16 BC Augustus reorganized the political administration, consolidating the changes of the previous generation. The bulk of the armies were concentrated on the Rhine, and the Rhineland received the name Germania, divided into an upper and a lower province. Its inland frontier ran due south from the mouth of the Scheldt, approximately where the modern cities of Antwerp, Brussels and Charleroi now stand, and then turned westward along the Ardennes, to turn south again, roughly parallel with the river, at a distance of twenty to forty miles. The rest of Gaul was divided into three provinces, without combatant troops, which corresponded to the threefold division Caesar had found when he came: Belgica extended from the lake of Geneva to the mouth of the Somme, Lugdunensis in the centre was separated from Aquitania in the south west by a frontier that ran parallel with the Loire, some fifteen to twenty miles to the south and west of the river. The Three Gauls, sometimes called *comata* or *bracchata*, 'long-haired' or 'trousered', were each bounded on the south by the original Provincia of the Mediterranean coast, known from its first capital as Narbonensis (see Map 9, p. 136).

Each of the three Gauls contained many separate nations. Large confederations were broken up, and very small peoples were absorbed by their larger neighbours, to form sixty-four separate states, or *civitates*. The accumulated experience that Rome had brought from Italy and the east was immediately applied. Each of the *civitates* became a self-governing state. Each was equipped with a single capital town, termed *caput civitatis*, where its council met regularly. The notables of each state were confirmed as substantial landowners, and in several states one or two individuals of proven loyalty were rewarded with the privilege of full Roman citizenship. Annual elections chose two or more of these notables to serve as magistrates for a year, and ex-magistrates became councillors for life. Roman governors adjudicated upon disputes between states, and heard cases that involved Roman citizens; otherwise, each state was governed by its own council and its own laws.

Gaul was reorganized by Caesar's heir, but the policy was Caesar's own. Little is recorded of the foundation of individual cities, but in the short interval between his triumph and his assassination, Caesar drafted standard constitutions for the newly-founded and newly-incorporated cities of the western empire. Large sections of these laws survive, and so do the charters of one or two later cities. Many thousands of inscriptions witness that cities throughout the western Mediterranean were governed for centuries by Caesar's constitutions. The rules adapted the constitution of the city of Rome to the needs of local towns, with one important modification: all authority was vested in the local landed aristocracy, and the political power of the Assembly was limited to the election of magistrates and council. These standard constitutions made the cities uniform. The numbers of the magistrates and council, and similar detail, varied, but the substance of government was everywhere similar; and though Caesar's surviving laws concern only towns with Latin or Roman status, the rest of the towns, legally termed *foederatae* or *peregrinae*, 'allied' or 'foreign', were similarly governed.

Caesar made the rules. His successors enforced them, and created the towns themselves. Often the inhabitants of a pre-Roman stronghold formed the nucleus of the new urban population, and often the new town was sited within a mile or two of the old stronghold, sometimes on the same site. Well-engineered main roads soon linked the new towns, and posting stations, which often grew into small market towns, were placed at convenient intervals, for the use of government travellers and transport. They remained parts of the state wherein they lay, subject to the council and magistrates who ruled in and from its capital, but they acquired their own internal government, similarly modelled.

Experience soon showed that the single, well-defined territory of Gaul, divided among dozens of local capitals and scores of growing market towns, needed a common centre. Two years after Caesar's death, a Roman colony was founded at *Lugdunum*, Lyon, where the Saône flows into the Rhone, and a generation later Augustus made it the *caput Galliarum*, capital of all three Gauls. An altar of Rome and Augustus was erected where the rivers met, and there delegates from the councils of all sixty-four states met annually, to offer formal religious honour to the divinity of Rome and its ruler. The formal act was the equivalent of an oath of loyalty, but the business of the Assembly soon extended beyond its formal commitment. It elected a chief priest of the Gauls, *sacerdos Galliarum*, who held office for a year. Neither he nor the Assembly held formal administrative power, but from the beginning they were a sounding-board that warned the government of the strength and direction of changes in public opinion, and in time they acquired formidable political influence (see below, p. 190).

The real political strength of the Assembly of the Gauls took time to mature; but from the outset it enabled the leaders of the separate states to meet one another, and to discuss problems and policies of wider import than the local internal concerns of each; and it enabled the government to keep its finger on the pulse of the nation. It was centred on the national capital. There it maintained an office and a staff, and thither the chief priest and the governor attracted all manner of persons with public and private business. The city acquired the manifold attributes of an important capital; its situation made it an important commercial centre, and it prospered, useful both to the government and the provincials. The success of Lugdunum became a precedent that was to be a powerful influence upon the authorities of a later age, who founded and developed the city of London.

A century's quiet growth ripened Gaul into a secure and peaceful Roman province. Throughout the empire, the victory of Augustus brought lasting peace. Wars continued on the distant frontiers, but in the interior all that men knew of war was what they heard from retired and returning soldiers. A single battalion proved sufficient to police each province, with the separate states responsible for internal law and order. The peace endured for nearly three hundred years; Gaul and Europe had not known peace so long-lasting or so secure before, and have never known it since. Security made agriculture prosperous, and the expense of government was light. The advanced urban technology of Rome flooded the market with relatively cheap consumer goods, and, except in remote infertile regions, greatly raised the material standard of living of all classes.

The Roman peace guaranteed some degree of personal security, protected by law, even to the humblest. Caesar had remarked that before he came to Gaul the aristocracy had reduced their plebeian inferiors to the level of slaves by arrogant, merciless repression; but the bitter experience of her own recent history taught the government of Rome to rule lightly, and to discourage the native aristocracies of the new cities from the harsh and illegal exploitation of their own citizens. Gradually men came to acquiesce in permanent Roman authority. The armed force of Rome proved too strong to challenge. In Caesar's own time, rapid conquest fired all Gaul with a patriotic determination to expel the invader, and popular enthusiasm swept along with it the kings and nobles who had made their peace with Rome.[1] But the patriots were beaten, and their children discovered that life was safer and easier under Roman rule, less exciting than in the past, but also less dangerous. Society was no longer polarized between a narrow aristocracy and a servile mass of sullen peasants. Commerce enriched many men of lowly birth, and some seventy years after the conquest their prosperity and loyalty were evident. An altar to the ancient Celtic gods in Paris was inscribed in Latin by the men who paid for it, the Shipping Association of the Seine, and was dedicated to the emperor;[2] and many memorial stones demonstrate that settled, urban civilization had taken root. Its stability was tested in AD 21. Debt and high interest rates emboldened a small group of noblemen to organize a rebellion. For a few weeks the rebels prevailed in five of the sixty-four states, but they were speedily suppressed by the Rhine armies. They did not inspire significant support in the other fifty-nine states, and even in the rebel states many notables supported the government; among the Treviri of Trier, Julius Indus raised a cavalry regiment of his own countrymen to put down the rising.[3]

The revolt was a feeble failure because men had no strong incentive to risk their present security, and viewed the distant days of independence with mixed feelings. When Gaul again rebelled, nearly fifty years later,[4] the rebels did not repeat the cry of liberation from Rome, but sought to replace one emperor with another, and justified revolt by appeals to the glories of the Roman past, not to memories of Gallic national freedom. Rome was the unchallengeable sovereign, and the leaders of the several states were themselves Roman. Many more had received Roman citizenship; and by the time that the Roman armies again crossed the channel to conquer Britain, the grandsons of the first Roman citizens of Gaul, whose fathers had fought against Caesar, were themselves admitted to the senate of Rome itself in some numbers, and took their place among the Roman governors of provinces, and the commanders of Roman legions. The Roman government had already learnt from its own history how to turn resentful conquered barbarians into loyal Romans in a few generations, and had put the lesson into practice in Gaul. The disaffected were sternly punished, but those who submitted were not merely spared; they were encouraged, rewarded, and cherished.

The organization and the policies that made Gaul Roman were the models that Rome later adapted in conquered Britain. But they developed slowly over several generations; and the immediate impact on Britain of Caesar's Gallic victory was quite different. Britain received numbers of refugees, who fled from their homeland to escape the Roman conqueror. A single anecdote in a later text names and dates one among them. Commius was a young nobleman, whom Caesar installed as king over the Atrebates, north of the lower Somme, whose capital town is today called Arras. He undertook a fruitless and dangerous embassy to Britain on Caesar's behalf, but he was carried along by the great Gallic revolt of 50 BC, and became an implacable enemy of Rome. His escape to Britain is reported by a writer of a later age, Frontinus, who published a collection of successful military stratagems: Caesar was in hot pursuit, and Commius' flotilla was stuck upon a sandbank at low tide, within easy reach of land, but while he waited for the tide to rise and float him, he spread his sails, and fooled Caesar into believing that he was already under way and out of reach.[5]

A substantial part of the Atrebates settled in Britain, and later Roman geographers locate them in north Hampshire and southern Berkshire, with their capital at Silchester, ten miles from Reading. In their territory, coins stamped with the names of Commius and his sons are frequently found. They are one part of a whole series of coins, that constitute an unusually important historical source; for, normally, coins add no more than interesting footnotes to the recorded history of an age, but the history of Belgic Britain is otherwise almost entirely unrecorded, so that the exact modern study of its coinage explains most of what we know of its political and social history. The inferences drawn from coins rest on certain assumptions, that are valid, but need explanation. In most societies, including our own, the circulation of currency is almost entirely confined within the borders of the political state that issues it; in modern Britain, Scottish pound notes and Irish pennies are common currency in Scotland and Ireland, but rarities in England, and continental coins are very few. So it was with the Belgae. Each particular type of coin is concentrated within its own area, with relatively few outliers in alien territory, save in one or two ports, notably Selsey in Sussex, where merchants from different peoples each brought their own currency to pay the foreign trader.[6]

The first Belgae and their coins reached Britain about fifty to seventy years before Caesar's time. The earliest coins were minted in Belgic Gaul, and in Britain are most numerous in Kent, in Buckinghamshire and Hertfordshire, and in western Essex; in between, they are found upon routes that link Kent with Hertfordshire, and traverse the London region. Their evidence is suggestive but uncertain, for the reasons why they reached the places in which they have been found can only be guessed. It is obvious that a single coin, found where no other signs of human life have been observed, is no evidence that men lived where the coin was found; it is, however, likely that a continuous line of find spots may mark a road or route, where travellers were robbed or lost their coins. But when coins are found in numbers at the same place, or close to sites where pottery and tools and other signs of settled life are known, then it is probable that the coins were used and lost by the men who lived there.

Map 2 shows the coins found in Greater London that were in circulation before Caesar's invasion (Gallo-Belgic), and the traces of human habitation in the late Iron Age. They hint at a possible first use by men of the site of the future London. Towards Kent, coins at Plumstead and Erith lead to a group of half a dozen at Gravesend, with Southfleet and Tilbury (off map, to the east). Further east they are more numerous, and their distribution suggests that Gravesend may have been the main crossing place of land traffic from Kent to Essex. North of the Thames, coins are few, but significantly distributed. Three of them run in a straight line from the city to Enfield Chase, where some doubtfully recorded pots may be of the pre-Roman Iron Age. A fourth coin at Hatfield (off map, to the north), where surer signs of habitation have been reported, continues the line, that leads directly to Wheathampstead, the probable site of Cassivellaunus' stronghold, that Caesar stormed. The route that these coins mark is the line of the medieval and modern Great North Road by Potters Bar, that remained in use until it was superseded by by-passes quite recently. If this route was in use before Caesar's time, it crossed the Thames at or near the site of the future London; and the few pre-Roman pot-sherds from Southwark may have been the property of those who manned the ferry.

Half a dozen other coins suggest a possible east–west route north of the river; those from Southall, Ealing and Golders Green are reinforced by two more from a slightly later period at Harlington and St John's Wood, and imply the possibility of a route from Windsor to a crossing of the Lea opposite Walthamstow. These are possibilities, no more. The distribution of a dozen casual finds of coins need not be significant; yet since that distribution marks two lines roughly at right angles to each other, they may be more than coincidence. Though they may or may not indicate routes, the fact remains that the coins are isolated and far apart; this argues strongly that they were lost in untilled wooded countryside where no man lived.

South of the Thames, the distribution of the coins points to a different conclusion. They are quite plentiful on the cultivated lands of the North Downs, and half a dozen are reported from its foothills, where plenty of other evidence records the presence of poor farming communities. Some might have been brought to where they were found in Roman times, for they lie either beside the Roman road to Lewes (compare Map 5, p. 83), or by the later Roman settlements of Mitcham and Croydon. But there is no such uncertainty about the coins from Kew and Kingston, for there is abundant evidence for a riverside population from Staines and Shepperton downstream to Kew and Barnes, but no further. This is the oldest continuously populated district in the London region. It lacks a comprehensive modern name, and is most conveniently described as the Thames Reaches.

Elsewhere in the Greater London region in Caesar's time, men moved but did not settle. In the century thereafter, the wars and migrations of the Belgae transformed southern Britain, and prepared it politically for

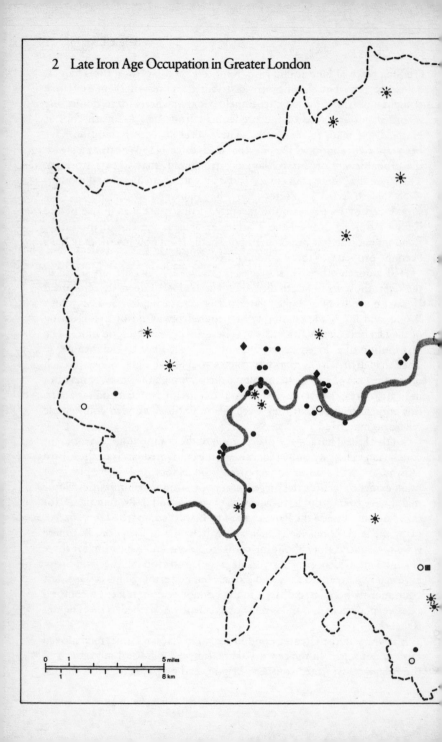

2 Late Iron Age Occupation in Greater London

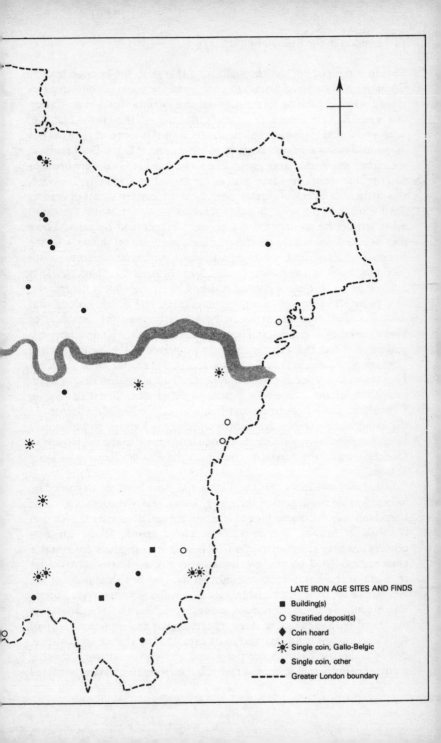

LATE IRON AGE SITES AND FINDS

■ Building(s)
○ Stratified deposit(s)
◆ Coin hoard
☀ Single coin, Gallo-Belgic
● Single coin, other
‑ ‑ ‑ ‑ Greater London boundary

Roman conquest; but they brought little change to the London region. Commius had come to Britain in 50 BC, and the coins of the Atrebates spread widely, reaching to the edges of the Thames Reaches at Walton and Sunbury. One chance text records their migration to Britain (above, p. 29), but other evidence implies that substantial groups of refugees not mentioned in any text emigrated from other parts of Belgic Gaul at about the same time. A last large group of coins minted in Gaul were brought to Britain at much the same time as the arrival of Commius.[7] In Gaul, they are widely but thinly spread near the north-eastern coasts of France, northward from the Seine, but they are thickly concentrated in one small area, astride the modern border between France and Belgium. There they are confined within precise frontiers, bordered on the west by the river Scheldt, and on the east by an almost mathematical north–south line, westward of the modern road from Brussels to Charleroi. It is marked by no prominent natural features, but it was clearly the frontier of a particular people in Caesar's time, for it was roughly along that same line that Augustus drew the boundary between the provinces of lower Germany and Belgica. The name of the people who dwelt there is plainly recorded; that territory was the homeland of the Nervii, both in Caesar's time, and in later Roman Gaul. In Britain, the coins from the Nervian territory are found in numbers in two main districts, in Kent, and north of the Thames in a narrow band extending from Luton through north Hertfordshire and Essex to Colchester and Clacton. In the London region they are numerous near the Kentish stronghold of Ightam, or Oldbury, west of Maidstone, and spread along the Downs to face the limit of the Atrebatic coinage in the Thames Reaches at Long Ditton.

Other evidence hints that the Nervii may have been accompanied by a considerable contingent of their neighbours, and that contact with the homeland was maintained for at least two generations after the Roman conquest of Britain. A remarkable localized feature of the late first century AD was the construction of large burial mounds for notable persons, modelled on the great tombs of Rome. These barrows are frequent in three small regions only, in the two British regions of the Nervian coins, from Bedfordshire into Essex, and in Kent; and in Europe they are found only on the borders of the Nervii.[8] Both coins and barrows are found only in the same three separate small areas; the similarity of their distribution is too marked to be explained by chance coincidence. But in Gaul, the barrows are not found in Nervian territory; they lie across the frontier, in lower Germany, but on its extreme edge, bordered on the east by the river Meuse. There, they are certainly the peculiar monument of a specific people. In Caesar's time, that territory was the homeland of the Eburones. He all but exterminated them; the small remnant was absorbed by the Tungri of lower Germany, who took over their ancient stronghold, and gave it its modern name, Tongres or Tongern, in the centre of the barrow district. The Eburones themselves minted no coins. The probable interpretation of this evidence is that a considerable part of the Eburones who escaped destruction by Caesar moved to Britain with the Nervii; and that in the late first century, when the Eburones who remained at home among the Tungri took to building tombs in the grand Roman manner, their kinsmen in Britain imitated them, perhaps because they shared a particular variety of Celtic religion, whose priests remained in communication with each other.

The arrival of the newcomers powerfully reinforced the Belgae of Britain, and was followed by their rapid expansion. The Nervii and their neighbours did not permanently retain their identity in Britain, and were merged with greater peoples after the Roman conquest; but from the beginning, their fortunes marched with those of the Catuvellauni. Just before Caesar's arrival, Cassivellaunus, king of the Catuvellauni, had overwhelmed the Trinovantes, whose chief centre was Colchester. Caesar reinstated the son of the defeated king of the Trinovantes, and forbade Cassivellaunus to molest them. But the Trinovantes did not retain their independence. The coins of the newcomers spread inland from Colchester, and in the next generation the coins of Tasciovanus, the successor of Cassivellaunus, take their place. He ruled from a new royal stronghold at Verulamium, by St Albans, five miles from the old fortress of Wheathampstead, and he was the first of the Catuvellauni to cause his name to be written, stamped in Roman letters upon his coins. Many of these coins are also marked with the place where they were minted; the most frequent mint mark is VER, for Verulamium, but some are marked CAMVL, for Camulodunum, Colchester, firm proof that Tasciovanus annexed and ruled the kingdom of the Trinovantes. His power also crossed the Thames, for coins of the kings who ruled in Kent stopped short at the Medway, and the coins of Tasciovanus succeed the earlier coins at and near Gravesend, controlling communication between Essex and Kent, and follow the coins of the Nervii in and near the stronghold of Ightham. But elsewhere in the greater London region they are few.

Tasciovanus founded the empire of the Catuvellauni. It was extended over almost all southern Britain by his son Cunobelinus, who reigned for thirty or forty years, dying in or about AD 40. He made Colchester his principal royal residence, and the coins that mark the extent of his rule reach through the eastern midlands over Northamptonshire and into Nottinghamshire, westward to Hampshire and the Dorset borders, and up the Thames to Gloucestershire (Plate 2). Roman record confirms the implication of the coins, for the kings of the Atrebates and of Kent took refuge with the emperor Augustus at Rome;[9] and excavation adds further confirmation, for Belgic pottery spread north and west with the coins of Cunobelinus, and the remains of a few western fortresses that were stormed, burnt, and left empty by the shores of the Bristol Channel, shortly before the Roman conquest mark the limit of Catuvellaunian advance. They were still advancing at the time of the Roman invasion; for the Romans found that the Catuvellauni ruled a portion of the Dobunni, who straddled the lower Severn and peopled Gloucestershire and the Cotswolds, but that part of their territory was not yet conquered (see below, p. 55). Their advance evidently enlisted and rewarded pioneers from the Belgic kingdoms they had earlier subdued, for when the Romans came to reorganize Hampshire and Wiltshire, they gave their territory the general name of Belgae, not of any particular Belgic people; the probable reason is that it had been colonized by settlers drawn from a number of different Belgic peoples.

The evidence of the coins suggests that Tasciovanus' earlier conquests were greatly helped by the Nervii, but that they were incorporated within his kingdom. They seemed to have retained a considerable autonomy for some time, for in all the regions where the newcomers' coins are found, a plentiful cheap coinage of tin has also been discovered, that does not spread to other parts of the Catuvellaunian empire. Its most marked single concentration is in the Thames Reaches; there, the individual coins are found on both sides of the Thames, but on the Middlesex shore four large hoards are reported, containing between them several thousand coins, in sheer numbers more numerous than any other coinage of Belgic Britain. The coins cannot be closely dated; they evidently came into use some time after the migration of about 50 BC, and did not remain in circulation for more than a generation or two, for they are rarely found with Roman coins.[10] It may be that the Nervii took over the Thames Reaches, a tiny isolated populated region, and there for a while maintained independent identity; the hoards on the north bank of the river were plainly buried by men who had to flee quickly, and could not take their money with them, perhaps when Cunobelinus' advance overwhelmed them, for his coins are thereafter found in their territory.

The long reigns of Tasciovanus and Cunobelinus brought not only conquest to southern Britain, but also a changed economy. Its most striking witness is the craft of the potter, for the Belgae developed for the first time in Britain the use of the wheel. The importance of the new technique was that it enabled a full-time professional to produce large numbers of vessels that could be distributed over a wide area, by pack horse, cart or other means; and because the potter could work faster, making more pots in an hour, he could sell his wares more cheaply than his predecessor, whose inferior products cost more labour and were sold less far afield. Change is easily recognized in the pottery industry, for though pots are easily broken, the broken pieces are virtually indestructible, and remain undamaged in the soil for archaeologists to find and recognize. Their durability makes pottery the index of change in other commodities, made of textiles, leather, wood and other perishable materials less often found in recognizable shape.

Specialized production, producing cheap goods for a wide market, required a new currency. The earlier coins were all of gold, save in parts of the west country, where silver was available. Gold coins alone are the currency of wealthy men, useful for the purchase of sword or shield, of cattle or sheep, but no use at all for the purchase of smaller items. When potters and other craftsmen first began to market cheap commodities, they had no means of receiving payment except by barter; and the travelling salesman who returned from his round with a quantity of chickens, eggs, bags of flour, pieces of leather and cloth and other small payments in kind suffered obvious inconvenience. It was not long endured. The Catuvellaunian kings soon began to issue coins of smaller value, suitable for the purchase of small domestic needs. When Caesar arrived, copper coins as well as gold were already in use, though the evidence of the coins themselves suggests that they were then a very recent innovation, and few in number. But under Tasciovanus they are more numerous, and under Cunobelinus plentiful. They chiefly circulated in and near the great royal strongholds, at Verulamium, Colchester, Braughing and elsewhere, and gold was still proportionately more frequent in outlying districts. In the London region, five coins found at Walthamstow, opposite the apparent early crossing point of the Lea, are all of gold, and so are a few others at Kew, Poplar and elsewhere. Copper coins are reported only from the Thames Reaches by Kew and Barnes, where also the cheap coins of tin were much used. There alone in the London region the monetary economy took shape.

Elsewhere in the London area, coins are fewer than in most parts of the Catuvellaunian kingdom. After the Catuvellaunian capital was moved from Wheathampstead to Verulamium, there is no further sign of the northward route by Potter's Bar and Hatfield; instead, a small Belgic stronghold at Pear Wood, near the future Roman town on Brockley Hill, above Elstree, and perhaps two coins, at St John's Wood and Westminster, mark the new route to Verulamium, the line of the future Roman Watling Street, that crossed the Thames near the modern House of Commons (see Maps 2 and 5, pp. 32 and 83). A few coins have been found within the City, but they may well not have got there before the Roman city was founded, for the later Belgic coins remained in circulation for several generations after the Roman conquest, and no routes, pottery, or other signs of settlement suggest any movement or residence of men within the City area, between the time of Caesar and the conquest.

Conquest enriched the Belgic aristocracy, but only the aristocracy. A Roman writer lists the exports of Belgic Britain as corn, cattle, hides and dogs, metals and slaves.[11] They were the product of war, for metals were mined in the west country that Cunobelinus subdued, and Catuvellaunian conquest imposed upon the conquered a tribute of corn and cattle whose surplus the conquerors might sell abroad. But slaves were the richest prize of victory, and a standing incentive to continuing war. A number of slave collars and chains have been excavated in Britain; most are found in the Belgic districts, and almost all of those that can be dated belong to the Belgic period. The slave trade was an inescapable consequence of the proximity of Roman Gaul, for demand stimulated supply. In previous generations, the Roman presence in the eastern Mediterranean had instigated the kings of Asia Minor to enslave their own subjects, or to make war upon their neighbours, in order to acquire valuable cargoes that they might exchange for the wealth of Rome; and the Roman wars of the first century BC had greatly increased the supply. But the peace of Augustus ended in Europe the wars that had earned cheap slaves, and had made Britain an important source of supply. The kings and nobles of the Catuvellauni might gain some small increase to their substance by annexing the western mines, by exacting tribute from the conquered, or by forcing their own peasants to grow a larger agricultural surplus. But their surest road to wealth was war; they fought in the sure knowledge that victory over the Dobunni, or the peoples of Northamptonshire or the Thames Reaches or any other region would earn them many prisoners, whose sale abroad would win a rich return.

The wealth that the kings and nobles won by the export of their people and their produce has left ample archaeological trace. The Roman coins that circulated in Gaul in the Belgic period are plentiful in Britain, though it is rarely possible to discover whether they were imported in Belgic times, or brought to Britain by the Roman conquest. Other evidence is clearer. Elegant and expensive pottery, Roman jewels and ornaments, quantities of wine jars, are common in the first decades of the first century AD, and are most commonly preserved in the elaborate tombs of noblemen and kings, as at Welwyn at Hertford Heath,[12] and in a splendid burial at Lexden, by Colchester, that may well be the tomb of Cunobelinus himself.[13] Wealth sealed in tombs is safeguarded for easy modern discovery; but it is no more than an index of the greater wealth that men used in their lifetime. Yet wealth was almost entirely confined to the strongholds of kings and noblemen, and very little of it penetrated into the countryside.

Belgic Britain matured under the shadow of Roman Gaul. Wherever the Roman frontier faced groups of small barbarian peoples, with a loose political organization, the barbarians learnt from Rome. In Dacia on the lower Danube, in Bohemia, and later on among the Germans beyond the Rhine, barbarians were impressed by the wealth and might that Rome assembled under the authority of a single, centralized government, ruling a vast territory. Men of might observed that Roman noblemen, in the provinces as in Italy, lived well, in obedience to a single monarch; and when the ambition of kings grasped after wide empire, it found powerful support, and broad sections of ordinary opinion remarked the obvious, that only a large army under the command of a single ruler could hope to withstand the immense power of Rome. The lesson was learnt early in Britain, for when Caesar invaded, the separate Belgic kings, at odds with one another, sank their differences and entrusted the overall command to Cassivellaunus. When Caesar went, the urgency passed, and lesser rulers no longer voluntarily accepted the permanent supremacy of the Catuvellaunian kings. But the threat remained, visibly and permanently present upon the cliffs of Roman Gaul. Men might boast that they alone had driven back the legions, but they were well aware that the invaders might come again. The arguments that urged the southern British to unite in a single, powerful kingdom were never silenced; and in the end, enabled the greatest of the Belgic dynasties to subdue the lesser kings and absorb their subjects.

The quick success of Tasciovanus and Cunobelinus provoked resentment, and their successors were not given time to let the resentment die down into acquiescence. Rome had observed the danger from too powerful neighbours, and in the eastern Mediterranean had early learnt how to disrupt and enfeeble strong kings. The policy of divide and rule was adapted to the west; the short-lived Bohemian kingdom of the Marcomanni, the men of the March, or frontier, was destroyed from within by dissident noblemen and underkings whom Rome encouraged to withstand the centralized rule of the new monarchy; and Roman diplomacy long hindered the formation of powerful German states on the Rhine. The growing power of Belgic Britain aroused apprehension. Exiled lesser kings were welcomed and comfortably entertained in Rome; and in time the heir of the house of Commius of the Atrebates was to prove a powerful ally.[14]

Rome intervened before the strength of the Belgic kingdom was consolidated, while the passions aroused by the wars of conquest were still enflamed. The Belgae as a whole were relatively recent foreign masters, ruling over the descendants of earlier Iron-Age peoples, who were not yet reconciled to conquest. Belgic expansion was still unchecked. Nations beyond their borders feared the next attack, and were disposed to welcome Romans or any other enemies of the Belgae. Fear of the Belgae pressed hardest upon the still independent Iceni of Norfolk. Within the Belgic peoples, the lesser kingdoms overwhelmed by the Catuvellauni still smarted from defeat. The exiled kings of Kent and the sons of Commius, Tincommius and Verica, were guests of the Roman government, and looked to the Roman army to restore them to their kingdoms. At home, some at least of the notables kept faith with the exiled kings across the seas, and humbler folk mourned relatives sold into slavery, and suffered from the agricultural taxation that paid for the jewels and wine imported by the victors. The fear of Rome was still present, and argued in all men's minds against these immediate resentments. Yet the discontents persisted, varying in strength among different individuals and regions; the Catuvellauni and those who benefited from their victories had nothing to gain and all to lose from Roman success; but some were wholly committed to the overthrow of the Catuvellauni, at whatever cost, and others looked upon Roman invasion with mixed feelings, welcoming liberation from the oppressor of the moment, but also fearing the might of the liberator.

To the rulers of Rome, the invasion of Britain was a project inherited from Caesar. Britain had been conquered in name, but let go. It was in practice independent, paying no tribute. The mass of small warring states constituted no threat, and did not justify the cost of conquest. The growing power of Cunobelinus brought into being an overmighty border kingdom, that would certainly have prompted Roman counter-measures if it had lain upon a European frontier. But the channel was a natural frontier stouter than the Rhine and Danube, and there was no real danger that Belgic Britain, however powerful, would undertake the invasion of Roman Gaul; at the worst, it could serve as a base and refuge for dissidents and exiles from Gaul, but in Cunobelinus' time the failure of the Gallic rebellion of AD 21 had amply demonstrated that in Gaul itself open rebels were few and ineffective, little to be feared.

The pressures that argued for and against an invasion of Britain bore equally upon the Roman government, and there was no compelling reason that made the decision to invade in the long run inevitable. The chances that tipped the balance in favour of invasion had momentous consequences for the future of Britain and Europe; for if Britain had remained an offshore barbarian island, beyond the end of the Roman world, it risked conquest and subjection by the powers of the mainland for the whole of its future history, an impotent victim, as much at the mercy of the rulers of France as Ireland was to be at the mercy of English invasion and exploitation in the Middle Ages and later centuries. The Roman conquest incorporated Britain within its advanced and sophisticated economy, and left behind it long traditions of acknowledged government and law, and social cohesion, centred on and symbolized in its cities and in the national capital of London. The Roman decision to invade was taken with no such lofty hindsight. The considerations that resolved long indecision were the outcome of a particular short-lived political crisis, which was a by-product of the wider struggles that shaped the imperial monarchy. It was no more essential to that struggle than the motives which decided Caesar to hazard the bulk of his army in Britain in 54 BC; but, like Caesar's decision, it emerged from the complex history of Rome in the previous century.

Claudius' armies invaded Britain in AD 43, ninety-seven years after Caesar left Britain. It was seventy-four years – three generations – since Augustus' victory at Actium had founded the imperial monarchy. The monarchy disciplined the aristocracy of Rome and created an executive government capable of controlling the empire and those who ruled its provinces; but it left all-important offices in the hands of the senatorial nobility. The powers and titles assigned to them respected aristocratic convention, avoiding the practices as well as the language of despotism. The religious term 'august' meant then what it now means in English, majestic, revered, and sacred. The ruler was not termed king or lord, but *princeps civitatis*, chief citizen of the state; the word adapted to Latin usage the title that Alexander and his heirs had used in Greek cities, *hegemon*, 'leader', of the citizens, and Augustus' successor is said to have defined his threefold power as '*imperator*, commander-in-chief, of the soldiers, despot to the barbarians, and first among the citizens'. Augustus claimed that he excelled all others in personal authority, but held no higher legal power than other Roman magistrates. The claim was literally true. Powers similar to those once entrusted to Pompey were revived in his favour; he was made proconsul for ten years of an extended territory, with superior authority over neighbouring proconsuls, and empowered to choose legates to exercise command under his direction where he was not personally present. The territory assigned was that where the heaviest fighting was expected, Gaul and northern Spain in the west, and the disturbed lands of the eastern Mediterranean. The central territories, the Balkans and north Africa, with southern Spain and the Mediterranean islands, remained under the command of annual proconsuls chosen by lot. He protested that he had taken the difficult areas of the empire, and left the fairer and pleasanter parts to others. The claim was true; but his critics emphasized another truth, that his proconsulate gave him command of most of the armies; and that command was widened when the Balkan armies marched north to the Danube, for the lands they conquered formed new provinces, and new provinces, with the armies in them, passed to the emperor's proconsulate.

The special powers were granted for ten years, but were renewed and renewed again, and were granted for life to later emperors. The powers were wide and long lasting, but they comprehended an equally powerful limiting restriction. All the legates whom Augustus and his successors appointed to the actual command of troops were without exception senators, and convention soon decreed that all armies should be commanded by a consular legate, termed *pro praetore*, invested with praetor's powers of executing Roman citizens; lesser legates, without a praetor's power, commanded the separate legions within each army, and were younger men, not yet consuls. The convention mattered greatly, for throughout Augustus' reign only the upper nobility of patricians attained the consulate, with two or three exceptions in half a century, and most of the consuls belonged to the same few families who had held the office in the great days of the second century BC. Augustus ruled, but the aristocracy governed. One incident reported by the historian Tacitus emphasizes their strength. Twenty years after Augustus' death, the patrician Cornelius Gaetulicus, legate of lower Germany, heard a rumour that he was to be recalled to Rome to stand trial. He wrote to the emperor, before he was charged, refusing to attend, and struck with him a 'kind of treaty', that if Gaetulicus was suffered to rule his province, Tiberius might continue to rule elsewhere.[15] The epigram expressed political reality, for Gaetulicus' army comprised four legions; on the upper Rhine his father-in-law commanded another four, and on the Danube his brother-in-law probably already commanded four more. Between them, they controlled twelve of the twenty-five legions in the Roman army, almost half its total force.

Augustus had come to power as the champion of Italy against the powers of the resentful eastern provinces, headed by the renegade Antony and his paramour Cleopatra. His power endured because Italians feared above all else the renewal of civil war. His powers passed to his personal heirs, for the army and the provinces easily accepted the authority of a hereditary monarchy, but men rightly feared that the ending of the special powers or the appointment of an outsider would encourage rivals to compete for a vacant throne. Augustus therefore shaped the government of the empire to forms acceptable to Italy. The Senate met fortnightly, except in the summer recess, as a legislative assembly concerned with the routine business of Italy and the provinces; a two-thirds quorum compelled regular attendance. Augustus strove successfully to make the Senate representative of propertied Roman citizens everywhere. It was recruited by the election of the junior magistrates, the quaestors, who became senators for life. Until Augustus' last years, all the new senators whose origins are known were eminent citizens of the towns of Italy, some of whom were at first reluctant to accept promotion, for fortnightly attendance obliged the senator to live in or near Rome, and neglect his native city. Augustus tried to make the Senate a representative assembly in a formal sense, proposing that magistrates be elected by a secret ballot of senators and of councillors of the colonies of Italy. Though the initial franchise was tightly limited, the proposal anticipated the techniques of modern parliamentary government. It came to nothing, and junior magistrates were ultimately elected by existing senators; but its intention was realized in a different form. Individual senators, and other influential persons, accepted the patronage of particular cities in Italy and the provinces, and undertook to represent their interests in Rome, at all levels from coaxing a government grant for a local water supply to soliciting a commission in the army for a young citizen. The function of the patron extended under later emperors, as wealthier provincials were admitted to membership of the Senate, at first from the old established provinces of southern Gaul and southern Spain, under Claudius from the Three Gauls and north Africa, and later from other provinces.

A working legislature designed to represent the localities within the empire required a cabinet council to prepare its business and to advise the emperor. Augustus began with a Council of fifteen senators, chosen by lot like the councillors of ancient Athens, and replaced every six months. Such rigid constitutionalism did not endure, and by Claudius' time the most eminent senators, termed *primores*, were normally summoned; later a smaller group of about a dozen, including the great officers of state, formed the regular Council. It was advisory, without formal power; but emperors who consistently overrode its advice on matters of moment were soon replaced by others more amenable. In practice, the Imperial Council was hardly less influential than the Privy Council of Tudor England.

The monarchy soon learnt the truth of a fundamental political maxim that is sharply focussed by an epigram of Disraeli, who defined a statesman as 'a politician held upright by equal and opposing pressures'. The emperor was at the receiving end of all the pressures within the empire, and in the Council he found a means of assessing their relative strength; for it was to the members of the Council that the patrons of cities and provinces made suit and lodged their protests. The effective curb upon government was finance. The taxes that Augustus stabilized remained immutable, and were light; direct taxations brought the government hardly more than ten per cent of income, and indirect taxes, death duties, purchase tax, and customs dues, averaged about two per cent of assessed value. Public opinion successfully refused new taxes or increased rates, and all other financial expedients depended on the good will of the magnates, which could not be expected when the Council disapproved.

The limited finance of government dictated its policy. Its chief expense was the army, and Augustus cut the army down to some twenty-eight long-service citizen legions, each composed of five to six thousand heavy infantry. An approximately equal number of auxiliaries, which comprised the cavalry, the light-armed and specialized troops, were raised from provincials and maintained by volunteers, attracted by the reward of Roman citizenship and a gratuity on discharge after twenty-five years' service. An army of a little over a quarter of a million men held some ten thousand miles of frontier, and sufficed to rule and to protect a population that numbered something between fifty and a hundred millions. The task stretched its resources. At first, it was engaged in subduing untamed mountaineers within the empire, in Spain, the Alps and the Balkans. Thereafter Augustus and his principal generals, his step-sons Drusus and Tiberius, matured a grand design to advance the European frontiers from the Rhine and the Danube to the line of the Elbe and the Carpathians. The advanced line would have halved the length of the frontier, and might in time have been held by a much smaller army. But after various mischances, the attempts proved too costly. In AD 9, a German revolt destroyed three legions. Augustus did not and could not replace them. Forty years before, at the close of the civil wars, the Roman world had sustained some sixty or seventy legions under arms; now it could not raise half a dozen legions to wipe out the disgrace of a crushing defeat at the hands of insolent border barbarians. The body of Roman citizens ruled the rich lands of the Mediterranean without risk of resistance; they were no longer to spend their lives on the conquest of unprofitable German forests. Augustus accepted their refusal, and urged his successors to be content with their present frontiers.

The empire ceased to expand territorially. Instead, Roman civilization spread internally. Energy and wealth were diverted from warfare to the development of cities. Ever since the great days of Athens, rich men had been obliged to meet some public expenditure from their own pockets; instead of any general surtax, wealthy Athenians were obliged to pay for the building of a warship or the production of plays. The democracies had had to compel the reluctant rich to undertake such 'liturgies', or public burdens. The aristocratic government of Rome was able to encourage voluntary liturgies; landlords and financiers took pride in spending a portion of their income on education, libraries and public health in their own local cities, in constructing theatres, temples and aqueducts, and were honoured for their munificence by countless statues with flamboyant inscriptions erected by their grateful fellow citizens. The cost of public sport was borne by elected magistrates, and each city strove to outdo its neighbours in the magnificence of its performance; the convention guaranteed the enduring rule of the local nobility, for no man who could not afford the cost of sport could hope to win votes.

Augustus is said to have boasted that he found Rome built of brick, and left it built of marble. The lesser cities of Italy and the provinces were turned from wood and plaster to stone and brick. They were the means and symbol of Roman sovereignty, and the imperial government energetically encouraged private expenditure on public services. Sophisticated towns bred men who gladly conformed to Roman ways, and Roman citizenship was extended to individuals and communities who had proved themselves Roman in outlook and behaviour over several generations. The citizen body was augmented by the descendants of veterans discharged with citizenship from the auxiliary provincial regiments of the army, and further increased by the manumission of slaves. The peace of Augustus had cut short the supply of unskilled barbarian foreign slaves; but the disorders of the previous century had glutted the market with cheap slaves, whose descendants were born and bred in Roman territory, and spoke Latin as their native tongue. Many acquired a skilled or semi-skilled training, and they were too numerous for their owners to employ profitably. Masters preferred to sell freedom to their slaves, and be quit of the cost of feeding and clothing them; the freedmen became clients of their former masters and their heirs, who, as their patrons, protected them, and exacted from them respect and services. The legislation of Augustus gave Latin citizenship to the freedmen, Roman citizenship to their descendants. Some among them rose high in wealth and office, and it became a widespread fashion for noblemen born to sneer apprehensively at the growing power and influence of men of low-born freedmen origin. But the Roman state upheld the opportunity for a few able men to move quickly upwards in the social scale, and before the end of the second century a freedman's son who had risen by merit in the army was created emperor by the Senate, to defend the wealth and privilege of aristocracy.[16]

These developments matured for more than two hundred years after Augustus' time. But by the time that Claudius' armies assaulted Belgic Britain, they were already far advanced. The empire of Rome was made of a multitude of self-governing city states, of varied status, all dependent allies of Rome, grouped for administrative convenience into provinces. Throughout the empire, provincial notables had learnt to regard the physical city as the embodiment of each state, and to take pride in its appearance and amenities. They knew that they might look to the government for support, for their devotion to their own cities was the surest guarantee of continuing obedience. In Gaul, Rome had pioneered and tested an efficient means of transforming a rural barbarian land into a province ruled through cities. The experiment in Gaul had advanced slowly and unevenly, by trial and error, for in the first forty or fifty years after the conquest of Gaul, the central government of Rome was still undeveloped, and the taming of the Gauls was left to the chancy initiative of individual commanders. But by AD 43 the imperial government was well established. It already knew exactly what it wanted to do with newly-conquered barbarians; and it had the means to achieve its ends quickly, cheaply and easily. The future towns of Britain were to become the testing ground of Greek and Roman urban civilization at the peak of its development, where Rome might prove that its forms of government were instantly valid for aliens still uncivilized.

Chapter 4

The Roman Conquest

THE INVASION OF Britain was a military project bequeathed by Caesar to his heirs. Augustus put it aside, for his armies were fully committed to the conquest of Germany; and when they failed, he abandoned further wars of expansion. When he died in AD 14, he was succeeded by his elderly stepson Tiberius, whose many hard-fought, victorious campaigns had already ranked him among the ablest generals of Roman history. But Tiberius' wars were over. He carefully observed Augustus' behest, to stay within existing frontiers; and he also withdrew from Rome and from the management of public affairs, abandoning the government of Rome to the Senate, and appointing trusted and able commanders to the armies, who kept their commands for ten or twenty years.

Faction and dynastic struggle tore the aristocracy apart, with hatreds as passionate as in the civil wars before Augustus' victory. But the existence of Tiberius prevented armed conflict, and limited the violence to an extravagant succession of political trials and impeachments. The ageing emperor remained in scornful seclusion on the island of Capri, hated and feared for his unpredictable irritable intervention, to quash a sentence or to bolster or abandon a minister. Men feared the future. When Tiberius died in AD 37, his immense fortune passed to his great-nephew and heir, who bore the honourable name of C. Julius Caesar; reluctantly and with apprehension the Senate bestowed the powers of the monarchy on the young man who inherited the name and wealth of his predecessors.

The new emperor was twenty-four years old. His father, Germanicus, had died young, leaving a golden name as a successful general, and as a nobleman who went out of his way to be agreeable to humbler men. The son inherited his father's popularity, symbolized in his nickname, Caligula, or 'Little Boot'; for army slang distinguished the other ranks, *caligati*, who wore boots, from the officers, *calceati*, who wore shoes, and the child, born when his father commanded the armies of the Rhine, was adopted as the soldiers' darling. He was the first of the emperors to be born and reared as an imperial prince, heir to the monarchy, and the first to win sovereignty before experience had matured and tested him. The young emperor retained his popularity with the army and the plebs;

but he gravely displeased the nobility, for he delighted in extravagant parties, and his passion was sport, in particular horse racing. The wits protested that if he had lived longer he would have nominated his favourite horse as consul, and various noblemen lost their lives and property, accused of real or pretended conspiracy. The monarchy no longer seemed secure, and the future was uncertain.

It was in this uneasy political context that the projected invasion of Britain was revived. The official pretext was the 'refusal to return refugees',[1] and there is no doubt that responsible Roman statesmen viewed with displeasure the growing strength of Cunobelinus, whose kingdom offered an attractive escape for any dissident or criminal in Roman Gaul. But Roman Gaul was already secure, and no sane man could credibly argue that Belgic Britain threatened to invade Gaul, or even to weaken Roman authority. Other motives gave weight to the formal complaint. The Senate was still dominated by noblemen whose ancestors had founded and repeatedly renewed the glories of each family by military triumphs; but for more than a generation no significant wars had given their descendants the opportunity to emulate their forebears. Chief among them was the emperor himself, named Julius Caesar, patently destined to bring his predecessor's conquest of Britain to a triumphant conclusion. The prospect seemed easy, for the European frontiers had been quiet for thirty years, and the strains that had deterred Augustus from further wars were now eased; moreover, the rigours and rewards of a major campaign might serve to distract the emperor from his light amusements, and stablize the government.

The invasion was seriously organized. Two new legions were raised, and the army was concentrated on the coast at Boulogne, ready for embarkation in AD 40. But it never sailed. The sensational headline reports of hostile historians describe the lunatic behaviour of the emperor, who sailed out alone, and finally ordered his troops to fill their helmets with sea-shells, proclaimed as the 'spoils of Ocean'.[2] The probable explanation of these vagaries is that Caligula faced a mutiny, as did Claudius three years later (see below, p. 44), and was forced to accept the troops' refusal to embark. Whatever the reason, the invasion was abandoned, and Caligula returned to Rome, where he was assassinated by a conspiracy of Guards officers in January, 41.

The immediate sequel decided the future of the monarchy. The Senate met under the presidency of the surviving consul, Sentius Saturninus and named no successor. Instead, it passed a motion censuring all four Caesars; the memory of Augustus and of Julius Caesar was condemned, as well as the memory of Tiberius and Caligula. The decision was superficially reasonable. Seventy years earlier, special powers had been entrusted to Augustus for a limited period to regulate a particular crisis. The powers had been renewed time and again, but the emergency for which they had been designed was long since over; there was no reason to renew them, and no outstanding individual who was equipped to receive them.

A single motion abolished the monarchy and restored the sovereignty of the consuls and of the senatorial aristocracy. The restoration lasted less than a week. The plebs of Rome demonstrated in the streets, demanding the punishment of the assassins and the appointment of a new sovereign, for, as an acute contemporary observed, they regarded the emperors as a 'curb upon the arrogance of the aristocracy'. It was soon apparent that an emperor must be named, and parties began to form, canvassing support for their respective candidates. The allegiance of the Guards and police battalions in Rome was divided, the attitude of the frontier armies uncertain. A darkening future threatened renewed civil war when a private soldier, at large in the almost deserted imperial palace, discovered the person of the late emperor's uncle, Claudius. The problem was instantly resolved; the Guards acclaimed him eagerly, and compelled the Senate to ratify their decision.

Claudius was a freak, brought to power by chance. He was an ungainly retired scholar, an expert on ancient Roman and Etruscan history, an amateur philologist devoted to the reform of illogical Latin spelling. In his youth Augustus had treated him as mentally defective; he had never been allowed to make public speeches like other princes, and held no public office until his nephew named him consul. Once enthroned, he demonstrated a common-sense ability to adapt his antiquarian understanding to present-day reform, thwarted only by a pedantic want of judgement and perception.

The crisis of January 41 made the monarchy permanent. Hitherto, it had been possible to believe that the institution was a temporary expedient that might one day be discontinued. Henceforth, the abolition of the monarchy ceased to be practical politics; future struggles were concerned with who should be emperor, who should choose him and guide his government, no longer with whether or not there should be an emperor. Claudius rapidly reorganized the administration of the empire into its permanent shape. Hitherto, numerous imperial freedmen had been employed to manage the many different sources of the emperor's income and expenditure, personal and public, and to act as secretaries to the emperor and his Council. Claudius streamlined them into permanent ministries, each with its own departmental head. A Treasurer, termed *a rationibus*, supervised and controlled the finances of the whole empire; a Secretary of State, *ab epistulis*, drafted orders and letters of appointment to every office from subaltern to army commander, and kept the files; a parallel department was added, under the Secretary for Petitions, *a libellis*, which enabled a subject to complain to the central government direct, through his patron, over the heads of governors and their staffs.

Claudius consolidated and tidied the experience of the previous century. His State Secretariats are the direct ancestors of all modern ministries; they were modified by later emperors and imitated by the papacy, prolonged throughout the Middle Ages by the eastern Roman empire, and adapted by the Turks; and they were shaped into their modern form by renaissance and later Europeans who were soaked from their childhood in the literature and history of Rome. Claudius appointed his own freedmen to head his ministries. It was normal practice. All great men entrusted the supervision of their estates and finances to trusted freedmen; and Augustus and Tiberius had employed their freedmen on their own and on public business. Few had objected when a multitude of imperial freedmen each managed a small portion of the public business; but the heads of centralized ministries wielded enormous political power, and the nobility fiercely resented the jumped-up eminence of slave-born creatures of the sovereign, personified in the ostentation of the Treasurer Pallas and the Secretary Narcissus, whose slave names aped the mythology of ancient Greece. The resentment was short-lived, for it was allayed a generation later by the appointment of respectable Italian knights, *equites*, as departmental heads over the freedmen; but in Claudius' time the freedmen ministers provoked fury and ribald contempt.

Conservative hostility was also enflamed by Claudius' overhaul of citizenship and of the Senate. Tiberius had in his last years opened up the consulate to new men, whose fathers had not been ancient noblemen or even senators. Claudius greatly increased the numbers of the consuls, standardizing earlier experiments and replacing the consuls with substitutes, or suffects, every few months. There were soon many more consulars available, from whom army commanders might be selected, and the majority were new men, senators of modest fortune, notables of the towns of Italy, enriched by large salaries earned in successive offices, career officers and administrators. Greater numbers of qualified consulars enabled army commands to be changed more frequently, and three years soon became the normal term of office.

Army command was no longer in practice confined to the greater nobles; and their control of the Senate was also undermined. Claudius, like Augustus before him, enrolled new families among the patricians, endowing them with a status not lower than that which the title Duke conveys in modern England; and the men he chose were the grandsons of the Italian notables whom Augustus had brought into the Senate. He also recruited many new men to the Senate, and proposed and carried in the Senate a formal motion approving the acceptance of senators from the Three Gauls, a century after their annexation. The gist of his speech is reported by the historian Tacitus, and the grateful citizens of Lugdunum obtained a verbatim transcript, which they engraved and exhibited on bronze tablets, some of which survive.[3] The language is uncouth and pedantic; but Claudius enunciated and justified a clear-cut philosophy and theory of Roman imperial government. Rome had grown great by absorbing and benefiting the conquered, admitting them to citizenship and to the highest public office as soon as they had proved their loyalty and their attachment to Roman manners and Roman laws. Seven centuries before, the emperor's patrician ancestors had been foreign Sabines; but Rome gave citizenship to the conquered Sabines, and the Sabine leader became a consul, founder of the Claudian house. Claudius cited numerous examples that repeated the precedent, and said that in recent times Augustus and Tiberius had 'wished to see the flower of all colonies and municipalities everywhere in this Senate'. Citizenship was considerably extended, and a number of Gauls and Spaniards were admitted to the Senate.

Conservative opinion sneered at the inferior origin of the new men, complaining that half the Senate was of servile origin, descended from freedmen, and that if Claudius had lived a little longer, he would have made citizens of all the painted British. But the reform had deeper causes than the quirks of a liberal-minded, academic emperor. A few incidents illustrate the real pressures that gave strength to Claudius and found in him a champion. Some years earlier, the father of the Roman general Agricola had been admitted to the Senate as the first senator from southern Gaul. When he stood for the office of praetor, which obliged him to pay for expensive games, a couple of powerful patricians obligingly offered to pay the cost for him; he declined their offer, refusing to become their client, and his fellow Gaulish noblemen, not themselves senators, raised a voluntary subscription to defray the expense. The discomfited patricians vowed vengeance on the stubborn independent Gaul, and he lost his life in the troubled years of Caligula; but the willing response of the Gallic notables is evidence enough that they actively wanted representation in the legislature of the empire, and saw their one senator as their own representative and spokesman.

Influential conservatives tried other means to retain control of the Senate. One of them tried unsuccessfully to compel the quaestors as well as the praetors to provide expensive games in order that membership of the Senate should be restricted to men of great wealth. Some years later, when a rising young lawyer of obscure origin, named Veiento, was elected praetor, the horse-racing teams refused to race unless their pay was doubled. Mid-first-century Rome was not the place for industrial strikes led by militant trade unionists, and the strike of the teams was certainly the work of powerful nobles. Veiento overcame them by ridicule; his adoptive father, Didius Gallus, was then legate of Britain, a principal source of fast and powerful dogs, and Veiento laid on dog races instead of horse races. Rome laughed with him and mocked the teams into submission.

These and other incidents mark the attempts of the die-hards to block the devolution of political power within the empire. They failed, and for the next hundred years policies that Claudius defended and practised continued to prevail. In his own time, they were prosecuted with deliberate energy. He was acutely conscious that his predecessors had made Gaul Roman in three generations, and that his own action but sealed and recognized their success. In Britain, the policies that had succeeded in Gaul might be applied with conscious vigour, with the express intention of turning the barbarian island into a model Roman province, in a shorter time than the civilizing of Gaul had required.

The projected invasion that Caligula had abandoned was resumed, and the legions were again assembled on the coasts of Gaul, in the summer of 43. The motives that had prompted the attempted invasion three years before still operated; and were reinforced by the policies of the new emperor, for the conservatives welcomed the revival of Roman military glory, and the prospect of an easy triumph over important enemies promised to strengthen the emperor, adding the conventional dignity of a successful soldier to the novel and untried ingenuity of a scholarly ruler.

The only surviving connected account of Claudius' invasion of Britain is the work of Cassius Dio.[4] He was himself a senator and a consular army commander; he wrote nearly two hundred years later, and in

Greek, but he used Latin sources, some of them probably contemporary with the invasion, and other writers preserve incidental detail that amplifies his narrative. According to Dio, it was 'Vericus, who had been exiled by internal conflict', who 'persuaded Claudius to send a force to Britain'. Verica, as his coins call him, was the last surviving son of Commius; his coins are found all over the Atrebatic kingdom, but are commonest on the Sussex coast, from Eastbourne to the neighbourhood of Portsmouth, especially about Selsey, Bognor and Wittering. He was plainly a very old man, for his father had been in his prime a hundred years before, and his brother Tincommius had been driven out, to take refuge with Augustus in Rome, more than thirty years before.[5] His own exile was perhaps more recent, for the coins of his kingdom were minted right on the sea coast, at Medmerry by Selsey, as far from the inland powers as possible, and he may have retained Sussex for some time after Cunobelinus annexed Silchester; but before the Roman conquest, the coins of Cunobelinus appeared in Sussex too, and there is little doubt that the expansion of the Catuvellauni was the cause of the 'internal conflict' that exiled Verica.

The virtuous intention of restoring the exiled Verica to his rightful kingdom doubtless formed the official pretext for invasion, for Roman armies had often enough before advanced as the champions of exiles against usurpers, and might expect to find in Sussex substantial support for the allies of a recently deposed native king, and lively resentment against the conqueror. But the Roman army commanded by the patrician Aulus Plautius fought for its own success. It comprised four citizen legions, with provincial auxiliaries in roughly equal numbers, constituting a total force of some forty to fifty thousand men, about the same size as Caesar's army in 54 BC, perhaps a little larger. But it was a reluctant army, for according to Dio:

Plautius had great difficulty in getting the troops to leave Gaul, since they strongly resented fighting beyond the limits of the known world. He could not persuade them to obey until Claudius sent Narcissus. When he mounted Plautius' tribunal and tried to speak, they shouted him down. He could not get a word across, until they suddenly took up the cry: 'Io Saturnalia' (Happy Christmas); for at the feasts of Saturn slaves act the part of their masters. Then they immediately followed Plautius, with willing enthusiasm.

The point of the story is that Narcissus was Claudius' freedman Secretary, the butt of popular jests at slaves who rose to high authority. The mid-winter festival of Saturn was a safety valve, celebrating the mythical golden age, before Jove displaced his father Saturn, when men were not yet divided into master and slave, rich and poor. The jest was an anti-climax that broke the tension. Senior officers faced with a mutiny stood on the brink of violence, that might cost them their lives if tempers turned ugly. Once the jagged passions of the mutineers turned to laughter, the danger passed. Fears of the wild unknown ocean were real enough, but they were irrational, when Roman power had stood for a century on the coasts of Gaul, able to see the British cliffs twenty miles away in reasonable weather, across waters that plainly held no terrifying monsters or abominable whirlpools. The release of tension turned men's minds from imaginary terrors to the actual easy passage that their eyes could see.

Dio continues:

Because of these delays, the expedition sailed late. The forces were divided into three, to deal more easily with anticipated resistance. During the voyage, they were at first discouraged, because they were blown back, and then encouraged by a meteor, that shot from east to west, the direction in which they were sailing. They landed without opposition, for the British had not expected them to come, judging from what they had heard, and so had not assembled against them. Even when the army landed, the British did not attack, but fled to the forests and marshlands, hoping to wear the Romans down, so that they would sail back with their mission unaccomplished as Julius Caesar had done.

Plautius had difficulty in finding the enemy ... when he did, he defeated first Caratacus, and then Togodumnus, the sons of Cunobelinus, who was now dead. When they fled, he won over a part of the Boduni, who were subject to the Catuvellauni.

Leaving a garrison, he came to a formidable unbridged river, whose crossing was forced by units who swam across in full armour, and required a hard-fought, two-day battle. The Britons then 'withdrew to the Thames, where it discharges into the Ocean, and at high tide floods a marshy lake'.

Only the later places are identifiable. The broad river before the Thames is plainly the Medway; east of the Severn, no other southern river but the Thames presents such obstacles. Interpretation of the earlier campaigning has been influenced by a curious modern assumption that Plautius, like Caesar, landed in east Kent, and advanced directly to the Medway. But it is difficult to compress the long search for the British and the separate campaigns against the two kings into the narrow space between the Medway and the east Kent coast; and Dio's statements virtually rule out the possibility of a landing in Kent. The port of embarkation was almost certainly Boulogne. The fleet sailed westward, but east Kent lies north of Boulogne; westward lies the Sussex coast and Southampton water, the territory of Verica, where Rome might hope to find allies. The three divisions of the armada were separately organized to facilitate landing, but apparently sailed in the same direction, and are unlikely to have remained apart when they discovered that their landing was unopposed. The first encampments of the invading force have not been located in this area, but the most likely location would be in or about the Chichester–Portsmouth region.

After the defeat of Togodumnus, Plautius received the surrender of a part of the 'Boduni', who were subject to the rule of the Catuvellauni of Verulamium, St Albans. It has long been assumed that Dio's 'Boduni' is a mis-spelling of the Dobunni of Gloucestershire and neighbouring counties; the assumption has been much strengthened by the recent excavation of the huge Belgic fortress of Bagendon, by Cirencester.[6] It was the stronghold of a ruler whose pottery and artefacts were Catuvellaunian. A few miles to the south, a fort for an an auxiliary cohort was placed, early in the conquest period, garrisoned by the Ala Indiana, the cavalry regiment first raised twenty years before by Julius Indus of Trier to help the government of Tiberius repress the abortive rising of the Gauls.

Excavation at Richborough has uncovered a supply base of the conquest period; numerous granaries and storehouses were protected by a long ditch and bank, with a single narrow entrance.[7] It is quite unlike the usual defences erected by Roman combat forces, and would have been a death trap for an army attacked by an enemy since it lacks the gateways that permit sallies and counter-attack; but it constitutes an efficient defence against robbers and raiders who might seek to steal or fire the stores. Since Plautius approached the Thames from east Kent after his encounter with the Dobunni, it is to be presumed that he first fell back upon this base, to supply his forces and secure his link with Gaul.

The geography of the invasion cannot be illuminated by the evidence of archaeology, for its dates are too imprecise; pottery and other artefacts may be dated to the time of Claudius, or thereabouts, but cannot distinguish a fort contructed in 43 from one laid out three or four years later; it cannot therefore hope to distinguish the movements of the army in the first few weeks and months of the campaign, from those of the next few years. The geography must depend upon the narrative of Dio; and his directions are westward from Gaul, then the surrender of the Dobunni, then the battle of the Medway and the retreat of the defeated

British to the Thames. The interpretation and elaboration of these few directions will remain a matter for speculation, for the archaeological evidence is incapable of disputing or confirming them.

Dio's subsequent account is the earliest description of the London area:

> The British easily crossed the river, for they knew the firm fords. The Romans pursued, but failed to catch up with them. German units swam across, and others crossed a little higher up stream by a bridge. They attacked the British on all sides, and cut off many of them; but rash pursuit led them into trackless marshes, where many were lost.

The Thames is not now fordable in the London region. But until the later Roman centuries, its level was some fourteen feet lower than it is today. The dramatic and decisive evidence was discovered forty years ago by Sir Mortimer Wheeler; seeking pre-Roman weapons in the Thames mud by Brentford, he discovered the floor of a Romano-British house at low tide mark, deeply drowned at high tide.[8] Since the British did not live under water, it is clear that when that house was built, the high water mark was well below its floor. Since that discovery, ample evidence has been observed of a late Roman transgression, of a water level higher in relation to the land, in eastern England and on the Netherlands coast, and in many other parts of the Atlantic and Mediterranean seaboard. The evidence has not yet been systematically studied, and it is not yet possible to say how gradual or sudden was the change, or when it occurred; but it certainly did not begin until some centuries after Claudius' time.

The tide limit, and the marshy lakes flooded at high tide, are therefore plainly not far from the site of the future city; the Pool of London, the marshes of the Lea mouth, Lambeth marsh may be intended. The bridge a little way upstream cannot be identified; Dio is translating from Latin, and without the Latin original, it is impossible to say whether he meant a permanent pre-Roman bridge, or a pontoon bridge built by the invading army. The layout of the roads (see Map 5, p. 83) suggests that traffic along the Watling Street crossed the Thames at Westminster before the Romans arrived, perhaps long before, but does not say whether the crossing was by ford, by ferry, or by bridge. If the army crossed by pontoon bridge, then the firm fords are likely to have been near Westminster, the bridge towards Chelsea or Hammersmith, the subsequent engagement in the neighbourhood of Kensington, Westminster and Hyde Park. The trackless marshes to which the British withdrew, north of the river, indicate Hackney and Stratford, the line of incautious pursuit by Long Acre and Old Street.

The advance was delayed:

> Though Togodumnus was dead, the British did not surrender, but rallied to avenge him. Plautius was apprehensive, advanced no further, and consolidated his gains. He had been ordered to do so, if difficulties arose, for substantial reserves, including elephants, had been prepared. On receipt of the news, Claudius left Rome ... and joined the army near the Thames. He took over the command, crossed the river, defeated the barbarians who assembled against him in battle, and took Camulodunum (Colchester), the royal stronghold of Cunobelinus. ... Later [in AD 44] he returned to Rome, after an absence of six months, sixteen days of which he had spent in Britain.

Colchester was clearly not taken until the late autumn. Since Claudius himself had to cross the Thames in arms, Plautius had evidently encamped his main force south of the river, somewhere within the bounds of Greater London, though he might have maintained fortified posts to secure his bridgehead on the north bank. Claudius' personal campaign has inspired endless antiquarian fancies, serious and weird. The military eye of Robert Graves selected the ridge of higher ground that blocks the Colchester road by Brentwood as the sensible site for the last stand of the British, and equipped the imaginary Claudius of his novel with unusual tactical ingenuity. But even the fact of the battle is uncertain. The biographer Suetonius, a respectable second-century senior civil servant who strongly disliked the eccentric authority of Claudius, flatly contradicts Dio:[9]

> He undertook only one campaign, and that a modest one. ... Since he wanted a regular triumph, he selected Britain as the most suitable place to earn it ... he received the surrender of a part of the island within a few days, without any battle or bloodshed, and returned to Rome in the sixth month after his departure.

Such direct conflict of evidence on a well-known event is rare; Claudius' own ambiguous words suggest the explanation. The inscription which he caused to be erected on the Capitol in Rome records the surrender of eleven British kings, and the conquest of the island 'without any loss' (*sine ulla iactura*).[10] The words recall Tacitus' satisfaction that Agricola later won the battle of Mons Graupius by the effort of his auxiliaries, with the legions held in reserve, so that the battle was won without the loss of Roman blood. In the critical language of Suetonius, a skirmish that did not involve the legions scarcely deserved to be called a battle. It may be that the contradictory texts can be so reconciled; or it may be that either Suetonius or Dio is plain wrong. There is no further evidence.

Early modern thought bothered little with evidence. The ground now occupied by Kings Cross Station was once called 'Battle Bridge', doubtless after some long forgotten medieval riot. When the station was constructed in the nineteenth century, labourers unearthed some huge tusks, probably mammoth tusks from glacial deposits. But the tusks were naturally credited to Claudius' elephants, and the battle that named the site attached to his invasion. It is just possible that the tusks were elephantine and Claudian, though no evidence suggests that they were; but it is impossible that the battle site should have been remembered through four Roman centuries, the name thereafter translated from British or Latin into English. Such fancies, however, linked Islington with Claudius in popular imagination; a vanished earthwork of unknown origin in Lloyd Square was linked with Claudius as readily as with Caesar, and one northern museum proudly exhibited, until recently, a couple of large rusty medieval keys, tied to a label which bore the ink inscription 'Keys to Aulus Plautius' Roman camp in Islington'. The words evoke the ludicrous concept of Plautius locking up his camp while he went out for the evening; by exaggeration they epitomize the romantic nonsense that has haunted the archaeology of Roman London until quite recent times.

What is certain is that Claudius quickly conquered the Belgic kingdom, and captured Colchester. Caratacus fled to Wales, and held out for eight years, to end his days with dignity, as a prisoner in a comfortable Italian villa, honoured by Romans who respected the stature of a formidable enemy. In one short campaign the Roman army had annexed the realm of Cunobelinus. On and beyond its edges, forts and camps of the conquest period are plentiful; within its borders they are known only within or beside the future towns of the Roman province; for here, in the lowlands, the establishment of Roman control was more quickly and effectively accomplished.

With the Belgic kingdom conquered at one blow, it is likely that the army was immediately deployed upon its borders, in the last months of 43 or the first months of AD 44. Beyond the borders there was fierce fighting. A little is preserved of the campaigns of the Second Augustan Legion, since its commander was the future emperor Vespasian, whose early life is well reported. It fought in the south-west, where it 'overcame two powerful peoples, took more than twenty fortresses and the Isle of Wight'[11] against stiff opposition. One of the two peoples was clearly the

Durotriges of Dorset. The excavation of their principal fortress, Maiden Castle by Dorchester, produced lurid evidence of its last resistance; by the main gate, the fallen were hastily buried where they fell, one of them transfixed by a Roman artillery bolt, still embedded in his skeleton.[12] The other 'powerful people' were doubtless either the Dumnonii of Devon and Cornwall, or perhaps the Belgae of Hampshire and Wiltshire. The other fortresses will be among the Iron Age earthworks of Wessex and the Cotswolds, in some of which small Roman auxiliary forts were inserted after their capture.

Of the other legions, the Fourteenth Gemina reached Wroxeter by Shrewsbury within a few years; large earthworks near Lichfield are likely to have been its earlier winter quarters. The Ninth Hispana was established at Lincoln, perhaps from the beginning.[13] The excavations of Cunobelinus' Camulodunum at Colchester contained sufficient Roman military objects to suggest that a considerable body of troops, probably the Twentieth Legion, was quartered there for some time.[14] Numerous auxiliary forts are disposed between the legionary fortresses. The central part of Cunobelinus' kingdom passed under the direct rule of the Roman legates, Aulus Plautius and his successors. On either flank an independent allied kingdom continued. To the north-east, the Iceni of Norfolk were not annexed to the province until after the rebellion of AD 60–61 (below, pp. 107ff). To the south, Tacitus reports that:

some states were entrusted to king Cogidubnus, who remained loyal till within living memory, perpetuating the ancient long-standing custom of the Roman people, of employing kings as the instruments of enslavement.[15]

Tacitus' 'living memory' stretches back to the 70s AD; and Cogidubnus is located by an inscription at Chichester, now preserved on the wall of the Civic Hall in North Street, a few yards from where it was unearthed in the eighteenth century.[16] It runs

> This temple (was erected) to Neptune and Minerva
> for the well being of the imperial family
> by authority of king Tiberius Claudius Cogidubnus,
> legate of the emperor in Britain.
> The expense was born by the Artisans' Association,
> severally and collectively. The site was presented
> by [Pud]ens son of Pudentinus

Cogidubnus' names declare him to be a Roman citizen. Romans, like moderns, but unlike most ancient peoples, used both a family and a personal name, the first name usually abbreviated, as with moderns. C.

Iulius, P. Cornelius, Ti. Claudius, T. Flavius and the like are the normal basic forms. But Romans, like the modern Welsh, suffer from a shortage of names, particularly among the higher classes. They resorted to the same solution, the addition of an epithet or 'cognomen' that might in origin be a trade, a place, a colour, a personal characteristic. As the Welsh distinguish Dai Jones Post from Dai Jones Baker and Jones the Pony, so the Romans distinguished P. Cornelius Scipio (the staff) from P. Cornelius Lentulus (the sluggard); although the Roman names, once bestowed, became hereditary. By the time of the emperors, most Romans used three names, though in some areas, notably Cisalpine Gaul, whence came very many of the western legionaries, two names remained normal until the time of Claudius and Nero.

New citizens took the name of the Roman whose good offices earned them citizenship; Cicero's friend Cratippus of Smyrna became M. Tullius Cratippus, because his patron's full name was M. Tullius Cicero. Under the imperial monarchy, the great majority of new citizens took the emperor's name, most of the rest the name of the governor, legate or proconsul. The study of names therefore affords a map of the spread of Roman citizenship throughout the provinces. Virtually all provincials named C. Iulius date back to a grant by Caesar or Augustus, though a few might derive from the short reign of Gaius Caligula; and they are for the most part men of native royal families, or of status almost as high. Three emperors bore the three names Tiberius Claudius Nero – personal name, family name, cognomen – and are known to history as Tiberius, Claudius and Nero. Tiberius' citizens were named Ti. Iulius, for he was the adoptive son of Augustus, grandson of Caesar. The name of Ti. Claudius Cogidubnus demonstrates a grant of Roman citizenship by Claudius or by Nero. The names of later emperors mark the continued extension of the Roman citizenship; the T. Flavii owe their citizenship to Vespasian and his sons, M. Ulpii to Trajan, P. Aelii to Hadrian, T. Aelii and T. Aurelii to Antoninus Pius. Some of the M. Aurelii derived citizenship from the emperor Marcus, but most from the emperor Caracalla, who, in AD 212, enrolled the entire freeborn native population of the empire as Roman citizens.

Roman citizens were rare in northern Gaul and Britain in the time of Cogidubnus. He was a king in Sussex; and it is therefore likely that he was the heir of Verica, perhaps his grandson. The approximate area of Cogidubnus' kingdom is known, since the people of Sussex, whose chief town was Chichester, retained the name 'Regnenses', the inhabitants of the kingdom, or *regnum*. The number and extent of the states entrusted to Cogidubnus is not known. They must have included the remainder of the Atrebates, about Silchester, and doubtless also the Belgae about Winchester and Salisbury, once Vespasian had reduced the Isle of Wight and passed on to the Durotriges of Dorset, and possibly the whole of Britain south of the Thames, including Surrey and Kent. In 47 Aulus Plautius' successor Ostorius 'consolidated the country this side of Trent and Severn' and thereby prompted a revolt of the Iceni, who objected to being disarmed.[17] One consequence of this consolidation was the construction of the Fosse Way, from the Humber and Lincoln in an almost straight line by Leicester, Cirencester and Bath to Ilminster in Somerset and to Exeter, a road, or *limes* laid down behind the forward positions of the troops. A second consequence was the entrusting of the states mentioned by Tacitus to the Sussex king. It is unlikely that Cogidubnus' colleague Prasutagus, king of the rebellious Iceni, received comparable authority. His energies were necessarily concentrated on restraining anti-Roman enthusiasm among his own people.

The physical evidence of Cogidubnus' extraordinary authority has recently been revealed by the excavations of Fishbourne, two miles south-west of Chichester. An enormous and luxurious palace, containing many dozens of rooms, was completed somewhere about AD 75, about the time of Cogidubnus' last years; there is no doubt that it was his residence. Exceptionally skilled investigation exposed not only the remains of the building, but also the plan to two huge, formal rose gardens, reaching down to the sea. The Fishbourne palace is far and away the largest and most imposing Roman residence yet known north of the Alps, and compares with the greatest houses of Italy. Its lavish grandeur emphasizes the scale and speed with which Roman civilization transformed the province, faster, more deeply, and more impressively than in northern and central Gaul.[18]

There can be no doubt that Cogidubnus' was a principal voice in decisions that shaped the future of the province. Chief among them was the decision to organize Britain into political states, each equipped with a capital town, on the model of Gaul, and to establish a chief town of the province, London. As a 'consistently loyal' native king, his experience necessarily showed the way in which the precedents of Gaul might be adapted to the conditions of Britain.

Two main kinds of evidence contribute to our understanding of how the Roman towns of Britain began: the archaeological investigation of particular towns, and texts from Europe that describe how Rome set about the foundation of new towns. In the political philosophy of the mature empire, the organization of new provinces, and the well being of old provinces, depended upon thriving towns. A second-century emperor exhorted his legate in Galatia to remember that 'we have an inborn desire to increase the number and the dignity of cities throughout our world', and a fourth-century emperor gave like encouragement to the neighbouring province of Asia: 'we must strive to found new cities and develop old ones'.[19] Claudius' legates tackled the virgin province of Britain with like enthusiasm. Hitherto, the conquered territories had known fortified royal strongholds and country farms, but neither town nor village in the modern sense. The experience of Gaul was quickly applied. Each separate, sizeable people was recognized as a distinct political unit, a *civitas*. The word is best translated 'state'. In the usage of Caesar and Cicero it means only a political community, a collection of *cives*, citizens, bound to one another by a common organization; in the time of the early emperors, it retained this meaning, but was also used to distinguish the physical city from the rural districts; in the late empire it meant only the chief town, which subsumed the political life of the community, and in the clipped speech of late Latin languages was abbreviated to 'cite', English 'city'.

The political form of the states was new. Their separate identity was not. Each was a coherent people, long accustomed to regard themselves as a unit; it is the simple fact that each was a political reality that has prompted modern writers to describe them by the supercilious appellation 'tribe', whose misty connotations imply primitive social habits. The usage of antiquity was more accurate: to Greek writers they were *ethnoi*, rendered in Latin *gentes*, peoples, or, in some specialized senses, *nationes*, nations. The principal change was a certain standardization of size. The swollen kingdom of the Catuvellauni was reduced to its original territory, centred on Verulamium; the Trinovantes of Essex and Suffolk formed a separate state, but several small peoples, including those of the Thames Reaches, are not separately recorded, and were presumably absorbed within the larger states. South of the Thames the Cantii of Kent, the Atrebates of Silchester and of the kingdom of Cogidubnus (the Regni), the Belgae, Durotriges and Dumnonii, were all allotted fixed frontiers. The Dobunni of the Cotswolds and lower Severn, the Cornovii of the upper Severn and modern Staffordshire, the Coritani to their east, in Leicestershire, Nottinghamshire and Lincolnshire, were of comparable size. (See Map 3.)

Each of these dozen states acquired the institutions of a normal Roman dependent foreign ally; they were *tributarii*, *peregrini*, *socii* – taxpayers,

3 The *Civitates* of Roman Britain

○ Colonia or Municipium

● Civitas capital

--- Approximate Civitas boundaries

CALEDONIAN CONFEDERACY

DAMNONII

SELGOVAE

VOTADINI

NOVANTAE

CARVETII

BRIGANTES

Aldborough
(Isurium Brigantum)

PARISI

York
(Eburacum)

Brough *(Petuaria)*

DECEANGLI

ORDOVICES

Lincoln
(Lindum)

CORITANI

CORNOVII

Wroxeter
(Viroconium Cornoviorum)

Leicester
(Ratae Coritanorum)

ICENI

Caistor-by-Norwich
(Venta Icenorum)

DEMETAE

Carmarthen
(Moridunum)

DOBUNNI

CATUVELLAUNI

SILURES

Gloucester *(Glevum)*

Cirencester
(Corinium Dobunnorum)

St. Albans
(Verulamium)

London
(Londinium)

TRINOVANTES

Colchester
(Camulodunum)

Caerwent
(Venta Silurum)

ATREBATES

Silchester ● *(Calleva Atrebatum)*

BELGAE

CANTIACI

Canterbury
(Durovernum Cantiacorum)

DUMNONII

Winchester
(Venta Belgarum)

REGNENSES

DUROTRIGES

Chichester *(Noviomagus Regnensium)*

Exeter
(Isca Dumnoniorum)

Dorchester
(Durnovaria)

0 10   50 miles

10   80 km

foreigners, allies. These institutions are well enough known from the several surviving codes that Rome laid down for other allies. Substantial sections of particular constitutions laid down for individual cities, notably in Spain and Asia Minor, also survive. These were all towns with developed internal differences; rich men owned land, cattle, houses and slaves, artisans practised their trades, labourers worked for hire and tenants paid rent. Belgic conquest had accustomed most of the British states to similar social inequalities; and in the remainder, the preparation of a military force to withstand the Belgic threat had also created a class of notables.

The first step was to create a government in each state; thereafter to prompt and guide its work. An individual Roman was responsible for the first initiative; the law that Caesar provided for Urso (Osuna) in southern Spain provided that 'C. Caesar, or whoever shall found the city on his orders' shall appoint the first priests and magistrates. The first nominees shall hold office until the 31st December next', and then be replaced by elected magistrates.[20] Each state had its council, similarly initiated, its size varying with the town; two hundred years after Caesar's time, when the district of Tymandus in Galatia became a *civitas*, the imperial legate was instructed: 'You should establish the number of *decurions* (councillors) for the time being at fifty.'[21] Thereafter, in normal practice, the decurions, collectively known as the *ordo*, or local senate, were recruited from magistrates, who automatically became councillors for life, like the senators in Rome. The regulations took account of the individual past of each province. Since Rome first undertook the organization of provinces outside Italy, a standard procedure developed. A law of the Senate and People of Rome laid down the overall working rules of each province; and the law was named from the senator who moved it in the house. The *Lex Rupilia de Sicilia, Lex Pompeia de Bithynia*, Rupilius' Law on Sicily, Pompey's Law on Bithynia, were formulated according to normal Roman practice, and their essentials were modified in detail as Roman practice changed.

There would certainly have been a *Lex Claudia de Britannia*, establishing the overall rules. Standard policy required a clause providing for the appointment of the foremost notables as magistrates and decurions by 'Claudius Caesar or whoever founds the *civitas* on his orders'. The immediate agents of his orders were his legates, who would in turn appoint a particular individual to supervise the institution of each separate state. The date at which this process was initiated was clearly 47, the year in which the new legate Ostorius 'consolidated' the province 'this side of the Trent and Severn'.

The pace was forced. Claudius made gifts of money to the leading British notables; and the philosopher Seneca, then tutor to the young Nero, and for a while effectively chief minister of the government, after Claudius' death in 54, 'lent the British forty millions, against their will, in the hope of high interest'.[22] The use of political force to compel reluctant private persons to borrow capital was a current evil, which later emperors denounced and forbade.

The institutions of state governments needed the physical cities in which they could be exercised; and each of the dozen states speedily acquired its town: Canterbury, Chichester and Silchester in the south east, Winchester, Dorchester and Exeter to their west, Cirencester, Verulamium and Leicester north of the Thames. Miscellaneous excavated objects of mid-first-century date argue that these nine towns came into existence soon after the conquest; but their initial size and extent cannot normally be determined, for the evidence of archaeology cannot easily distinguish shops and houses constructed in the first few years from those built fifteen or twenty years later. The scale of these first foundations can at present only be approximately observed in three towns that were burnt down in the rising of Boudicca, in AD 60 to 61: Verulamium, Colchester and London. In these towns, a thick layer of burnt debris lies over buildings put up and used only in the years between 47 and 60; it does not of course indicate the total area of the towns, for fires do not necessarily consume every building, but it accurately marks the concentrated centre of each town.

Although archaeological evidence cannot trace the origin and growth of these towns in their first few years, one or two peculiarities suggest their probable early development. Many of them are located within a mile or two of an earlier stronghold, the residence of one of the eleven kings who submitted to Claudius. Winchester lies below St Catherine's Hill, Cirencester by Bagendon, Dorchester a few miles from the Durotrigian fortress of Maiden Castle, Roman Verulamium between the Belgic capital on Prae Wood and the river, Colchester above Belgic Camulodunum. Two, Salisbury and Silchester, were built upon the site of the previous stronghold. A second peculiarity is that a number of these towns grew up within or by a fortified enclosure, whose ditch proclaims the work of army sappers, the legionary *fabrenses*. Such a ditch, of about the size and shape of a legionary camp, encloses the first Roman city of Verulamium, while Cirencester grew up around the auxiliary fort of Watermoor Park. Several of the smaller towns had a similar beginning: Dorchester-on-Thames lay within a small fort; Durobrivae, Water Newton by Peterborough, close to such a fort; Sulloniacae, Brockley Hill, at the northern extremity of the Edgware Road, is placed upon a hill-top that commands an extensive view from the Kent hills towards Verulamium, whose military utility cannot have escaped the notice of Aulus Plautius.

Several considerations concern the siting of towns by native strongholds and Roman forts. It is natural that for at least a short period an impressive force should be posted beside the native strongholds, that their inhabitants might see the strength of Roman troops and learn to fear and respect them. It does not necessarily follow that every such enclosure was a military fort or encampment, though some certainly were. Military engineers could have provided the civil city of Verulamium with a ditch and rampart, though it is at least equally probable that an army first encamped outside the old native stronghold, and that the civil town shortly afterwards was developed within its bounds.

It is, however, unlikely that sizeable forces stayed for any length of time within the borders of Cunobelinus' kingdom. The known permanent forts lie on or beyond its borders; Dorchester-on-Thames lies upon the probable frontier between the Catuvellauni and the Atrebates, the probable fort of Ixworth, on the watershed between the Waveney and the Little Ouse, by the frontier of the Icenian kingdom. Cirencester, Water Newton and many others lie beyond or by the further frontier of Belgic conquest. The main body of the troops was soon established on or beyond the Fosse Way. The extended front needed communications, and the roads that linked it with the south-eastern coast had to be laid down by military detachments, or at least under their supervision. Such detachments necessarily stayed for a few weeks at particular points while the roads were cleared and laid, and needed a temporary, defended camp while so engaged. Such encampments are the likely origin of many of the post stations and some of the towns. The short distances between them are equally suitable for road-building parties and for the subsequent remount stables.

These urgent military considerations were a problem of the first year or so after the initial conquest. By their nature, they were quickly resolved. When the troops departed, they left behind them at least a few government personnel to supervise the supply of fresh horses, carriages, and waggons; and it may well be that the needs of men passing along roads, and collecting taxation at roadside stations, already attracted some native settlement even before 47, while the legate and his staff were still preoccupied with organizing the military frontier. But the early development of Verulamium, where Boudicca's fire enables the first city to be studied, demonstrates that the growth of the town was not left to haphazard casual settlement. One main street by the town centre was flanked by a long building containing several shops, planned and erected as a single unit; one of the shops contained a bronzesmith's hearth, and when the entire block was rebuilt as a unit after the fire of 61, a new hearth was placed above the debris that covered the old one. Here the new town was deliberately planned and developed; one man, or conceivably the public authority, erected a row of shops upon a desirable street frontage, and rented them to shopkeepers. The plan is not the work of individuals, each selecting his own site, and putting his own building upon it separately from his neighbours.[23] Similar property development is necessarily implied by the rectangular street grid of most towns; they were the work of Roman town planners, acting on behalf of a constituted civic authority. Such planning implies a consequence of the consolidation that began about 47, or in the immediately following years, when the frontier was firmly established.

The towns were new, not only individually but collectively, for towns in themselves were a novelty in Britain. Their purpose was political, only incidentally economic. The town was the seat of government; it also held prisoner its citizens, for when the notables held Roman office in Roman towns, and bought property and commodities with the money they were given or lent by Romans, they had a great deal to lose if they ran foul of the imperial government. The town seduced the native leaders of the British into a necessary compliance with the conquerors and, novel and imposing, overawed the rural population; and artisans who set up business in the new towns also acquired a valuable personal interest in Roman survival.

The political town was a threat to rebels; and those who took up their residence within it thereby gave the government a pledge of good behaviour. But once it was founded, it began to transform the economy of its territory. The towns were linked by roads, and traffic moved upon the roads. The Watling Street linked the Thames with Canterbury and the ports of the short sea crossing, Dover and Richborough. North of the Thames, roads radiated to the principal military centres: Colchester, Lincoln, the Lichfield area, and Gloucester (see Map 8, p. 132). Official traffic required frequent change of horses; and at intervals of eight or ten miles, posting stations were established. Where monied travellers passed, persons in need of money settled to serve their needs and receive their cash. The armies required food and other supplies, paid in kind by the taxation of the province; the towns and posting stations became the centres at which these tax renders were delivered. The towns themselves also needed food; a poll tax was imposed, and peasants were induced to bring foodstuffs for sale in the town.

Men and goods moved further and more often than before, and this movement enriched some of the British. Farmers fortunately placed beside a growing town or post station prospered; and within a generation the men who lived within a mile or two of a town, and a few hundred yards of a road, were rich enough to build themselves rectangular farm houses with stone footings, with six to ten rooms on the ground floor, planned by architects trained in Roman skills. These homes, the so-called smaller 'villas' of Roman Britain, were comfortable properties that might fetch something of the order of £20,000 today,[24] if still standing intact and fully habitable. They began to be built a generation or so after the conquest, and attest the accumulation of profits rising over thirty or more years. Most of the post stations they served grew into small market towns, when they were sited in a region of good farmland; one or two, on the edge of the Sussex Weald, did not so develop, and their excavation demonstrates the early form of the post station, a ditch and bank enclosing half an acre or so of stabling, sleeping accommodation and shops.[25] Some were larger than others, for the distance between two of them is roughly the distance that a man might walk conveniently in a day, or a military detachment march, or a waggon travel; but a horseman might as comfortably cover thirty miles, or three stations, in a day. Elsewhere in Europe, the Roman itineraries, road guide books, distinguish between the *mansiones*, where mounted travellers might stay the night, and the *mutationes*, where they might change a tired for a fresh horse; and a similar distinction determined the size and scale of the first British stations.

Towns in Roman Britain, as in later societies, including our own, had differing formal status. The modern town may be a city, a borough, a county borough, an urban district.[26] The usage of Roman Britain and Roman Gaul distinguished similarly between the urban district, *vicus*, and the rural district, *pagus*. The *civitas*, alternatively called the *res publica*, comprised all the *vici* and *pagi* within its territory, including its chief town, the *caput civitatis*. The chief town of the newly-defined Atrebatic state was Silchester, Calleva Atrebatum, that of the Kentish peoples Canterbury, *Durovernum Cantiacorum*. Brough-on-Humber,

Petuaria, was the *caput*, head or capital, of the *civitas* of the Parisii of Britain, just as Lutetia Parisiorum, the modern Paris, was the *caput* of Gaul. But Brough is attested on a second-century inscription as a *vicus*.[27] The same word was used for the subdivisions of the city of Rome; modern Greater London has similar divisions, with the minor difference that current administrative language has elected to call them boroughs rather that urban districts. The word *vicus* was also used for the small towns that grew up around the later settled Roman forts in Britain; it was the normal status of the non-Roman town, inhabited by 'foreigners', *peregrini*, the subject allies. A few towns were in addition accorded the higher status of Roman towns, *coloniae* or *municipia*. Centuries before, Rome had held down the Gauls of northern Italy by planting among them military colonies, *coloniae*, of Roman citizens, while the commonest term for the Latin cities of Italy was *municipium*. In the early empire, *coloniae* served the additional purpose of housing discharged veterans from the army, and the title *municipium* was bestowed upon successful cities; the higher status bestowed by both these titles was an honour eagerly sought by the developing towns of the Roman provinces. Both *coloniae* and *municipia* might consist either of Roman or of Latin citizens, though in practice almost all *coloniae* were Roman, almost all *municipia* Latin; but in Latin communities the magistrates, and therefore the decurions, received Roman citizenship on election.

The status of the towns of Britain is known only when a chance phrase used by a writer, or an official inscription, proclaims its official title at a particular date. Beyond the Fosse Way, the Cornovii of Shropshire and Staffordshire were still officially a *civitas* in the early second century,[28] the Silures of Monmouthshire and Glamorgan a *respublica* a hundred years later. But Tacitus described Verulamium as a *municipium* at the time of its destruction in AD 60.[29] His evidence has had a rough reception until recently. When the splendid public buildings and large extent of early Verulamium were misdated, in the course of earlier excavations, first-century Verulamium was held to be too tiny a place to justify the rank of *municipium*, and unwise examiners sometimes asked their students to explain why Tacitus was 'wrong'. Now that a Claudian boundary ditch suggests the considerable size of the first-century town, and an inscription dates the opening of its immense town centre to the later first century, there is no longer an incentive to dispute the evidence of contemporaries; for the authority for Tacitus' statement was his father-in-law Agricola, who was in Britain when the *municipium* was overrun. But even when accepted, the statement was abused: since it was the only explicit written reference to a *municipium* in Britain, in 60 or at any other time, Verulamium has not infrequently been described as the only *municipium* in Britain throughout the Roman period; and this strange assertion tempted some at first to deny the evidence that shows Leicester to have become a *municipium* also in the later first century,[31] probably in the late 70s AD.

The formal difference was expressed by the official name of the state. Not merely the town itself, but the entire territory, became a *municipium*. Italian inscriptions distinguish between *intramuri* and *extramuri*, citizens within and without the walls; the constitution of the *municipium* of Tarentum prescribed that a necessary qualification for a councillor was that he should own a house with not less than 1,500 roof tiles, either in the town of Tarentum, or within the boundaries of its *municipium*.[32] The name of the state therefore changed – the *civitas Catuvellaunorum* was replaced by the *municipium Verulamiense*.[33] There is little evidence for other towns. One stone from Silchester refers to the town still as Calleva, without the prefix 'municipium', in the second century,[34] but it is not official, and unofficial usage will still call Luton a town more readily than a county borough, so that the exact status of Silchester is still in doubt. Similarly, when a military 'diploma', the official certificate of citizenship of an auxiliary soldier, granted on discharge, describes its recipient as a 'Belgus', a citizen of the state of the Belgae, at the beginning of the second century,[35] it is evidence that Winchester was not then a *municipium*, but no evidence for its future history.

Coloniae were fewer than *municipia*, more honourable, and different in their purpose and their population. Claudius founded two *coloniae*, more or less simultaneously, in the military north: Cologne and Colchester. Both were already major native towns, both centres of respectful worship of the state gods of Rome. Tacitus' brief notice of Colchester explains its double purpose: 'the colonia of Camulodunum was founded in conquered territory by a strong body of veterans, a help against rebels, a means of training the allies to observe law and order.'[36] The *colonia* had from the beginning been a community of armed Romans settled in the midst of alien allies of uncertain loyalty; under the early emperors, it was also a principal means of allocating land to retired soldiers.

The relation of a *colonia* to the surrounding peoples was in a state of change. When the *colonia* of Lyon was founded in the territory of the Segusiavi in 43 BC, a Roman *colonia* could not simultaneously serve as the chief town of a Gallic people, and *Forum Segusiavorum*, some thirty miles to the west, became the centre of the native allied *civitas*. But by the time of Trajan, at the beginning of the second century AD, the town had been upgraded to the dignity of *Colonia Forum Segusiavorum*. The word had ceased to denote a special kind of town, for Romans only, outside the native local organization; it had become an honourable distinction, grading a town higher than others, comparable with the superior status of 'city' or 'county borough' over plain 'borough' in our society.

The foundations of Claudius lay half-way between these dates; and the *colonia* at Colchester related to the Trinovantes, in whose territory it stood, in a manner intermediate between these extremes. It was a city of Romans, at first physically distinct. Old Camulodunum, the capital of Cunobelinus, was situated at the foot of the hill; the new *colonia* was established on top of the plateau, laid out as a Roman rectangle, with a grid of streets intercepting at right angles. The old city continued to be inhabited for some five to ten years after the conquest, and was then abandoned. It is probable that its inhabitants migrated, to live as inferior inhabitants beside the Roman citizen population. There is no evidence to suggest that Chelmsford or any other Trinovantian town became a new capital for the *civitas*; but a few miles south-east of the town, by Gosbeck's Farm, well within the territory of the *colonia*, an isolated theatre and temple, standing by themselves remote from any town, could be a new meeting place for the annual assembly of the Trinovantes.[37]

Within the town, the principal building was the colossal and magnificent temple of the emperor Claudius.[38] Later a fortification, then a Norman castle, it is now the museum, and still stands upon a foundation of vaulted concrete constructed in Claudius' time. Tacitus described it as a 'citadel of everlasting domination' in the eyes of the British; whose notables were 'picked as priests, and compelled to spend their whole fortunes' in honour of Roman gods.[39] The temple corresponded to the *Ara Ubiorum*, altar of the Ubii, the older name of Cologne, and the *Ara Augusti* by Lyon, the annual meeting place, not of one *civitas* but of the representatives of the *civitates* of the whole province. They elected one of their number in turn to serve as *sacerdos provinciae*, chief priest of the province, presiding over the meeting of the Provincial Assembly, and of the games that he provided for it at his own expense. In most provinces, at most times, when the expense was tolerable, the presidency of the province was an honour keenly sought; when, as in Claudian Britain, it was a ruinous burden, men strove to avoid it. It is likely that a few individual British notables, either independently wealthy, or those to whom Claudius gave money, accepted nomination with satisfaction; but there were not yet enough such men, and others had to be coerced into accepting. Those who borrowed Seneca's money at high interest are clearly included among the unwilling nominees whom Tacitus described.

The scale of expense necessarily matched the scale of the temple itself. Its excavated ruins, visually illustrated by an impressive model now to be seen in Colchester Museum, attest its magnificence. Columns of gleaming white marble, the interior and the surrounding wall picked out with dazzling coloured marbles imported from Italy and Africa, shone out from the hill-top over the neighbouring lands, visible for many miles, a 'citadel of dominion' inescapably awe-inspiring, in a land whose grandest palace had previously been no more than a timber hall with little architectural pretension. At the time of its first construction, it was one of the most ambitious public buildings north of the Alps, a witness of the lavish scale of Rome in Britain, as striking as the palace of Cogidubnus.

The organized formal worship of the Roman gods, including the image of the emperor's divinity, was a political act of loyalty to the state, the equivalent of the drinking of the royal toast or the singing of 'God Save the Queen' in modern society. Its initial weakness in Britain was simply that its pace was forced upon newly-conquered notables who had not yet learnt to wish that the gods might preserve the emperor, at a time when many still hoped that the gods might destroy him and all his works. The *colonia*, with its imperial worship, its gleaming temple, its arrogant Roman population, overawed the natives, but imperfectly attracted them to sympathy with Roman government. The more modest layout of the ordinary *civitas* capitals, and of the post stations that linked them, was better adapted to the double purpose of deterring the defiant and encouraging the loyal. These were the essentials of the ordering of the province, beginning in the years 48 to 50. The defence and extension of the territories first acquired needed a stable rear; its organization was the work of imperial legates. This speedy construction of an urban society within a land that had hitherto known neither towns nor political unity is the context in which London was founded.

Chapter 5

The Founding of London

LONDON BEGAN WITH a bridge. Like Rome itself, the city was placed at the lowest crossing place of a major river. The Thames had to be crossed before Colchester could be taken; thereafter, when the legions marched northward and westward to winter quarters deep inland, they needed a secure link with the Roman mainland, by way of the Channel ports. The site was chosen because it was the best place for a bridge, and the city came later, a consequence of the bridge.

There is no direct evidence to pinpoint the exact places where the army fought, encamped, or crossed the river; but there is evidence to suggest some of the most probable sites, where excavation may one day find traces of Aulus Plautius' campaign. Plautius first crossed the Thames where the high tide made a marsh (above, p. 55). The geology of the London region (Map 4) shows the approximate limits of the tidal marsh, before the river was confined by man-made banks. It extends to Vauxhall and Pimlico, confined to the north of the present river, from Tower Bridge to Westminster, by an extensive bank of gravel, cut only by the Walbrook and the Fleet river. Fords were known to the British, but, with one exception, they are likely to have lain above the tidal marsh. The exception is a tiny patch of gravel that rose above the surrounding shallows where the Tyburn joins the Thames. When it had reverted to nature in the troubles of the fifth and sixth centuries, the first English gave it the descriptive name of Thorney Island, before they built upon it the western monastery, Westminster; and that was its appearance when the Roman armies first arrived. Dividing the wet ground and water, the island of Westminster is a likely site for a ford, and the obvious siting for a Roman military engineer, who needed a firm bridgehead defended by a natural moat on the opposite shore. The alignment of roads laid down a little later, discussed below, suggest that the obvious site was in fact selected.

The army crossed, very probably by a pontoon bridge, and ran into trouble while pursuing the enemy in swamps north of the river, presumably about the Isle of Dogs and the mouth of the Lea. Plautius 'advanced no further, and consolidated his gains' (above, p. 58), while he awaited the emperor with his reinforcements. The writer whom Cassius

Dio quotes, very possibly a contemporary, adds that Claudius joined the army before crossing the Thames. Plautius had therefore consolidated south of the river. He kept his gains, and therefore stayed in the London region, in or about Southwark. He could hardly have done otherwise; he could not afford to withdraw behind the Medway, whose crossing had already cost him a bloody two-day battle, and the ground affords no position as defensible between London and the Medway. It was also an elementary and inescapable precaution that an army so encamped should hold a bridgehead on the opposite bank, and should build a military bridge, a floating pontoon easily destroyed in case of a successful attack on the bridgehead.

There is no further written evidence of what Plautius did, and where, before Claudius came, but certain inferences may be drawn. Plautius was an experienced commander, the senior general of his day. He is most unlikely to have disregarded the normal military precautions and practices of the time. Compelled to stay put for several weeks, he was obliged to concentrate his main force in a defended encampment, to secure his lines of communication, and to guard against surprise attack in force.

Roman field encampments could be of almost any shape and size, but in the first century, unless the ground dictated otherwise, they normally favoured an oblong layout, or playing-card shape, most often with its shorter sides about three-quarters of the length of the longer, and with two gates in each of the long sides, one in the middle of each shorter side. It needed to be the right size for the number of troops it contained. Two Roman writers at different dates describe ideal sizes for these forts, but known earthworks are a surer guide. The closest parallel in Britain is a series of encampments in southern Scotland, probably constructed a little over a century and a half later, for a campaigning army a little smaller than Plautius' total command. They enclose an area of 165 acres. But Plautius had to detach a considerable part of his force for the eighty-mile-long communications with his coastal base, to garrison bridgeheads north of the Thames, and perhaps to guard and patrol the Thames upstream from London, to give warning of any threatening concentration of enemy forces; and similar precautions might have been deemed necessary on the North Downs. There are no means of guessing at the numbers of the detached units beyond the obvious, that they are likely to have been numerous, but are not likely to have been as much as half the total force. The concentrated army is therefore likely to have required an encampment of well over a hundred acres.

4 The Geology of the Greater London Area

(drawn by L. Schaaf)

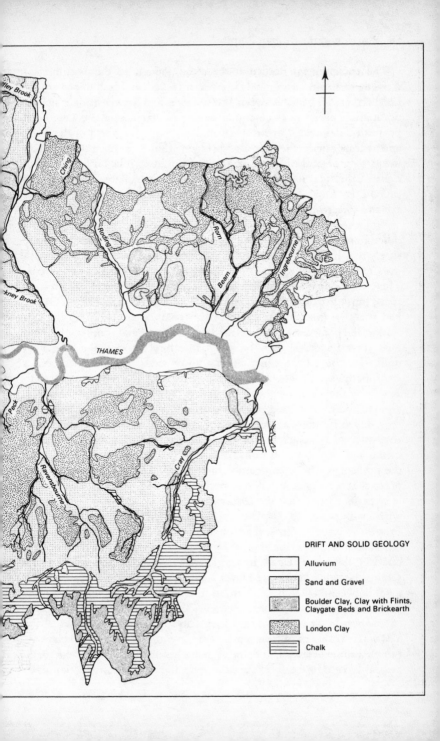

DRIFT AND SOLID GEOLOGY

Alluvium

Sand and Gravel

Boulder Clay, Clay with Flints,
Claygate Beds and Brickearth

London Clay

Chalk

The encampment needed to be close enough to the Westminster crossing to reinforce it quickly if it was attacked, and also to protect the northern gravel bank, between Westminster and Tower bridge, against occupation by enemies emerging from the marshes of the Lea. Such protection demanded one to two small strongpoints north of the river, and at least one further pontoon bridge within easy reach of reinforcements to protect them. The encampment needed to be on firm ground, clear of the tidal marsh, which coincides approximately with a street called Long Lane. No trace of such an encampment, probably of about 100 to 150 acres, has yet been found.[1]

Wherever he sited his encampment, Plautius had to undertake one other major construction in the weeks of waiting, whose traces are more surely recognizable. He had to build a good road to link his army with the Channel port of Richborough, and perhaps also Dover and Lympne. There can be no doubt that the wheeled traffic of the Belgae had brought roads into use before the Romans came. A hundred years earlier, Caesar had found a road, a *via*, north of the Thames, probably up the Lea Valley, the predecessor of the Roman north road; and some sort of road must have joined the London and Canterbury regions. But it is most unlikely to have been either engineered or straight or metalled, and a worn pathway, although serviceable enough for the advancing Roman armies as they first fought their way to the Medway and the London region, was hardly good enough for the needs of the entrenched army that stayed by the Thames. Plautius needed to construct a well-made roadway, solid enough for the passage of the emperor, with his reinforcements and elephants, his numerous heavy waggons and the coaches of the noblemen who accompanied him. The imperial dignity as well as practical necessity required a properly engineered, metalled road, and it is virtually certain that the Dover Road, at least as far as Canterbury, with its extension to Richborough, was the first Roman road built in Britain. The road from Richborough, through Canterbury and Rochester, aims straight for the bank of the southernmost bend of the Thames, opposite the Isle of Dogs. Its last known stretch, by Greenwich Park, retains the name of the Old Dover Road. Its course implies an encampment between Lambeth and Rotherhithe. Within that region, the Southwark area is the most probable, with bridgehead fort and pontoon bridge somewhere in the region of the future City.

Roman trunk roads were engineered, with a cambered surface of rammed stone or gravel, and drainage ditches on both sides. These roads are easily recognized in excavation, and their solid construction gave them a long life. But these engineered main roads were no more than the framework of the road system, and were fed by a multitude of secondary, unpaved roads, whose Roman origin can rarely be proved when they survive, enabling wheeled traffic to reach every farm and mansion.

The only irrefutable proof of the course of a Roman road is the excavation of a section of it. But when two or more sections have been excavated at different places on the same line, it is common sense to assume that the road continued between them, without verifying every yard of the road. A second sensible assumption stems from later history.

In Britain, many roads were little used for some centuries after the fall of Rome, and few new trunk roads were constructed before the fast coaches of the late eighteenth century. Sections of the road became waterlogged, or obstructed by fallen buildings, and when the volume of road traffic resumed, from the twelfth century onward, trunk roads were obliged to make deviations, of a few yards or a few miles, to avoid the obstructed sections, which had often become cultivated land, or served as floors for barns. Most of these deviations remain, but sometimes modernization reverts to the straight Roman course. In the few cases where modern trunk roads link towns of Roman origin in straight stretches, it is usually and properly assumed that the modern road is built upon its Roman predecessor.

The Dover road is such a road. A few sections have been shown by excavation to overlie the Roman surface, and there is no reason to expect extensive deviations elsewhere. As with many other Roman roads, much of it lies on a straight alignment between terminal points, but some stretches deviate from the alignment, to avoid unsuitable ground, or to take in places that lie off the alignment. The proper understanding of these roads requires the record not only of their actual course, but also of their alignment, and of the relation between course and alignment. In the flat lands beneath the North Downs, nature required only one significant bend in a straight line. The site chosen for the bridging of the Medway was at the top of a sharp S-bend in the river, guarded on the east by the fort of Rochester. To cross the river, the road had to veer sharply towards the north, and turn westward beyond the river. From the river crossing at Canterbury to the beginning of the Medway bend by Rochester, the overall alignment is 103° (13°) 30′. West of Canterbury, the road deviates slightly to the south of the alignment, but returns to it at Bapchild, east of Sittingbourne. It then runs straight along the survey line for ten miles to the Medway bend, with one slight kink at Rainham. These minor and tiny variants may have been due to differences in the soil, or may have been the result of slight errors in the surveying. From the other end of the Rochester bridgehead, in the centre of Strood, to Shooter's Hill in Blackheath, the alignment is 103° (13°) 24'.

For the first eight miles west of Rochester, the Roman and medieval roads depart from the straight line, to take in the considerable Roman sites in Cobham Park and Springhead. What survives is the permanent road of settled empire, after the conquest, and the first road laid down by Plautius did not necessarily swing from its course to serve these places; it may be that the earliest road followed the straight line, but was disused a few years later when roads needed to serve existing places. But whatever its early course, the road follows its survey line precisely for twelve miles, from Swanscombe Park through Dartford to Shooter's Hill. From Shooter's Hill the survey line continues to meet the Thames bank precisely opposite Westminster, the probable site of the first crossing. These precise alignments are neither a coincidence nor an oddity. They simply mean that the survey points chosen for the layout of the road were Westminster, Shooter's Hill and the Medway bridgehead. But the road did not follow the line when the ground was unfit. If the road had been continued direct from Shooter's Hill to Westminster, its course would have crossed the wettest part of the tidal marsh, shaving the south bank of the present river in the extensive mud of the mouth of Deptford creek, requiring an immense, unnecessary labour of building heavy causeways, at risk of flooding. The Roman engineers were not so foolish. From Shooter's Hill the road turned sharply south-westward. The first mile of this turn is still in use, now named Charlton Way, and its further course across Blackheath is marked upon eighteenth-century maps. The nature of the ground explains its line, for it met the Ravensbourne, the Deptford river, at the one point where its soft banks were hardened by a tiny outcrop of chalk, cut through by the stream, immediately north of modern Lewisham station. The contrast between the surrounding soil and the chalk is marked by the medieval and modern road beyond it, Loampit Lane, or Hill and Vale. The point where it turned to resume its original line is not now discoverable, but its course is picked up again in less than a mile; the line of the medieval Dover Road, to New Cross Road and the Old Kent Road, as far as Albany Road points directly to the Elephant and Castle and the Westminster crossing (see Map 5).[2] There is no evidence to suggest that a road was ever built on the last stretch, and the actual course of the Old Kent Road does not follow the line; for from Albany Road the Old Kent Road swings to the north-west, and is continued by Great Dover Street to the junction of Long Lane and the Borough High Street. It is possible that the earliest line led to Westminster, but it is unlikely to have retained its importance after the city was established, for little of the traffic from the Midlands to Kent would have wished to by-pass London. It is likely that it never received more than a slight, initial surfacing, and was soon reduced to a little-used lane. Whatever the course of the last mile of the road, it is highly probable that Plautius constructed an engineered and metalled road from Westminster and Southwark to Rochester, Canterbury and Richborough, while he awaited the arrival of Claudius, and that the line of that road was surveyed from Westminster to the Medway bridgehead on an alignment of $103\frac{1}{2}°$ ($13\frac{1}{2}°$).

These great stretches of straight road, pointing to distant places, seem remarkable on the ground or upon the map. But there is nothing odd about them. They are the consequence of Roman surveying techniques, efficient but simple. Before the road was made, the surveyors controlled both ends. Between two points a straight line is not only the easiest to survey, with limitless cheap labour, sighting-poles and flags, but also the easiest to build, when the soil permits, and no existing buildings or property rights get in the way. The same simple explanation applies to the layout of urban streets in London and elsewhere; and is emphasized by the practical simplicity of the main Roman surveying instrument, the *groma*. It consisted of a pole driven into the ground, with an equal-armed cross pivoted upon its top. The cross at once gave a sighting on a straight line, or at a right-angle. Any other angle was more difficult. The instrument was so universally used that it provided the Latin word for surveyors, *gromatici*. Repeated sightings with the *groma* enabled lines of ranging-poles to be planted over long distances to mark the base-line of the road, before the surveyors walked over it to select its actual route; and the ranging-poles drew them back to the base-line when the country and forests and river crossings so permitted. When the Fosse Way line was marked, trial and error easily allowed the surveyors to discover the point upon it that made a right-angle with Colchester, for though military considerations determined the exact sites of the fortresses at Lincoln and Chester, no natural reason demanded that Leicester should be where it is, rather than a mile or two up or down stream. A *groma* placed in the centre of the forum of Roman Leicester, with one arm along the Fosse Way alignment, points its other arm at a precise right-angle to the temple of Claudius in Colchester, a hundred miles away (see Map 8, p. 132). Such precise rectangular alignments are plentiful among the known Roman roads of Britain.

Plautius' army camped in or near Southwark, and its bridgeheads across the river were the beginnings of London. But they did not long remain. Claudius came, led his army across the Thames to capture Colchester, and returned to Rome. The Belgic kingdom of the sons of Cunobelinus was annexed, and the army advanced to the borders of the conquered kingdom, the Ninth Legion to Lincoln, the Second to the south-west, to the Hampshire and Dorset coast, and thereafter to Gloucester, the Fourteenth north-westwards to Wall by Lichfield, and to Wroxeter by Shrewsbury. Within four years a frontier line was established, with its base-line on the Fosse Way. For a few years the Twentieth Legion probably remained in reserve at Colchester. From the time of their advance, in the last months of 43, the forces needed supply routes, linking them with headquarters at Colchester, and with the Channel ports, and across the Thames bridges at London. The course and alignment of these roads in the London region argues that they were laid down before the lasting Roman bridge was built, and before the city was founded (Map 5).

The north road (Ermine Street) runs for a dozen miles dead straight towards the Thames, to a point a little north of Liverpool Street Station; there it angles south-westward towards the bridge of the Roman city. But a continuation of the straight line would meet the Thames some way to the east of the Roman city bridge, towards the Customs House, halfway between the bridge and the Tower. There is no evident reason in the soil why it should not have been surveyed and laid out from the Roman city bridge if the bridge had been there when it was surveyed. The probable explanation is that it was aligned on a pontoon bridge of the invading army, before the permanent city bridge was built. It is evident that a garrison must have been left to keep the fort and Plautius' military crossing by Southwark, during the Colchester campaign, and that crossing plainly afforded the first connections between Richborough and Ermine Street, the north road to the legion at Lincoln and its supporting troops. However, in the south-east, between Kent and the Solent, where Cogidubnus was king, there is no record and no likelihood of serious campaigning, and the southward roads, to Lewes and Seaford, to Brighton and to Chichester, are aligned on the city bridge, and were therefore probably not built before its erection. But the roads that linked Colchester and the Channel ports with the western legions altogether avoided the future city, and therefore probably follow the course of roads laid down in the first months after the conquest. The ports and the Kent road were linked with the north-western legions in and about

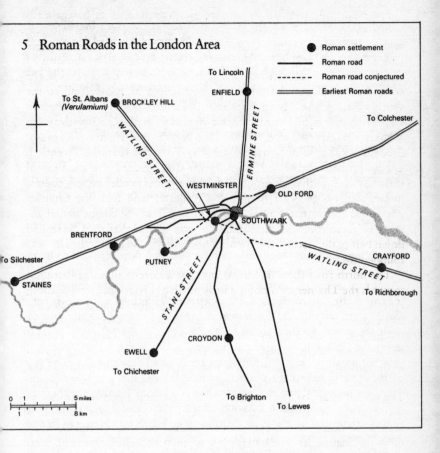

5 Roman Roads in the London Area

● Roman settlement
━━━ Roman road
╌╌╌ Roman road conjectured
═══ Earliest Roman roads

To Lincoln
ENFIELD
To St. Albans (Verulamium)
BROCKLEY HILL
To Colchester
WATLING STREET
ERMINE STREET
WESTMINSTER
OLD FORD
SOUTHWARK
BRENTFORD
CRAYFORD
To Silchester
PUTNEY
WATLING STREET
STAINES
STANE STREET
To Richborough
CROYDON
EWELL
To Chichester
To Brighton
To Lewes

0 1   5 miles
1   8 km

Staffordshire, not through the city, but by the Watling Street, from the Marble Arch down the Edgware Road, plainly by way of the Westminster crossing.

Another road ran south-westward from Colchester to serve the Second Legion, then commanded by Vespasian, the future emperor. It crossed the Thames at Staines, and forked at the Atrebatic capital, Silchester, southward to Winchester, straight on to Salisbury and Exeter, right to Cirencester, and Gloucester, with another fork a few miles further on, to Bath and Bristol. In the London region its course is marked by a continuous, dead-straight stretch from Notting Hill, along the Bayswater

Road and Oxford Street, to Holborn as far as Lincoln's Inn Fields. Its line continued straight to Bow Bridge. However, no road has yet been observed on this line beyond Holborn, and no medieval or modern road preserves one. For though some Romans settled early at Bow, the permanent Roman crossing was soon shifted northward to Old Ford, and the bridge at Bow was not built until the twelfth century. If any Roman road was built from the site of the present bridge to Holborn, it did not long remain a main road, and perhaps was never metalled.

The layout of these roads implies that, in the first year or two after the conquest, there was not yet a London. The encampment at, or near, Southwark was doubtless held by a small garrison, for whom a temporary crossing was sufficient, but when the country was securely held, heavy regular traffic clearly required a more permanent and stouter crossing than the pontoon bridge of the campaign. Colchester was taken, the Belgic kingdom annexed, the troops deployed upon its borders. Their supply and command required a permanent crossing place. Vessels might sail direct from the Rhinemouth to Colchester, and its supply base at Fingringhoe, and thence their cargoes and passengers might conveniently be carried by Cambridge to Godmanchester (Huntingdon), forking right for Water Newton and the legion at Lincoln, left for Leicester and the military concentrations about Lichfield. But Colchester was ill-sited to serve the armies of the Lower Severn and in Devonshire and Dorset; and seamen much preferred the shortest crossing of the open sea. The safe harbour of Richborough, in the navigable channel that separated Thanet from the mainland of Kent, was the site of a large Claudian supply base, and soon became the official entry to the province of Britain, its formal status celebrated by the erection of a splendid arch, whose inscription proclaimed it the gateway to Britain. But no convenient roadway could link Colchester with Kent; travel must either be by sea, or by the long land detour through London. The previous history of the Belgic kings had made Colchester the principal town of Roman Britain, where the military headquarters of the conquering army must necessarily be located for the first months, perhaps the first years; but the estuary of the Thames made the London region the most convenient centre for the control of the deployed armies, and for the future administration of the island. It had the further advantage of a large and secure port. Where alternative routes were available, by water or on land, the high cost of land transport made water the necessary route for bulky goods, while roads served passengers, short haulage, and the carriage of costly commodities. Most of the interior of Britain is ill-supplied with good natural navigable waterways; but while the Dover Road gave passengers and light goods quick and easy access to London, the Thames offered a safe channel for the transport of weighty goods in ships to the port of London, whence they were considerably more easily dispersed than from Colchester.

Military communications therefore required a bridge and a port somewhere in the London region, close to one another. Various considerations favoured the site chosen. The river cuts its way through clay-lands that in nature are thickly forested; from Chelsea downstream, the river is flanked by a thin spread of low-lying alluvial deposit, easily flooded, widening from Tower Bridge to Erith, evidently the 'marshy lake' formed by the flood-tide that Plautius encountered. Behind the alluvium, a stretch of gravel intervenes before the wooded clay-lands are reached. The gravel is naturally more lightly wooded, is easily drained, and offers a plentiful supply of well water, drawn from its junction with the underlying clay at no great depth. Above Westminster and Chelsea, beyond the tidal reaches of the Roman period, the navigation of sea-going vessels ceased to be easy. Below Chelsea, the gravel touches the northern bank only at the site of London, with gravel on the south bank very near to the river (see Map 4, p. 76). Both gravel patches constitute the largest available open land; and upon the northern gravel rise two small hills, about fifty feet high, now crowned by St Paul's Cathedral and Leadenhall Market, separated from one another by the broad shallow stream of the Walbrook. These natural advantages served the need for efficient communications in the newly-established province.

Caesar published a detailed description of how his engineers constructed a bridge across the Rhine, resting on piles angled and tied together to withstand the formidable current. That was a hundred years before Claudius' time, and half a century later Roman sappers bridged the Danube. The construction of a bridge resting on piles or piers across the Thames was no problem. Plautius' bridge may well have been on the site of London Bridge. The future Colchester Road, Aldgate and Aldgate High Street, strikes out in one direction to the crossing of the Lea at Old Ford, and in the other direction points towards the northern end of London Bridge. It did not become a thoroughfare of the central portions of later Roman London, for buildings overlie its course, in and about the eastern portion of Fenchurch Street; but Aldgate itself bears no evident relation to the street plan of Roman London. It was a Roman gate; and the only apparent explanation for inserting a gate in the later wall at that point is that a road was already there, pointing towards the bridge, but no longer leading directly to it. It is therefore likely, though not certain, that the first London Bridge was constructed by Plautius' sappers in the first year or two after the conquest.[3]

The exact position of the bridge abutment cannot of course be determined. There have been successive London Bridges in later centuries, and it is probable that the bridge was renewed once, perhaps more than once, during the Roman period. It is not probable that a single bridge survived for four hundred years, unscathed by several fires and violent assaults on the city. When an old bridge is replaced, it is commonly not knocked down until the new one is completed, so that the new bridge is necessarily placed alongside its predecessor, its abutment a few yards up or down stream. The sites, however, were doubtless not numerous, as the builders of a third bridge might conveniently utilize the abutments of the first bridge, so that sites might alternate. It is probable that the site of the bridgehead in the developed Roman London was about thirty yards downstream from the present London Bridge, opposite the end of Fish Street Hill. The Roman north road, when it approaches the modern intersection of Shoreditch High Street and Bethnal Green Road, veers a few degrees to the south-west. It is preserved by the southern end of Shoreditch High Street, that points directly to Bishopsgate. The prolongation of this line strikes the Lower Thames Street embankment, the river frontage of the Roman town, at Fish Street Hill, the site of the medieval bridge.[4] The Old Ford–Aldgate road alignment appears, however, to point somewhat nearer to the abutment of the modern bridge. It is quite possible that Plautius' bridge proved too small for the needs of the city; it might have lain on, or by, the site of the modern bridge, replaced a few years or a few decades later by a wider bridge, a little down stream. These are, however, no more than an illustration of the possibilities. They cannot demonstrate where particular sites were; they argue the probability that from the beginning a bridge was constructed in the immediate neighbourhood of the medieval and modern bridges, and that attempts to determine its exact site are not likely to succeed.

The south end of London Bridge was also connected by an early road with Chichester, Noviomagus Regnensium, the chief town of Cogidubnus' kingdom, and with its ports on Selsey Bill. From the northern end, in addition to the Colchester–Aldgate road, the Ermine Street ran, by Bishopsgate, due north to Lincoln; and Newgate Street, by Holborn, Oxford Street, and Bayswater Road, led westward to Staines and Silchester, where it forked three ways – south to Winchester, straight on by Salisbury to Dorchester and Exeter, or north-west to Cirencester and Gloucester. Cirencester and Gloucester might also be reached by the

Watling Street, whence a road from Verulamium, by the Vale of Ayles-
bury, pushed west to Cirencester; and an eastward road by Welwyn,
probably pre-Roman, to the Belgic fortress and Roman post town of
Braughing, in Hertfordshire, provided a direct connection from Gloucester to Colchester.

The laying down of the roads and the construction of the bridge
necessarily entailed the lasting presence of Romans. It is evident that
both a defence force and some traffic supervisors were required as soon
as the bridge began to be used. They needed houses, persons to supply
them with food and other necessities; and easy transit of heavier commodities – leather, iron, perhaps at first some corn – required the construction of some kind of quays or wharves, where goods might be
unloaded onto waggons for further inland transport, or onto barges for
transport up the Thames and Lea. Even before the founding of the city,
a small Roman community, part military, part civil, must have developed
at both ends of the bridge, that it might fulfil its function; and must from
the start have served traders, who imported the goods that the notable
British bought with the moneys given them by Claudius.

London was built around two low hills, Cornhill and Ludgate Hill. In
between lay the stream called the Walbrook, draining from Moorfields,
nowadays covered by Finsbury Circus, to the Thames at Dowgate Dock.
Its course was short, but broad and shallow, spreading a thick deposit of
soft, alluvial mud. To the west of Ludgate, the longer and stronger
course of the Fleet entered the Thames at Blackfriars. The houses of the
first Londoners have not been detected. Their approximate location is
known from a quantity of very early pottery. It was analysed more than
forty years ago, and though more has since been found, the distribution
shown by that analysis (Map 6) does not seem to have been modified
significantly by later discovery.[5] The earliest of all comprised expensive,
decorated wares made in Italy, termed Arretine or Italic. It was already
old by AD 43, most of it made by potters whose products were commonly
used thirty or forty years before. It has therefore sometimes prompted
the belief that it must have been imported nearer to the time of its
manufacture, by the inhabitants of a supposed British London, founded
a generation or two before the Roman conquest. The Italic pottery
cannot support that belief. Similar vessels have been found elsewhere in
Britain, in similar or slightly larger quantities, the great majority of them
in or near the royal residences of Belgic kings; but they have always been
accompanied by much larger quantities of native pottery and other
artefacts, proofs of the habitations that there existed. No such native

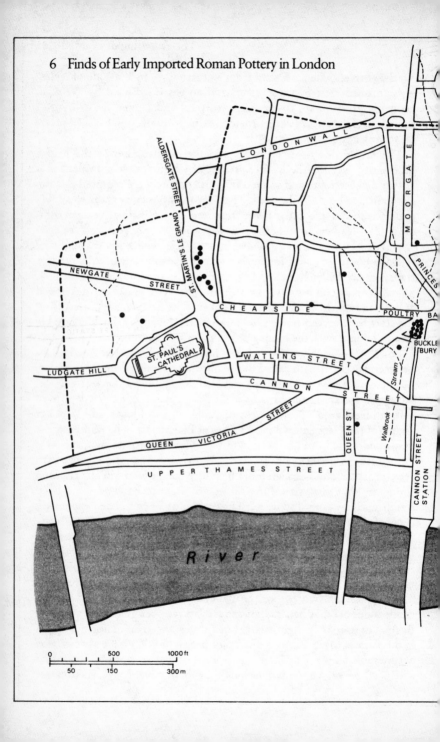

6 Finds of Early Imported Roman Pottery in London

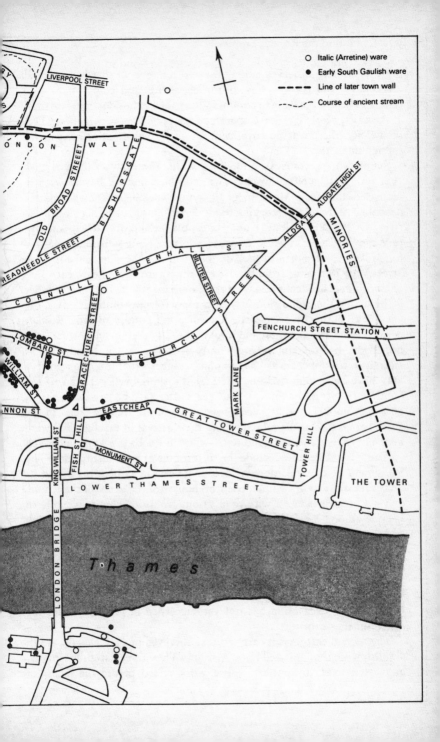

LIVERPOOL STREET

ONDON WALL

OLD BROAD STREET

BISHOPSGATE

ALDGATE HIGH ST

ALDGATE

MINORIES

THREADNEEDLE STREET

CORNHILL

LEADENHALL ST

BILLITER STREET

STREET

GRACECHURCH STREET

LOMBARD ST

WILLIAM ST

FENCHURCH

FENCHURCH STREET STATION

MARK LANE

CANNON ST

EASTCHEAP

GREAT TOWER STREET

TOWER HILL

KING WILLIAM ST

FISH ST HILL

MONUMENT ST

LOWER THAMES STREET

THE TOWER

LONDON BRIDGE

T h a m e s

pottery has been observed among the vast numbers of sherds excavated in London; and the very few brooches, sherds and coins of the two centuries before the Roman conquest unearthed in London indicate that, at the most, a ferry may have operated for a period in the neighbourhood of the city; there was no royal centre rich enough to afford expensive foreign imports.

Simpler inferences explain the Italic ware. There is very little of it; in 1928 only sixteen pieces were known, and their number has not greatly increased since then. More than half came from sites unknown, vaguely described as 'London', referring to modern London, on either side of the river. Of the seven pieces whose findspots were more closely known, four came from Southwark, downstream from London Bridge; one was found well to the north of the later city wall, by the side of the Ermine Street; only two came from the area of the future city, one on each side of Cornhill, in Leadenhall Market and Lombard Street. The total number is slight, and the proportions, twice as numerous in Southwark as in the City, may be partly accidental; but since the pottery of later Roman periods is many times more plentiful in the City than in Southwark, it is not likely that the emphasis on finds of Italic ware in Southwark is entirely a freak of chance. That emphasis suggests that this older pottery may have been imported and used by the short-lived garrison of the Southwark fort in the three or four years after 43. The vessels were old, and were unlikely to have been bought new from their makers. In the years between their manufacture and their arrival in Britain, they were kept unbroken; and the conditions wherein goods are kept unbroken and unused for decades include the storerooms of large institutions. The equipment of an expeditionary force in 40 and in 43 plainly obliged its quartermasters to draw upon the storehouses of the army of the Rhine; and a storekeeper faced with requisitions from other units is likely to include among his deliveries old stock long left untouched in the high and distant corners of his storehouse. The army is the most likely agent in the import to Britain of very old, fine vessels, required in small numbers for the use of officers; and it may be that the two fragments found in the city got there because Cornhill was the site of the fort beyond the river that guarded Aulus Plautius' encampment and bridgehead, though excavation has not yet succeeded in locating either the encampment or the fort.

The second category of early pottery surveyed in 1928 was the south Gaulish ware that imitated Italic Arretine. The survey carefully isolated all vessels made by potters whose work ended before the death of

Claudius in 54, and worked in the twenty years or so before, and rigidly excluded the work of potters whose output lasted longer, into the reign of Nero. Precision in this generation is relatively easy, for the nature of the evidence permits close dating of high-class products in the half century from about 40 to about 90; thereafter the margins of error are wider, and the basis of the dating is increasingly less secure. The reasons are twofold. As the provincial imitations of Italic wares, usually termed 'samian ware' by modern archaeologists, were first developed, potters experimented; each selected individual details of decoration, and very many vessels were signed with the manufacturer's name, often with the name of the individual slave or freedman who threw the pot as well, and many potters abandoned early decorative forms and devised new ones at recognizable stages in their working life. But as the conventions of the industry hardened during the second century, though individual variation and signed products continued, innovations and personal peculiarities decreased, conformity and similarity grew. The second reason that makes close dating relatively easy is that the local military history of the first century A D was recorded in considerable detail by Tacitus and other writers; and they wrote in an age of change, when military units still moved frequently from fort to fort, and towns were founded, or sometimes destroyed. There are therefore a considerable number of sites whose earliest and latest dates are known; and the pottery that is plentiful on these sites is that which was in common use in those years. But in the second century movement was much less, and what movement there was is reported in less detail.

The very early pottery of London is closely dated by well-established evidence from Europe. After the dates had been established, and after the distribution of these wares had been surveyed in London, the conclusions drawn were submitted to a rigorous test. Excavation at Jacklin's Café in the High Street of Colchester demonstrated that the modern café, with its flanking buildings, was built upon party walls first constructed about A D 50, when the *colonia* was founded, that were reused when the city was rebuilt after its destruction by Boudicca in 60, and have remained as property divisions ever since. When the shop was first built, it sold pottery. When it was burnt in the Boudiccan revolt, the stock displayed upon its shelves for sale in A D 60 was thrown to the floor, and, in the rebuilding of the city soon after, was covered with levelled burnt debris.[6] The goods then on sale included the produce of twelve potters who signed their names upon their wares; when this hard evidence was compared with the dates assigned to these potters by modern scholars, the modern dates were proved to be right in eleven instances; in one instance only a potter assigned to the Flavian period, 70 to 90, was shown to have begun his production earlier than was thought, before 60. This is the measure of the reliability that may be placed upon the evidence of early Roman pottery in London.

The early Gaulish vessels surveyed in London are those that were in common use in the 40s AD, when the city was founded, and in the years between the conquest and its foundation. Before Boudicca burnt London, they had been superseded by later fashions. The sharp evidence of the Colchester pottery shop is matched by evidence hardly less strong from London; for most of the vessels and sherds were found in the region that Boudicca's fire consumed, where vessels of the 50s are commonly found to be burnt. But very few of the earliest wares were scorched; they had been broken, lost, or buried before the sites where they lay were burnt. The evidence of their distribution is also clear. The findspots of a little over a hundred vessels are known, in contrast with only seven known findspots of Italic ware. They lie in three main concentrations: flanking King William Street, most of them discovered when the street, together with Moorgate and the new London Bridge, was laid out in the 1830s; by the Bank Underground Station, at the junction of Queen Victoria Street and Walbrook, on the bank of the Walbrook; and on the site of the General Post Office, east of St Martin's le Grand. More than half the vessels came from these three sites; half a dozen more came from the centre of the earliest city, in the middle of Lombard Street, about its junctions with Birchin Lane and Clement's Lane; the remainder, about twenty vessels, were widely scattered over the area of the future city, half a dozen upon the road line from the Fish Street Hill bridgehead to Shoreditch, the rest in single finds, with half a dozen in Southwark.

The areas in which they were found were those where extensive building operations were undertaken in the nineteenth century. But they were not reported in very many other parts of the city, where equally extensive building disclosed pottery of later Roman generations, in particular in the central portions of early Roman London, in and about Cornhill. Their distribution and their date argues that they reached the places where they have been discovered before the city was built. They are likely to have been the property of the first civilian immigrants, from Gaul and elsewhere in Europe, who settled as soon as the bridge was built. They were relatively expensive vessels, owned by well-to-do persons who profited from servicing the army with supplies, and from the first impetus to native imports from abroad, stimulated by Claudius' grants of money to the foremost Britons, which were designed to help them to learn Roman ways and buy the material and external paraphernalia of Roman civilization. Several among these substantial immigrants, the chief exploiters of the new market, are likely to have been Roman citizens. As such, they needed a formal organization; the inscriptions of Europe amply attest the proper and normal style of a small body of first-century Romans who made their homes among provincial *peregrini* – the *cives Romani Londini consistentes*, Roman citizens established at London.[7]

The largest of the three centres of immigrants lay about King William Street. The newcomers avoided the low-lying lands between the bridge-head and the Fleet crossing at Ludgate Circus, but they did not yet settle upon Cornhill, possibly because it was still in the occupation of the army, or retained by the government as army property. The recorded area is tiny, not more than two hundred yards in length; its breadth is not known, for discovery was limited to the areas excavated for the construction of nineteenth-century buildings on the frontage of King William Street. It cannot have extended far to the north and north-east, for Roman sites beneath Lombard Street are extensively recorded, and few pieces of the early Gaulish vessels are recorded from these sites; it may have extended somewhat further to the south and south-west, for there discoveries of Roman sites are very few. The area has not been explored, and whatever was there found has escaped record, save for a few sites.

The second concentration of the first immigrants lies no more than a hundred yards away, at the crossing of the Walbrook, and was doubtless the extremity of the same settlement, for in the short space between the two areas, Roman finds of all periods have also escaped record. But what is known is sufficient to show that the first Romans in London lived in a small space east of the Walbrook, between the Bank and Cannon Street, extending no further east than the line of the road from the bridge to Shoreditch, on the eastern side of Gracechurch Street, if that far, and covering barely more than a dozen or fifteen acres.

New roads soon served the immigrants, and became permanent. From the Fleet at Ludgate Circus a road led direct to the southern edge of the Roman citizen area. It is preserved by the modern Cannon Street, and excavation has established the course of its metalling, along the northern side of the modern street, between the Station and Gracechurch Street. From the north-west corner of the settled area, on the Walbrook by Bucklersbury, a road led towards Oxford Street, near to the point where it forks to Bow and to Old Ford. The course of this road is preserved by Newgate Street and the western end of Cheapside, and has been excavated at several points; the Roman and modern course of its Cheapside end veered slightly to achieve a staggered junction at the point where it was intersected at right-angles by a road running south from the later fort at Cripplegate, but the slight diversion was probably not earlier than the construction of the fort.

The date and purpose of these two roads is necessarily inferred from the location of the inhabited areas they served, and the road junctions they reached; archaeological enquiry is unable to confirm or deny the inference they suggest, for the investigation of a road surface is not able to distinguish a road laid down in 43 from one laid down in 48 or in 53. Its margins of error are necessarily much wider. But the roads built to serve the immigrants who used the early Gaulish pottery were surfaced and resurfaced throughout the Roman period, and substantial stretches of them remain in use today, with modifications occasioned by a multitude of casual causes in the intervening centuries. These two roads between them are the base-lines upon which are aligned a majority of the streets and buildings of the Roman city, whose exact direction is known. When the city was later walled, gates were positioned at the points where the wall crossed them, and they are most conveniently known, from the names of these gates, as the Newgate and the Ludgate alignments.[8]

The precise dates of the coming of the first settlers, and of the foundation of the city, are not recorded. It is probable that the first civilians made their homes by King William Street and the Walbrook crossing shortly after the Belgic kingdom surrendered. But London did not grow gradually by the spontaneous, unaided growth of such a bridgehead station. The account of Tacitus and the evidence of excavation both attest the existence of a city planned on an elaborate scale within a very few years of the building of the bridge. So early a plan could only follow from a deliberate decision to found a city, taken and implemented by the appropriate officers of government.

The date of that foundation may be fairly closely determined. The *Annals* of Tacitus record the decisions to consolidate the province and to found the colony of Colchester under the year AD 50; that entry outlines the achievement of Plautius' successor Ostorius, which culminated in the capture of Caratacus in AD 50, and comprises the whole of Ostorius' tenure of office, probably the years 47 to 50. The consolidation is listed early in the record, the founding of Colchester somewhat later, probably at least a year later. It is likely that the decision to consolidate was taken late in 47, and began to be implemented in 48. It is therefore likely that the formal foundation of London, the delimitation of its borders, took place in the year 48, with the erection of its principal buildings undertaken during 48 and the following years.

The first steps that such a decision entailed are plainly laid down in Caesar's regulations for new towns:[9] 'No one may bring, burn or bury a dead person within the boundaries of the town, as they shall be defined by the plough.' The first step, doubtless explicitly outlined in the earlier chapters of the law that have not been preserved, was to define the limits of the town by ploughing a furrow around them. A single furrow, subsequently outlined by flags of fencing before the builders began work, is not a feature that could leave recognizable archaeological trace; the city bounds might or might not have been marked, or protected, by a ditch, but no evidence of such a ditch has yet been observed in London.[10] The next clause of Caesar's law offers a more substantial pointer to the location of the city: 'No new crematorium shall be established within half a mile of the town.' Laws are not always observed to the letter for ever; but the distribution of Roman burials in London closely conforms to Caesar's provision. All the known burials of London dated to the mid-first century are found in the area of three large cemeteries: near Newgate, from St Martin's le Grand to Warwick Square; about Bishops-gate and Finsbury; and about the Minories. A fourth, whose first burials possibly date from the mid-first century, lies in Fleet Street about Shoe Lane, just west of the River Fleet.[11] All the new cemeteries where burials continued for centuries, are approximately half a mile from the nucleus of the first city between Cornhill and Cannon Street. During the next hundred and fifty years, buildings spread outwards from that nucleus while individual burials encroach nearer towards it, though cemeteries do not. But the burials rarely came close enough to suggest that they crossed the formal boundary; it is therefore probable the limits drawn by the plough are defined within the central area in which very few burials of the first two hundred years of London are recorded.

The dating of the earliest, mid-first-century burials is too vague to show whether they are the tombs of early settlers who died before the foundation of the city, or of those who died a few years later. The nearest edge of the cemeteries lies just under half a mile from the probable limit of the first city. It may be that these burial grounds first came into use just before the foundation of the city; for the law expressly forbids the

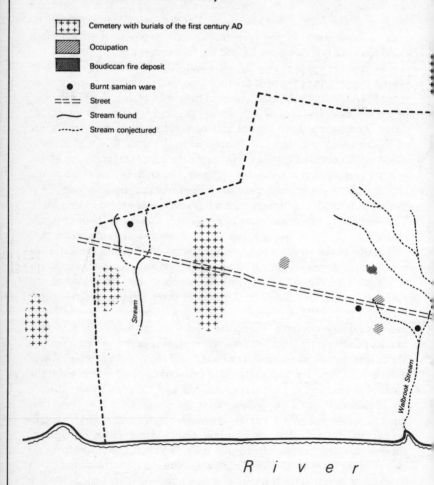

7 London in the Boudiccan Period, with Cemeteries of the First Century AD

+++ +++	Cemetery with burials of the first century AD
▨	Occupation
▧	Boudiccan fire deposit
●	Burnt samian ware
===	Street
⁓	Stream found
------	Stream conjectured

Stream

Walbrook Stream

R i v e r

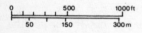

0   500   1000 ft
0 50 150 300 m

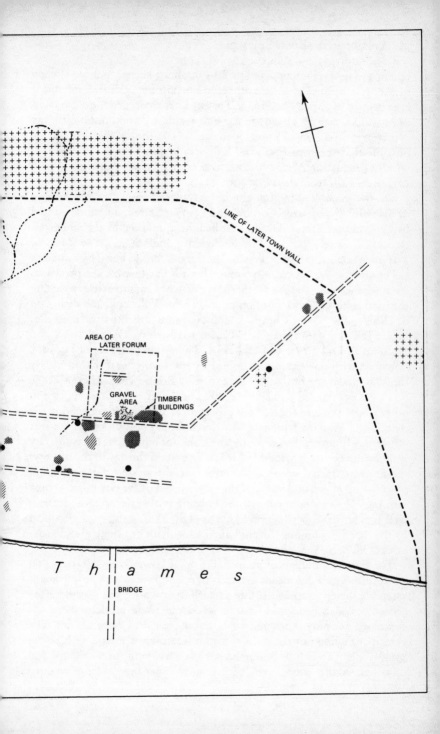

LINE OF LATER TOWN WALL

AREA OF
LATER FORUM

GRAVEL
AREA

TIMBER
BUILDINGS

T h a m e s

BRIDGE

opening of new cemeteries, and thereby implies a licence to those already in use to continue, so long as they do not intrude upon the inhabited area defined by the city boundary. For city laws envisaged the conversion of provincial centres already in use into regulated cities, not merely the construction of houses upon open land. It is, however, also just as possible that the prescription of half a mile was liberally interpreted, with the reduction of a few score feet, or that cemeteries early spread slightly inward from their first site.

The town centre of the first London was placed upon the more easterly of the two hills, between Cornhill and Lombard Street, its ruins bisected by Gracechurch Street. To the west its limit is marked by the numerous traces of fires securely dated to the time of Boudicca, in AD 60 (Map 7). The main concentration of sites and pottery of the 50s burnt by Boudicca lies east of the Walbrook; its southern limit is fixed with some precision, for it reaches down to the northern frontage of Cannon Street, touching the road from Ludgate. The fires extend to the Walbrook, and thence on or close to the line of Cheapside and Newgate Street, by the road that linked the city with the earlier Roman road, along Oxford Street and Holborn to Old Street and Old Ford. The reported traces of burning, however, with one exception, do not extend further east than the early road line from the bridge to Shoreditch by Bishopsgate. Their absence further is perhaps an accident; that area of the city is poorly reported in all periods, though at ten sites observed at different times about the junction of Mincing Lane and Fenchurch Street, no sign of the fire was noticed. Moreover, the fact of the fire does not imply that the entire city was consumed; if the wind blew from the east on the day of the fire, and the fire was started in the city centre, then the western portion would meet its full effect, and much of the eastern part of the city might escape burning. The northern edge of the burning is also uncertainly defined; its traces have not been reported north of the area of the future basilica, by the meeting point of Cornhill and Leadenhall; but there also discoveries of all periods are few.[12]

The central buildings of almost all Roman towns concentrated upon the forum. The word means in origin an open space, where people might assemble, listen to speeches, buy and sell their wares; and it is therefore sometimes ineptly termed 'market place' in some modern works. It contained not only shops and stalls, but a great deal more besides. The principal building of the normal forum was the town hall, or basilica, usually filling the whole of one side of a square, with rows of shops and offices of roughly equal length enclosing the other three sides of an open space approximately square. Such a layout is nowadays called a town centre.

The accident of modern discovery has made the forum area the most excavated and best understood portion of Roman London. The excavated structures belong to three successive town centres; but they do not give foolproof dates to these three periods. They do, however, suggest probable dates, which must be accepted as working hypotheses until more decisive evidence is discovered, and are so accepted by all who have studied them in detail.[13] The three periods conform to two alignments; the earliest lies by the modern frontage of Lombard Street, and Fenchurch Street by Gracechurch Street, on the axis of the later great forum and of the bridge itself; the second is aligned on the approach road, Newgate Street, and the third reverts to the first alignment. The second layout contains pottery in use in the years between approximately 60 and 80, and it is therefore probable that earlier buildings buried beneath it belong to the first foundation of the city. The second layout included a small temple and an oblong building with a nave and two aisles, about 150 feet long and 70 feet wide, that may have served as the basilica, or town hall, during these years. (Map 10, no 5, p. 156.)[14] In the third period, at the north of the forum area, the final form of the great basilica appears from the pottery wedged between its walls to have been built not earlier than about AD 80, but, from the absence of later pottery, not long after that date. But the future discovery of even a few sherds or coins of later date may make the whole sequence of building later. No such evidence has, however, yet come to light; and dates cannot be calculated from evidence that we do not have. Present evidence warrants provisional conclusions but warns that they may have to be revised in the light of future discovery.[15]

The forum area would normally be located roughly in the centre of the city borders 'as defined by the plough'. The size of the city as suggested by the distribution of early imported pottery, all found fairly close to the town centre, and the burials of the first two hundred years, almost all of which must be presumed to lie outside the boundary, suggest a rectangular area of the order of about 60 acres, with the forum more or less in the middle. Such an area is somewhat larger than the space required to encamp one legion, and is the shape of a military encampment. It might possibly have begun as the defences of that part of Plautius' army posted forward of the bridge, while he awaited the arrival of Claudius in 43; but such an encampment must necessarily have been defended by a military ditch, deep enough to be observed by modern archaeology. No such ditch has yet been detected, though very little excavation is recorded along the line that it is likely to have taken. There is therefore as yet no evidence to show whether London, like other Romano-British towns, began within the defences of an abandoned military site. It could have been so; it is equally possible that the boundaries of the town were defined from scratch when its foundation was first determined.

The foundation of a city was a formal affair. It required a defined city boundary, and also a *territorium*, land around it. A possible indication of the western limit of its first *territorium* is given by the third, outlying concentration of Gaulish ware, by St Martin's le Grand. The street itself marks the boundary between an early inhabited area on its east, and an early cemetery to its west. The discoveries made when the General Post Office was built suggest the possible purpose of the detached early settlement, for among the finds were an unusually large concentration of very early pottery and a stamp issued by the Procurator of the Province of Britain.[16] The isolated area was perhaps a station of the *portoria*, the collection of local customs dues, close to the border of the *territorium*. The likely site of the border is suggested by excavation some 150 yards to the west; there lay the course of a little stream, that flowed southward to the Thames, leading towards Puddle Dock, immediately downstream from the modern Blackfriars Station, and at some date a substantial Roman wall, eight feet thick, was built against the eastern bank of the stream. Beyond it, burnt earth and pits with ash may indicate that the land was neither inhabited nor tilled, but used for the extraction of clay and the firing of bricks during the construction of the city.

Little is known of the city's internal street plan. But the city is likely to have been laid out in a rectangular grid, on the same axis as the Ludgate road. Its buildings were unpretentious; the traces that remain in the burning almost all indicate houses of lathe and plaster, sometimes built upon a foundation of stone, usually ragstone from Kent. Agricola visited it just before the fire, and described it to Tacitus as a busy commercial centre, full of persons in transit. The use of the roads shows something of the direction of transit. Burnt samian ware has been found on the Colchester road, at the eastern end of Fenchurch Street, probably outside the city limits; some also borders the Newgate road, with an area of burning removed a hundred yards or so to the north of the road. The Fleet Street cemetery, which may have begun in the mid-first century, argues that the Ludgate road was already continued eastwards beyond the Fleet; later buildings mark its course and destination. It ran by the

Thames towards Westminster, where a few Roman buildings and burials lie by the northern side of the early ford or ferry that linked the Watling Street from St Albans and the midlands with the Dover road, before London was planned or built. The sites observed are very few; they suggest that the Westminster crossing remained in use, but that the volume of traffic which required to use it and to by-pass the city was not great.

Roman Fleet Street may also have served an additional, more distant destination, perhaps by extension in the second or third century. To reach Westminster it was obliged to change direction at least twice, roughly on the line of the modern Strand and Whitehall. After the first of these kinks, the western end of Fleet Street points in the general direction of Hyde Park Corner, where the alignments of the Dover Road and the midland Watling Street meet each other. It may have continued to another river crossing. A Roman road or roads reached the southern shore of the Thames a hundred yards upstream from Putney, where a considerable Roman settlement lay beside them. One road points across the river to Fulham, where a few Roman sherds have been observed within an earthwork that surrounds the medieval palace of the bishop of London, and seems to be older than the palace. The greater part of the modern Fulham Road lies directly upon the line from Fulham Palace to Hyde Park Corner. It may lie over a Roman road, that may or may not have been engineered and cambered. No such road has yet been detected; but recent discoveries have established that there was a river crossing above Putney Bridge, doubtless by ferry. The crossing implies that a road fit for wheeled traffic linked Fulham with the Roman city, and lies somewhere undiscovered – it is also possible that another road from Fulham, beneath or beside the modern Fulham Palace Road, led to the west road from Oxford Street to Brentford and Staines, joining Gold-hawk Road at right-angles, somewhere about its junction with Hammer-smith Grove.

The first city grew quickly. At least four main roads radiated from the northern end of the bridge; at least two diverged from the Southwark end of the bridge, to the Kent coast and to Cogidubnus' Chichester. The people who dwelt in the new city about these roads were chiefly foreigners, most of them probably Gauls, who understood the language of the British, and profited from the import of Roman goods. With them were army personnel in transit, and government officials. The most important official was the procurator of the province. His job was the supervision of government finance, and the appointment was open only to men qualified with the income and rank of a Roman knight. In AD 60 the procurator was Caius Decianus, whose exactions both Tacitus and Cassius Dio list among the principal causes of the rebellion. All that is positively recorded of his location is that it was not at Colchester, and that it was served by a small body of troops. He was able to despatch two hundred ill-armed men, and no more, to the relief of Colchester. It is likely that he had under command a single auxiliary battalion of five hundred men, intended for police work. Since their station was not Colchester, it was most probably London; and at London the likely site is the outlying cluster of buildings and early pottery by St Martin's le Grand, where the stamp of the procurator was observed. The site was conveniently situated for a customs and control post, commanding the main exits from London to the west and north-west.

The status of London, as of most Romano-British towns, is not recorded. The normal conventions of the western empire, and a single ambiguous contemporary statement are our only evidence. In his account of the rebellion of Boudicca in AD 60, Tacitus describes London as 'not yet distinguished by the title of *colonia*, but renowned for its very large population, particularly of traders and travellers' (*cognomento quidem coloniae non insigne, sed copia negotiatorum et commeatuum maxime celebre*).[17] Each of Tacitus' evocative words was deliberately chosen for the association it was intended to stimulate in his readers' imagination; they are therefore impossible to translate literally, since their English equivalents do not comprehend the same set of associations, and Tacitus' meaning depends on the cumulative impression of the phrase, including all shades of meaning attached to its component words. The overall purpose and impact of the phrase is clear; Mediterranean Latin readers are tersely told that London was a much bigger place than they would have expected in a newly-conquered province. But the individual words that tint the overall picture defy exact equivalence. The word *celeber* means both 'populous', 'famous' and 'celebrated', and is intended to convey both meanings; *copia* means 'abundance', 'large number', 'wealth' and 'riches', implying that the traders were both numerous and prosperous; *commeatus* means persons or goods that pass through a place, or stay there temporarily. It includes travellers proceeding to or from the more distant parts of Britain, soldiers on leave, or in transit, or in temporary garrison, and also government officials who serve a term of duty for a limited number of years. *Maxime* has the sense of 'greatly' and of 'especially'; *quidem . . . non* means 'not yet', or 'not even', or 'not indeed'.

The emphasis on the fact that London was 'not yet', or 'not even' a *colonia* jerked the contemporary reader into realizing that this was the scale of London; it was a place such as they might normally expect elsewhere to be a *colonia*. The words contrast with Tacitus' comment a few paragraphs before on the decline of the ancient Italian *coloniae* of Tarentum and Antium, Otranto and Anzio, whose 'shrunken population a settlement of army veterans failed to restore'.[18] There Tacitus deplores the tendency of old soldiers to drift back to the provinces where they had served their time, in preference to strengthening the Italian heartland of the empire; his remarks upon London are the counterfoil to his complaint about Tarentum and Antium: provincial cities prosper while Italian cities decay.

The facts behind the message are harder to determine than the message itself. There is no reason to suppose that Tacitus was personally acquainted with Britain or with London. His source of information was his father-in-law Agricola, who was in Britain in 60, in 69, and again for seven years from 77 or 78 onward. But Agricola was not concerned to trace the growth of London between his three visits; he simply reported that London was an exceptionally large and prosperous provincial city, and that it was surprising that it was not a *colonia*. The comment might apply to London both in 60 and in 80; but need not necessarily fit both, or distinguish one date from the other.

Agricola's words have a point; they are not idle gossip. Agricola had a disciplined, tidy mind, and believed that what was fitting should be done; his comment that London was not a *colonia*, in spite of its size and wealth, implies a view that it should have been a *colonia*. Tacitus' account of Agricola throughout emphasizes his efforts to correct what was wrong; and the comment suggests the probability that Agricola recommended that London be granted the status of *colonia*, or at least considered such a recommendation. The words 'not even', or 'not yet', might mean either that London had not received the higher status when Tacitus wrote, some years before 120, or when Boudicca sacked the town sixty years before. It is perhaps a more probable inference that the city had not yet been upgraded by about 120, but no sure conclusion is warranted.

More important are the words that Tacitus does not use. He does not add '*vel municipium*', 'or a *municipium*'. The reasons that prompt a careful writer to leave out words are many and complex, and include his sense of the balance of a sentence as much as his record of fact. Tacitus' silence does not justify the inference that London was a *municipium*, on the basis that he pointedly refrains from saying that it was neither *colonia* nor *municipium*, but the wording leaves open the possibility that it was one. The possibility is much strengthened by the exceptional circumstances of the city's foundation, and the nature of the administrative practice that bore upon the government of Claudius, who had to determine the new town's status. It could not be the principal *vicus*, town, within a non-Roman *civitas*, like the other towns of Britain, for there was no such *civitas* in the sparsely populated woodlands where London was set. Its first inhabitants were not recruited from native country people, as in other Roman towns in Britain. They consisted principally of prosperous traders and officials, most of them necessarily immigrants from abroad, many of them already Roman citizens, some doubtless Gauls or Spaniards who had not yet attained citizenship, and whom the hope of gain and advancement had induced to settle in the newly-acquired province.

The most abundant source for the nature of a Roman town's population is its inscriptions. The inscriptions of London are not numerous, the recorded names very few. But the few that are known are all Roman; there are no signs at all of freeborn persons with native names, who formed the overwhelming bulk of the population of all classes in the normal cities of Gaul and Britain in the early empire. Though the quantity of information is exceedingly small, what it says is clear; as far as the limited available evidence goes, the early population of London was of foreign, continental, Roman, not of British origin.

The status of a city so constituted admits of little doubt. Before the formal founding, the early residents might be 'Roman citizens living at London'. When a city was established, it could not easily have any status but that of a *municipium*. It could hardly, like Verulamium or Leicester, be a Latin *municipium*, for the status of Latin was in practice limited to freedmen, and to provincial *civitates*. Its most probable status, from its foundation, in or about 48, was the rarity, a *municipium civium Romanorum*, a Roman citizen borough. London was an exceptional town in its Roman context, and would easily have fitted such an unusual status.

The first phase of London's history was abruptly terminated by the disaster of AD 60. That disaster was very largely the consequence of the central government's behaviour. Much had changed in twelve years. Claudius was poisoned in 54 by his forceful wife Agrippina; her sixteen-year-old son was proclaimed as the emperor Nero, in preference to Claudius' own twelve-year-old boy, Britannicus, whom Nero poisoned at dinner a year later. Claudius, like Augustus before him, was deified, canonized as a divine being in the halls of heaven; but he was mocked by men. The philosopher Seneca, now promoted to the post of tutor to Nero, lampooned the dead emperor in a skit entitled the 'Pumpkinification of Claudius', in which he sneered that, given a little more time, Claudius would have turned all the savage Britons into Romans wearing the toga. Claudius' principal freedmen ministers, Pallas and Narcissus, lost their lives, and a pattern of lawless violence became the accepted practice of central political government. Little effort was made to pretend that the death of the emperor and his heir was anything but murder; but even contemporary opinion was startled when the brash, teenaged Nero boasted in liquor that 'mushrooms must indeed be the food of the gods, since my father was made a god by the eating of one'.

Worse followed. Agrippina proved an overbearing empress, and an overbearing mother. Seneca struggled to break her aggressive political dominance, and enlisted the aid of her son, resentful of his mother's authority. For his pupil's formal education he enunciated the principles of his *Epistulae Morales*, 'Moral Letters', composed some time later; but for his evening's entertainment he took care to provide an attractive and well-trained mistress, whose pleasing tongue inflamed the boy's resentment against his domineering mother. Nero proved an apt pupil, and framed his conduct upon the precedents that had made him emperor. Since his mother had murdered his father when he proved an embarrassing nuisance, he murdered his mother when she became a nuisance to him. Contemporaries were shocked at a crime that outstripped even the violence normal to their age; but were still more shocked that the parricide made no serious attempt to disguise his mother's murder as an accident.

When Agrippina was murdered in 59, Nero was twenty-one years old. During the previous five years, in the absence of an adult emperor, effective political initiative reverted for a brief spell to the senatorial nobility. Their most prominent elder statesman was the stern Cassius Longinus, descendant of the lean and hungry Cassius who had headed the aristocratic conspiracy against Caesar, and fallen with Brutus upon the field of Philippi. Longinus honoured and revived his ancestor's severe ideals. One sharp incident told by Tacitus reveals their concept and effect. In the year 58, the oligarchic Council and the popular Assembly of the Greek city of Puteoli, on the Bay of Naples, sent rival delegations to the Roman Senate. The ancient social struggle of the parties of the rich and poor persisted in numerous Greek cities; but petitions to the Senate replaced the civil war and massacres of the pre-Roman age of independence. The councillors complained of the violence of the mob, the commons of the avarice of the magistrates and notables. Since the riotous plebs had thrown stones and threatened to burn down buildings, the affair was entrusted to Cassius. But 'his severity proved intolerable', so, at his own request, he was replaced by a milder Roman senator who 'restored harmony to the town with the aid of a battalion of guards and the execution of a few'.[19]

Three years later, the prefect of the city of Rome, an elderly senator placed at the head of the police force and civic administration, was found murdered in his bed. Since he had four hundred slaves in his house at the time, it was plain that their number must include the murderer and his accomplices. Cassius revived and upheld the ancient letter of the law, that when a man is murdered and the culprit not identified, then all his slaves who were present at the time are deemed guilty of the deed, or of conniving at it, and are to be executed. Cassius won a narrow majority in the house for the literal enforcement of the law. The execution was prevented by a mighty demonstration of the city population, who assembled and threatened to stone the executioners and burn buildings. The Senate thereupon appealed to Nero. Open street conflict between the plebeians and the nobility is not reported from Rome itself in the previous eighty years, save for the disturbed days when Gaius Caligula was murdered. Its renewal faced Nero with an insoluble dilemma. He was already detested by the nobility; but the name of Germanicus, and even the excesses of a headstrong young prince combined with affection for the emperor, the holder of a tribune's power, to make him the popular champion of the people. Yet if the emperor aligned himself with a violent popular demonstration against the constituted authority of the state, he made himself the patron of a social rebellion whose consequence was unpredictable. The emperor was himself the greatest of the wealthy nobles, and could not make himself the leader of a revolution. Nero turned out the guards, ten thousand strong, and they lined the streets while the savage executions were carried out. They were no further signs of popular enthusiasm for the living Nero. Cassius' severity triumphantly asserted the ancient standards of aristocratic rule.

It is precisely in these years, when the executive of government was weakened, that extensive speculation and private exploitation of provincial subjects begins to be again recorded. The narrative of the *Acts of the Apostles*, and the *History* of Josephus describe the misgovernment of Judaea, that culminated a few years later in the great national revolt of the Jews. In southern Gaul, the swelling volume of malpractices by financial officers underlay the revolt of 68, whose outcome was to cost Nero his throne and his life. In Britain, Tacitus describes some of the abuses that remained for Agricola to cure nearly twenty years later (see below, p. 143), and in general terms, he asserts that in AD 60 it was the financial procurator, Caius Decianus, who incurred 'the hatred of the province, that his avarice had driven to armed rebellion'.[20]

The particular causes of the great rebellion are set forth with quite differing emphasis by Tacitus and by Dio Cassius, who wrote much later, but used contemporary accounts. Their narratives are complementary rather than contradictory. Tacitus describes the rising in his notice of the year 61,[21] when it was suppressed; but the progress of events requires a long time, long enough to suggest that the first incidents took place in the late summer or early autumn of 60. The consular legate Suetonius Paullinus, 'ambitious for the glory of a military triumph', was engaged in reducing the island of Anglesey, that 'sustained the strength of the resistance' from its numerous 'sacred groves', guarded by the Druids, and by 'women wildly dressed like the Furies, with streaming hair'.

The island was subdued and the groves destroyed, but fearful news came from the supposedly submissive interior. The wealthy king of the Iceni, the allied kingdom in and about Norfolk, died after a long reign.

He left a written will, bequeathing his kingdom and his family property to the emperor and to his daughters, hoping thereby to preserve them. But, on the contrary, kingdom and property were looted like conquered territory by the officers (of the legate) and the slaves (of the procurator).

Tacitus passes over the political realities. From the time of Augustus onward, in lands effectively controlled by Rome, allied kings were recognized for life, with no guarantee of succession for their heirs. Rome required rulers loyal to the empire, able to keep their own people in order, and was not ready to endorse a king's heir unless he seemed fully competent. The kingdom of Galatia was taken over as a province when its king died without a suitable heir. When Herod of Judaea died, his son was constrained to promise concessions to an angry crowd; he was punished by the loss of the fairer portions of his father's kingdom, because concession proved him too weak to rule like his father, and his acceptance of authority before endorsement by Augustus was presumptuous. There could have been no question of automatic succession to the kingdom of the Iceni by the late king's son, if he had had one; it was not conceivable that any Roman government could endorse the division of political authority between two women, even if the Iceni had shown themselves docile and easy to rule. In fact, they had revolted in 48, and were ready to revolt again. It is possible that the imperial government might have recognized an exceptionally able son, acceptable to the Iceni and to Rome; in the absence of such an heir, the practice and policy of the empire could hardly avoid a decision to end the kingdom and incorporate its territory within the province.

When the king wrote a will, he adopted a Roman practice. In phrasing it, he was aware of the tendency of government policy, of the likelihood that his kingdom would be ended with his life, and took what desperate measures he could devise to avert the inevitable. Native tradition accepted inheritance customs alien to Rome. Tacitus does not say whether the king had a son or not; the will implies the succession to male authority of the daughters' husbands; and, since there were two daughters, implies a division of the territory. The division of a territory between the king's children is common enough among the later Welsh, the Franks and many other peoples; and the succession of the daughter's husband in preference to the son survives in some parts of the modern world, notably in southern India. In first-century Britain, the armies of the Brigantes of the Pennines were commanded by whoever was the husband of queen Cartimandua for the time being. Among the Picts beyond the Forth, succession through the women survived into the ninth century, to the distress and puzzlement of Bede, and of later historians. It is likely that in native custom the husbands of the king's two daughters were the normal and natural heirs of the Icenian kingdom. But Tacitus was writing for Romans. He was concerned with the politics of Rome rather than the anthropology of Britain. His bare statement that the king named Nero and his daughters as heirs invites his readers to compare the king's will with the wills of numerous Roman notables, whom Nero's oppressive tyranny constrained to include the emperor as a substantial legatee.

Well-informed realists among the Icenian notables must have foreseen the probability that the kingdom would be incorporated into the province. But the violation of native custom evidently provoked considerable resistance. Tacitus reports that the widow, Boudicca, was flogged, her daughters raped. He does not report the incidents that led up to so violent a situation, beyond a generalized reproach against the arrogance of the army officers sent to supervise the take-over of the kingdom, and of the slaves sent by the financial procurator to impound its revenues and treasury. He continues with an explanation of the support the Icenians found immediately beyond their own borders, in the territory of the Trinovantes:

The veterans recently settled in the *colonia* of Camulodunum (Colchester) turned the native Trinovantes out of their homes, seized their lands, called them captured slaves; serving soldiers encouraged the outrages of the veterans, for their own behaviour was similar, and they looked forward to similar opportunities themselves on their own retirement.

Moreover, the gleaming temple of Claudius shone forth provocatively, a 'citadel of everlasting domination', and British notables, who had not yet learnt loyalty to the emperor, were forced to 'spend their whole fortunes in the name of religion', picked as priests who must pay for the entertainments provided at the temple festivals.

Tacitus describes the immediate causes of a local revolt in East Anglia. Cassius Dio reports the wider context of misgovernment that earned the rebels wide support throughout the province.[22] The procurator asserted that the gifts Claudius had made to British notables were loans; he demanded instant repayment, and confiscated what property he could. This was the first cause of the rising. The second was that Seneca, presumably sensing danger, called in the forty millions that he had lent the British, all at once, and used force, presumably the soldiers of the procurator, to ensure repayment. It was then that the British of the province responded to the leadership of the rebel Icenian queen, who was now able to put an army of 120,000 men into the field. The total Roman force in Britain amounted to about half that number, but it was so widely scattered that Suetonius could bring no more than 10,000 under his immediate command.

Boudicca's army crossed the frontier of the province, probably the Waveney river, and advanced on Colchester. The over-confident settlers had omitted to fortify the *colonia*, protected only by a small force. The settlers appealed for help. The procurator could spare them only two hundred ill-armed men. Colchester was stormed, its defenders holding out for two days in the temple of Claudius. Soon after, the Ninth Legion from Lincoln, hurrying to the relief, arrived too late and proved too weak; the victorious British destroyed the whole of its infantry, its legate, Petillius Cerialis, barely escaping with his cavalry escort to the shelter of Lincoln. The procurator Decianus despaired of resistance and embarked for Gaul.

Meanwhile Suetonius rode to London, leaving his infantry to follow down the Watling Street from Anglesey. He passed 'through the midst of the enemy'; evidently much of the province had taken arms in Boudicca's support. A few dramatic archaeological discoveries may concern their supporting actions; at Margidunum – East Bridgford, near Nottingham – the hastily interred remains of a middle-aged couple and a teenage boy, whose physical structure suggests the marriage of a Roman soldier with a British girl soon after the conquest, lie beside a mass of oysters pressed together in the shape of a barrel, whose staves time has rotted.[23] The date is probably mid-first century, the occasion probably the activities of Boudicca's supporters upon the flank of Suetonius' march.

Suetonius reached London and

considered whether to give battle there. But in view of his small numbers, and of the grave and obvious penalty incurred by Petilius' rash failure, he decided to save the whole province by the loss of one city. He withstood the tearful pleas of the citizens who implored his protection, and gave the signal to march out, and allowed those who could keep up with him to join his force. Those who stayed, women, elderly people, and people captivated by the delights of London, were slaughtered by the enemy. A like disaster overtook the *municipium* of Verulamium. ... Some 70,000 Roman citizens and allies are estimated to have been killed in the places named. The British took no prisoners to sell as slaves, and observed none of the usages of war; they promptly cut down, crucified or burnt their captives.

Tacitus' vivid tale is epitomized by Cassius Dio, or his source; but Dio adds grim detail of the atrocities inflicted by the British upon their captives:

The worst was the following. They hung up naked the noblest and most eminent women, cut off their breasts and sewed them to their mouths, so that they seemed to be eating them; and then speared them through the length of their bodies. This they did ... in their holy places, especially in the Grove of Andate, their name for the goddess of Victory.

Suetonius fell back to join his infantry, marching at all speed down the Watling Street. The Second Legion, from the south-west, was ordered to join him. Its acting commander disobeyed the order; doubtless he regarded Suetonius' destruction as inevitable, and reckoned to be able to transport his own legion by sea to Gaul. Boudicca's force is now quoted as having almost doubled, set at nearly a quarter of a million by Dio's source. Suetonius had only one legion, the Fourteenth, with a small detachment of elder, time-expired men of the Twentieth, and a few of the nearer auxiliary battalions, about ten thousand in all. He sought to postpone and avoid battle, evidently in the hope of joining forces with the Second; but dwindling food supplies amid hostile lands forced him to fight. 'He chose a site enclosed between narrow defiles, and a wood at the rear', designed to prevent the enemy deploying more than a fraction of their full force against him. The site should lie somewhere in the Midlands, north of Verulamium, not far from the Watling Street; but cannot sensibly be more nearly identified. After an all-day battle, in which the defenders held the slopes against British chariots, a Roman counter-attack prevailed; the figures that Tacitus quotes claim eight thousand British slain, with Roman casualties totalling four hundred killed and somewhat more wounded. Enough of the British escaped to contemplate further resistance; but Boudicca died, poisoning herself, according to Tacitus. Her followers gave her a lavish funeral, whose site the fancies of early antiquarians have located in half a dozen different Midland parishes. With her death, hopes of resistance died, and the remnant of her forces dispersed to their homes.

Dio reports eighty thousand Romans slain and two cities sacked before the battle, as against Tacitus' seventy thousand in three named towns. Excavation confirms Tacitus. In Colchester, London and Verulamium, in the town centres and adjoining streets, a thick layer of burnt debris covers pottery and coins dated earlier than AD 60. In London, many dozens of skulls, with few other bones, were reported from the bed of the Walbrook, mostly concentrated between Finsbury Circus and the south side of London Wall (Plate 4); and the fantasy history of Geoffrey of Monmouth, written in the twelfth century, invents a mass beheading on the banks of the Walbrook, placed in the year 297, probably to explain much earlier discoveries. The only positive evidence of date is that one skull was covered by the third-century Roman wall, and that others lay upon the gravel banks and bed of the stream, that was subsequently embanked, early in the Roman period.[24] It is therefore very probable that the skulls are those of Boudicca's victims, the first Londoners, their bodies thrown into the stream somewhere immediately north of Finsbury Circus, possibly in a sacred grove, the rounded skulls washed further downstream. A few of the skulls have been preserved, though their measurement and type has not yet been studied and reported. Their number must have been very large; the great numbers found in modern times, together with probable extensive discoveries in or before the twelfth century, with due allowance for those that passed without record in other centuries, or have not yet been revealed, suggest a total of several thousand. The first London was totally obliterated. The victorious army of Suetonius recovered empty, blackened ruins, their boundary stream blocked with the rotting corpses of a slaughtered population.

Chapter 6

Flavian Rome

SUETONIUS AND HIS troops were embittered. They had narrowly escaped merciless destruction. In the ruined towns they saw the aftermath of the hideous atrocities that the British had inflicted on their fellows, in many cases on their friends and relatives. They were reminded of the tortures they would have suffered individually if the British had won the war, and were in no mood to spare enemies guilty of such outrage. The army was reinforced by two thousand legionaries drafted from the Rhine to replace the lost infantry of the Ninth, and was augmented by a further five thousand auxiliaries.[1] Punitive campaigns finished the war before winter, and the army was dispersed in new forts. Hostile or suspect peoples were wasted, their families cut down, their homes burnt. Survivors starved, for the British had sown few crops in 61; able-bodied men of all ages had been drawn into the army, and had hoped to live upon supplies captured from the Romans.

Even so, the British were not yet prepared to accept defeat, accompanied by continuing revenge. The dangerous situation was eased by the new procurator,

Julius Classicianus ... who was at odds with Suetonius, and hindered the public welfare by his private intrigues. He advised the British to await the appointment of a new legate, free from the rage of an enemy and the arrogance of a victor, who would deal more kindly with the conquered. He also reported to Rome that no end to the fighting could be envisaged, until Suetonius was replaced.[2]

Classicianus brought to the problems of Britain an experience allied to that of Cogidubnus. He was himself a Rhinelander, son-in-law to Julius Indus of Trier, who had raised a cavalry force to help Tiberius suppress a Gallic rising forty years before. His ancestors and his wife's ancestors were Gauls. Classicianus was born some two generations after his forebears had resisted the conquest of Caesar, and in his childhood would have known plenty of elder men who remembered the rebellion of Vercingetorix and its aftermath. Trier was now a Roman *colonia*. In the history of his own family and his elder acquaintance, Classicianus had experienced how in a few generations Rome had turned sullen, conquered Gauls into loyal Roman officials; now he applied that cumulative experience to the sullen, conquered British. It taught him that terror brought no lasting cure. He appealed to the ancient Roman tradition of the Scipios and of Claudius, against Suetonius, who revived the brutal force of a Cato. Rome had grown great by absorbing former enemies, by teaching and inducing their nobles to govern on behalf of Rome, in a manner acceptable to the governed. The cause that he pleaded was immortalized in the political morality that Virgil epitomized in the age of Augustus, *parcere subiectis et debellare superbos*, 'spare the conquered and knock down the proud'.[3] That cause was so deeply embedded in past Roman experience, that even the government of Nero listened to his protest. The imperial secretary Polyclitus was sent to Britain to investigate, and on the basis of his report, a convenient excuse was found to replace Suetonius by Petronius Turpilianus, the consul of 61. He 'forbore to harass an enemy who was no longer enflamed, and imposed the honest name of peace upon his own sluggish inertia'.[4]

Tacitus condemned the protest of Classicianus and the peaceful policy of Turpilianus, but it was continued by his successor. Yet a dull decade, free of disturbance, with little military effort to strain the shattered economy, gave the province time to heal its wounds, and to establish the basis upon which Agricola and his successors were to construct the mature civilization of Roman Britain. Classicianus remained in Britain until his death. His monumental tombstone, recovered in two pieces, in 1852 and in 1935, from a fourth-century bastion by Tower Hill, was presumably originally erected in the nearest cemetery, in and about the Minories. It reveals his full name, Julius Alpinus Classicianus, with the names of his wife and of his father-in-law, whence his own origin is inferred;[5] a third portion, not yet discovered, would have summarized his earlier career. Its culmination, in Britain, shaped the future of the province. His representations closed the period of conquest; their implementation opens the history of the province that became Roman.

The years between 61 and 70 were quiet in Britain, disturbed in Rome. When Nero came of age and murdered his domineering mother, he also emancipated himself from the control of his tutor Seneca. Like most unsuccessful, 'bad' emperors, he abused his position because his principal interests did not concern politics and government. Gaius before him, and Commodus after him, were devoted to sport; Nero's passions were drama and music. Each year he attended the major Greek festivals, where well-born Romans were accustomed to enter their horses, and occasionally to compete in athletics and foot races; but Nero submitted his verses and musical compositions, and was naïvely delighted to receive a succession of first prizes, which he ascribed to his talents rather than to his position as emperor. In Rome he organized amateur theatricals, and these, combined with the flamboyant dining and drinking of an unrestrained, millionaire boy, deeply offended aristocratic opinion. The bitterest complaint of his detractors is that he forced the last bearers of the most honourable and ancient Roman names to disgrace their ancestry by appearing on a public stage like common players.

The *Annals* of Tacitus close with a mournful account of the feckless conspiracy of 65 which failed to destroy Nero.[6] Headed by a Calpurnius Piso, whose name stood out in the public eye as the symbol of aristocratic arrogance, the conspirators discussed matters for two years, until everyone in Rome knew of the existence of the plot, save Nero. At last, the remonstrances of a forthright freedwoman shamed the plotters into action; but instead of determined, planned action, they drew lots for the honour of doing the deed. The lot fell upon a middle-aged knight, who did not seek the most expeditious weapon, but sent to an ancient Etruscan temple for a knife of particular sanctity, and spent the evening anointing it with holy oil, and in preparing his will. One of his freedmen concluded that action was at last impending, and hastened to the Palatine to warn Nero. The elderly designated assassin was arrested, and betrayed the names of friends; they in turn named other accomplices, and in the ensuing trials large numbers of the heirs of great families permitted themselves to be exterminated one by one, grateful only if the tyrant's mercy permitted them to commit suicide before sentence, thereby allowing them to bequeath their property to their heirs, instead of leaving it for the Treasury to seize, as was the custom with condemned criminals. The deaths were reinforced by a considerable plague. Their combined effect destroyed the tight group of aristocratic families that had ruled Rome for centuries before the emperors. Old families had long been faced by a dilemma; custom expected that they should provide equally for all their children, but an excess of children risked the splintering of great properties, so that each individual was too poor to maintain his station; too few children risked the extinction of the family, by the normal hazards of infant and youthful mortality. Plague and execution, followed by civil war, reinforced the natural risks. The heiress of the Fabii buried her son, heir of a name scarcely less distinguished, with the sad epitaph *ultimus gentis suae*, 'the last of his line'.[7] Her words were the epitaph of a dying society, not of one family. Of the great patrician houses that had dominated political society since the time of Augustus, no more than three or four survived the fatal years of Nero's fall, and none but the Acilii played any significant part in the political life of Rome thereafter.

The end came in 68. Exploitation by uncontrolled financial administrators urged the Three Gauls to rebellion; and the legate of Aquitania, Julius Vindex, put himself at the head of the revolt. Like Classicianus, he was the heir of a native family that had acquired Roman nobility; but the sentiments that are put into his mouth by later historians do not voice the resentment of Gauls at Roman domination. Instead, he is made to complain of the degradation that Nero's irresponsible conduct brought upon the heirs of ancient Roman nobles; though the words may be those the historians would have liked him to utter, the absence of all sign of national hostility among the disaffected Gauls is an eloquent comment on their full acceptance of Rome.

The armies of the Rhine were directed to suppress the rebellion. Their commanders had begun discreet negotiations with its leader, when he was killed by an over-zealous officer. Negotiations were thereupon opened with the legate of Spain, Servius Sulpicius Galba. Nearly three hundred years before, an ancestor of the same name had persuaded the Romans to attack Philip of Macedon, and begin the rapid subjugation of the eastern Mediterranean. But the Galba of 68 was the last of his line. Like nearly all the emperors chosen by the aristocracy, he was selected as a caretaker, who might discuss with his peers the choice of a suitable successor, whom he might then adopt as his son and heir; he therefore shared the necessary characteristics of a caretaker emperor, being a nobleman of honourable ancestry, aged seventy or more, without sons of his own.

Under Galba's command the army of Spain, with portions of the Rhine army, advanced upon Italy. Troops despatched by Nero to resist them deserted to the rebels as they drew nearer. As power slipped from him, Nero innocently proposed to the Senate that if he abdicated the empire, he might be appointed Prefect of Egypt, for he would find congenial company in the *Mouseion* of Alexandria, the renowned centre of the arts and of scientific research long since established by the Ptolemys, the kings who succeeded Alexander. Though the proposal was not entertained, the Senate took no action, until the commander of the guards, in relieving the battalion on duty at the Palatium, omitted to supply a replacement battalion. Nero, left alone with his personal slaves, lost his nerve, and appeared in prudently empty streets, banging on the locked doors of notables. The name of Nero Germanicus had once been popular with plebs, and later on was to win support for impostors who claimed to be Nero, but there was in 68 no sign of popular support for the emperor who had turned out his guards to enforce the execution of four hundred innocent slaves. Abandoned by all, Nero jumped on a horse and rode from Rome. Then at last the Senate proclaimed him a public enemy, and despatched a force to kill him. When they found him, he is said to have died with the protest 'What an artist the world has lost in me.'[8]

The army of Britain stood apart from these disturbances; and, like the rest of the Roman world, at first accepted the authority of Galba. It did not long endure. The Rhine armies proclaimed Vitellius, son of Claudius' principal senatorial colleague. The record of those who knew him, and the portraits on his coins, depict him as the grossest of the boorish, over-eating Roman nobles of the age of Nero. In Rome, Galba indulged the unwise choice of the aristocracy, and adopted as his son and heir another Piso, a relative of the conspirator of 65. The city plebs were indignant at the prospect of enthroning a name so thoroughly hated, and lynched Galba and Piso in January 69. Salvius Otho replaced them. His ancestors, like Vitellius', had first entered the Senate under Augustus. He had been a favourite companion of Nero's youth, but had for ten years been relegated to honourable exile as legate of Lusitania, covering most of modern Portugal, when Nero annexed his ebullient wife, Poppaea Sabina.

Vitellius' army invaded Italy, and destroyed Otho's weaker forces, near Cremona, in April. But his victory was not endorsed by the powerful armies of the east. They were considerably enlarged, for the Jews had risen in national rebellion in 66, and an army of three legions was despatched to suppress them. The choice of commander had presented unusual difficulty. Very many of the experienced generals qualified for such major command had perished in the conspiracy of 65, or in the plague; and many of the survivors were men of note whose loyalty was uncertain, and whose status might tempt others to raise them as rivals against Nero. The choice fell upon the elderly Flavius Vespasianus, son of the principal citizen of the small, central Italian town of Reate. His elder brother Sabinus had served as Aulus Plautius' principal subordinate general in Claudius' campaign in Britain twenty years earlier, sharing the credit for the Medway victory with Hosidius Geta, and sharing a consulship with him in 45 as his reward. Vespasian had served in the same campaign as legate of the Second Legion in the south-west, but did not receive his consulate until the end of 51. Thereafter, he had commanded no armies, but had in due turn served as proconsul of Africa, normally the last office in a senatorial career, and ranked as retired.

Vespasian had incurred disgrace, and been banished from the court; he had been observed to snore while attending one of Nero's concerts in Greece. His immediate misfortune proved to be to his ultimate benefit, for he was out of the way during the troubles of 65. In 66, an elderly senator, whose comparatively obscure origin made him an improbable rival to Nero, with a commendable record as a legionary commander, seemed a sensible choice as general of the army in Judaea. When news of Vitellius' conquest of Rome reached the east, considerable diplomatic consultations among the aristocratic officers there present were organized by Mucianus, the legate of Syria. Their consensus proclaimed Vespasian emperor in Alexandria on 1 July, AD 69. Further diplomatic missions secured the effective neutrality of the Danube armies, many of whose commanders discovered dangerous threats from barbarians beyond the frontier, whose urgency demanded immediate action, and prevented them interfering with the passage of armies from Syria to Italy in their rear.

Vespasian's vanguard, instructed to secure the Alpine passes, exceeded its instructions, and destroyed Vitellius' main forces in October, on the same north Italian battlefield at which Vitellius had secured Italy in April. But the victors were unable to reach Rome in time. Vitellius' defeat had robbed him of authority over his own troops in the city; on their own initiative they besieged Vespasian's brother Sabinus, then Prefect of Rome, in the Capitol. They took the hill, killed Sabinus, and in the fighting burnt down the temple of Jupiter. It had served as the government record office, and the destruction of its documents deprived Tacitus and later historians of a principal source for their narrative. But the local victory of disorderly troops did not benefit Vitellius. He was soon removed, and Rome accepted Vespasian. He was so securely established that he did not himself need to travel to Rome until the sailing season opened in March 70. He entrusted the Judaean army to his son Titus; and to Rome despatched the king-maker Mucianus, and one of his principal legionary commanders, the Spaniard Ulpius Trajanus, father of the future emperor Trajan.

Britain played little part in these momentous events. The legate Trebellius Maximus had continued the 'inert' policy of his predecessor Turpilianus. When the civil war broke out, his authority was challenged by Roscius Coelius, legate of the Twentieth Legion, then probably at Wroxeter, near Shrewsbury. Coelius protested that Trebellius' corruption had fleeced the legions; and when Trebellius accused Coelius of undermining discipline, he found that discipline had gone. Mutinous troops compelled him to flee to Vitellius, and the province was administered by a consortium of legionary legates, Coelius pre-eminent among them. Vespasian speedily removed Coelius. The new legate was Vettius Bolanus, the most prominent citizen of Milan, whose second name preserved the memory of his Gallic ancestors. Tacitus regretted that he too continued the 'inertia' of his predecessors, improving upon their record only in that his blameless conduct won him affection, if not respect.[9] The poet Statius, praising his sons years later, credits him with campaigns among the 'Caledonii',[10] but the word was probably chosen because it symbolized in the public imagination the barbarians of Britain at the time the poem was published, and is unlikely to mean that Tacitus is wholly wrong, that Bolanus did in fact inaugurate ambitious campaigns far beyond the then frontiers of the province. Coelius was replaced as commander of the Twentieth by Agricola, who had already served as a military tribune in Britain at the age of twenty, under Suetonius, at the time of the great revolt. Agricola was Tacitus' father-in-law, the source of his information about Britain; Tacitus relates that he found the Twentieth still mutinous, and reluctant to admit the authority of Vespasian, but managed to persuade the legionaries to accept the new government and the restoration of discipline voluntarily, rather than having it imposed from above. He also represents him as accepting the inactivity of Bolanus, which he personally deplored, in the name of discipline.

The dynasty of the Flavians comprised Vespasian, who died in 79, and his two sons, Titus, who died young in 81, and Domitian, who survived until 96. The government of Vespasian inaugurated new moral and political standards. By the end of the century, the extravagant excesses of Nero's Rome seemed as remote and incredible to Tacitus and his contemporary, Pliny, as they did to Victorian England. Tacitus' austere account has indelibly implanted upon all future ages the image of the gross Roman boor, the stock character of the romantic novel and the film epic. The story of Flavian Rome is less sensational, and is told by pedestrian writers who made less impact on posterity. In their own day, the energies of the political leaders who served Vespasian and Titus were less absorbed by the high politics of the Senate and city of Rome, and more fruitfully directed to the guidance of maturing provinces.

The new dynasty set to work to reconstruct the government of the empire. New moral and political standards, a new attitude to citizens and provincials, new people to advise and direct the control of public affairs, all combined to establish a stable and secure imperial administration. Reform began at the top. Conspiracy, plague, civil war, and the customs of the last generation had suddenly removed the old patrician nobility that had dominated Roman political life for five or six centuries. The few old families who survived were no longer numerous enough to constitute a class, and Vespasian and Titus held a census in 73 and 74, creating a number of new patricians.

The new patricians were men of one kind, the most eminent citizens of the principal regions of Italy, and of the most Italianized Mediterranean provinces; the individuals selected among them were principally those who had held useful command during the civil war. They included Vettius Bolanus of Milan, and the Neratii of Saepinum, in the Benevento region, on the edges of Samnite and Campanian territory, whose heirs are said to have been considered as possible emperors on two occasions in the early second century. Others were ancestors of men who were later selected as monarchs. T. Aurelius Fulvus, at home both in Nemausus (Nîmes) and in Cisalpine Gaul, was the grandfather of the emperor Antoninus Pius, Annius Verus, grandfather of Marcus Aurelius. Two non-Italians were selected: the elder Trajan from Spain, father of the emperor, who was said to have been of native Spanish ancestry rather than the descendant of Italian colonists; and Cn. Julius Agricola of Forum Julii (Fréjus) in southern Gaul, whose name likewise proclaims a native Gallic ancestry.

Vespasian ennobled those upon whom his government relied. The new patricians included men who had served him well in the crisis that made him emperor; but not all his prominent adherents were so rewarded. Patrician rank was bestowed upon the heads of the wealthiest and most notable families of Italy, and of the western Mediterranean provinces whose outlook was wholly Italian. Rank meant more than formal honour. It formally recognized a profound change in the political government of the Roman empire, long overdue. Hitherto, the aristocracy of Rome had been dominated by noblemen whose remote ancestors had conquered Italy, and who remembered their superiority to the heirs of the conquered. Henceforth, the empire was to be governed for more than a hundred years by the well-to-do landowners of Italy, and by those in the provinces who shared their standards and thought like them.

The change bit deep enough to be termed the Italian revolution. It was not a social revolution, dispossessing an entire ruling class; but it transferred political power and social distinction to a new kind of nobility, as firmly and as decisively as the English revolution of 1688. It was the reassertion in new terms of an old political outlook, that Rome ruled by absorbing the conquered, and making Romans of them. It was the philosophy that Claudius had preached, pedantically and in the face of scornful critics, a quarter of a century before. It entailed important consequences for the provinces as well as for Italy, for the Italian leaders governed in the light of their own experience.

Five generations back, the Italians had been subject allies of Rome, and had won citizenship only by armed revolt. Some Italians sat in the Senate, and during the civil wars a few were numbered among the consulars, who mastered Rome before the emperors. But such men became Roman only by uprooting their local origins. Distinctions remained. In Caesar's time, Cicero frequently boasted that his political eminence was unique among new men of Italian origin. Augustus made a nation of Italy, and filled the Senate with the notables of its towns, but few of them reached the consulate until the last years of Tiberius. Under Claudius they multiplied, and their rise provoked stubborn resistance among the old urban aristocracy; Agricola's father refused to become a client of the mighty, and soon after lost his life (above, p. 52). Others accepted dependence, and attempts to exclude men of modest means by raising the cost of office were repulsed with difficulty.

These memories were recent among the men who enthroned Vespasian. Through him they acquired a political authority that had long been denied them. It came to them through crisis and disaster, but the troubles were not of their making. They did not rebel. They came to power in a vacuum, when the old order was already dead. It had died violently. Until 65, the ghosts of ancient names remained predominant among the *primores*, the foremost men, to whom belonged the right and the duty to advise the emperor, to marshal and to focus those pressures which could discourage policies and activities detrimental to the aristocracy as a whole. For half a century they had failed to curb the public violence of a rudderless government and the private extravagance of a dying nobility. They perished with the futile irresolution of the conspirators of 65, and in the disorders that caused and followed the fall of Nero. But their ruin involved much else. Civil war killed many men, encouraged extremist violence, and destroyed many useful political illusions; Agricola's son-in-law, the historian Tacitus, acidly observed that men had learnt that an emperor might be made elsewhere than at Rome. In the long run, Romans did not forget the lesson that they then learnt; but the victors of 70 were concerned to see that they had no fresh occasions to remind them of the possibility. They and their children and grandchildren avoided further civil wars for more than a hundred and twenty years.

The new patricians became the *primores*. They inherited the deep-rooted instincts of the Italian towns, that Cicero had voiced, and that had been the basis of his authority. They craved stability, and they knew that its only guarantee was political moderation; the ideal of Solon of Athens taught men to deplore the stasis that ruined the Greek cities, and the ambition that brought down the consular government of Rome. Clever men and novel ideas spelt danger; wisdom counselled the traditional rule of *pars sanior et maior*, 'the wiser and the greater part'. The strict etiquette of constitutional form, the rigid niceties of precedence, set limits to argument between the balance of wisdom and individual weight, and of formal majorities. In the first months of Vespasian's reign, the men of moment sharply discouraged extremist attempts to place the financial control of the emperor and his executive in the hands of the Senate, at the mercy of uncertain voting. Instead, they made sure that in the long run the pressures that they commanded were effective enough to render the assembly's votes unnecessary. They had learnt the truism that innumerable later governments were to face; when the executive government drifts into head-on collision with its legislative assembly, then the government must fall, or take arms to maintain itself. Such a crisis had been reached in 68; when it was reached, either the victory or the defeat of the government equally entailed disorder and ruin. What mattered was to prevent the recurrence of such a crisis in Rome, and to ensure that each city in the empire enjoyed a like immunity.

The new rulers understood, better than most earlier or later aristocratic governments, that if a government and legislature does not fairly represent the powerful social and political interests within the state it governs, then it will provoke rebellion and disorder, and will be unable to command the support of powerful groups when it seeks to suppress insurgents. Vespasian and his *primores* had learnt the hard way. They set out to create a stable society wherein the ruled accepted the authority of government without question, without serious resentment, and without significant opposition, grumbling against it only as they grumbled at the weather. They succeeded beyond measure. To Edward Gibbon, writing seventeen centuries later, in the twilight of a later age of enlightened aristocracy, the empire that they fashioned constituted the happiest age of mankind. It became the lasting pattern of an élite government, wherein a few hundred men ruled many millions without visible discord.

The first essential was to reach agreement upon a code of political and personal conduct, that the vast majority of the well-to-do accepted and endorsed at all levels, as the natural and proper convention of civilized behaviour. The polite customs of the new age were not established at once, nor without stress and difficulty. They were shaped in the first dozen years of the new regime, in the lifetime of Vespasian and his elder son Titus, who died in 81. But his younger brother drifted into improper autocracy. The statesmen held their hand and were rewarded. He was removed in 96 by the dagger of a humble freedman, without the provocative flamboyance of aristocratic assassination that had fired plebeian riots at the murder of Gaius or of Caesar, and without the rebellion and civil war that had brought down Nero. Another caretaker emperor was installed. Nerva, like Galba, was an elderly, childless patrician, but he chose his heir more wisely. Trajan was the son of a Spaniard raised to the patriciate by Vespasian, and was himself a general of proven ability. On his accession, in 98, the new age reached maturity. For a hundred years, new emperors were selected by the magnates, with little more disturbance than intrigue among the mighty. Trajan was succeeded by his cousin Hadrian in 117, and before his death in 138 Hadrian appointed both his immediate successor, Antoninus Pius, and Pius' successor Marcus Aurelius, who reigned from 161 to 180 and bequeathed the empire to his unhappy and unlucky son, Commodus.

The age is commonly termed the Antonine, for the emperors Pius and Marcus both used the cognomen Antoninus. Its philosophy was sharply and consciously formulated from the moment of Trajan's accession, above all by two eminent writers, Tacitus and Pliny the Younger, close friends, but wholly unlike in temperament. The severely moral Tacitus published the biography of his father-in-law Agricola in the year of Trajan's accession. The short book was more than the pious record of a respected relative. It displayed the ideal portrait of a Roman ruler, loyal in counsel even to an evil emperor, a wise and kindly guide to the provincial subjects committed to his care. It chanced that the province in which Agricola governed was Britain, and that twice before he had served in Britain, on both occasions in times of great crisis, during the rebellion of Boudicca in 60 and during the civil war of 69. The *Life of Agricola* underlined the central political concepts that distinguished Flavian and Antonine Rome from earlier times. The health of the empire was not to be gauged by the well being of its magnates alone, or of the population of Rome, or even of the privileged who held Roman citizenship; the empire included its remotest provinces, and its stability depended upon the proper ordering of each city, state and territory within its borders.

Vespasian and his advisers reorganized the Roman state, integrating the provinces with the central government. Britain especially benefited, for it was the most recent major province, neglected since the time of Claudius, retarded by the rebellion of 60 and its aftermath; and since it was also Agricola's province, it became a pattern of how Roman ways could and should be encouraged to take root quickly in an alien land. But the development of Britain was a part of a policy that embraced the whole empire. Vespasian's census greatly widened the body of Roman citizens, and the Senate, in line with changes that had come about since Claudius' censorship twenty-five years before. Many more notable Gauls and Spaniards were admitted to the Senate, with no sign of the sneering opposition that Claudius' enrolments had aroused; and a few were advanced to patrician rank. Several prominent Greeks from Asia Minor and the Aegean coastlands also became senators, most of them descendants of kings to whom Augustus had granted citizenship; the first African reached the consulate, and many more entered the Senate.

Roman and Latin citizenship was carefully distributed, and developed towns were advanced in status. Almost all the foreign communities of Spain became *municipia*, and so did many in Gaul; in Britain, Lincoln and Gloucester became *coloniae*, at first peopled by discharged soldiers, and Leicester and perhaps some other towns became *municipia*. Many individuals received Roman citizenship. In most provinces a few families, often of royal or princely origin, bore the name Julius, in virtue of a grant of citizenship by Caesar or Augustus. Within the provinces, many of the larger cities record at least one family named Claudius, from a grant by Claudius or Nero. But the name of Flavius, inherited from grants by Vespasian and his sons, was borne by several families in the greater cities, and by outstanding local families in lesser towns.

Vespasian brought the Senate and citizenship of Rome up to date. Care was taken that it should remain in step with social change. Hitherto widespread expansion of the Senate and large-scale revision of the register of citizens had been undertaken only on the occasion of a formal censorship; and a censorship was an elaborate and rare occasion, held only once in the 60 years since the death of Augustus. Domitian took the title of perpetual censor, and flaunted the honour upon his ceremonial inscriptions. His successors discreetly dropped the title, but retained the powers. Thenceforth, the government was able to expand the institutions of state from year to year, as opinions slowly changed on who was worthy of advancement, without the need for drastic reconstruction in successive generations.

Vespasian's reforms made Romans of the most influential provincials throughout the empire, and assembled in the Senate the wealthiest and most eminent Romans of all provinces. Means were found to perpetuate the process, to make men Romans and senators as soon as they demonstrated reliable adherence to the values of Rome. Conflict hardened instead upon the proper relations between Latins and Greeks. Some westerners, like the poet Juvenal, feared and loathed the corrupting influence of smooth and cunning *Graeculi*, but others, like the emperor Hadrian, passionately championed the culture of Greece as the inheritance of Rome, in equal partnership with the Latin west. In the Greek-speaking eastern provinces some, like the philosopher Epictetus, still regarded the Roman as an arrogant and boorish conqueror, but many others strove eagerly for citizenship and senatorial dignity, welcoming the security of the Roman peace and accepting the Roman state as the common bond of all Greek lands. The conflict was never resolved, and in the end had much to do with the fall of the western empire. But in the age of the Antonines it was stilled and latent, and within both halves of the empire Roman ways and Roman institutions eroded former internal differences, bringing the several provinces to an even civilization.

Chapter 7

Flavian Britain

SUCH WAS THE context in which Britain and the west were reorganized, in which London was restored and transformed into a major city. The integration of the empire required the emperors' legates to shape each city in their provinces into local copies of Rome, adapting their institutions to a common model, and encouraging among them the ideals of the reformed government. Their scope was larger in Britain than in Gaul, for in 70 neither the institutions nor the sentiments of the British were yet aligned to Roman ideals. Men more than forty years old still had lively memories of Britain before the Roman conquest, wherein they had been born and bred; and all adults remembered the Britain that had responded to Boudicca's revolt. The integration of Britain within the empire was urgent, and needed especial effort.

In the year 70, the first concerns of the government were military. The loyalties of the armies needed to be consolidated, and to each main frontier Vespasian despatched a close relative. In the west, both the affection of the legions and the security of the frontiers needed immediate remedy. Their cure was entrusted to Petillius Cerialis. On the Rhine, Civilis, a chief of the Batavians, who lived between the arms of the Rhine in what is now the southern Netherlands, had taken the opportunity of the civil war to assert *de facto* independence, and had suborned the disarrayed legions of the Rhine. Eight battalions of Batavian auxiliaries had abandoned their allegiance to the legate of the Upper Rhine at Mainz, and had marched to join their countrymen. Cerialis gave no heed to Civilis' protests that he had served Vespasian's interests against his rival Vitellius. He was reduced and punished; the disgraced legions were disbanded, their men enrolled in other legions with loss of seniority; the eight Batavian battalions were similarly treated, and re-formed as four double-strength battalions. When the Rhine was quietened and disciplined, Cerialis was transferred to Britain, and brought the Batavians with him. There the frontier was still insecure, and weakly sited. The revolt of 60, and the ten years' standstill thereafter, had halted expansion, and the army still held little more than it had gained in the first years of conquest, the kingdom of Cunobelinus in the south and Midlands, with Devon and Cornwall. The troops were stationed on or near the Severn and the Trent, their communications resting on the Fosse Way, from Lincoln to Exeter. Most of Wales was still unconquered, much of it actively hostile, and the large Pennine kingdom of the Brigantes was retained in uneasy alliance only by the intervention of Roman troops, to protect its queen against her own subjects.

Vespasian's generals undertook the conquest of the rest of Britain. Cerialis subdued and annexed the Brigantian kingdom in a battle at Stanwix, in the angle of the roads of Scotch Corner, where the natural open routes of the north fork left for Carlisle, northward to Newcastle. His forward troops pushed on to the isthmus between the Tyne and Solway. His successor Frontinus overran most of Wales, and in 77 or 78 Agricola was despatched to complete the conquest of all Britain. The legions moved forward from Wroxeter, near Shrewsbury, to Chester, from Gloucester to Caerleon, and from Lincoln to York. The three highland areas were separated from each other, their territories sliced by a grid of new roads, patrolled and secured by relatively small garrisons housed in small forts by the roads. The strongest peoples of Britain had been quickly broken; only the wilder backward peoples of the far north remained unconquered.

The completion of the conquest of Britain was an urgent strategic priority for the Roman army in Europe. The maintenance of the army was the principal charge upon the slender financial resources of the imperial government. Its force, not far short of half a million men, constituted the largest long-service, professional standing army that the world has yet known. They were strung out thinly and unevenly over some ten thousand miles of frontier, nearly two-thirds of them in Europe. Augustus had tried and failed to advance the frontier to the line of the Elbe and the Carpathians. The line from Hamburg to the mouth of the Danube was half the length of the frontier upon the banks of the Danube and Rhine, and if it were attained, the running cost of the European army might in time be halved. But the cost of conquest proved too high. Augustus was compelled to relinquish the advance, and to counsel his successors to rest content with the long, expensive river frontier. Neither he nor they were able to raise the men or money to equip a large expeditionary army; they could dispose only of the standing army of twenty-five to thirty legions, with its attendant provincial auxiliaries and foreign border units. Augustus' advice was in principle heeded, but the aim of shortening the northern frontier of the empire was never wholly forgotten. Vespasian initiated a fresh step towards it, that his successors maintained half-heartedly; the awkward salient of southern Germany between the upper courses of the Danube and the Rhine was annexed piecemeal by the slow extension of roads and forts, for a frontier that ran straight from Mainz to Regensburg was half as long as a frontier that followed the rivers; and once achieved it might offer an easier base for the penetration of central Germany.

The straight line was never achieved, and the frontier was not significantly shortened. But in the 70s it was an immediate aim, and its speedy realization demanded more troops, who must be disengaged from some other sector of the frontier. That need was the context of the Flavian campaigns in Britain. When Wales was subdued, the bulk of the campaigning force stood upon the narrow line between Carlisle and Newcastle. One-eighth of the entire Roman army was bogged down on eighty miles of frontier; eight times as many men held each mile of frontier as on the Rhine and Danube, against enemies far fewer and weaker than in Europe. If these few enemies could be quickly subdued, and all Britain made Roman, then its garrison might soon be reduced. One legion now sufficed to secure the whole of Spain, where formerly three had been required. It was reasonable to suppose that Britain also might in time be held by a single legion, or even by auxiliaries without a legion. Two or three much-needed legions might be freed to hold and shorten the European frontier.

Agricola undertook the final subjection of the north. He did not succeed. The campaign did not fail by reason of military mistakes. It was thwarted by the scale of northern geography, hitherto unknown to the Romans, and still today ill-understood by the inhabitants of southern Britain. To a southerner, Newcastle seems to lie far away in the north; but it is nearer to London than to the north coast of Britain. The moors and mountains of the north are thinly peopled, but hard to police and hold; they were not effectively subdued by southern rulers until the end of the eighteenth century. Agricola's methodical campaign lasted more than six years; his command was extended to twice the normal length of time, and in the end he forced the elusive armies of the Caledonians to stand to battle. No other southern commander achieved as much until 1745. Agricola won the battle, with few Roman casualties. But he could not use his victory. The enemy dispersed, and the vast spaces of the empty north lay open to his army. But he had not the men to hold them. In a later age, Hanoverian England was able to expend much money and many men over two generations in the slow and ruthless subjugation and depopulation of the highlands, but only after the lowlands had been English in speech and culture for very many centuries. If the Roman government had attempted a comparable investment of men and money, when even the Pennines had been Roman for barely ten years, it would have cost far more than the distant prospect of freeing legions for service in Europe warranted. It was cheaper and easier to contain the north than to conquer and hold it.

The push to the north failed. But the campaigns transformed the economy and the political needs of Britain, and made a great city necessary at London. The armies, having made as much progress north-ward as they could, stayed at the natural frontier zone they had reached. Detailed information is much less for the military history of the following years. The campaigns of Agricola and his predecessors were described by Tacitus not only in the *Life of Agricola* but in the *Annals* and the *Histories*, which trace the history of the empire to the year 70. Thereafter, political and military events are poorly recorded throughout the empire for centuries to come. The political disturbances of the sixty years from 180 to 240 are recorded in some detail by two contemporary writers, Cassius Dio and Herodian, and many other documents amply illustrate the social and political life of the empire; but no other narrative, com-parable with Tacitus, is again available until the history of Ammianus Marcellinus, whose surviving books cover the twenty-five years from 354 to 379. Thereafter, a great quantity of contemporary notices describe the dark days of the fall of western Rome.

Within this faulty record, references to Britain are few. Those that survive are almost entirely limited to obscure references to military campaigns, and to incidents that concern important visitors to Britain. Agricola's doings are described year by year, but not even the names of his immediate successors are known. A little archaeological evidence reveals something of their activity. Agricola had moved a legion's winter quarters north to Inchtuthil, near Perth, to hold the Vale of Strathmore against the Caledonians of the Grampians. It was withdrawn within two or three years of the end of his command; its timbers were carefully dismantled and removed, presumably for storage in York. Some of the lesser forts between Perth and Newcastle were held for some years more, but at the beginning of Trajan's reign the army pulled back to the line of Newcastle and Carlisle. Twenty years later, Hadrian fortified that line with a stone wall, some miles of which remain as the grandest monument of Rome in Britain.

Hadrian's Wall was intended to be permanent, but it was forsaken almost as soon as it was completed. In or about 140, his successor, Pius, moved the frontier garrisons forward to the shorter isthmus between the

Clyde and Forth. Given time, the shorter line could have been held by fewer troops, but time was not given. Immediately, the saving in mileage was more than offset by the need to garrison longer lines of communication, guarded by troops moved northward from the Pennine forts. The move was premature. Rebellion in the Pennines, in or about 155, entailed heavy fighting, and constrained the high command to pull the frontier back to Hadrian's Wall. Some years later, the wall of Pius was again occupied, and again abandoned, at dates not yet clearly established. About the time of Marcus' death, in 179 or 180, the Roman army was badly beaten, with very heavy casualties, and it was long before settled order was again restored. In the years from 208 to 211, the emperor Severus tried again to conquer the far north, but failed, without even approaching the military success that Agricola had achieved. He died at York in 211, and his successor, Caracalla, established the permanent frontier, based upon Hadrian's Wall, with a screen of outpost forts along the Cheviots from the neighbourhood of Carlisle to the mouth of the Tweed. Time hardened Caracalla's line, for it followed a natural divide; though it was long obscured in the centuries after the Romans, it ultimately reasserted itself as the lasting border between England and Scotland.

The northern half of Britain was never subdued by Rome; but the establishment of the northern frontier determined the future of the Roman province. The first need was the supply and maintenance of the troops, and food was the first priority. No evidence yet known suggests that there was any extensive arable cultivation in northern Britain beyond the Trent before the coming of the Romans. The British lived chiefly on meat and milk in and beside the hills, but the armies of first-century Rome fed on bread and porridge. When they first advanced beyond York, they still depended on the corn of the south. The legates of the Flavian emperors in the late first century built a waterway to carry the corn northward. Canals joining river to river linked the Cambridge-shire Ouse with the Ouse of York. Together, the whole waterway is known as the Car Dyke. It served its purpose, but its purpose did not long endure. Within three generations, the British of the north had learnt to grow corn enough to feed the army from their own acres. By the middle of the second century, most of the Car Dyke was silted, filled in, out of use; only the short stretch that joins Lincoln to the river Trent was kept permanently open, and still today, termed the Foss Dyke, makes inland Lincoln a sea-port.

Waterways were all-important in the economy of antiquity. Horse power was still weak and costly, ox power costly because it was slow, and demanded the time of men and animals. The padded horse collar was not yet known, and the horse pulled a waggon by means of a wooden yoke and traces; and though the heavy horse was known to the Roman world, it was bred in numbers only in limited regions, notably in Noricum, roughly the equivalent of modern Austria. The pulling power of the northern working horse was barely more than four times the strength of a man; and in agricultural lands, a horse cost almost four times as much to feed and maintain as a man. Long-distance transport of bulky, low-priced commodities like corn by road was uneconomic. Later, the collar quadrupled the pulling power of the medieval horse, and made the heavy horse a cheap and frequent animal for cartage and ploughing over much of Europe, and therefore also made it a serviceable weapon of war; but the collar, probably brought from China by the Slavs and Avars, and spread by the initiative of monks, was not widely known in western Europe until the ninth century or later, and the heavy horse that used it to best advantage was not extensively bred until two or three hundred years later.

Roads served other purposes. Waggons, more commonly drawn by mules and oxen, transported goods of less weight and higher value over long distances, and carried all goods for shorter distances. Persons of importance travelled by carriage, and government messengers rode by relays; and before they could ride at ease, armies marched, and needed roads behind them to keep them supplied. The first paved roads, of the time of Claudius and Nero, are not often easily distinguished from those of later generations; but where they can be recognized they were commonly small affairs, twenty or twenty-five feet wide or even less, no wider than a modern main road in the years before motorways. But the trunk roads of the Flavian age were engineered more amply. The central, hard, cambered surface commonly measured from twenty-five to thirty feet, and was flanked on either side by a broad, softer track, with the road ditches set from sixty to eighty feet apart. They clamped the economy of the lowlands together. A square of main roads rested with its corners upon the estuaries of the Severn and Dee, Humber and Thames, with diagonals, the Fosse Way and the Watling Street, that ran from Lincoln to Bath and Exeter, and London to Chester (see Map 8). Other main roads served the regions outside the rectangle of the estuaries; the Pennines were flanked by northward extensions of its eastern and western sides, from the Mersey by Warrington to Carlisle, from the Humber and York to Newcastle and Corbridge, with several Pennine

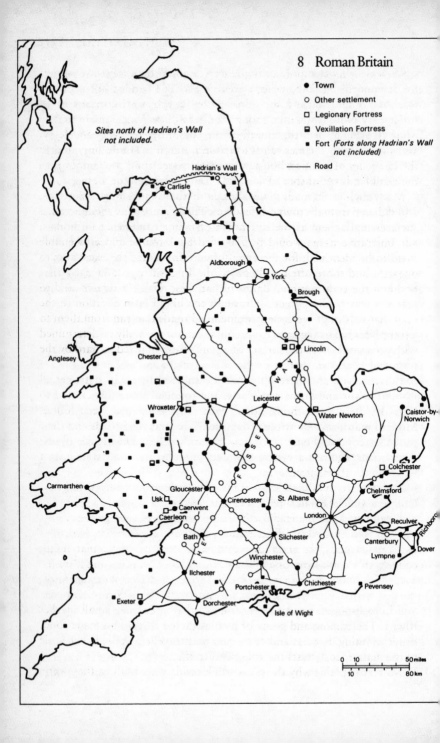

8 Roman Britain

- ● Town
- ○ Other settlement
- □ Legionary Fortress
- ▣ Vexillation Fortress
- ■ Fort *(Forts along Hadrian's Wall not included)*
- —— Road

Sites north of Hadrian's Wall not included.

Hadrian's Wall

Carlisle

Aldborough

York

Brough

Lincoln

Anglesey

Chester

Wroxeter

Leicester

Water Newton

Caistor-by-Norwich

Carmarthen

Gloucester

Usk

Caerwent

Caerleon

Cirencester

St. Albans

Colchester

Chelmsford

London

Bath

Silchester

Reculver

Richboro[ugh]

Canterbury

Dover

Lympne

Winchester

Ilchester

Portchester

Chichester

Pevensey

Exeter

Dorchester

Isle of Wight

FOSSE WAY

THE

0   10   50 miles

10   80 km

traverses, the most important of them the Stainmore Pass by Bowes, that forks from the York-Newcastle road at Scotch Corner to Penrith and Carlisle; other roads stretch from London to Colchester, and to Caistor-by-Norwich, with a fork to the left that provided an alternative route to Lincoln over the mouth of the Wash, by causeway and ferry; and south of the Thames roads led from London to Canterbury and to the harbours of Kent and Sussex, to Winchester and Southampton, to the chalklands of Salisbury Plain and on to Exeter and the west.

Many engineered roads joined the country between to the trunk roads, and radiated from the towns upon them. Their camber and their metalled surfaces mark them as the equivalent of major routes that in modern administrative usage would be classified as A-roads, and also enable them to be identified; for the metal often remains for the excavator to unearth, and more often still caused the English of a later age to fix beside it the enduring boundaries of parishes, farms or estates, and to name nearby places 'Street', 'Strat-' or the like. But in addition to the main A-roads there were many unmetalled roads that ran from them to lesser places, whose age and exact course cannot normally be determined with precision. Often the surface of an old road is packed so hard by the traffic of centuries that it cannot be loosened without the aid of a pneumatic drill, and there is no clear evidence to reveal its date; yet all Roman towns and farms used carts, and roads of some sort existed to bear the carts, even though their exact course has not been found. Modern maps, that show the proven course of metalled roads and their probable continuations, accurately report modern knowledge of the main roads, but are a very incomplete guide to the road system as a whole in the Roman centuries.

Roads were many, and the needs of government made them busy. Couriers, officials, and supply waggons needed relay points where tired horses might be exchanged for fresh, and where men might sleep. Post stations were early established at intervals of about eight to twelve miles along main roads, the *mutationes* and *mansiones*. In a day a man might comfortably walk from one to the next, and so a waggon might travel; a rider in a hurry might manage three stations in a day. Once established, the post stations grew. They became centres for the collection of taxes, and in well-populated agricultural lands they grew into small market towns. The coming and going of men attracted those who made food, drink, clothing, harness and other gear that travellers needed. The scale of the main roads attests the volume of traffic.

No text explains why the great trunk roads were built as they were, but such roads were built by others as well as the Romans, and elsewhere their use is known. Many main roads of modern India are similarly planned, with a hard, cambered centre and soft side tracks, sixty feet or more in total width. The bulk of the traffic is slow moving, men and women walking, or ox carts travelling more slowly than people; but when the approach of a fast, light car or cart is heard, the walkers and the oxen spread away to the side tracks, and pour back on to the road when the occasional faster vehicle is past, like water parted by a ship. Such roads presuppose that most traffic is slow and local, but that fast through traffic is also expected. Many of the great roads were laid out in the time of Domitian, in the last years of the first century; they imply that considerable local traffic was then expected, and doubtless already experienced. Much of it was concerned with the feeding of the towns, large and small; and by the early years of the second century, many farmers who lived within a mile or two of a town and close to a main road prospered enough to rebuild their homes on an ampler scale, as good roads promoted easier contact with a wider range of customers.

Towns and roads, trade and property, government and taxation required a great deal of administration. The legates of the emperor were responsible at all times both for the civil administration of the province and for the command of the armies. Elsewhere in Europe Rome had faced the differing needs of frontiers and of peaceful interior lands. Augustus had resolved the problems of the frontier in his day by creating new provinces. The large territory of Gaul was divided. A narrow territory along the Roman bank of the Rhine became the new province of Germania, with two armies, stationed in its lower and upper portions; the rest of Gaul was split into the three divisions which Caesar found in existence before he came. The north-west, peopled by the Belgae, was henceforth the province of Gallia Belgica; the prosperous south-west became the province of Aquitania; and the central territories, called 'Celtica' by Caesar, formed a third province, termed Gallia Lugdunensis, from Lugdunum, Lyons, the city that Augustus made into *caput Galliarum*, the capital of the Gauls. It held together the three provinces, recognized as an entity distinct from Mediterranean Gaul, Gallia Narbonensis, ruled from Narbonne, that had been a Roman province long before Caesar's time. (See Map 9.)

Similar solutions were elsewhere easier. When the armies of the Balkans moved north from Dalmatia and Macedonia to the line of the Danube, Augustus made new provinces of the newly-conquered lands – Noricum, roughly the modern Austria, Pannonia, roughly equivalent to

Hungary south and west of the middle Danube, and Moesia on the lower Danube. The frontier provinces contained a number of important civilian towns, and needed civil government; but in each of them the army predominated, and all were small enough for the legate who commanded the army to administer conveniently. Behind the frontiers, no legions remained, save in Dalmatia, where they stayed until Domitian's reign. The interior provinces were termed *provinciae inermes*, 'unarmed provinces', and were governed by imperial legates, who soon found their precise niche in the orderly hierarchy of the senator's career. The frontier provinces were governed by propraetorian legates who were consulars, men in their forties with previous military experience, who had under them legates in command of each legion, of praetorian rank, commonly in their middle thirties. The unarmed provinces were governed by propraetorian legates who were not yet consuls, but were commonly older than legionary legates and senior to them. After he had commanded his legion in Britain, Agricola was appointed legate of Aquitania, and Tacitus described the appointment as *spe consulatus*, carrying with it the promise of the consulate. In due course, Agricola left Aquitania, held his consulate, and was then sent as consular propraetorian legate to Britain.

Vespasian might have divided Britain as Augustus had divided Gaul, and as in fact Britain was divided somewhat over a hundred years later.[1] But in the 70s Vespasian appointed a Roman legate from Italy, for whom a new title was devised, *legatus iuridicus*. No text explains the office; only its title, 'judiciary legate', and the nature of the men appointed, explain its purpose and its function. The first two *iuridici*, Salvius Liberalis and Iavolenus Priscus, were both lawyers of outstanding distinction.[2] Both were senior in their careers; both had already commanded legions, and both received their consulate soon after their return from Britain. They held office while Agricola was campaigning in the far north. They were the men who set the new system on its feet; only a few of the later *iuridici* are known, but all those whose status is known were junior in the hierarchy, recent ex-praetors who had not yet commanded a legion, and are not known to have been lawyers. When the trained lawyers had done their work, in Agricola's time, they left behind them a well-ordered administrative machine, whose continued functioning might be supervised by men of less experience, without specialized training.

The geography of Britain dictated Vespasian's decision. The army depended upon supplies from the south; the propraetorian legate could

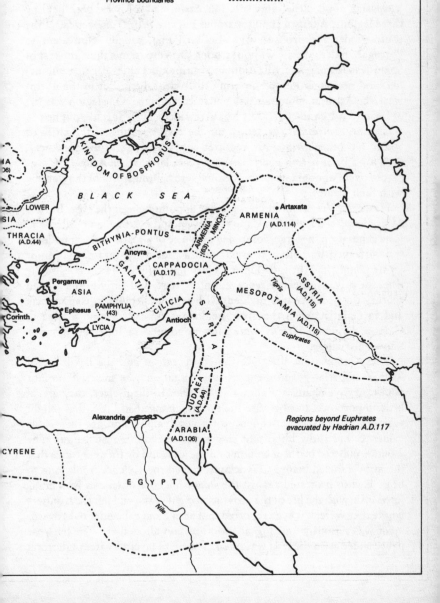

9 The Roman Empire up to the time of Trajan (AD 98-117)

Frontier of Roman Empire A.D.14 ----------
Frontier of Roman Empire A.D.117 -- -- -- --
Province boundaries ....

KINGDOM OF BOSPHORUS

BLACK   SEA

LOWER

SIA

THRACIA
(A.D.44)

BITHYNIA-PONTUS

ARMENIA
(63)
MINOR

• Artaxata

ARMENIA
(A.D.114)

• Ancyra

GALATIA

CAPPADOCIA
(A.D.17)

Pergamum

ASIA

ASSYRIA
(A.D.115)

MESOPOTAMIA (A.D.115)

Tigris

Ephesus

PAMPHYLIA
(43)

CILICIA

S
Y
R
I
A

Corinth

LYCIA

Antioch

Euphrates

JUDAEA
(A.D.44)

Regions beyond Euphrates
evacuated by Hadrian A.D.117

Alexandria

ARABIA
(A.D.106)

CYRENE

E G Y P T

Nile

not afford to have his base cut off under the command of a separate, independent legate, not under his command, governing a distinct province. But he needed a subordinate who could be trusted to supervise civil administration. One other province had a similar problem, and to it Vespasian applied the same solution. Spain had formerly been held by three legions; Augustus had separated Further Spain, or Baetica, in the south, under a proconsul, and also Lusitania, roughly equivalent to Portugal, under a legate without troops. By Vespasian's time, the rest of Spain was Roman in civilization and outlook; its cities became *municipia*, and no longer needed an army to control them. But in the northwest, the Asturian mountaineers remained untamed. One legion was left at Léon to watch them, and its legate retained consular rank; but he too was given a *iuridicus*, evidently for the civil ordering of the cities of Spain. No other *iuridici* are reported anywhere else in the provinces, save for a brief period nearly seventy years later, when a *iuridicus* was placed over Pannonia while the legions were fighting north of the Danube with their legates.

However, Vespasian made a similar appointment in the east. In Asia Minor he placed legions in Cappadocia, upon the Armenian border, and for a generation the large, combined province of Galatia and Cappadocia was governed by both a consular and a praetorian legate; the junior legate plainly had the functions of a *iuridicus*, though he did not use the title, for it was not easily rendered into Greek, and early in the second century the province was divided, with separate legions in Cappadocia and in Galatia, when the army no longer depended upon a base in Galatia. Regional *iuridici* were later appointed in Italy, but none is known elsewhere.

These innovations illustrate the conservatism and the flexibility of Roman imperial government. A new situation was met with minor administrative changes within a set system. In themselves, they are of little importance, but because the system changed so little, these slight variations were the consequence of potent causes, and are the visible evidence that show important stages in the evolution of Britain. The wounds inflicted by the rebellion of Boudicca, and by the vengeance that the army exacted before Classicianus stayed the violence, took long to heal. Tacitus protested against the sluggish inertia of legates who interfered little with the life of the province for ten years, and left the frontiers where they were; it is even reported that at one stage the imperial government was seriously urged to abandon Britain altogether.[3] The ten-year pause ended with the civil war of 69. The first Flavian legates undertook the ordering of a province that had been Roman for a generation, and had begun to recover from the bloodshed of rebellion.

Their chief concern was to conquer the rest of Britain. Their campaigns fell short of full success, but they achieved a lasting frontier far from the fertile lowlands. Their second priority was to regulate lowland life. Their measures had twin motives. One was straightforward military prudence. The army could not hope to free its full strength for northern wars unless the lands already conquered were tame enough to be held with a small police force. Tacitus reports in a sentence the policy that Agricola practised, and repeats what Agricola himself had told him. After powerful military force had demonstrated that resistance to Rome was bloody, costly and unavailing,

when he had instilled sufficient fear, he returned to forbearance, and displayed the inducements of peace. Consequently many states that had hitherto asserted independence put aside their hostility.[4]

Agricola was speaking of his own policy towards the nearer peoples first subdued in the early 70s; but it was also the policy that Classicianus had counselled in the lands that had earlier been conquered by Claudius and had rebelled against Nero, and that had operated under Agricola's immediate predecessors. It was the only sensible military policy, but it was also the realization in Britain of the outlook of the new government of Vespasian and his advisers. Agricola was one of his patricians, selected above others to formulate and fashion the principles upon which the empire was governed. He and his son-in-law used events in Britain as practical examples from which general principles, valid for the whole empire, might be abstracted and lucidly expressed.

The paternal outlook of the Roman patricians persisted throughout the Flavian and Antonine century. It was voiced in very many comfortable remarks, by noblemen who felt themselves secure, and strong enough to be gentle in all their dealings. Any threat of serious dissidence, or obstinate defiance, would merit firm punishment; but rulers could afford to be indulgent towards the grumbles, the criticisms and the complaints of the great majority, who accepted submission to authority, but retained the right and the means to protest against particular decisions. The historian Florus saw his time as 'the old age of the world', when all history was past. Emperors stayed quietly in Italy, living as great country gentlemen, and trusting their legates to rule their empire well. He felt confident enough to publish a lampoon on the unusual and unseemly travels of the emperor Hadrian, who visited most of the provinces, including Britain, to inspect and improve their government. His journeys excited remark, for no other emperor visited provinces, save to command in war or deal with an urgent political threat; and not all comment was favourable, for men of influence who sought the ear of government preferred to have it easily accessible in Rome, and disliked uncomfortable journeys in rough strange lands to find it. Florus protested

> I would not be a Caesar
> Wandering among the British ...
> Enduring Scythian frosts.

His freedom brought him no punishment or disfavour; he suffered only the sting of sharp rejoinder, published as prominently by the emperor,

> I would not be a Florus
> Wandering from pub to pub ...
> Enduring buxom tarts.[5]

The motives that sent Hadrian on his travels were the inherited motives and attitudes of a class who saw themselves as shepherds of their flocks, providing paternal guidance for their subjects in the interest of the state, chastising only the incorrigible. Their care extended to all their subjects, and included the responsibility to protect the humbler subject against abuse by his mightier neighbour or by government officials. The law laid down that the prime duty of a governor was to keep his province 'quiet and composed'. Tacitus' friend, the younger Pliny, spelt out the ways in which provincials were best kept quiet. He wrote to congratulate his colleague Calestrius Tiro on

your excellent administration of your province. Your tact ensures its good reception, ... for you manage to win the good will of the humble without forfeiting the respect of their betters. Nowadays many governors are so scared of seeming to yield to the influence of provincial magnates that they gain the opposite reputation of *sinisteritas*. You altogether avoid this danger.[6]

The literal meaning of *sinisteritas* is 'leftism'; but its meaning here is nearer to the French 'gaucherie', awkwardness or clumsiness. Pliny wrote a personal letter to a friend, but he edited his letters and published them; and they proved best-sellers. He was a provincial governor himself, and, like Tacitus, his published work preached a model of public and private conduct. As a lawyer, he had prosecuted governors accused of misconduct by provincials, and had also defended other governors so charged. His generation had learnt that a successful governor must not only be just, but be seen to be just; he must therefore decline even the most modest gifts from those he ruled and must not appear in his judicial capacity to favour his social equals, the notables of the province with whom he wined and dined. His delicate words to Tiro indicate that by the early second century the Flavian lesson was well learnt, and taken for granted; the opposite danger tempted a governor unsure of himself to fall over backwards to avoid the appearance of favouritism, and to be therefore unduly prejudiced against powerful interests.

Flavian legates could afford impartiality. They were Mediterranean millionaires, made cosmopolitan by senatorial rank and residence in or near Rome. They were above the conflicts of provincials, free of interest that might attach them to one faction or another; and the corporate vigilance of the Senate had learned to punish swiftly corrupt practices among individual senators, for history had taught them that their whole order was endangered if men believed that it was corrupt. They were wealthy enough to stand in no need of bribes; and when they had secured themselves against temptation, they were eager to suppress corruption and injustice among lesser officials. They were ready to listen to complaint, and had the means to see that complaints reached the government. Each city and province had its patrons in Rome; and even the humblest might petition. Several records instance the effective working of the right of complaint. In one second-century instance, the protest of some poor African tenant farmers reached Rome; they lived upon an imperial estate supervised by a procurator, who leased its portions. The customs of the district permitted the lessee to exact six days a year unpaid labour on his home farm from the dependent farmsteads, but their lessee demanded more, and the procurator connived at his demand. The cultivators protested over their heads, and the government ruled in their favour. The grateful peasants took care that the imperial ruling should be engraved on bronze and publicly exhibited, to deter future lessees and procurators; the inscription survives,[7] one among the many witnesses to the care which Pliny, Agricola, Tiro and their fellows exercised to see that provinces remained quiet and composed, that the government did not appear as the champion of oppression by the ruling notables in each province.

The lofty patronage of the imperial aristocracy was calculated common sense, learned in the hard experience of past centuries. It was not motivated by radical idealism, or by any eagerness to reform society. Good order was preserved by just and fair decisions, but good order rested on the maintenance of a stable social hierarchy, whose heads were

the nobility of each state and province, their apex the senatorial aristocracy. The preservation of the ordered hierarchy was paramount, itself
the reason that enjoined just rule. Pliny concluded his letter to Tiro with
further congratulations, on

the way you maintain differences of class and rank; once they are muddled or
set aside, nothing is more unequal than so-called 'equality'.

He and his fellows remembered with horror the chaotic past when the
riots of the urban plebs in Rome had provided gangs for electioneering
agents, and armies for generals who raised civil war against each other,
promising either to win better living standards, greater freedom and
equality for the masses, or else to terrorize the mob into submission. A
century after Pliny's time, Cassius Dio described those dark days in
similar words, as a time when the 'so-called freedom of the mob proved
the bitterest servitude of the better classes'.[8]

Quiet and justice were the watchwords of the age. Many stories
emphasize them. Whether they are literally true is of small moment; they
were believed, and were put about to stress the outlook that the government wished to encourage. Men identified the Roman empire with
civilization; civilized standards required the embellishment of all its
parts, with greater distinction for each regional and provincial capital,
the greatest of all for Rome, the capital of the world. The blessing that
the Roman church still formally bestows, *urbi et orbi*, upon the 'city and
the world', underlines their identity. In the middle of the second century,
when a pompous professor of Greek from Smyrna was invited to address
the assembled academics and statesmen of Rome in the presence of the
emperor Pius, he piled cliché upon cliché, imagining the vast length to
which the cities of the empire would stretch if they were placed end to
end. Among his rhetorical flourishes were the boasts that Rome was 'the
workshop of the world' and ruled 'an empire upon which the sun never
sets'.[9] It is not an accident that an unknown reader centuries later
pillaged his ornate discourse to seize upon these phrases, and give them
a new currency in honour of the nineteenth-century British empire.
Much else in Antonine Rome asserted the same self-conscious rectitude
that pleased the leaders of Victorian England. A story was told of Pius to
the effect that when he was first appointed emperor, his wife expected
larger household expenditure, but was rebuked by Pius with the words
'Fool, now that we have become imperial, we have lost the property we
held before'.[10] Because he was emperor, his personal property had
become state property, a public charge entrusted to his care. All that errs
in the telling of the model tale is that Pius was too much a gentleman to

have called his wife a fool. Other stories match. As he lay on his deathbed twenty years later, the aged emperor was asked for the watchword for the relief battalion at the changing of the palace guards; with his dyingbreath he murmured 'Equanimity', and turned his face to the wall.[11]

These were the standards that the Flavian legates brought to Britain. They were new in the empire, and Roman ways were still new to Britain. Wounds were healed, and lost time must be made good. The first need was to win the sympathies of the principal citizens in each state. Tacitus outlines Agricola's means and methods, and the success he claimed. The preliminary step, undertaken in his first months in Britain, was to clean up the small-scale corruption that had lingered in the years of inertia, and during the first campaign of the Flavian legates. It principally concerned taxation. The government imposed a tax on land, often payable in kind, and a poll tax; the principal delivery was in grain, and in the early days, when the north did not yet grow sufficient crops, strains were heavy upon the Car Dyke, and the roads that fed it. The government therefore also required and used the right to buy additional foodstuffs, over and above the yield of taxes, by compulsory purchase at fixed prices.

The officers of foreign conquerors had ample opportunity to line their pockets at the expense of farmers who did not know their language, and stood in awe of military force, whose unrestrained anger had been felt a few years before, after the rebellion. Instead of ordering farmers to deliver their grain to the nearest forts, local officials instructed them to deliver to distant destinations at their own cost. Tacitus' terse language does not explain in words their reasons, but the implication is plain; farmers faced with ruinous transport charges were ready to bribe the officials to accept delivery at a nearer collecting point. Tacitus also complains that the government granaries were overfilled with grain, and that farmers had to buy back their own corn at outrageous prices. Compulsory purchase had evidently swallowed up more than the available surplus in some regions, and impounded more than the armies actually received or needed. The population was short of seed-corn at least, perhaps also of corn for consumption; and local officers offered for sale the collections additional to government requirements, charging inflated prices, whose excess went into private pockets. Tacitus emphasized that the weight of the tax itself was relatively light, and caused no widespread grievance; but resentment flamed against abuse. A burden 'that should have been light served to enrich a few individuals'.[12]

The abuse was smartly ended, and its cure began to win the subjects' trust. When the head of the Roman government in Britain was seen to protect the native British against Roman misbehaviour, men who had growled at the evil ways of Rome began to distinguish between good and bad Romans, and were ready to champion the virtues that the new government preached. Agricola then took trouble to instil those virtues into the leading British of each state, and to offer them the practical material advantages of conformity with Roman ways. His second winter

was spent in fruitful enterprises. Uncivilized people, whose homes were scattered, were prompt to take arms. He therefore used pleasurable inducements to accustom them to quiet and ease. He offered state aid for the construction of temples, town centres and private houses, and also encouraged individual undertakings. He lavished praise on those who co-operated readily, and poured scorn on those who were slow to respond. Men acted because they strove to earn respect, no longer because they must. He offered advanced education to the sons of leading men, and said that he preferred the native wit of the British to the laboured application of the Gauls. Soon a people who had spat upon the Roman tongue began to strive for fluency in Latin. Our dress became a mark of honour, and the *toga* became a common sight. Gradually men succumbed to the corrupting charms of colonnades, baths and elegant dinners. They are a part of the process of subjugation, but to men who had not known them before they bore the name of culture.[13]

Tacitus' short paragraph describes an energetic, many-sided drive, and explains its purpose. Government money and effort was devoted to taming the British, to reducing or abolishing the risk of renewed rebellion, to transforming the settled regions into peaceful states, whose leaders might be trusted to run their own communities without cost or disturbance to the resources of the Roman government. A relatively small capital investment in the form of state aid to new building saved much expense in the future. The effort was made in the interests of Rome; but it was made by men who held that the interests of Rome rested upon the docile prosperity of each corner of the empire. It eliminated conflict between the interest of the government and the interest of the more powerful subject.

A first inducement was the grant of Roman citizenship. The *toga* was the citizen's normal dress, and those who wore it in Britain were men whom Agricola had recommended for citizenship, the ancestors of the British who bore the names T. Flavius. But citizens required cities in which to live. The buildings that made up a city were both public and private; temples and town centres, colonnades and baths, were the essentials of a town; but those who used them also needed houses. In the first years of conquest, when men still lived chiefly in houses of timber, building was not expensive; ample timber grew near to every town, and its use required no more than the traditional native skills of the carpenter. But substantial buildings of brick and stone needed money: the materials were more expensive to dig out and to manufacture; they often necessitated costly cartage from kiln and quarry to the building site, and demanded sophisticated skills new to the British. When the towns were built, their administration needed records, and therefore knowledge of reading and writing. British remained the normal spoken language, and still endures today, modified through many changes into modern Welsh, but British was never written; reading and writing were possible only in Latin, so that the management of towns required the advanced education that Agricola provided.

The effort was considerable. Agricola drew upon the resources of a vast empire whose government and private citizens considered it right and proper to spend time and money freely in order to raise an undeveloped province to the level of Roman civilization elsewhere. Chance notices in several writers, and a quantity of excavated evidence, attest the scale of the Flavian initiative in Britain. One incident illustrates the importance attached to the development of Roman education. The most prolific writer of the age was the scholar Plutarch. He was a priest, housed with a stipend in the wealthy, ancient religious establishment of the oracle of Delphi. He was a Greek who indulged some nostalgia for the vanished glories of past independence, but who warmly welcomed the quiet security that the Greek lands enjoyed under Roman rule. His life's work was to demonstrate to his fellow Greeks that Rome was the heir, champion and extension of Greek civilization, that Greeks and Romans had similar origins, and shared a common culture and interest. His best-known work was his *Parallel Lives*, wherein short biographies of a notable Greek and a notable Roman were paired, and a concluding summary stressed their similarity. His writing earned him Roman citizenship and world distinction. His well-furnished academic apartments at Delphi invited the visits of men of note, governors of the province of Achaea, governors of other eastern provinces on their way to or from their appointments, literary and political personages who travelled eastward. His guests included Demetrius of Tarsus. A hundred years before, Augustus had selected Tarsus, in south-eastern Turkey, on the borders between the Greek lands of Asia Minor and the Syrian provinces of the Levant, as a principal centre of higher education, where the political and moral philosophy of Rome might be mingled with the Greek, and a joint Greek and Roman viewpoint taught to men of Syriac and Phoenician backgrounds. One of the earliest pupils of the schools of Tarsus was Saint Paul, whose cosmopolitan education, blending Greek and Hebrew experience, epitomized the culture that Tarsus was encouraged to spread, although Saint Paul's use of his education ill accorded with the aims that Augustus foresaw. In the Flavian age, Demetrius, the principal academic of Tarsus, was among the foremost educationalists of the day, a Greek of Levantine antecedents who was also a Roman citizen. He stayed with Plutarch on his return from Britain to Tarsus, while Agricola was legate, and told him stories of the Hebrides, which he had visited, presumably with Agricola's fleet. Plutarch reported and published only his anecdotes,[14] but so eminent a teacher had not visited Britain for the sole purpose of sailing in remote western waters. His business was education, and it is plain that Agricola had brought him over to help and advise upon the development of the schools in the rising British towns. His work endured, and so did the intellectual vigour of Tarsus, to offer similar aid to a greatly altered Britain in a later age; for it was another scholar of Tarsus, Theodore, who was to remodel the Christian church of the English, and give it its enduring modern shape, six hundred years after the time of Agricola and Demetrius.

A few other notices show the rapid spread of Roman letters and Roman manners. The poet Martial, friend of Pliny and Tacitus, delighted with the wide sale of his poems, was especially gratified to learn from his publisher that his books were sold and read as far away as Britain;[15] he also wrote a verse for the wedding of a friend of his, a respectable Roman knight of Italy, whose bride was a Claudia, a British girl born among the fabulous blue-painted savages of the far north.[16] She was evidently the daughter or granddaughter of one of the eminent Britons who had received citizenship from Claudius or Nero; she might have been the heiress of Cogidubnus, or of some other nobleman. The image of savage Britons of the age of conquest was implanted into Roman literature by Caesar and Tacitus, and long remained as a colourful literary cliché; but the poet Juvenal reveals something of a more sophisticated Britain. He had himself served as an officer in the army of Britain in later Flavian times, and in his older years his sour and crusty morality satirized all novelties that invaded the stern simplicity of ancient Roman tradition. Among the many targets of his tongue were the silly fashions of giddy young ladies in Rome; among their follies was the craze for a new, modish style of handbag, a type woven of reeds by the

British and imitated in Rome, termed *bascauda* in the outlandish British tongue.[17] The word is probably preserved by the modern English 'basket', one of the few English words borrowed from the speech of the British, and was perhaps something of the nature of a Sussex trug, though its precise form is not clearly described. Nonetheless, the fact that a British fashion was embraced by well-to-do young women in Rome implies acquaintance with matured urban life in British towns, where British girls commonly walked the streets with their purchases in the same kind of carrier that their mothers had brought from the countryside to the new cities. The granddaughters of the blue-painted savages were already passing into the common civilization of Rome.

Fair and firm government, the building of cities, and Latin education bound considerable sections of the notable British to the civilization of Rome. The towns in which they lived are known from their archaeological remains. Their scale and early date is impressive. It cannot yet be comprehensively observed, for only a few towns have been systematically excavated, and the smaller towns are at present less well understood than the capitals of the several states. Dates vary in precision. They rely chiefly upon pottery, and it is sometimes possible to distinguish early from late Flavian pottery, when there is enough of it to make the absence of later or earlier types significant. More often, it is possible only to say that the pottery is of the late first century in general. Moreover, pottery and other objects sealed beneath the floors or walls of a building show only the earliest possible date at which it could have been built, while objects found upon floors often show only a date after it had ceased to be used, for rubbish was not normally allowed to accumulate upon a floor that remained in use.

The dating of buildings therefore depends on deductions from random instances. From these it is possible to outline the level of urban life in broad terms, with dates unlikely to be overset by future discovery, through the fertile lowlands of Britain as a whole, although the precise dating of individual buildings is seldom possible. The large public buildings, however, are frequently dated more easily, either by inscriptions, or because poorer houses of an earlier age were often cleared away to make way for them. In most of the state capitals, and in several of the smaller towns, where evidence is available, these buildings are of Flavian date. They were large and opulent. The baths of Exeter occupied some 20,000 square feet; at Chelmsford, in origin a post station, possibly later the capital town of the Trinovantes, the external drains of the baths were lined with imported marble. Town centres were as spaciously designed, and were commonly built under the Flavian emperors. They normally comprised a large basilica, or town hall, that formed one side of the forum, with at least two other sides occupied by shops and offices. The basilica was normally of much the same size as a medieval cathedral; at Cirencester, the basilica is within a few feet of the dimensions of Gloucester Cathedral, if its Lady Chapel be ignored; the measurements of the Verulamium basilica are very nearly the same as those of the medieval abbey and modern cathedral of St Albans; and the great basilica of London was somewhat larger than the present-day Cathedral of St Paul.

Only one sure date exactly indicates the construction of any of these Flavian buildings. A monumental inscription was placed in the wall of the Verulamium forum, over one of its main entrances, presumably matched by another over the other main entrance. The normal purpose of slabs was to mark the completion of a building, and to celebrate its official opening; the stone cannot have been put in position before the wall was finished, and elsewhere there is firm evidence that the forum was normally constructed after, rather than before, the town hall which it accompanied. The stone fell in time, and a few fragments have been recovered, enough to indicate its size and preserve the date inscribed upon it. The whole slab had measured about 13½ feet by 2½ feet, and commemorated the opening of the town centre by, or by authority of, Agricola in the second half of the year 79.[18]

The date discloses that the forum cannot have been begun and initiated in Agricola's time. The building of so huge a complex must have taken several years. None of the great medieval churches that compare with it in size and in demands upon manpower is known to have been completed in less than thirty or forty years. Roman building was certainly very much faster, for no such forum is known to have been planned or built anywhere in Britain before the time of Vespasian. The Verulamium basilica and forum are therefore not likely to have been begun before 71 or 72 at the earliest, and cannot have taken much more than eight years to build; but it is scarcely credible that the work was begun and ended in less than two years, the longest possible interval between Agricola's arrival in Britain and the erection of the inscription. Agricola doubtless hastened the work, an outstanding instance of his drive to build temples, fora and houses; but he plainly continued a policy initiated by his immediate predecessors, Cerialis and Frontinus, that was part and parcel of Vespasian's provision for all provinces.

Not all state capitals finished their great buildings so speedily. Verulamium was a *municipium*, in all probability long before the work was undertaken, and was probably then the only *municipium* in Britain (above, p. 70). A comparable inscription is known only from one other capital, Wroxeter, the chief town of the Cornovii of Shropshire and Staffordshire. The district was poorer than the fertile lowlands, and developed somewhat later. The place had been the fortress of a legion that was not moved forward until Agricola's time; Chester took its place, probably about 77. Then public building of comparable size was under-taken, possibly starting from scratch, possibly continuing an uncom-pleted legionary building. But the work was not hurried through, and was discontinued for long periods. It was revived half a century later, when Hadrian came to Britain, and at Wroxeter the stone that marks the completion of the building is dated to the year 130.[19] Elsewhere, the evidence is less positive, for the pottery that underlies these great build-ings normally points to the date at which building was begun, not when it was completed. Many such buildings were begun under the Flavians; and in several towns, among them London, the evidence argues that the basilica was probably completed under the Flavian emperors, or soon after, but that the forum around it was added in Hadrian's time.[20]

Towns so lavishly appointed were built to impress. Such extravagant construction, beyond the previous experience, was clearly backed by the state aid which Tacitus reports. The encouragement to individuals prompted them to build private houses suitably proportioned to the public buildings, to invest in shops and commercial property, and per-haps to contribute towards the construction of temples and places of entertainment. But grandeur was the purpose of the Flavian towns. Present evidence does not suggest that the appearance of the state capitals in the time of Claudius and Nero was particularly striking. Then the might of Rome was emphasized at Colchester, where the colossal temple of Claudius gleamed in white and coloured marbles from its hill-top across the surrounding lands. But no comparable monuments yet daunted the rest of the British. The Flavian cities, however, were laid out in most states of the fertile lowlands, probably in all. They served both of the twin principles of government that Agricola and Tacitus formulated, to instil fear into the ill-disposed, and to comfort and reward the co-operative. These huge buildings were set down in a countryside that had hitherto known no structures more elaborate than a large timber hall, or the high bank and deep ditch around the hutments of a royal centre. They spoke plainly to the native population. Rome was too great to challenge; the empire that could place such palaces in every state was more than able to contain any counter-attack that the British might hope to organize.

But though the buildings were Roman, the men who ruled in and from them were British. The notables among the British, whose children were taught to strive for fluent Latin, constituted the town council and the magistrates who made laws and sat in judgement in the newly built town halls. They had become great landlords, enriched by rents whose continued payment the government of Rome ensured. They dwelt in comfortable houses, importing Roman wine, wearing Roman clothes, and took their ease in Roman baths. The leaders of each British state were irrevocably bound to Rome, some few of them already Roman citizens, many more with a hope of citizenship. Rebellion threatened the loss of all that made their lives, with no hope of success, and no prospect of a better life even if victory were possible. The mass of the poorer population had not yet received significant material benefit, save that they had in Agricola's time lived at peace for some twenty years, with every prospect of continuing peace. But when they were deprived of the possibility of leadership by the great men of their own nation, renewed resistance was no longer thinkable. It was not merely reduced to the level of grudging submission by men who kept alive their resentment, as in later empires, where the officers of a foreign conqueror directly ruled the natives. The memory of resistance was forgotten, and men speedily accepted without question their status as Roman subjects, directing such resentment as remained against the British nobles who ruled each state, looking to the Roman governor for protection against undue exploitation by lords of their own speech and nation.

The town was at once the means and the symbol of stable Roman rule, and London was the greatest of the Roman towns in Britain. Its maturity was reached when the Flavian initiative was spent. The first priority in the creation of a province permanently quiet and composed was to make each of its parts whole. The frontier was secured and stabilized; each state received its own government and administration, seated in its own capital town. Then came the need for a permanent centre for the imperial government that co-ordinated the several states. At the time of conquest, Claudius had established a *colonia* at Colchester, because Colchester had been the capital of the greatest of the kings before the Romans, who ruled most of the fertile lowland. Time dimmed the causes that had prompted the building of the temple of Claudius in Colchester, and made it the centre of Roman control of Britain. When Britain matured, Colchester was in the wrong place. It may be that it long retained some of the ceremonial attributes of its early prominence; and Roman conservatism may possibly have caused the Provincial Assembly to meet in its original centre, regularly or occasionally, long after the original reason had gone. But only London could be the centre of day-to-day administration. From London the roads radiated, to the armies and to the state capitals; at the lowest practical crossing place of the Thames, London bridge joined them to the roads that led to Europe. Bulky cargoes might sail up the estuary to the port of London, but travellers more conveniently used the short sea crossing from Boulogne to Richborough, near Sandwich, and posted ninety miles up the straight road, through Canterbury and Rochester, to London. London grew as the administration and trade of the Roman province of Britain expanded.

Roman rule endured. What did not endure was the rule of a foreign nation termed Romans over alien subjects termed British. That contrast was valid only for the first generations after the conquest. The aim and concept of Agricola and Vespasian and their successors was to integrate the provinces, and make them fully Roman. The busy politics of the major towns, the lively traffic upon the broad roads, the commercial activity of the post stations that grew to market towns, soon sufficed to transform Britain. Peace, and the pressures that guaranteed the food supply of towns, greatly expanded agricultural production, and as it expanded many men won moderate wealth. Britain before the Romans had been polarized between a large number of peasants, equal in their poverty, and a small number of warrior lords, enriched by kings. The maturing of Roman Britain created a hierarchical society, akin to that of Italy and the provinces of Europe, with infinite gradations between the very rich and the very poor. Slowly, in Britain as in other provinces, more and more men attained Roman citizenship, until the ancient distinctions between citizen and *peregrinus*, non-Roman provincial subject, ceased to correspond with social reality. In any given city, a large proportion of the notables had won citizenship, but no other clear distinction divided them from their wealthier colleagues who remained *peregrini*; moreover, many descendants of discharged soldiers, and of slaves freed by citizens, were now in law full Romans. Citizenship had reached substantial numbers of humbler folk, while many of their betters were still denied its privilege. The process advanced so fast that early in the third century the emperor Caracalla was able to make all freeborn inhabitants of the empire into full Romans. Though the old differences took some generations to iron out, by the end of the century every Briton, every Syrian, every Macedonian was as Roman as an Italian. New social differences replaced the old legal categories, and the law henceforth distinguished between *honestiores* and *humiliores*, the better people and the humbler. But within his own class every Briton was Roman, and all civilian Romans long resident in Britain became British; there was no more contradiction between a man being a Briton and a Roman than there is today between a Somerset man and an Englishman. Britons, Spaniards, Africans, Asiatics, could and did command armies and govern provinces; at times the Roman world obeyed emperors of British, Arabian, Balkan or other origin. Rome remained the capital, the centre of the empire, even when it had ceased to be the centre of government, and men from Italy and the provinces moved up to the City, permanently or for a short stay, as men move from the provinces of a modern country to London or Paris.

These processes that made the empire one were initiated and encouraged by the Flavian rulers. They were built upon the principle that the empire was composed of an ordered hierarchy of men, in which each knew his own station and his fellows', accepted his position, and observed the rules that permitted men to change their social standing, to augment or decrease their wealth. The political, financial and commercial structure of that hierarchy required that each person in the empire should belong to a particular state; that each state should have its well-regulated capital; and that each province or region should have its administrative and commercial centre. London became a great city, different from others and distinguished above them, only as the empire and Britain were gradually integrated. Its growth measured and matched the expansion of Roman civilization within the empire. Because it was not the capital of a particular state, it was early a cosmopolitan centre, its contacts, outlook and experience more Roman than those of the local towns it supervised. London, unlike any other city in Europe, began as the capital city of a large, self-contained country, and has never known any life save that of a political or commercial capital.

Part Two

Roman London

Chapter 8

The Maturing of London

THE REVOLT WAS over. Classicianus was the new procurator, and the new legates of the province shared his outlook, that the province must be given time to heal its wounds in quiet, without strenuous efforts to subdue border peoples, or energetic compulsions to learn Roman ways and erect Roman buildings. They were the authorities who supervised the restoration of the city. A few buildings, dated by pottery in use in the years between 60 and 80, can be identified, but many more can only be assigned on present knowledge to the late first century in general, and most of them were more probably erected under Domitian than in the time of Nero or Vespasian, after 80 rather than before. Except in the town centre, not many buildings of the 60s and 70s are known, and though some of these are more substantial than their predecessors, with walls or wall footings of ragstone and tiled floors, they do not extend significantly beyond the area of the earlier city. Few burials can be closely dated to these years, but the splendid tomb of Classicianus, recovered from a bastion on the eastern wall, implies that he was buried nearby and that the Minories cemetery continued to be used in these years.

Evidence from the town centre is more abundant. The area has been relatively well reported in modern times, and the reports record a number of well-constructed public buildings. After the gutting of the first city, destruction was so thorough that the reconstruction was laid out on new alignments, the original directions and streets had been obliterated. Thanks to the accidents of nineteenth-century rebuilding, the footings of the Roman structures have been reported in considerable detail in the northern and western halves of the forum area; but the south-east area remained a blank upon the map, for no one observed and noted the Roman walls and floors that there underlay the medieval and modern houses and streets.[1]

The western side of the forum area was rebuilt upon the Newgate Street alignment, and that alignment thereafter became the most frequent of all in the layout of Roman London. The Ludgate–Cannon Street road formed the southern limit of the earlier city, for it cuts between the southernmost habitations and the northernmost riverside burials. From the Walbrook crossing by Bucklersbury, Fenchurch Street was laid out parallel to it, and formed the southern border of the known early area of public buildings. South of the forum area, and for a little length eastwards, the surfaces of both these roads have been detected, as far as the probable eastern edge of the early city. But they were not permanently extended eastward, for when the city wall was built, no gates were provided at the points where their continuation meets the wall. However, where an extension of the Newgate Street road eastwards from the Bucklersbury crossing of the Walbrook was intersected by the wall, on Tower Hill, a gate was placed (Merrifield G 1).[2] It has not been excavated, but the *Survey of London*, undertaken by John Stow in Queen Elizabeth's time, reports a gate on Tower Hill built partly of the Kentish ragstone most commonly employed in Roman London, and rebuilt with Caen stone after the Norman Conquest, that was a principal eastern exit from the city throughout the Middle Ages. It is not probable that the English kings before the Norman Conquest inserted a new gate there, and unlikely that English kings should site any gate upon a Roman alignment, unless a road lay upon it. It is therefore probable that the Tower Hill gate, reduced to a postern after its collapse in 1440, was a Roman gate, and that a Roman road led straight to it from Newgate and Bucklersbury.

The new buildings in the west forum area were aligned upon the axis of such a road. They are however quite unlike the buildings usual in the centres of the towns of Roman Britain (Map 10, No. 5). One (Merrifield 235) was probably a small temple; a larger building to the north (Merrifield 229) might have been a basilica and was plainly a public building of some sort.[3] Whatever the exact date and plan of these buildings, the first reconstruction of London was on a somewhat more substantial plan than the first building of the city.

Map 10

Key to numbered sites (see note to Map 10, p. 351)

1 Walls at Knightrider Street (Merrifield 93–102)
2 Remains of two or more buildings at Watling Street (Merrifield 69–80)
3 Late first-century building at St Mildred's Church, Bread Street, excavated 1974.
4 Late first-century building at Watling Court, excavated 1979.
5 Buildings underlying the great forum. The building to the west is a temple (Merrifield 235). Other buildings to the east (Merrifield 228, 229, 229A, 236, 240) may all be part of an earlier basilica-forum complex, and have been reconstructed as such here, after Marsden 1978, 1980.
6 Late Roman building with baths, probably a large private house, at Billingsgate, Lower Thames Street (Merrifield 353)

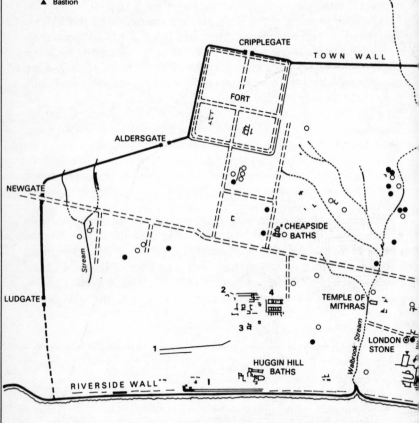

10 Roman London

○ Tessellated pavement

● Polychrome and/or patterned mosaic pavement
(pavements within buildings not shown)

==== Street

▲ Bastion

CRIPPLEGATE

TOWN WALL

FORT

ALDERSGATE

NEWGATE

Stream

CHEAPSIDE
BATHS

LUDGATE

2
4
TEMPLE OF
MITHRAS

3

1

LONDON
STONE

Walbrook Stream

HUGGIN HILL
BATHS

RIVERSIDE WALL

River

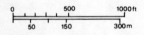

0   500   1000 ft

50   150   300 m

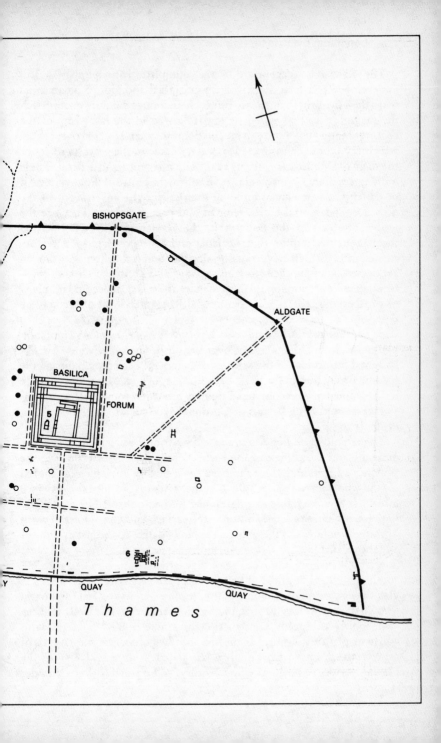

The scale was appropriate to the administrative capital of a still undeveloped province, somewhat more settled and more Roman in its ways than the Britain of AD 50. But these buildings did not yet approach the magnificence and grandeur that followed in the last years of the century. Many public and private buildings were constructed over earlier structures, whose debris included pottery dated to the years 80 to 90, or the reign of Domitian, or simply to the late first century in general. These buildings include a greatly enlarged basilica, the centre of the government of the city, a vast official building that housed the government of the province, and several baths, temples and private houses. They are the visible products of the policy that the Flavian government initiated throughout the empire, that Agricola and his immediate predecessors carried through in Britain, transforming the foremost Britons into landed gentlemen, winning them to Roman ways and Latin speech and dress, helping and encouraging them to acquire the physical accompaniments of prosperous, genteel and commercial Roman civilization. It may be that some of these developments were planned by Agricola, but they were not realized until some years later, after Agricola's long command had ended, for buildings erected over demolished premises whose owners had used the pottery of the 80s are likely to have been put up during the 90s and soon after, in the years on both sides of 100. Many however are unlikely to have been completed significantly later, for several were consumed in another disastrous fire, probably accidental, dated on present evidence to the 120s.

The rebuilding of London in the last years of the first century was the outcome and the climax of the earlier Flavian policy of reshaping the province of Britain. Before the need for a mighty and splendid capital for the whole province was fully felt, the states that formed the province must first become stable and developed Roman centres. The ample and impressive centre of Verulamium is the earliest known completed work of the new policy, and the only one securely dated, to the last months of 79 (above, p. 148). Since it was also the capital of the largest and most powerful British state, the centre of the Catuvellauni, who had ruled all southern and south-midland Britain before the Romans came, and was also the earliest known municipality, it may well have been the first in its own day, as well as the first among those recorded. It is likely that the same policy of speedy construction of ample public buildings with adequate private housing was pushed ahead vigorously in the capitals of other states. Many such buildings are dated in a general way to the Flavian period, or to the late first century, and it is likely that a number of town centres, accompanied by baths, temples and residences, were completed at various dates during the 80s and 90s.

The rapid increase in the numbers of people who thought and lived like Romans made an enlarged London necessary. Roman notions of freehold private property, of large-scale commerce in low-priced commodities, entailed a great deal of law and administration. Greater intercourse between members of different states required remodelling of the laws; for, though there was doubtless a generalized body of common, customary law, its detail necessarily varied from state to state, and often differed from Roman civil and commercial law. Three hundred years before, when Roman power first extended beyond Italy and began to impinge heavily upon all cities within Italy, a similar problem had faced the Roman Senate. Then, in the third century BC, the problem had been solved by the appointment of a new law officer, the *praetor peregrinus*, the foreign praetor, whose office in the capital, Rome, was responsible for cases between foreigners of different nationality, and between foreigners and Romans. In the mid 70s, the same kind of difficulties were beginning to arise in Britain. They were met by the appointment of *iuridici*, and the two senior lawyers who were first appointed were obliged to hammer out a lasting framework for the legal practice and administrative conventions of the province of Britain (above, p. 135). They worked at a time when Verulamium and the other state capitals were beginning to take permanent shape. As those capitals matured, the volume of legal business inevitably grew quickly and greatly, throwing added work upon the offices of later *iuridici*. Their offices, like the procurators', were plainly in London, and needed extension.

At the same time, commerce expanded rapidly. New Roman houses, town centres, baths, and temples where none had been before involved extensive imports from abroad, or from other regions of Britain, before local industries were founded to make the new towns self-sufficient. The late first century was necessarily a boom period for the manufacturer and merchant. Their vigorous activity is plentifully witnessed throughout the country. A few scraps of business correspondence survive on the wooden frames of wax tablets in London, and the earliest of them is dated to the reign of Domitian. Elsewhere there are many towns, large and small, and many areas within towns, where the pits and gullies, sleeper-beam trenches or post-holes of the dwellings of relatively poor people, sometimes accompanied by iron slag, traces of bronze smelting and other signs of new local industries, are abundant. Often the pottery and coins of the late first century are more numerous than those of earlier or later generations upon such sites. Earlier, the trade and manufacture was not yet in being; later, a stable population, with centres of production and distribution geared to a steady demand, often maintained by great men, reduced the volume of new enterprise.

Similar evidence is sometimes found outside towns. Among the commodities most in demand as the new towns rose were building materials, especially bricks and tiles. The construction of bath houses and centrally-heated rooms in private and public buildings required chimney flues. The normal fashioning of a chimney flue, commonly called a 'box-tile' by modern archaeologists, involved the scratching of deep grooves upon the wet clay, designed to key in the plaster of the wall that would be set upon it. Tile makers made rollers to key the tiles quickly, and the rollers had their own patterns, that may be recognized on excavated tiles. One tiler, who worked at Ashtead in Surrey, used rollers whose products have also been recognized in Hertfordshire, near Potters Bar. There, in the uncleared woodlands nearest to Verulamium, clay and timber for fuel were easily to hand, with the least transport costs. Similar kilns cluster about the Watling Street immediately to the north of the Roman post town of Sulloniacae, Brockley Hill, near Edgware; their products served not only the small post town, but lay within a short land haul of Verulamium, and close to convenient rivers that flowed south to the Thames and London. The peak period of their activity is also the end of the first century and the early years of the second, when the towns were still expanding.

The tilers were among the craftsmen who could supply goods made locally. The industry of antiquity differed greatly from modern industry in that the tools of the manufacturer were light and portable, relatively cheap in relation to the cost of his product; but transport charges were relatively high, except when good waterways ran straight from his factory to his market, as the Car Dyke led from the southern cornlands to the northern armies, and as the Thames and its tributaries led to London. There was therefore little impetus to draw workmen towards an industrial area; the craftsman more easily moved himself and his bag of tools near to his market, or as near as his raw materials would let him come. The incidence of these pressures upon differing trades varied greatly. The manufacturer whose goods were unusually light and unusually costly, like the goldsmith, had less need to move, and must live where gold could most easily be acquired, usually near to a centre of government; the cartwright, the miller or the brickmaker must live near his market, while the leather-worker and cobbler must live where hides were easily obtainable, usually in a town where cattle were commonly slaughtered.

Gradually, production was decentralized, but slowly and unevenly. The pottery industry is a useful guide to the evolution of industry in general. At first, Roman civilization meant the importation of pottery by sea from Europe. The production of coarse pottery in Britain took a generation to establish; native fashions remained in use in most of the province for thirty years or so after the conquest, but during the 70s they virtually disappeared, driven from the market by the commercial output of large numbers of kilns, that manufactured Roman fabrics in a large number of local centres.[4] Their rapid expansion suggests that their more refined techniques made cheaper products possible, undercutting the markets of the older native producers; their relatively sharp and sudden growth suggests that their owners may have also been among those who received government aid and encouragement, a small part of the policy of forcing the pace of voluntary adherence to Roman fashion. But this expansion was confined to everyday wares. No extensive manufacture of the elegant and expensive red wares, termed samian, succeeded in Britain; vast quantities were imported from Gaul for many generations. It was not until the beginning of the third century, five or six generations after the conquest, that fine wares made in Britain effectively replaced the imports; then their output was centralized within Britain, in a limited number of regions where the right clay was available, and where a community of potters could mature their skills. The most important of such areas was among the Northamptonshire clays, about Peterborough, that nowadays make bricks on a considerable scale; there, the output of pottery, commonly termed Castor ware, began before the middle of the second century and took the place of imported fine wares after a couple of generations. Its profits enabled the owners of the land whence the clay was dug to build many large and extravagant country houses, and also turned the owners of the pottery works themselves into men of means. But their industry took long to develop. For a century and a half the British market for fine wares had depended almost entirely upon imports from Europe.

The variations in trades whose products were less durable are more difficult to observe; but there is no doubt that considerable quantities of goods were imported throughout the first and second centuries, and that the rate of imports increased most sharply towards the end of the first century, and in the early years of the second, as the Flavian impetus to Roman material civilization began to be felt most strongly. Roman merchant shipping used many ports, but the short seaways, and the roads that radiated from the bridge, guaranteed that by far the largest single section of these imports passed through the port of London. Under the early Flavian legates, until the end of Agricola's rule, the effort of government was chiefly directed towards the conquest of the rest of Britain. That objective was abandoned when Agricola's victory and exploration had shown that total conquest was impracticable. The impetus to the spread of urban civilization was already well under way; in Britain, the end of vigorous military expansion freed the resources of the province and the energy of legates for continuing internal expansion. Britain was equipped with a number of substantial towns, whose multifarious political, legal and commercial affairs required coordination. A province that was quickly growing rich needed a capital; London was the only place suitable for the capital of the province. The city and its buildings needed to be enlarged beyond their early modest scale, hitherto little more impressive than those of the regional state capitals. The fulfilment of the Flavian and Antonine concept of the empire, a hierarchy of states each centred upon a city that was a local copy of Rome, imposed the need to make London a city outstandingly and obviously greater and more splendid than Verulamium or Cirencester, Chichester or Leicester, the visible representative of Rome in Britain, queen and mistress of its regions.

The evidence of the pottery tends to argue that the enlargement of London was not undertaken until the closing years of the century. In itself, it is not conclusive, for individual vessels can only rarely be dated to within ten years or so; and the evidence that dates them indicates not the time of their manufacture but the time when they were most commonly used. Individual vessels may survive unbroken for a very long time, but the majority have a relatively short life. The combined evidence of a number of sites in London, whose latest wares were the normal fashion of the last years of the Flavian dynasty, point to a general date. The political circumstances of the reign and fall of Domitian equally tend to suggest the same conclusion, that the generous replanning of London was undertaken at about the time of the assassination of Domitian, of the reign of Nerva and of the accession of Trajan. The political attitudes of the Flavian and Antonine nobility, that Agricola had applied in Britain, lasted and gathered strength; but Domitian himself was out of tune with their philosophy. His view of the empire was mirrored by the poets, especially Statius, for poets who sang the praises of the emperor and received his favours conveyed the propaganda that the government encouraged. Domitian was hailed as Augustus and as Dominus, as the Italian master. He was master of the aristocracy; and the empire consisted of foreign subjects ruled by Italy. Various new measures were designed to benefit Italy at the expense of the provinces, including an embargo on the vineyards of Gaul that might threaten the Italian wine trade. Outside Italy, the emperor's concern was with frontiers and barbarians. The occupation of south-western Germany was vigorously prosecuted, and the armies campaigned northwards from Mainz beyond the Rhine, with inconclusive results. The Rhine armies were reinforced by detachments taken from Agricola's force in Britain, even before his campaign was over; and a legion was withdrawn soon after Agricola's office was ended.

More serious fighting broke out on the lower Danube, where the strong foreign kingdom of the Dacians, roughly the territory of modern Romania, threatened the frontier. The defeat of the Dacians required three major campaigns. The first, under Domitian, ended in a disastrous Roman defeat; the second war, in Trajan's early years, proved indecisive, and the third campaign, Trajan's second Dacian war, achieved total victory in 106. Dacia proved in the future a useful bastion beyond the Danube; for a hundred and fifty years or more the Roman province of Dacia split the Sarmatian peoples north of the river, and long delayed the alliance of Sarmatian and German. The conquest was costly, and prompted bolder adventures. Trajan was an able and ambitious commander. He forsook the traditional policy of Augustus, of stabilization within existing frontiers, and turned his effort eastward against the Parthians of Mesopotamia, the only great power that bordered upon Rome. After years of careful preparation, he attacked and won quick and decisive military success. The Parthian empire was overrun and Trajan hastened to the Persian Gulf, looking towards India. Men hailed a new Alexander, who would revive and extend the conquests of the distant past, bringing within the orbit of Greek and Roman civilization those few distant corners of the world that were still unsubdued. But the expense of war had overstrained the finances of the government; attempts to restore the Treasury at the expense of the newly-conquered peoples of the Levant inspired a general revolt. It was contained by force of arms before Trajan died, in 117. But the cost of the prolonged repression of immense territories, peopled by skilled and civilized enemies who hated the name of Rome, was too great. The name and power of emperor passed to Trajan's cousin Hadrian, who was known to have opposed wars of expansion, and would devote his own energies to the fostering of civil well-being within the empire, to the extension of citizenship and of the senatorial dignity, especially to the Greek-speaking provinces of the Aegean and of Asia Minor. Some of the notable marshals of the empire endeavoured to prevent his accession, but they lost their lives, and the consensus of ruling opinion accepted Hadrian, in the full knowledge of the policies that he championed.

The government of Britain and the development of its capital waited upon the course of imperial policy. Vespasian had sent Agricola to complete the conquest of the island. His campaign achieved its military objective; the last and furthest army of the independent British was brought to battle and routed. Agricola, and Tacitus on his behalf, rightly acclaimed a victory and a conquest. But it proved a conquest no more enduring than Caesar's conquest of southern Britain long before. The enemy surrendered, but could not be held in permanent subjection without the employment of an army vastly greater than the Roman state could afford to maintain in Britain. As Tacitus had himself said of Caesar, Agricola had revealed northern Britain to Rome rather than subdued it. Domitian wrote off his losses, for the European frontiers of the Rhine and Danube claimed priority. Tacitus reports Agricola's complaint, that Britain was 'conquered and forthwith neglected'.[5] The complaint looked chiefly to the end of military expeditions in the north. But it was also valid for the civilian south. The processes that had already begun to transform the leading British into loyal Romans, and equip them with towns and trade, continued to develop naturally of their own momentum; but there is no sign of a renewed or sustained government impetus, so long as Domitian lived. Italy and the frontiers received all the energy that his government generated.

Domitian was removed in 96, and his fall brought back to power the children of the men who had enthroned Vespasian. Tacitus published his biography of Agricola, preaching the just, paternal effort that Roman rulers should exert upon their provinces; and because Agricola had governed Britain, Britain was the model and example. Trajan's chief concern was with wars; but he was himself the son of one of Vespasian's patricians, selected by the men who had inherited their fortunes and their views. Some of his correspondence is preserved by the younger Pliny, and some other contemporaries report his civil actions and attitudes. He fully shared the prevailing outlook, that the empire was as healthy as the sum of its parts, and that health depended upon fair and conscientious administration, careful of detail, honest and competent at all levels. The men named to offices in Trajan's early years, and while

Trajan was colleague and heir of Nerva, included some unusual appointments, designed to cure the consequences of neglect. Julius Frontinus,
who had governed Britain before Agricola, was recalled in old age from
twenty years' retirement to take charge of the metropolitan water board
in Rome. He was an established writer, and when his job was done, he
published a short book describing how he had cleaned up corruption
and inefficiency in an important department of city administration.[6]

Even more unusual was the appointment of Neratius Priscus to the
upper Danube, as legate of Pannonia. Priscus, like Trajan himself, was
a second-generation patrician, ennobled in boyhood because his father,
the wealthiest landowner of the region about Benevento, in south-western Italy, was made patrician in 73. For the last half-century, military
commands had been entrusted chiefly to men of lesser rank, career
senators who spent half their adult lives abroad, and in a succession of
public offices earned high salaries, that they invested in land, leaving
their heirs among the very rich who stayed in Italy; and the command of
a major army rarely went to a man who had not previously commanded a legion. As in the nineteenth-century British empire, where Earls
or Viscounts commonly governed Dominions and Colonies, but Dukes
rarely sought or accepted such posts, so in Flavian and Antonine Rome
second-generation patricians rarely governed provinces. Moreover, Priscus is not known to have had previous military experience; he had been
head of the Treasury, and he was the outstanding lawyer of his generation, one of the half-dozen most influential Roman jurists of all time. A
few years later, when the Dacian wars were over and quiet was restored
to the Danube frontier, the province of Pannonia was reorganized and
divided into two; it may be that Priscus organized a division whose
realization was delayed until the wars were over.

Priscus' command on the Danube was matched by an even more
remarkable appointment to Britain. His brother Marcellus was legate in
Trajan's early years. His full career is known from the inscription of a
statue bequeathed to his home town by his widow.[7] In youth, as military
tribune of a legion, he accompanied his father, then governor of Vespasian's new border province of Cappadocia, in north-eastern Asia Minor,
in time of peace, but had otherwise seen no military service, and had
held no public office beyond the routine magistracies of a senator's
formal career, quaestor, praetor and consul. He was consul in 95, and
was sent to Britain about five years later, the first of Agricola's successors
whose name is known. When he returned to Italy, he was appointed to
the water board after Frontinus' reforms, and lived on to the age of

seventy or more, an influential political leader, adviser of Trajan and Hadrian.

The unusual appointment implies an unusual assignment; for Trajan chose men whom he deemed apt for the specific task in hand. Marcellus was unfitted for active military command but suited for administrative and legal responsibilities. A man of his rank, close to the centre of imperial counsels, came to Britain when decisions of unusual significance needed to be taken, and important policy innovations implemented. The scanty record of British archaeology pinpoints a few such innovations, dated by material evidence to about the time of Marcellus' government. In the north, the forward troops were pulled back somewhere about the year 100, and the lasting frontier line from Tyne to Solway was consolidated. Throughout Britain, the earth and timber forts of the first century were replaced by more permanent ones, with at least the headquarters' buildings and gateways, and sometimes the walls, of stone and brick.

In London a new stone-walled fort was built at Cripplegate, immediately north of the early site at St Martin's le Grand.[8] There had always been troops in London, since the bridge garrison that guarded the Thames crossing when Claudius moved forward to Colchester in 43. In 60, Decianus had a few hundred troops at his disposal. They had probably consisted of an auxiliary battalion five hundred strong, for such a battalion was the normal force allotted for police duties in an unarmed province. Though Britain was not formally divided into an unarmed and a frontier province, its geography created such a division in practice. In provinces commanded by a legate, troops were not formally responsible to the procurator, whose business was finance; but he needed to use them. In Britain, they were plainly assigned to the civil legate, the equivalent of the legates of unarmed provinces, from Vespasian's time the *iuridici*.

It is possible that in the special circumstances of Britain the *iuridicus* controlled a somewhat larger force, of two or more battalions, and that one was assigned to the procurator, another stationed elsewhere, and the force directly commanded by a civil legate might properly include legionaries, detached from the frontier armies. The new London fort was large, enclosing twelve acres, a greater area than any other permanent fort in Britain, other than the legionary fortress. It was of a size to house 1,500 men or more. Its garrison may have included an auxiliary battalion, but it allowed for other troops as well. The tombstones of the city cemeteries suggest who some of them were. The surviving tombstones are not numerous, barely thirty in all, but half a dozen of them marked the graves of legionaries, all of them buried in the second or third centuries, after the construction of the fort. They were officers or infantrymen; no stone yet suggests that any of the *equites singulares*, the legate's Horse Guards, were detached for duty in London. One stone, of the early third century, suggests a more obvious purpose; it commemorated a *speculator* of the Second Legion, whose headquarters were at Caerleon, and was erected by three of his colleagues, also *speculatores*.⁹ The *speculator* was the regular title of the executive officers of legates and proconsuls, their eyes and ears, their watchmen or policemen. The *speculator* informed the legate of suspect criminals, and made arrests; and in the few transcripts of court cases that survive, most of them concerned with Christians, the common formula that ends the proceedings is the command of the legate or proconsul as judge after sentence, 'Speculator, take him away.' The London fort plainly housed a police force, under command of the *legatus iuridicus*. Its size suggests that it also fulfilled a function comparable with that of the *castra peregrinorum* in Rome, the 'strangers' barracks'. It accommodated officers and men in transit, or posted to temporary reserve lists, or seconded to the capital for interviews, training courses and the like. In London, where individuals commonly arrived from Europe by road from Richborough, to pass on to other destinations in the province, or made the same journey in the opposite direction, the numbers of military and official personnel in need of such accommodation must at all times have been considerable.

The fort housed troops, but it was not the seat of government. Recent excavation has revealed the central offices of the administration of Britain, under and beside Cannon Street Station (see Map 10 and Plate 7). A huge building, full of office rooms, covered about five acres, slightly larger than the modern British Museum. It was constructed upon three different alignments; it fronted upon Roman Cannon Street on the Ludgate alignment, and its east wing was laid out at a precise right-angle to the excavated course of the Roman road. But the central courtyard, the northern and the southern ranges, lie slightly askew to the street, and are built upon the Newgate alignment. And a massive wall, ending in large projecting apses, running from east to west across the middle of the area, was constructed upon the same alignment as the great basilica.¹⁰ Its purpose is indicated not only by its layout, but by a considerable number of procurators' stamps found within it; it doubtless also contained the offices of the *iuridicus*, whose duties did not entail the issue of stamps to mark his headquarters precisely.

Across the road, some thirty or forty yards to the east, an inscription in monumental letters six inches high has been recovered, dedicated to the *Numen*, the divine might, of the emperor, set up by the province (Merrifield 284). The inscription probably stood in the courtyard of a large temple, that served as the centre for meetings of the Provincial Assembly. Immediately opposite the main entrance to Government House stood London Stone (Merrifield 268). It was there in the twelfth century, already a respected antiquity whose origin had been forgotten, and is said to have been observed in the tenth century. Most of it is probably still there. Its top was discovered in the wall of St Swithin's Church in 1960, and is preserved upon the same site, now the Bank of China. It is made of Clipsham stone, imported from the Midlands, and is shaped like an oven loaf, with two wide grooves upon the top. Since the sixteenth century, antiquaries have guessed that it might have been the central milestone of the province, whence all distances were measured, equivalent to the Golden Milestone in Rome. Since it is now known to have lain at the gateway of the provincial government centre, their guess appears more probable. It may have been earlier than the government building, and have determined its siting; for it also lies at the point where the Cannon Street–Ludgate road reached the lip of the Walbrook estuary, approximately at the south-western corner of the early city.

The construction of the Government House is, on present evidence, closely dated. Part of the eastern wing was built over a goldsmith's workshop, dated by pottery to the period 60 to 80; the southern range covered pottery assigned to the years 80 to 90. The intervals are too narrow to permit close distinction, but the differing alignments indicate that the building grew by stages, and was not built all at once. The eastern wing, aligned upon Cannon Street, may have been extended or rebuilt as administrative offices of some sort, connected with the goldsmith's workshop, for its southern end lay upon the waterfront, on the nearest firm ground to the outflow of the Walbrook; and the goldsmith may have worked for the government. Its original purpose was perhaps concerned chiefly with the landing of official persons and goods, from vessels able to sail above the bridge. The main layout and the central cross-wall, on the alignments of Newgate and of the great basilica, reflect the same changes of plan that affected the layout of the town centre. The southern range, and therefore probably the whole main complex offices, was not built before the 90s; it therefore forms part of the same reorganization of London that caused the building of the fort and of the great basilica, about the year 100.

The great basilica was also constructed over pottery and buildings still used in the later Flavian period. The portions so far excavated do not permit a thorough and complete explanation of its architectural history. It is probable that it was all one great building; but a considerable stretch of its southern wall was doubled; at least the footings of a fresh one were built against an existing wall. Its size is staggering. Over five hundred feet long, and about two hundred feet wide, it was a little bigger than the modern St Paul's Cathedral. It was not only big in relation to modern buildings. It is not easily matched in the Roman empire; it was twice the size of the basilica of Trier, that became the largest city of the Gauls and the frequent capital of later emperors. If it was built at the beginning of Trajan's reign, it was perhaps the largest basilica in the Roman world at that time; though it was very soon exceeded by the Basilica Ulpia, built by Trajan in Rome, and Rome had a dozen basilica buildings, not simply one. But whatever the ultimate solution of its many problems, it was planned on a magnificent scale, disproportionate to earlier Roman building in Britain, and to the public buildings of most of the rest of the western provinces. Those who designed it intended London to become one of the greatest cities of the empire.

The dates indicated by pottery sealed beneath a building show when that building began, not when it was completed. But the basilica was probably finished in a few years, for its floor was covered by the ashes of a great fire, probably the fire of the 120s. They suggest that it was gutted, but on present evidence the walls stood, and did not require reconstruction. The forum that accompanied it, however, was not built until Hadrian's time; the Flavian buildings aligned upon Newgate Street, at an angle to the great basilica, remained for a generation before they were deliberately demolished to make way for the completion of the forum.[11]

The great buildings were matched by an enlargement of the city. New buildings of the late first and early second centuries multiplied west of the Walbrook. They were more than the straggling ribbon development of timber houses that flanked the roads of the mid-first century, for they included at least two large bath establishments (Map 10). The limit of known building did not yet extend nearer than about 150 feet to the walls of the fort; for the protection of fort walls required some space of clear ground within the range of defenders' weapons, unencumbered by buildings that might afford cover to an attacker. Eastward, the buildings aligned upon the great basilica reach as far as Mark Lane, whose medieval course preserved the same alignment. Southward, they extended to the river, but there is not yet significant evidence of the northward expansion of the city, save in a number of poor dwellings scattered along the upper branches of the Walbrook. Some, perhaps most, were industrial, and were placed by the stream to use its water; but the waterside extension of small industry is likely to have lain outside the city limits.

The extent of the early second-century city is also indicated by the same kind of evidence as the first city, by burials and the debris of a fire, as well as by dateable buildings and alignments. The relevant burials are few and indecisive, and concern only the eastern limit. One, dated to the years 80 to 110, on the edge of Mark Lane, lay immediately by the eastward limit of the basilica alignment, and might have been made before or after the reconstruction of the city;[12] an amphora, probably of the early second century, from All Hallows-by-the-Tower, may have come from a burial; and to the north, a few more on the southern edge of the Bishopsgate cemetery extend a little distance within the line of the future city wall, one of them as late as the mid or late second century.

The evidence of the fire of the 120s marks the extent of the city at that date (Map 11); and cannot distinguish its growth in the twenty or twenty-five years since the replanning. There is however no evidence at present that growth within that period was considerable. Nor does the evidence suggest extensive replanning after the fire; on many sites new floors were laid above burnt layers that held pottery of the late first and the early second century, but few involve new alignments of buildings and streets. The contrast with the aftermath of the fire of 60 is striking. The London that Boudicca burnt was built of timber and plaster, and the fire blanketed its ruins with a featureless layer of ash. But the fire of the 120s burnt many buildings of brick and stone; their footings and many of their walls survived, to enable reconstruction on the same frontages. There was heavy burning about the bridgehead. When the early nineteenth-century bridge was built, its builders recovered from the bed of the Thames a colossal bronze head of the emperor Hadrian (Plate 8), in excellent preservation. It had plainly stood upon the bridge, doubtless placed there when the emperor visited Britain in 122, or soon after, the top of a statue dominating the crossing. It fell. The date and the circumstances of its fall are not known. It is probable that it fell when the bridge fell, possible that the occasion was the fire.

The debris of the fire covered the early second-century city. The main area of burning lies in a broad sweep running north-west and south-east. It begins west of the Walbrook, well clear of the fort, and extends into the industrial area by the upper branches of the stream, and southward to the river. It is at its densest east of the stream, west and south of the forum area, fierce about London Bridge approach, but the sites thin out sharply before they end at Mark Lane. The distribution of these sites suggest a fire fanned by a wind from the north-east that consumed almost all the city. The evidence was summarized twenty-five years ago; but a recent check upon the pottery concerned has confirmed the accuracy of its dating, to the 120s. Burning on the site of All Hallows-by-the-Tower, sometimes associated with the great fire, but in a building outside the probable limit of the early second-century city, is said to have overlain Antonine pottery later in date than Hadrian's time, but if so it concerns a later local fire.[13]

There is no further fixed point in the growth of London until the building of the city wall. Views upon the dates of town walls in Britain have altered drastically and rapidly in the last half-century, as fresh evidence has disproved earlier assumptions. It was once assumed that walls, retaining-banks and gates were all of one build, and that all or most walls were constructed at about the same time. The first thorough investigation of a town gate, at Colchester in 1919, suggested a Flavian date.[14] In the 1930s the bank of Verulamium was shown to have been not earlier than Hadrian's time, and one gate was very probably constructed during his reign.[15] In the late 1940s, the ramparts of Canterbury were proved to be not earlier than the beginning of the third century;[16] at first they seemed exceptional, but soon further digging showed that many other walls were as late. Subsequently, some defences were found to date to the third quarter of the third century; and some of the earlier misconceptions were explained by the discovery that some towns were equipped with earthen banks, and doubtless timber palisades, in the second century, or even the first; that stone gates were sometimes inserted into earthen banks in the earlier or mid-second century; and that some stone walls were added later, sometimes inserted into a pre-existing bank, sometimes on a different line.

It is not probable that present views will remain unchanged indefinitely, for further excavation is likely to produce fresh evidence, that will modify assumptions now held no less severely than the discoveries of the last few decades. Present evidence strongly argues a date early in the third century for the building of the walls of London, and has some suggestive external corroboration. In the late empire the south-eastern coast of Britain from the Wash to the Solent was guarded by stout fortresses, and collectively termed the Saxon Shore. In several fortresses there is scattered evidence of an earlier fort or habitation; but at Reculver, the fort nearest to London, near Herne Bay, the firm evidence of an inscription dates the fort to the early years of the third century, and is

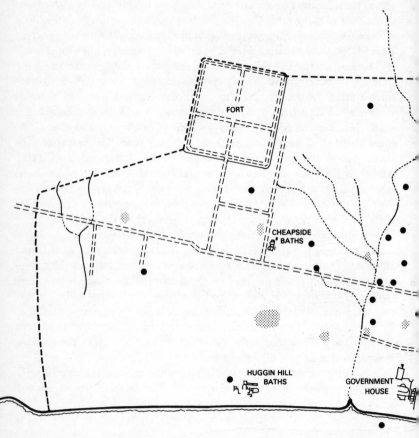

11 London in the Hadrianic Period
(After P. Marsden)

Fire debris

● Burnt samian ware

FORT

CHEAPSIDE
BATHS

HUGGIN HILL
BATHS

GOVERNMENT
HOUSE

River

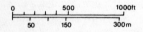

0   500   1000ft

50   150   300m

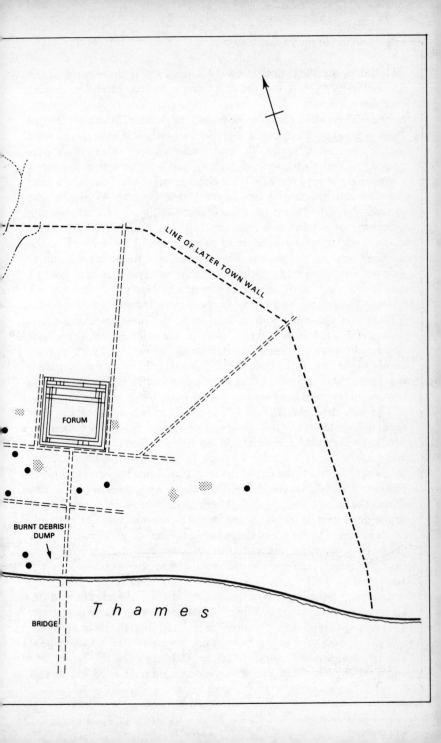

LINE OF LATER TOWN WALL

FORUM

BURNT DEBRIS
DUMP

T h a m e s

BRIDGE

matched by sufficient pottery of the same date. If the estuary of the Thames needed protection, then the heavy enterprise of walling the city was also justified.[17]

The wall was laid out as economically as possible, in straight lengths from point to point, changing direction only where it must. Gates were sited upon existing roads. The points selected were where roads converged, so that their point of convergence lay just within the gates, allowing the gate to serve two or more internal roads. From the Tower the wall ran by the gate on Tower Hill straight to Aldgate, at the intersection of the old road to the bridge and of the road from the forum; thence it changed direction and ran straight to a turn a few yards short of Bishopsgate, at a similar road junction, and thence direct to the north-eastern angle of the fort. The outer walls of the fort, northern and western, were doubled in thickness, and the wall continued straight to a turn a few yards above the road junction at Newgate. Thence it ran straight to Ludgate, and probably there turned south-eastward to the Thames, though some walling continuing the Newgate–Ludgate line directly may be Roman, and may indicate that here two walls were built at different dates, enlarging or contracting the extreme south-western corner of the city. A substantial embankment-wall upon the river frontage, whose course is now followed by Upper and Lower Thames Street, is of a different build and may be later in date.[18]

The wall chose the shortest line it could. It extended for more than three miles, and demanded a colossal effort, not lightly undertaken or needlessly expended. It included no more unoccupied land than it must, and excluded some, notably the northern part of the industrial area by the upper Walbrook, the region that was later termed Moorfields, where Finsbury Circus now stands. Its line marks the expansion of the city during the second century, in the hundred years between the replanning of the great central buildings and its own construction. The probable limits indicated by the fire of the 120s and the replanning of twenty years before enclose an area of about 80 to 100 acres, considerably larger than the first-century city; but the area enclosed by the walls is about 330 acres, three or four times the size of the early second-century city.

The second-century expansion utilized the old alignments, and developed new ones. Many buildings and some streets in the extreme west, about Newgate and St Paul's, were constructed upon the Newgate Street alignment; and so was the only building east of Mark Lane whose alignment is known (Merrifield 359), by All Hallows-by-the-Tower. But when the area between the Walbrook and the fort filled up, several buildings, some very large, were aligned upon a way that joined the southern gate of the fort with the Walbrook crossing; and traces of road metalling have been observed upon that line. In the north, several wealthy mansions were set close to the line that joined Bishopsgate to the middle of the northern wall of the great basilica (Merrifield 320–323). In the south-west, very long walls in Knightrider Street (Map 10, No. 1) are upon the same alignment as the straight way from Newgate to Aldgate, which is exactly parallel to the line from Ludgate to the Walbrook crossing. But a little to the north, between Watling Street and Cannon Street, earlier houses aligned upon Newgate Street and upon the great basilica were replaced by a large mansion laid out parallel to the course of the Thames embankment to its south (Map 10, No. 2).

The city wall marks the expansion of London during the second century; the alignments and buildings between it and the early second-century city mark the stages of growth then, and thereafter. It is clear that there was extensive replanning in some districts at some periods. The need to replan implies a dense population. The wall was designed to include as little empty space as possible; the sites that are known suggest that what empty space was left was soon filled with houses, mean and featureless, or grand, leaving easy signs to read. The blanks upon the map are many; but they do not indicate ground left open in Roman times. They are witnesses of areas where Roman layers beneath the modern city have not been recorded when drainage or the digging of foundations disturbed them, or where no such inroads have been made upon them. The greater part of the city has been disturbed at one time or another, and in some districts signs of opulent mansions, expensive buildings with stout foundations, mosaic and tiled floors, have been observed in large numbers. But the feebler signs of poorer houses, built of timber, clay and plaster straight upon the gravel soil, do not attract the casual notice of building workers and construction engineers, and escape notice, save when an experienced modern excavator has the opportunity to examine them closely. It is therefore likely that the larger part of the regions where nothing is reported over many acres were districts where poorer housing was proportionately greater.

Roman London had many mansions, and several wealthy regions, but also many more poor houses and slum districts. They were pressed together in great numbers, interspersed with temples, baths and other public buildings. The city expanded greatly in area until the wall was built; thereafter, as in other towns in Britain, the walls forbade further expansion until a distant age at the close of the Middle Ages, when towns ceased to need the protection of walls. Within the walls, the increasing population squeezed men together. Roman London did not expand beyond its walls, but within its walls it was a populous and thriving city. The walled area was larger than that of Lugdunum, the capital of the Gauls, and was exceeded by very few cities in the empire, by Nîmes, Trier, Milan and a very few others. It was about one-sixth of the area of Rome, walled in the later third century. Its public buildings were proportionate in size and number, the scattered distribution of its opulent mansions and squalid slums jostling each other as in Rome. Unlike the country capitals of the states of Britain, its anatomy made it a lively cosmopolitan capital, closer to the many-sided vigour of Rome than any other city in Britain, closer than almost any other in the empire. The Flavian and Antonine rulers set out to build the empire upon cities, and to make those cities copies of Rome as nearly as they could. The city that Ostorius and Classicianus established, that Agricola encouraged and that Neratius Marcellus helped to set upon a new course, fulfilled their aim as nearly as any city in the empire. They founded a city, and gave it the means to grow. It outlived the Roman empire, and long retained its strength, in centuries when towns mattered little to the kings of men, to re-emerge in greater splendour in more recent centuries. Rome founded many cities. None was better sited, and few were more successful than London, when it grew to maturity.

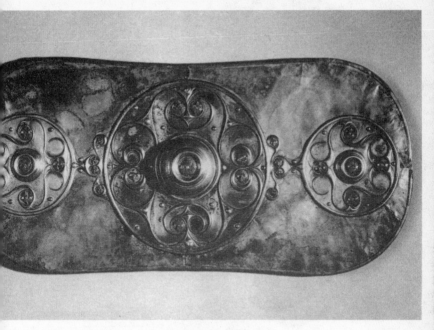

Bronze shield of Iron-Age date from the Thames at Battersea

Bronze coin of Cunobelinus

3 Bronze head of Claudius from the River Alde, Suffolk

4 Skulls from the bed of the Walbrook

5 Bronze coin showing head of Nero

6 Head of Vespasian, from Carthage

7 The Governor's Palace at Cannon Street, reconstruction by A. Sorrell

8 Bronze head of Hadrian, from the Thames near London Bridge

9 Roman mosaic depicting Bacchus riding on a tiger, from Leadenhall Street

10 Fragment of Roman wall plaster decorated with bird and flowers, from Queen Victoria Street

11 Marble relief of Mithras slaying the bull, found near the temple of Mithras, Walbrook

12 Marble sculpture of Bacchus and his companions, from the temple of Mithras, Walbrook

13 The Cheapside bath house, reconstruction by A. Sorrell

14 Roman boat found by County Hall, *in situ*

15 Gold medal struck by Constantius Chlorus to commemorate the recovery of Britain

16 Saxon brooch of fifth-century date, from the Roman bath at Billingsgate

Chapter 9

Government House

LONDON WAS PLANNED with generous ambition, and amply fulfilled the ambition of its founders. In its maturity, it was the largest and most prosperous capital of the western provinces. The archaeological evidence salvaged in modern times maps the Roman city. The map is unfixed and incomplete. It is incomplete not only because large areas are blank, but because many important buildings have not yet been located, theatres and amphitheatre, other temples and baths, and because the function of many of the buildings recorded is not known. It is unfixed, because the only outline plan that can be given is inferred from this incomplete evidence. Future discovery is bound to modify the inferences that present evidence suggests. No map set down today can pretend to accuracy.

The purpose of drawing maps that are known to be faulty is threefold. One, only recently made possible, is the provision of a framework whereby the significance of future discovery may be measured and quickly recognized. Ralph Merrifield's *Roman City of London*, published in 1965, assembled what is known of the plan and alignment of streets and buildings, and of their date and character. Though interpretation changes as new evidence is found, no interpretation at all was possible until the old evidence was disciplined. The maps here drawn rest upon that evidence. They will serve to throw into relief future discoveries that bring new knowledge, and to distinguish them from those which merely confirm what is already known or inferred; and, when new evidence causes the date, alignment or purpose of one small site to be revised, they will also help to show the implications of that change for a wider surrounding area.

The purpose of maps is more than technical. Despite their imperfections, they sharply display the dynamic of the city's growth, the interaction of self-generating impulses set off by earlier stages in the city's life, and of deliberate fillips given to its development by the decisions of governments and individuals. Though new discoveries may show that the street lines and the city limits differed at various dates from those that present understanding suggests, they are less likely to change our view of the motivations, the patterns and the pace of expansion that present maps imply. The third and most important purpose of maps is to highlight the city's individuality, to place it in the context of its own society, to point out how, where and why London resembled other Roman cities, and to observe what distinguished it from other towns.

These purposes are common to the maps of all cities, past or present. Maps show what buildings lay where, and often indicate the scale and purpose of the buildings; but they cannot by themselves say much of the behaviour of the men who used the buildings. So it is with archaeological evidence. It can provide an ample map. It can illustrate the tools and utensils, the furnishings and the art that accompanied the buildings it records. But, unaided, it cannot enter more deeply into the lives of the people who lived in them. It must be complemented by evidence that describes how men thought and acted, drawn from the miscellaneous writings of antiquity, and from the records that men caused to be engraved on stone and bronze and other materials.

To understand a town well, a man must visit it and live some time therein. The cities of antiquity cannot be visited by living men, for they are either gaunt ruins, or buried like London beneath the buildings of later ages. At best, ancient towns can be understood only as modern towns that have not been seen, by description: in maps, pictures and words. The understanding of the unseen town requires two distinct kinds of knowledge: the maps and pictures that describe the individual town, and also an understanding of the society in which that town is set. An Englishman is equipped by his own experience to understand an English town he does not know more speedily and more thoroughly than a French or German town; and he more easily understands a European town, whose life is nearer to his own, than an Arab or Indian town set in a different kind of society.

Next to nothing is known of the social and political history of Roman London. No documents describe the city or its people. But much is known of other Roman towns. London had much in common with them; the archaeological evidence of buildings mapped, and objects stored and exhibited in museums, helps to distinguish some of the features of other Roman towns that were more highly developed in London than in those less prominent, but that which was common to all western Rome must form the basis of understanding. So it is in modern society. A man does not need to visit Birmingham or Manchester to know that in these cities there are railway stations, churches, football grounds, large stores and small shops and all the other common furniture of modern society. A good map will tell him where they are; but if his map is torn and incomplete, he knows that they exist, though he does not know their precise location. So it is with many public and private buildings in Roman London; they existed, though they have not yet been located. But the bare knowledge of such buildings is idle. The town is poorly understood from maps and pictures by a man who has no idea what a church or football ground is for, who is altogether unacquainted with the function of a public house, a law court or an art gallery. A stranger unacquainted with the norms of modern English society must make many enquiries, that seem naive to those he asks, before he can make sense of an individual town. Roman London, unknown and unseen, mapped and illustrated but not described, can only be interpreted by inference from what is known of Roman society in other Roman towns.

Roman London reached full maturity in the third and early fourth centuries. Its excavated buildings match those of other cities, and are distinguished chiefly by their size and number, and by their unusually close resemblance to those of Rome. The city was rooted in an aristocratic authoritarian society, wherein a small number of eminent persons ruled a large, submissive population, whose discontents had only begun to find a voice at the beginning of the third century. Men of great wealth predominated, with infinite gradations below them, of persons well-to-do, of moderate means, of modest income, poor and very poor, slave and free, clients and dependants of the great, or men still independent. The principal evidence for the homes of the very wealthy are numerous mosaics, many of them of surpassing skill and luxury. Much more will be learnt of the growth and gradations of the high society of Roman London when these mosaics have been systematically surveyed, dated, and assigned to different schools and origins. The serious study of rural mosaics in Britain has quite recently been initiated.[1] Urban mosaics await study. Their history differs, for the tendency of present evidence argues that they begin in towns considerably earlier than in country houses. Some London mosaics have been tentatively dated to the early third century, others to later generations, but no systematic survey is yet possible.[2]

The map however reveals their location (Map 10, p. 156). Though fashionable districts may have changed from time to time, as in later civilizations, the wealthy houses of London do not concentrate in a particular quarter, equivalent to a West End or a Belgravia, though they are more numerous in some regions than others, as are well-made tiled floors. They are most in evidence between the forum and the Walbrook; and were built upon both sides of the stream after it had been partially covered over in the middle of the second century. They extend westward in smaller numbers, and a few lie near the river in the neighbourhood of the bridge. In most areas, they are interspersed with meaner houses, not set apart in comfortable residential areas. But in the north of the city, about Bishopsgate, in a quarter that was first developed in the late second century, shortly before the building of the city wall, fine floors have been found upon a dozen separate sites (though perhaps some may have been parts of the same house) and no poorer housing has been encountered. This wealthy Bishopsgate region is separated by a sharply marked border on the west, by the continuation northward of the forum western boundary street; beyond it the industry and poorer housing of the upper Walbrook spilled well to the east of the stream itself. In older areas, rich men bought the sites they could, and built upon them; but when the city grew, the new northern quarter became a rich man's region. Elsewhere it was otherwise; so far, wealthy residences are not recorded in the south-east or south-west, in the riverside regions beyond the limits of the early second-century city. The segregation of housing appears to have been a relatively late development, effective only in areas first built upon in the middle and late second century.

The wealthy Londoners who dwelt in these mansions were concerned with two centres of political power, Government House in Cannon Street, and the great basilica, whence the corporation of the city ruled its internal affairs, regulated its trade, and judged its fellow citizens. The size of these buildings points to the scale of the authority the London magnates exercised. Other indications give some idea of the absolute numbers involved. The faulty records of antiquity do not admit of statistical calculations; estimates of population must rest upon common-sense interpretation of many different kinds of evidence. Earlier calculations were disturbed by the political pressures that bore upon the thinking of nineteenth-century Europeans. Self-confident pride in expanding modern prosperity tended to patronize the memorials of antiquity, that the nineteenth century claimed to have surpassed for the first time, and implanted in the minds of its scholars the curious notion that it was more 'cautious' to underestimate than to overestimate. Absurdly low figures of ancient populations were commonly advanced, and have been revised more recently by an age that prefers accuracy to error in either direction, and deals more happily with facts than with the moral judgements purveyed by the loaded polemical adjectives 'cautious' and 'rash', 'speculative' or 'sober'. The population of Rome was once placed as low as half a million; more sensible modern inferences vary between the extremes of a million and a quarter and two million.

The walled area of third-century London is a little larger than a tenth of the walled area of third-century Rome. It was densely peopled, and it is not likely to have included spacious parks and gardens and other open spaces, nor so many wide-spreading buildings of such large proportions as in Rome; but it is also unlikely to have contained too many tall tenement blocks. The population of London is likely to have been less dense than that of Rome, to have somewhat less than one-tenth of the figure for Rome, not significantly above a hundred thousand. The figure has one later reference point. London in the sixteenth century was at least as densely populated as Roman London; the medieval limits of the city had been somewhat enlarged, but the overall area of London, with Southwark and its suburbs, did not exceed the area of Roman London, including Southwark and suburbs, by more than half as much again. The late sixteenth-century population is estimated, upon well-founded information, at about 150,000. The figure matches the Roman evidence, implying a third-century population of somewhere of the order of a hundred thousand.

The population of the province that London governed is reckoned upon a somewhat surer statistical base. Modern estimates have rocketed in the last forty years from half a million to two million, and estimates are still rising, as deep ploughing, the construction of motorways and other disturbances reveal rural Roman sites in hitherto unsuspected density; and usually destroy them. The density of sites affords some basis of comparison with the figures reported in the eleventh-century survey termed the Domesday Book. No overall comprehensive comparison is yet possible; but in selected small areas, it is already apparent that it is quite impossible to make the lowest estimate of the number of Roman families whose homes are already known by excavation anything like as low as the number of families there recorded in the Domesday Book, even without allowance for Roman sites not yet discovered. In some areas, the Roman population was several times greater than the eleventh-century population. The Domesday figures are not easily translated into total population figures; only able-bodied working men are recorded, without women and children, and without certain other categories of persons; several areas, including London, are not entered in the survey, and Wales and much of the north were not surveyed. Modern calculation must therefore arbitrarily guess the figure by which it must multiply the record of adult males, and what allowance it must make for the missing portions of the country. Estimates that rely upon different figures and allowances vary between one million and two million; since there is a real statistical basis for these calculations, the actual size of the population is likely to fall within these extremes of calculation. It is probable that twenty or thirty years hence, when more Roman sites are known, and when the populations implied by known sites have been more systematically investigated, it will be a commonplace that the Roman population much exceeded the eleventh-century figure, and should be seen as of the order of at least three or four million, perhaps more.

There were a lot of people to govern. Their government involved much administration, for it depended upon complex and often contradictory laws, whose surviving fragments fill some thousands of printed pages. Though laws might be bent in favour of the mighty, the rulers of the early empire were trained to strive for reasonable fairness. Their endeavours caused a great deal of clerical work, and a steady multiplication of government departments. Each province or allied subject territory was equipped at its inception with its own basic law, named from the Roman magistrate who sponsored it, that spelt out the main principles upon which the customary laws of the province and its constituent states should be reconciled with those of Rome. The names and dates of several are known, and portions of the text of a few are preserved. Some states were in law free allies, not subjects. An early law laid down the rights of a city named Great Termessus in Asia Minor.[3] It was not a treaty, but a law, moved by a Roman tribune in the Roman Senate, voted and approved by the Assembly of Roman citizens. Its provisions were simple, its language heavy:

Persons who were citizens of Great Termessus in Pisidia, or were created citizens of Great Termessus in Pisidia according to the laws of the said Great Termessus in Pisidia before the first day of April in the consulate of L. Gellius and Cn. Lentulus (72 BC) together with their descendants, born and unborn, ... shall be free friends and allies of the Roman people, and shall use their own laws.

Other provisions specifically guaranteed property, forbade the billeting of Roman troops, secured the city's customs revenue. Free alliance brought considerable advantages, lighter taxation, exemption from the attention of Roman officials, from conscription and other interference. But the advantages were not always straightforward. When the party conflicts of one free city deadlocked in a constitutional tangle, the city asked the Roman Senate to provide it with a new constitution, and received it. On another occasion, when an imperial legate undertook investigation of suspected corruption in a free city within his province, the city successfully pleaded that its freedom exempted its accounts from audit or examination by the government. Its legal rights were upheld; but not all its citizens benefited equally.

Freedom meant privilege, not independence. Cities that fell foul of the government on matters of importance lost their freedom, and those that kept it retained only advantage and honour. Among them was the city of Marseilles, that was in law never part of the Roman empire; but its status was formal, for a city entirely surrounded by enormous Roman provinces could make no practical use of theoretical independence, and retained its status only because it made no attempt to do so. The formal status of British cities is not known; it is quite likely that Cogidubnus' Atrebates of Chichester, who permanently retained the name of 'the kingdom', long after Cogidubnus and his dynasty vanished, may have been free allies in law, and so perhaps were the Demetae of south-west Wales. Such states presented no difficult problems; but their special status required special treatment and tactful handling, and probably required a separate clerical staff and separate offices in the government building to deal with their affairs.

Some specific provisions of the Sicilian law are recorded. It was proposed by the consul Rupilius, who had headed a commission of ten that prepared its draft, and was known as the *Lex Rupilia de Sicilia*, Rupilius' Sicilian Law.[4] It became a model for similar laws in the future, as did the procedure of the commission that prepared it, and the basic form of its provisions. There is not much doubt that a similar law, probably termed the *Lex Claudia de Britannia* passed in the late 40s, constituted the basic Law of Britain. The clauses of the Sicilian Law provided that

   I If a citizen has a legal dispute with a citizen of the same state, he shall sue in his own state according to its laws.

  II If a Sicilian is in dispute with a Sicilian of another state, the praetor shall assign judges according to the Rupilian Law.

 III If an individual sues a community, or if a community sues an individual, the council of a third city shall be assigned to determine judgement; each party shall have the right to reject the nomination of one city.

IV If a Roman citizen sues a Sicilian, a Sicilian judge shall be assigned; if a Sicilian sues a Roman, a Roman shall be assigned.

V In all other cases, the judges assigned shall be selected from Roman citizens resident in the appropriate assize circuit.

VI Suits between tax-payers and revenue officials shall be regulated by the revenue law, termed Hiero's law.

It is probable that Law of Britain was phrased in almost identical terms, with the substitution of Briton for Sicilian, legate for praetor, but without provision for a separate revenue law, that in Sicily was the outcome of its particular history. The subject states, like the free states, retained their own laws, but in practice maintained only those which did not conflict with Roman law. Over the centuries, a mounting series of rulings and of case-law precedents ironed out the differences, and assimilated local to imperial law, so that when all freeborn provincials became Romans in AD 212, there is little sign of any need for a drastic overhaul of local and provincial laws. In principle, there was no conflict; and some differences on minor matters were suffered to continue. On one occasion, for example, a few years after 212, a Greek city claimed the services of an eminent academic who lived elsewhere. Normally cities might claim upon men whose fathers' were their own citizens, but the city alleged and proved that by its own customary laws it might also claim upon men whose mothers were its citizens; and the claim was upheld. Such minor points of conflict endured, and were many.

The volume of civil law was large. In theory, men might appeal to the judgement of the 'Roman people', in the distant past to a citizen assembly in Rome. The judicial power of appeal was by law transferred to the emperor, and as Roman citizens multiplied, was delegated to numerous high officers. But the right of appeal was in practice open only to eminent persons convicted of grave offences, for it was exceedingly costly and involved inordinate delay. To ordinary civil suitors, appeal was more expensive than an unfavourable verdict. Even the normal courts, overwhelmed with business, cost much time and money. Roman legal practice therefore evolved, during the early empire, a simpler common-sense procedure for settlement out of court. The parties took the advice of eminent counsel, termed jurisconsults. Their decision was quick, their fees less expensive than the courts'; and though the party aggrieved by an unfavourable ruling might grumble, he knew that his chances of oversetting the ruling in a court were virtually nil. The government soon licensed reputable jurisconsults. Their rulings were published, and shelved in the libraries of lawyers and government offices. They were supplemented by imperial edicts; when legates and proconsuls referred knotty points of law, the imperial council consulted its law officers, themselves jurisconsults, and issued an imperial edict stating their interpretation of the law. Most of these rulings stemmed from individual cases, where counsel on opposing sides cited contradictory precedents. An uncertain point of law that the judge could not resolve was referred to the government of the province, in Britain to the *iuridicus* in London. If the law library in Government House found no clear solution, the problem was passed to jurisconsults in Rome. One such ruling probably dealt with a case in early second-century Britain. The foremost jurisconsult of the day was Neratius Priscus. He published his collected rulings in several volumes; one of them, cited from volume IV, was addressed to his brother Marcellus.[5] Since Marcellus' only known command was in Britain, it is probable that the issue was raised by a case in the court of Britain, that the lawyers of the Cannon Street offices could not themselves confidently settle. The issue concerned an inheritance, where the parties disputed whether a bequest of a house and its contents necessarily included all the books, ivories, furniture and clothing in the house. It suggests that in the years when Britain was reorganized and London expanded, one notable Briton left one or more comfortable mansions, with a fortune great enough to justify his heirs in expensive litigation upon its distribution. The property concerned might have been in London, or elsewhere in Britain; but plainly such houses were furnished and inherited in London, whether or not this particular case concerned the city; and many among them involved dispute.

There was much legal business. Government also involved many administrative and financial departments. The imperial postal service maintained a frequent and regular goods service of heavy waggons routed along the roads that radiated from London, with plenty of mules, oxen and horses, and also riding horses and light carriages. A provincial departmental office of the *praefectus vehiculorum*, traffic prefect, supervised the animals and vehicles, and required the assistance of the revenue departments to ensure that the roads were adequately maintained. The procurator supervised the collection and allocation of revenue; and from time to time procurators and legates were at loggerheads. Classicianus had challenged the policy of Suetonius Paullinus in the early 60s, and the government had upheld his criticism, but occasions of dispute more often arose from the allocation of funds. Such friction could not be satisfactorily eased by a set of rules, and a rescript of the emperor Pius wisely limited the law to advice, enjoining that it was 'better' for a legate or proconsul not to meddle with the finances of his province.

There were many revenue departments, and their central and provincial offices were normally headed by gentlemen of equestrian status, knights, whose social standing was not less than the status of those who are termed knights in modern society. The normal career of a knight, like that of a senator, combined military and civil experience. It began with three army appointments: the command of an infantry auxiliary battalion, service as one of the five equestrian tribunes of a legion, followed by the command of an auxiliary cavalry squadron. Some men held only one such appointment, and served no more; a few others went on to higher military command. Most of those whose career continued held a succession of administrative posts, at the head of a provincial financial department, service in Italy, and thereafter the procuratorship of a province. The most eminent equestrians might rise to the prefecture of the corn supply of Rome, or Egypt and of the Praetorian Guard in Rome. The sons of the few who reached such heights might safely reckon that their sons could become senators, and the children of many procurators also rose to senatorial rank.

The principal revenue departments were concerned with individual taxes. The direct taxation of men and land was at first the business of companies, who contracted for the right to collect taxes, at a figure which allowed them a margin of profit between the amount collected and the amount delivered to the government. The uncontrolled extortions of huge, wealthy companies had been a main cause of provincial resentment and rebellion in the disastrous years that ended with the victory of Augustus, and a chief concern of the procurators appointed by Augustus and his successors was to limit that exploitation to a level that no longer provoked serious disturbance. They succeeded in general, for complaints against the enormities of the tax companies, in the forefront of the political storms before Augustus, are rarely recorded thereafter, save under the loose conservative rule during Nero's minority, when the tolerated licence of procurators was an important cause of three major rebellions in the 60s: in Britain, in Judaea and in Gaul. In the main, tax companies were weakened, reduced to small and local enterprises, whose officials, termed *publicani*, were intensely disliked, but no longer feared as irresistible, millionaire exploiters. The publican employed by the early empire tax companies was more of the standing of Saint Matthew, a publican of Judaea. But the weakening continued until in time the margin of profit disappeared; individual contractors, termed *conductores*, for a while replaced the companies, but by the third century it was difficult to find men willing to bid for the contract, for its profit was gone; and the procurators were obliged to undertake the direct collection of taxes, through the agency of state councils.

Other departments collected particular revenues. The heads of the provincial departments of the customs, *portoria*, and of the death duties, normally at five per cent, the *vicesima hereditatis*, were normally knights. So were the lesser procurators, of imperial estates, of particular mining areas and ports, sometimes of specific functions such as the stage, the games, the census of a region. It is probable that at least the customs and death-duty procurators of Britain had offices in the government buildings in London, directly responsible to their central offices in Rome, but necessarily supervised by the procurator of the province of Britain. There too lay the main responsibility for ensuring that the states discharged their obligations to the central government, chief among them the upkeep of the roads. Early experience showed that such expenditure invited abuse; it was easy enough for large sums to be voted, and to achieve no more than the filling of a few potholes in the roadway, while large slices of public money reached the money chests of contractors who were the friends and relations of councillors. From the later first century it became increasingly common to appoint *curatores* to examine accounts and check peculation, at first in very large cities, later in cities of moderate size. The men appointed were commonly equestrian, but by the middle of the second century the *curatores* of important cities were commonly senators. In the nature of the evidence, the record of such appointments in northern Gaul and Britain is not preserved. They were plainly as necessary as elsewhere, and if *curatores* were appointed to London, men of senatorial rank were required by the third century; but it may be that the close proximity of the government offices to the city council eliminated the need for a specific appointment in London.

Plain administration needed many men and much detailed work. The principal evidence of how it worked is provided by the last book of Pliny's letters. He was, in his lifetime, a widely-read author, his nine books of elegantly edited letters published in a large edition. In his last years, Trajan appointed him legate of Bithynia, in north-eastern Asia Minor, in an extraordinary appointment necessitated by reports of extensive corruption, and by fervid clashes between rival parties among the provincial notables. He died in office, and an enterprising publisher managed to secure his official file, and issue it to the public, unedited and unpolished. The letters concern an immense range of small issues that bothered Pliny. Long letters to the emperor are sometimes accompanied by Trajan's courteous replies, usually brief, and usually giving a short quick 'yes' or 'no' to a request or a query, often with a gentle comment whose tenor is that the resolution of such problems is precisely the business that was delegated to Pliny.

The problems range widely. The provincial Law of Bithynia had prescribed that a man must be thirty years old before he held a magistracy, as in the Roman Senate; Augustus had subsequently altered the age for magistracy in Rome to twenty-five, and had extended the change to Bithynia, presumably also to other provinces. Elected magistrates became councillors for life; but the council might also co-opt men who had not held office. Could it co-opt men of twenty-five, since the amendment had concerned magistrates, without specific mention of co-option? In one city, vast sums had been spent on an aqueduct, whose footings had collapsed in soft ground. Could Trajan send a competent engineer? He could not; the Greek provinces had plenty of engineers. In another city, Roman citizens, immune from arrest and prosecution in the local courts, abused the natives; could Pliny have a Roman army officer and a few men to police them? He could not, for if all such cities had military police, there would be no army left. Recruits to the army included two men who were discovered to be slaves; should they be executed for passing themselves off as free men? Trajan replied sensibly that if they had volunteered, they were guilty; but if they had been passed off by their owners as free men, the owners and not the slaves were guilty. Throughout, Pliny was uncertain of his own judgement, but desperately anxious to judge fairly, and to be seen to be just and honest. When his wife's grandfather was dying in Como in north Italy, he gave her one of his official warrants to travel by imperial post, that she might quickly reach Como before he died; but he wrote immediately to Trajan, explaining the circumstances and seeking assurance that he had not acted improperly. Trajan reassured him, but also re-emphasized the strict control of warrants. Pliny was also disturbed by the prosecution of Christians; they were numerous and a nuisance, and had almost put the temples out of business. Pliny sentenced them only if they pleaded guilty; he was sure that their obstinate defiance merited punishment, but unsure of the law. Were they punished for crimes inseparably bound up with the name Christian, or for specified legal offences? He was, moreover, troubled by a spate of anonymous accusations. Trajan reassured him; those who refused a formal oath of loyalty were guilty; but it would be wholly contrary to the spirit of the modern age to heed anonymous accusation. The law must take its course, but Christians must not be sought out.

Pliny's worries entailed much correspondence, enquiries and delays, and kept his office busy. The principles that dictated his anxieties were those he had formulated clearly in his published letters:

A man invested with the power and emblems of authority cannot fail to inspire respect, unless his own conduct is evil and sordid, and breaks through the awe-inspiring reverence due to him. Power that inflicts injury is evil. Terror cannot command reverence, and affection is a much better way of gaining our ends than fear. For terror is only effective when the force that underlies it is present, but affection operates when force is absent, and where as fear turns to hatred, affection turns to respect.[6]

Pliny was not an original thinker. He put into words the philosophy of government that prevailed in his day, and tried to practise it when he himself had a province to govern. It was a policy plainly wise, but one that few governments after the early Roman empire have been able to adopt in practice, and teach to their officials. Pliny found its application more difficult than its expression in a phrase. It meant hesitancy, delay, and expense; it worked because it upheld authority, without serious division or open force against dissidents, for the best part of a hundred years. But it required many departments, many officials, and a tight supervision at all levels over their day-to-day business to work. In Britain that work and that supervision were concentrated at Government House in Cannon Street. There, men dealt with the kind of business that fell to Pliny in Bithynia, and gave the same care to detail, though doubtless not all were as unsure of themselves; for most legates and procurators had had more experience of the command of men than Pliny before they came to Britain.

The large government staff formed an important section of London society. They included several men of high social standing who served in Britain for two or three years, and then passed to other provinces or returned to their homes. The provincial procurator, the heads of the provincial revenue, and some other officials were knights. They were used to expensive, even luxurious, living and commonly brought with them their wives and children. They needed spacious, well-furnished accommodation within easy distance of their offices. It may be that the government itself owned and provided official residences for some of them; it is also probable that some enterprising Londoners built and owned suitable mansions, or high-class blocks of flats or apartments, to be let to short-term officials. It is in any case evident that many of the comfortable town houses by the Walbrook, and between the Walbrook and the forum, began their history in the late first and early second century as the homes of important personages employed in the government of the province. Their number was increased by the needs of persons who required good accommodation for a much shorter period, officers in transit who stayed for a few days, or those posted to London for short-term courses for some months, and others who passed through the city.

During the second century the number of Roman citizens increased. The state capitals prospered, and in the countryside farmers and landowners began to be able to afford substantial homes and country houses. The administrative, political and financial business of the province swelled. It was not all concentrated upon the offices of the imperial government. Much passed to the Provincial Council, whose offices were probably situated just across Cannon Street, attached to the temple that formed the official centre of its business, whose probable location is indicated by the large inscription to the *Numen* of the emperor (above, p. 168).

The workings of western provincial assemblies are best known from the inscriptions of Gaul, from a number of laws that concern them, and from a number of scattered texts. In the political philosophy of the early empire, loyalty to the state and government was exacted and expressed chiefly through respect and honour of the gods of Rome. The loyalties of ordinary citizens in their daily affairs were accommodated by the ordinary run of temples scattered throughout Roman cities, but the formal adherence of their official representatives to the government of Rome required a special form of expression. Oaths and sacrifices to the divinity of the city of Rome and of the emperor had little to do with the notions that are associated with the modern meanings of the word religion; they corresponded rather to the modern practices of saluting the flag and singing a national anthem while standing to attention, conveying respect for the government and all that it stood for.

The monarchy of Augustus took pains to establish such ceremonies, and to give them official centres. An *ara Romae et Augusti*, an altar of Rome and Augustus, was early consecrated among the Ubii, on the left bank of the Rhine, soon after Roman military control was secured. The city that grew around it became a *colonia* at the same time as Colchester, and preserves its title, under its modern name of Cologne, Köln in German. When the Roman army marched northward from the Danube to the Elbe, a similar altar was established, perhaps at or near the confluence of the Elbe and the Morava, in the north of Bohemia, in modern Czecho-slovakia. The early advance failed, and Rome did not retain central and northern Europe; the altar did not survive to become a great city in Roman or later Europe. But a similar altar in Gaul, at the confluence of the Rhone and the Saône, was accompanied by the *colonia* of Lug-dunum, *caput Galliarum*, the capital of the Gauls, nowadays called Lyon. There many inscriptions attest the continuing activity of the altar and the Assembly it served.

Delegates elected by the councils of each of the sixty-four states of the Three Gauls met annually at the altar of Lyon. Their official business was to pay respect by sacrifice upon the altar of Rome and Augustus. They chose a *sacerdos Galliarum*, chief priest of the Gauls, who held office for a year, and opened his year of office by entertaining the public with elaborate games paid for chiefly out of his own pocket. When the Gauls accepted Roman ways, his standing among his countrymen re-placed the former pre-eminence of the chief Druid of pre-Roman Gaul. The office was keenly sought for the honour and status entailed, so long as men respected the government, and so long as the cost of games remained manageable. The government took care to see that it did so. The only surviving report of a speech by a subject in the Senate of the Roman empire is an amendment to a government motion, moved in the later second century, imposing maximum prices and wages that might be paid to gladiators and others in the games at the annual assembly of the Gauls. The government motion had evidently laid down general principles; the speech fills in precise figures, and swells over with grateful thanks to the initiative of the government that had taken measures to cut the cost, and make the office again an honour that many men sought instead of an intolerable burden that all sought to avoid.[7]

The formal business consisted of an act of loyalty and a festival. Much more accompanied it. The assembled delegates consulted with the legate and with one another. Their legal executive authority was slight, their actual political weight considerable. In 48, the magnates, the *primores*, of Gaul conveyed a formal request to Claudius in Rome for the *ius honorum*, the right of Roman citizens in Gaul to hold office in Rome and sit in the Senate; the request conveyed on behalf of the magnates was clearly formulated in the annual Assembly, and was welcomed (see above, p. 52). Provincial Assemblies also had a powerful means of exerting pressure upon legates and proconsuls; when their term of office expired, the Council might vote a resolution of approbation and thanks, in varying degrees of warmth; or withhold such an address; or prosecute a legate or proconsul whose conduct had excited general disapproval.

The imperial government was disposed to listen to the protest of the subject, that its cause might be removed before it provoked serious trouble. But the government was acutely sensitive to the danger of its own senatorial provincial rulers becoming pawns to be pushed around by factions within the provinces. In the middle of the first century an imprudent magnate of Crete boasted that his influence in the island was so great that he could decide whether the outgoing proconsul received congratulation or prosecution.[8] He was a Greek, recently promoted to Roman citizenship, and his brash indiscretion infuriated the Latin conservatives. His impudence was swiftly rebuked by the Senate, but the power of the assemblies was not diminished. Many of Pliny's letters concern prosecutions by the councils of Bithynia, of Baetica, southern Spain, and of Africa against their former rulers; and in Bithynia the struggle within the nobility of the province was evidenced by a prosecution that was cancelled and withdrawn when power passed to an alternative faction, and was replaced by a vote of congratulation. The indecent pressures then manifest were among the reasons that induced Trajan to send Pliny to sort out the problems of the province; he was equipped to deal with them, for he had been retained as advocate in prosecutions by the province on more than one occasion, and knew its political complications.

One long inscription of the early third century records a similar dissension in the Gauls. Sennius Sollemnis was the principal delegate of one of the smallest states of Gaul, the Viducasses of Vieux, near Caen, in Normandy. Powerful forces in the assembly at Lyons moved to prosecute the outgoing legate, Claudius Paulinus, who subsequently governed twice in Britain, at York and at London. The able and well-timed intervention of Sollemnis blocked the motion, and secured a vote of thanks instead; and he was thereafter amply rewarded by the personal and public generosity of Paulinus, and of his friends. Other prominent politicians were involved, and the issues concerned touched upon the political struggles that then beset the central government. But the power of the Assembly was still real, and Paulinus was greatly concerned to win a favourable vote.[9]

The apparatus of the Provincial Assembly of the Gauls comprised more than an annual gathering. It included a treasury, *arca*, with a head who was also a leading citizen of one Gallic state. He, like the chief priest, held office for a year, as did another official termed the *inquisitor*, of whose functions nothing is known but his name, and his standing, also an eminent Gallic noble. These three constituted the nucleus of a standing committee; and a few inscriptions of clerks and slaves of the province and of its institutions attest the existence of their staff. Scraps of comparable information from elsewhere confirm the existence of annual assemblies and standing committees in several other provinces, and suggest that they existed in most provinces, though their power and influence doubtless varied in different provinces and at different times.

As the pressures upon government increased, and as the notables of the provinces became thoroughly Roman in outlook, more and more business devolved upon the provincial councils and their executives. Hadrian instructed the Council of Baetica that severe punishment of cattle thieves, sentencing them to fight as gladiators, was appropriate only when cattle thieving was particularly rife; in normal circumstances it was sufficient to condemn them to hard labour for a fixed term. Both Hadrian and Pius instructed the Thessalian Council that when cases involved both violence and rights of ownership, the accusation of violence must first be investigated. Pius assured the Council of Thrace of their right to appeal against an imperial edict, that had been issued on the advice of the governor or any other person; he acceded to a request of the Asian Council that incoming proconsuls should make their landfall in the province at Ephesus; and also charged the Council with the responsibility of seeing that an adequate number of doctors and teachers were maintained at public expense in its principal cities. Early in the third century, the Christian scholar Origen commented on an even more striking extension of provincial powers. Expounding on a difficult passage in the biblical story of Susanna, he drew a modern analogy:[10]

It is not at all unusual that when great peoples are conquered, the conquering ruler should permit the conquered to use their own courts and their own laws. The Judaeans nowadays pay tribute to the ruling Romans, but the emperor has none the less conceded considerable authority to them ... as I know because I have had first-hand experience. Courts are held, not publicly proclaimed, but nevertheless legally, and several people have been condemned to death, not of course with full and open licence, but nevertheless not without the emperor's knowledge.

The right of capital punishment was exceptional, recent, and still improper, though convenient. But the second-century rescripts indicate that the councils and their executives were already invested with considerable judicial and administrative powers, and their right of appeal against a central government ruling issued on the advice of the provincial governor, like the initiative of Sollemnis, demonstrate that their political power was considerable.

The precedent of the Council of the Gauls was followed in Britain immediately after the conquest. A colossal temple of Claudius was erected in Colchester; reconstructed as a Norman castle, it is still the most impressive building in the city. In its service, notable Britons were impressed to serve as priests, to the ruin of their fortunes, before time and custom had induced them to regard the worship of Rome as an honour; and their resentment constituted one of the reasons that helped the rebellion of 60 to spread widely. Nothing more is recorded of when and where the Assembly met. It may be that the formal annual meetings long continued at Colchester, for Roman convention respected established right, and if the citizens of Colchester maintained their claim to entertain the delegates, it may well have been confirmed. But the administrative offices were in London. It is attested not only by the formal inscription to the divinity of the emperor set up by the province of Britain, but also by the funerary monument of an imperial freedwoman, buried in the late first century on Ludgate Hill, to the west of the then city, but within the later city wall, set up by her husband Anencletus, a slave of the provincial council.[11] It is more likely that in time the pressures of convenient travel made London a more acceptable venue for the meetings themselves than Colchester, and that the whole of the business of the Assembly was concentrated in the capital.

It is highly improbable that the powers and functions of the Council of the states of Britain differed widely from those of other councils in other provinces. If they evolved normally, they turned the Assembly into a legislature, whose decisions had no effect until they were approved by the legate, with an executive investigating and judging theft, violence and other crimes, supervising health education and other public services throughout the province, but always under the authority of the legate. Its location, immediately across the road from Government House, emphasizes both its dependence upon the authority of government, and the large and expanding part that it is likely to have played in the government of Britain. Its officials also required lodging in London, for a year at a time when they were not themselves Londoners, and, as and when the Assembly met in London, its numerous delegates, probably of the order of a hundred persons, with their servants and attendants, needed accommodation for several days, perhaps weeks. They were added to the numbers of the government officials who created a demand for short-term rented property. The considerable clerical staff of the government offices and of the provincial council also had to be housed, in homes of less luxury, but nevertheless of reasonable comfort. The permanent staff, however, were for the most part people who lived their whole lives in the city, and might as readily own as rent their homes. Between them, the various grades of government employees and officers constituted an important element in the society of London.

Chapter 10

City Hall

THE SECOND MAIN centre of government was the basilica, whence the city was ruled. Its administration was also in part decentralized. Most large Roman cities were divided into wards, variously named *vici*, urban districts, *curiae*, courts, *regiones*, or by other names. One inscription, found near the Walbrook, between Newgate and Ludgate streets, gives the description of the London wards; it reads *Matr*[ibus] *Vicinia de suo res*[*tituit*] 'to the Mother Goddesses, the neighbourhood, or ward, restored (the shrine) at their own costs', and was presumably placed in the district temple.[1] Commonly, urban wards were headed by a *magister*, a master, with a committee of colleagues; their constitution is not clearly known, but the terms suggest that their officers and committee might be selected in consultation with the inhabitants, their authority derived from the city council, and that the *magister* owed his formal appointment to the city government.

The constitution of cities is better recorded. As well as the general laws for the government of cities enacted by Julius Caesar, the constitutions of two later cities in Spain were incised upon bronze that survived.[2] These constitutions repeated the three principal institutions common to all Greek and Roman cities, an assembly of free-born adult male citizens, a council, and magistrates elected annually, who combined the functions that in modern society are discharged by mayors and by justices. As in almost all Roman cities, the function of the citizen assembly was limited to the election of magistrates, and elected magistrates became councillors for life.

The council was usually known as the *ordo*, sometimes as the senate, sometimes by other names; a councillor was a *decurio*. The chief magistrates were usually termed the *duumviri iure dicundo*, the two men who deliver judgement, equivalent to the consuls of Rome; in larger cities aediles, quaestors and other magistrates were also elected. Normally they were junior in status, and men held the lower offices before standing for the duumvirate, but sometimes the magistrates formed a collective board, *sexviri* or more usually *octoviri*, of six or eight. The names and numbers of the magistrates of London are not recorded, nor is the official name of the council, nor its size, but they necessarily followed the universal pattern of city government in the western provinces. If the constitution adopted the names and numbers most usual in the larger cities, its council was an *ordo*, with at least a hundred members and probably more, its elected magistrates, *duumviri*, accompanied by at least a pair of aediles and a pair of quaestors, whose chief functions were the responsibility for public works and for finance.

At the foundation of new cities, the first magistrates and councillors were appointed, and their successors thereafter elected. The political principle behind the elections was simple. Only candidates of wealth and standing might be chosen, but the aristocracy of each city and state must be free to choose the individuals it preferred from among qualified candidates, men of the right age not disbarred by insufficient income, by birth or by conviction of serious offences in the courts.

The troubled history of the city of Rome had ended with the withdrawal from the Assembly even of the right to vote; for the high ambition of dissident noblemen had learnt to buy and arm gangs of voters. In Rome, after the various experiments of Augustus and his immediate successors, the Senate selected the candidates, and the electors were presented with one candidate only for each office; candidatures not supported by prior vote of the Senate were forbidden. The conditions of Rome were exceptional, not repeated in the provinces. In the Greek cities of southern Italy and the eastern Mediterranean, the assemblies of the plebs frequently continued to meet throughout the early empire, and exerted significant political pressure. Political and sometimes military authority was required to protect aristocratic rule from plebeian challenge. In the Latin cities there is little sign of an active plebeian assembly, but elections remained free and hotly contested. The western charters make elaborate provision for their conduct, and when Pompeii was overwhelmed in the Vesuvius eruption of 79, the ashes of the volcano covered walls that were painted with recent and current election slogans, eager and sometimes ribald. London plainly followed the practices of the west.

The sanction that securely confined office to the rich was the expense of office. Elected magistrates were obliged to provide games, gladiatorial and animal displays, horse races, theatrical performances, and to bear all, or a large part, of the cost themselves; and the duties of councillors involved considerable unpaid time and effort, and substantial expense. When all public sport and much of the essential city services depended upon disbursements by elected magistrates, no man of small or modest means stood a chance of winning votes. But the basic restriction was often strengthened by a formal property qualification. The clauses that listed qualification for office in the Spanish charters are not preserved; but the earlier charter of Tarentum in southern Italy, now Otranto, provided that

whoever is, or shall hereafter be, a councillor of the town of Tarentum, or whoever shall speak his opinion in the senate in the town of Tarentum, shall possess a building within the town of Tarentum, or within the borders of the territory of the town of Tarentum that shall be roofed with not less than 1,500 tiles.[3]

It is likely that the lost clauses of the Spanish charters, and of that of London, required similar property qualifications, within the city territory, though it is probable that their value was expressed in terms of money.

The constitution of Malaga, in south Spain, was promulgated in the 80s.[4] The conduct of elections is laid down in section 55:

The returning officer appointed in virtue of this law shall summon the citizens to vote by wards, and shall issue a single summons to all wards.

Each ward shall vote separately, by ballot, in its own enclosure.

In charge of the ballot box of each ward the returning officer shall place three citizens of the town, who shall not be members of that ward. They shall act as tellers, and before counting the votes they take oath individually that they shall count and return the votes in good faith.

The returning officer shall not hinder the candidates from placing their own observers at each ballot box, one observer for each candidate.

The person placed at each ballot box by the returning officer and by the candidates shall individually vote in the ballot box by which they are stationed, and their votes shall be legally valid, as though they had voted in their own wards.

The next sections laid down the manner of reckoning votes, that followed the ancient practice of the Assembly of Rome, but contrasts with modern methods. The votes of each ward were counted separately. The candidate who secured the largest vote in each ward was declared to be the candidate preferred by that ward, and was credited with the vote of one ward. The candidates who secured the votes of most wards were declared elected, and took oath. Elaborate rules provided for the contingency of a tie in the voting.

If in any ward two or more candidates shall receive an equal number of votes, the returning officer shall prefer a married man, or a man reckoned as married, to a bachelor, without children, or not reckoned to be married.

He shall prefer a man with children to one without children, provided that two children who have died after they have been named, or one child deceased after puberty, male or female, shall be deemed equivalent to one surviving child.

If two or more candidates receive the same number of votes, and are also of the same condition (in respect of children), lots shall be drawn.

Similar rules applied in the event of a tie in the number of ward votes credited.

Such elections were real, and aroused enthusiastic support for candidates, and opposition against them. The slogans painted on the walls of the houses of Pompeii proclaim who supported which candidate, and sometimes why. The wards of Pompeii, like those of London, were termed *vicinia*, their members *vicini*. Often individuals who deemed that names carried weight proclaimed their personal support. One of the fullest reads:

Vicini! Vote for L. Statius Receptus for duumvir. He is fine. Posted by Aemilius Celer, *vicinus*. A plague on any wretch who scrubs it out.[5]

More often trade corporations, sometimes with their patrons, proclaim support:

Cn. Helvius Sabinus for aedile! The bakers want him and so do the *vicini*.[6]
M. Holconius Priscus for duumvir! All the greengrocers are for him, with Helvius Vestalis.[7]
Trebius for aedile! The barbers support him.[8]

Some slogans voice differing policies:

Vote for M. Casellius Marcellus. A good aedile. He will give great games.[9]

but also:

Bruttius Balbus for duumvir. Genialis supports him. He will conserve the treasury.[10]

But personalities were more prominent than policies. Most slogans praise the candidates they support; but some satirize their opponents:

M. Cerrinius Vatia for aedile! All night drinkers back him. Vatia for aedile! The pickpockets back him.[11]

Slogans were painted, and were soon washed away. They survive only where disaster killed and mummified a town in an instant, jerked to an end in the full vigour of its life. The excited, easy-going contests they witness were common to most towns similarly governed. Only different individuals of the same class and inherited outlook might contest; elections therefore tended to turn upon personal attachments more easily than upon deeper social and political problems. Groups and parties turned upon likes and dislikes, family and commercial interests; their passions often ran strongly. At the beginning of the fourth century, the father of the poet Ausonius, a well-to-do landowner and doctor in Bordeaux, altogether eschewed the politics of the city council because he could not stand the tempers of its squabbling factions.[12] Yet disputes necessarily involved different views on the welfare of the city; the contrasting slogans displayed in Pompeii by the supporters of Marcellus and Balbus, 'spend for the public welfare' and 'keep the rates down', bear upon all elected public authorities.

The business of the city government, like that of the proconsul or the legate, was to keep its people 'quiet and composed'. If it failed to do so, it was itself at fault. More strongly than most subsequent authorities, the rulers of the early Roman empire judged that when a violence was directed against a government, the government was to blame for provoking the violence or failing to forestall it; city governments might rely upon the armed force of the empire to suppress rebellion and chastise rebels, but they must also dread punishment and rebuke for their own shortcomings if such intervention was needed. An incident in the life of St Paul illustrates their fears in the middle of the first century. One of the chief glories of the ancient city of Ephesus in Asia Minor was the great temple of its own goddess, the many-breasted Artemis, or Diana, whose silver images were sold to its inhabitants, and in large numbers to tourists and visitors. A silversmith organized a demonstration of protest against Paul, whose teaching made Artemis a thing of nought, threatened his own trade and insulted the city's pride. Large numbers filled the theatre, and the chief magistrate failed to quieten them. For about the space of two hours they cried 'Great is Diana of the Ephesians'. The English words excite no passion, but in Greek the syllables *megalé hé Artemis* have a rhythm wherewith a chanting crowd might daunt any officer who tried to soothe them. When the magistrate at length restored order, his concern was for the consequences:

> If the craftsmen have a matter against any man, the law is open, and there are deputies; let them implead one another. But if ye enquire anything concerning other matters, it shall be determined in a lawful assembly. For we are in danger to be called to question for this day's uproar, there being no cause whereby we may give an account of this concourse.[13]

The English word 'deputy' translates *anthupatos*, proconsul. The spontaneous assembly in the theatre was not duly convened, illegal, and therefore in itself an offence. Though the riot had been quelled, without damage to persons or property, there had been a risk of violence; the city feared punishment – a fine or loss of privilege, at the hands of the Roman government.

The council of London lay in the shadow of a powerful provincial government. It knew well that riots sprang from acute discontent, easily sparked by misgovernment, open corruption, visible corruption; and must contain and avert the possibility. It also felt the pressures to spend as much as was needed to keep its population acquiescent, if not content; and also the pressures that frowned upon local taxation. So did every other city in the empire. The chief means whereby the necessary expenditure was encouraged and controlled was the spread of a concept of civic responsibility among the wealthy. It was inherited from the Greek past, and vigorously encouraged by Augustus and his successors. Augustus himself spent vast sums from the fortunes he had acquired in the civil wars upon public works, and urged others also enriched by the wars to do likewise. He was disappointed by the response in his own time, but as stable prosperity matured in Italy and the provinces, men came to seek and accept honour by private benefactions to their cities. Innumerable inscriptions praise the generosity of rich men who built or enlarged theatres, baths, temples; who contributed to aqueducts, who bought corn dear and sold it cheap to the poor in time of famine or poor harvest, who voluntarily paid large parts of the city's taxes, endowed schools or libraries, or otherwise benefited their fellow townsmen. Social convention prompted great men in the Middle Ages to found abbeys, colleges and charities or contribute to the building of great churches for the good of their souls in the after-life; similar conventions prompted second-century Romans to adorn their cities and equip them with public services for the good of their reputations and self-respect on earth.

These conventions had much to do with the expansion of London in the second and third centuries, and with the increasing splendour of its buildings. Elsewhere, construction and public services were financed by a mixture of public moneys raised by taxation upon the citizens, and of private expenditure. The proportions between them can only be observed in lands where stone was relatively cheaply available, and fashion prescribed that much should be recorded upon stone inscriptions, or where chance record describes benefactions. It permits no more than the general inference that benefactions were numerous, increasing through most of the second century; but that they varied greatly from town to town, and from one period to another.

Expenditure was also supplemented by public duties undertaken without payment by councillors and notable persons. A third-century lawyer gives a long list of the unpaid offices normal in a large city, which included the supervision of the city's funds, when not undertaken by an elected quaestor or equivalent magistrate; for cities owned land that paid rent, accumulated surplus taxation, and invested it. Some cities endeavoured to force unwilling landowners to borrow at inflated interest rates, to swell current income; but Trajan forbade the abuse. Other offices were the obtaining of recruits for the army, and of horses and vehicles for government service, in particular for the imperial post. Such services did not mean that the man must pay for the horses and vehicles, but must spend the time and effort needed to see that they were where they were needed at the right time.

Other offices concerned the city itself. *Frumentarii* and *olearii* must see that corn and oil were available. A curator must supervise the city's baths, if they were not run by contractors, another must see that the aqueducts were kept in good repair. Police chiefs must control the police force, maintain public order and pursue crime. Inspectors must see that bread and other foodstuffs are of the proper weight and quality, and others must supervise the collection of market dues and of the city's other public revenues. Others must ensure that the temples are kept in repair, and take responsibility for public buildings, docks, post stations, and when necessary ensure that ships are built; others must supervise the bakeries, the nightwatch, the repair of city streets. Archivists, accountants, billeting officers are included; so are persons sent to plead the city's needs to the emperor, and barristers who act for the city in the courts.[14]

The list emphasizes that these are all duties which involve no personal expenditure. In many cities at many times, such duties were discharged directly by the magistrates; in others, the magistrates saw to it that individuals assumed the responsibility. Often, especially in the second century, many such services were farmed to contractors. The earlier laws lay down the exact staff to be employed by each magistrate, and the salaries to be paid to them. They also provide for contracts, auctioned every five years for a five-year period, for the leasing of public lands; for the upkeep of temples and public buildings, at set amounts paid to the contractor; for the maintenance of the baths and other amenities.

The laws of a government-controlled mining town in Portugal spell out the detail of some of these services:[15]

The baths contractor, with his partners, shall at his own cost and charges heat and provide the baths for which he has contracted.

He shall open the baths daily until the last day of June from dawn until one o'clock in the afternoon for women, and from two o'clock in the afternoon until two hours after sunset for men.

He shall provide properly running water, for women as for men, ... to the rim of each bath.

He shall charge one copper for each man and half a copper for each woman; entry shall be free for imperial slaves and freedmen, and for children and soldiers.

On the expiration of his contract, the contractor, or his partner or agent, shall return all equipment in good condition, save for fair wear and tear.

Every month he shall thoroughly wash and scour all bronze utensils, and grease them with fresh grease. . . .

The contractor shall not be permitted to sell wood, except for separate branches considered unsuitable for burning. . . . He shall at all times have sufficient wood in store for ... days.

Other regulations provide for the licensing of cobblers, barbers, laundries and other trades, and threatened heavy penalties against unlicensed tradesmen. Though in this instance the rules were promulgated by the procurator in charge of the mines, they were modelled on those enacted in cities by their councils. When contractors could be found, they were preferred. The job of the magistrates, or of curators appointed by the council, was to see that they kept to their contract. If the services were not contracted, the council staff must see to them.

The magistrates and council of London had much to do. The great basilica, as in other towns, was flanked by many rooms and offices. In some, the council and its committees met. In others, often provided with an apse to accommodate a tribunal, the magistrates sat in judgement in criminal and some civil cases; their judgement might be appealed against, but appeal was costly and dangerous if the cause was trivial. Other rooms were the offices of those who supervised the council's many-sided activity.

At all times the city council sat under the shadow of the government of the province. But the relationship between the two centres of government changed speedily during the second century. When the great basilica was built and London enlarged, in about AD 100, old men in their 70s and 80s still remembered the time of the Belgae, before the Romans came; men in their 50s and 60s, including many members of the council, retailed lively memories of Boudicca. Their personal antecedents were mixed. Most of the first population were Romans from abroad, probably in most cases from Gaul. The majority perished in the horror of Boudicca's sack. The origins of those who rebuilt the city in the 60s are less easy to discern. London was again to experience settlement from Gaul and elsewhere; but not all who saw the opportunity of enrichment in a new city in a new land can have wanted to face the risk at first, until experience had shown that the city was unlikely to be the victim of a second attack. But those of the British who accepted the Roman conquest are more likely to have seen safety in London, and more likely to have been welcomed therein. It is probable that the new population still included many foreigners, though somewhat more British than in the 50s; but it is evident that the dominant element in the population was still the government personnel, military, and civil. Thereafter, it is likely that in the forty years between the rebellion of Boudicca and the enlargement of the city, increasing numbers of British swelled the city's population.

Most of the settlers who came in the early 60s, with keen memories of the rising, were dead by 100, or too old to take an active part in the city's affairs. But the first councillors of the great basilica, and the citizens they ruled, were the sons of the men of the 60s and the 40s, or of more recent immigrants to the city from Britain or abroad. The British among them were exposed to conflicting sentiments. They knew their own peaceful experience, but all men's views are coloured by the attitudes implanted by their parents, and by the detailed stories told of their fathers' times. The outlook of Plutarch illustrates something of the divided feelings of subject peoples who accepted Roman power at the end of the first century. In an essay on how a Greek statesman should behave in his own day, he regretted with nostalgia that

the affairs of cities no longer include leadership in war, the overthrow of tyrants, or acts of alliance. ... But ... for a brilliant career there remain public lawsuits and embassies to the emperor ... many excellent policies that a man may take up in our cities ..., many evils that he may remove, and so gain honour.

But if you hold office as a subject, in an empire controlled by the emperor's proconsuls and procurators ... do not have over great pride and confidence in the power of your office, for you can see the jackboots above your head.

When city magistrates are foolish enough to urge people ... to imitate the glories of their ancestors ... they stir up the plebeians. A statesman and his state should behave irreproachably towards our Roman rulers, and should always buttress his administration by seeking a friend among the highest and mightiest, for the Romans are very eager to promote the interests of their friends. . . .

The statesman should make his state obedient to its masters, but not servile; if the leg is chained, there is no need to thrust the neck beneath the yoke, as some do. . . . Those who refer every decree of measure of the city council to the government's approval . . . force the emperors to be more masterful than they wish. . . . In the feeble state of our affairs, wise men grasp the one advantage we have gained, a life of harmony and peace, for fortune has left us no other prize to win.[16]

The Roman peace enforced internal order, ending the violent stasis of the Greek past, the continuing hostility of rich and poor; it ensured the unchallenged rule of gentlemen of property, and Plutarch strongly discouraged dangerous patriotic fancies that might arouse the passions of plebeians. Rome also gave a guarantee against external attack. But Roman rule was uninspiring and unwelcome, even to those who urged its acceptance. Men could not assert the independent glories of their cities; but they might muse upon them.

The attitude that Plutarch sensed and shared with the Greeks was deep rooted and lasted long, for the whole corpus of literature and learning of antiquity perpetuated it. All schoolchildren, Greek and Roman, were soaked in the stirring tales of ancient Athens and the Persian wars, and of the triumphs of Alexander. Greek memories of the time before the Romans were never stilled, and the Greeks remembered a civilization older and finer than the Roman. But in the west it was otherwise. Even if their history were remembered, nothing in the past could match the visible civilization of Rome in which the Gauls and British lived; at best men might share the respect which Romans themselves accorded to a generous native king, Caratacus or Cunobelinus; but even among the old who remembered these distant heroes were many from the states whom the Belgae had conquered, whose recollection looked no more kindly upon the Belgic conquerors than upon the Romans who destroyed them. But even this history was not recorded. British was unwritten, and had no literature. All that remained was oral tradition, preserved in living memory. Living memory is short, for though men learn vividly from the fathers they know well, they rarely learn more than remote scraps of information from their grandfathers' tales, of antiquarian interest that fire no present warmth. At most, living memory endures for a hundred years or so. Thereafter, even the barest outline of the past is forgotten, unless it is recorded in writing, or in living saga. In Britain, Roman rule effaced all memory of a time before the Romans came, so that in the end the later British had to invent an imaginary past concocted from a misreading of a Roman historian's record. Oblivion quickly buried the past as the last survivors of the age of Boudicca died; by the end of the second century, national antagonism to conquering Rome was dead, and the British, like other provincials, were ready to accept universal Roman citizenship.

These important changes dictated the relation of the city council to the Government in London, and matured its stature. In 100 the government personnel were basically Roman, with Roman freedmen and slaves, still largely drawn from the Mediterranean lands; they patronized inferior provincials, British or Gallic, both the majority who were still of peregrine, foreign, status and the few who had recently acquired Roman citizenship. A hundred years later, provincials and Romans were integrated. Men were divided by their social class. Men of wealth and education could and did travel to Rome and the Mediterranean, and take service under the government at all levels. They shared the cosmopolitan attitude of the rulers of the empire. Humbler men who stayed at home had little understanding or sympathy for foreigners, whether they were Gauls, Italians or Egyptians, save for the occasional foreign visitors and traders that they might encounter in their daily life in the streets of London. But all residents, including the permanent staff of Government House, were now Londoners and British born, save for the short-term visiting officials. No one any longer remembered whether his remote ancestor five generations back had originally come from Gaul or Spain, or from the nearby North Downs or some other part of Britain, anymore than the descendants of Flemish or Huguenot settlers in modern England remember their ancestry, unless the retention of a foreign surname reminds them of their origin.

Good houses increased in the second century. Many men prospered by buying and selling. In the traditional attitudes of Roman, as of other aristocratic societies, the landed gentleman looked down upon the sordid tradesman. Cicero had once prescribed the conditions upon which a nobleman might invite a merchant or a manufacturer to dinner; in essence, he must be exceedingly wealthy, and he must also have disposed of his business, and invested his profits in land.[17] In the middle of the first century, the earliest work of fiction of the form that is nowadays called a novel, Petronius' *Satyricon*, portrayed a nobleman's view of the brash and vulgar businessman who had risen from the lowly stature of a slave and freedman.

The practical experience of the second century retained the gentleman's disdainful philosophy, but modified its practical effect. The pattern of Roman industrial profit is most fully illustrated by the stamped bricks of Rome. All bricks for a short period, and many bricks for a longer period, were stamped with a wealth of information: the name of the estate from which the clay was dug and of its owner, the date, the names of the owner of the firm who made the brick, of his freedmen foremen and of the slave who made the individual brick. Two important conclusions emerge from the study of this information, and are amply confirmed by less complete information from a variety of other industries. The greatest profit went to the owner of the land, who leased or let it to the brickmaker; and during the second century the largest and most profitable estates concentrated in the hands of fewer and fewer owners. But secondly, in successive generations, the contractor who made a substantial fortune bequeathed his business to his freedman, often with a charge upon it payable to his son or other heir; but his profit, invested in land, passed to his sons, who became gentlemen, sometimes equestrians, themselves ancestors of senators.[18]

Noblemen born still derided the parvenu. Tacitus protested that many of the senators of his own day were descended from slaves and men of humble birth. He bemoaned a trend rather than a statistic, but the trend continued, and earned honour as a mark of the generous social mobility opened by enlightened rule to men of merit. Its most striking example was the second-century marshal, Helvius Pertinax. His father was a slave, who earned his freedom and prospered in the timber trade. Pertinax, born in the 120s, was well educated, but was at first denied an officer's commission as centurion in the army. Later, the influence of the patron of his city secured him a commission as prefect of an infantry battalion, at the opening of a prolonged period of frontier warfare. Long and distinguished service, some of it in Britain, and steady ability earned successive promotions until, in years of severe crisis his military rank and experience made him the obvious choice for the command of a legion. The proper commander of a legion was a senator, so in the emergency he was co-opted into the Senate, and further promoted to the command of armies, including those of Britain and of Syria, and the command of armies required also promotion to the senatorial status of a consular. At the end of the century, a veteran soldier and senior consular, he was appointed prefect of the city of Rome in a time of threatening political disaster, and when the disaster came, he was enthroned as emperor, as champion of the interests of the nobility.

Many societies have their stories of the private soldier who carried a marshal's baton in his knapsack. What distinguishes Rome is the frequency and likelihood of such promotion. The changing possibilities of second-century Rome are illustrated by many other instances; no individual rose so high in a single lifetime, but many families rose in successive generations from humble or servile origins to the status of gentlemen, their sons becoming knights, their grandsons becoming senators. Such careers are most frequently recorded among men who attained high military or civil office, but sufficient instances parallel them among men whose public life was restricted to their own cities. Social change prompted alterations in formal law. A cautious lawyer of the early third century recognized change that had gone far beyond the acceptance of men whose ancestors had been humble. A jurisconsult replied to a query that

Persons who earn their livelihood by the sale of articles in daily use ought not to be disregarded as vile, even if they have been flogged by the aediles. Such men are not forbidden to aspire to the decurionate or any other office in their own city. . . . However, it is in my view unseemly that persons of this condition . . . should be admitted to councils when there are plenty of respectable citizens available; but if a shortage of persons for public duties makes it necessary to call upon them, they may be admitted to municipal honour if they have the required property qualification.[19]

These are the conditions in which London grew. Many of the fortunes that were spent upon public buildings and private mansions are likely to have originated in the profits of trade; and the owners of those mansions constituted the men who held office and spoke and voted in the council chamber of the basilica. But not many among them are likely to have been working butchers or bakers or other tradesmen, or shop owners or haulage contractors. They were more probably the sons and grandsons of such businessmen, who invested their inheritance in landed property. The discoveries of the environs of London suggest something of their investment and of the return upon it. In most fertile districts well-built Roman country houses are numerous, especially near to large cities, and in the fourth century many are very large. The countryside about London north of the Thames, and close to the river on the south, is not easy and prosperous in nature; but the chalk downlands from Mitcham and Croydon southward are. Their fields offer to their owners as rich a yield as chalklands elsewhere, and the near and hungry market of the city promised even greater profits to their owners. But these lands have fewer fine houses than other similar soils in Britain. They contrast with the lands to the south-east, more removed from the city, where fine houses

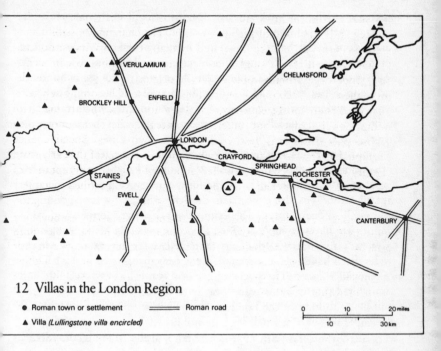

12 Villas in the London Region

- ● Roman town or settlement
- ▲ Villa *(Lullingstone villa encircled)*
- ═══ Roman road

0 ... 10 ... 20 miles
0 ... 10 ... 30 km

abound in the valleys of the Darenth and the Cray, and reach as near toward the city as Keston (Map 14). But in the Surrey hills the majority of the Roman homes that have been observed are among the poorest in Britain, little touched by the wealth of the city and the province, hardly improvements upon their pre-Roman predecessors. The likely inference is that these lands belonged to the city corporation or to wealthy citizens, who drew their rents and lived in city mansions, in its streets and within its walls.

Great houses spread through the city, and are most marked in the latest quarters to be developed, in the north of the city. They are the local sign of social changes common to the west. The men who lived in them had by the third century become the social equals of those who commanded in Government House, no longer inferior provincials; many of the equestrians, and many senators came from provinces as recently Roman in their ways, and most of their cities were smaller and poorer than London. The origins of the men who held equestrian and senatorial office are chiefly known from inscriptions erected in their homelands, either in their own honour, or in honour of relatives whose names and connections reveal their relationship. The evidence of the Mediterranean lands is abundant, for their provinces have tens of thousands of inscriptions, but the fertile lowlands of Britain have barely a couple of hundred, and London but thirty odd. Comparable evidence is lacking, but a few items of evidence suggest the kind of record that might have been, if stone inscriptions had been as common in London as in the towns of Africa, Spain and Italy.

About twenty inscriptions are known from Colchester. One of them is the tombstone of a citizen who was a Roman knight, and died at the age of twenty, probably early in the third century.[20] His youth suggests that his father was also equestrian, though he himself was too young to hold public office. Others of his family doubtless lived longer; and other families are likely to have attained the same rank. By his time, London was a far larger and wealthier city than Colchester; several of its citizens are likely to have been equestrian, some perhaps senatorial. Colchester was an old *colonia*. The status of London is not known. Agricola had commented that it was a place worthy to be compared with a *colonia*, doubtless thinking of the London that he had known in the 80s. Since the emperors who reigned after he published his account eagerly rewarded civic success with appropriate recognition, it is highly unlikely that London was long denied the title of *colonia* (see above, p. 102). It is equally improbable that a *colonia* of the size and importance of London lacked its quota of senators and knights by the end of the second century.

One discovery points mysteriously towards the personality of two of them. The nearest great country houses to the city were those of the Cray and Darenth valleys. In the fifth century, a political frontier allied these valleys with London, and sharply separated them from Kent. The frontier may well have been the boundary of the *territorium* of Roman London, but whether it were or no, the magnates of the Darenth are likely to have received London citizenship, even if they were not sons of London families who had bought country estates. One of the wealthiest of these villas was at Lullingstone.[21] There, a mysterious funeral ceremony was conducted towards the end of the second century, at a period when sharp political disturbances cost many senators their lives. An underground room was painted, with a dado line drawn the length of its walls; but the painter did not stay to wipe away the paint that dribbled as it dried. The room was sealed and never again opened. In it were placed two statue busts, with funeral meats in dishes, together with a cat, doubtless immured by accident. The statues are outstanding. Near life-size, they are among the finest portrait busts of the period from any part of the Roman world; their dress is senatorial, their cast and appearance that which is usually reserved for emperors. But they were not emperors, for sufficient portraits of the emperors remain to exclude identity. The purposes of this extraordinary monument can only be inferred. No bodies were buried, but funeral honours were accorded to two busts. The inescapable conclusion is that these were men who had died and been buried elsewhere; and further, the funeral ceremonies suggest that they were believed not to have had honourable burial. The honour paid to them at Lullingstone suggests that that was the home of their family. The circumstances suggest that they were eminent Roman citizens, British and probably Londoners, who came to an untimely end in the political disasters of their day.

Whatever the identity of these distinguished persons, the council and mansions of London were in the early third century of a scale fit for men of their rank. Some Londoners are likely to have commanded legions and armies, governed provinces and administered finances elsewhere in the empire. Such men, with their families, constituted the ruling group at the head of London society. They were the equals, no longer the inferiors, of the men who governed Britain from the Cannon Street offices. They might also serve to defend its interests abroad more fruitfully than in the past. The known constitutions of cities provide for the election of patrons, by a majority of not less than two-thirds of the decurions, when a quorum of not less than two-thirds was present. The purpose of patrons was to bring the city's needs before the central government in Rome; common sense required people who lived in Rome or went there frequently, and needed them at various levels, from notable senators who could bring matters of importance to the ear of the emperor and his chief ministers to equestrian gentlemen who might badger responsible departmental officers on matters of less moment, and barristers to cope with legal appeals. In cities of Africa and Italy whose lists are extant, some dozens of patrons are named, a quarter of them senators, the rest equestrian. Early in the second century, London was dependent upon securing the good offices of powerful foreigners; by the time that it included senators and equestrians among its own citizens, they might accept appointment themselves, or, if their presence at Rome was insufficiently frequent, were in a position to secure the services of personal friends. A closer intimacy furthered the advancement of individuals as well as of the city collectively; just as Pertinax secured his commission through the good offices of the patron of his father's city, so a patron whose friends knew the people concerned was in a position to further the advancement of ambitious Londoners.

Such men stood at the head of society. Below them were men of lesser fortune, and men still directly engaged in trade. Numerous tools and objects indicate some of them. One baker operated on a scale large enough to require a donkey mill (Merrifield 175) just north of the Walbrook crossing, and another perhaps operated immediately east of Government House (Merrifield 300). Immediately to its west, on the edge of the Walbrook estuary, a ton of animal bones may be the remains of a slaughter-house (Merrifield 259), as may others between the arms of the Walbrook, just south of the northern city wall (Merrifield 142). Slag and mould just south of the forum (Merrifield 288) suggests a glassworks. The permanent moisture of the Walbrook bed has preserved a great number of tools of many trades, in excellent or perfect preservation. They include dockers' and porters' hooks, carpenters', metal-workers' and many other specialized tools; and form probably the largest group of well-conserved metal from anywhere in the Roman world. They imply substantial engineering and building equipment, for one Roman shackle-hook is said to have stood up to re-use for a week in the building of Bucklersbury House in 1954, replacing a modern hook that had snapped on a bulldozer.

These trades were systematically organized. In the main, production and retail went together. Where the nature of the manufacture enabled it, the street frontage of a house served as a shop, the back rooms as workshops and storage sheds. In Pompeii, the ground floors of residential houses, often of ample proportions, were used as shops and workshops, either let to tenants, or worked by the slaves and freedmen of the house-owner; many London houses may have been similarly designed, and it is not unlikely that some buildings, whose only surviving trace is a ground floor of mean or modest appearance, may have had spacious and elegant apartments upon its upper floors.

Where evidence is available, as in Ostia, the port of Rome, trades were organized in *collegia*, associations, who enrolled respected noblemen as their patrons. Such associations began early in Britain; the inscription that names Cogidubnus in Chichester in the first century was erected by the town's trade association, *collegium fabrorum*.[22] At that date, in a new and relatively small town, a single association sufficed for a number of trades. In Ostia, and plainly in the developed city of London, each trade had its own association. The election slogans of Pompeii name very many such incorporated trades. They include launderers, dyers, tailors, goldsmiths and silversmiths, carpetmakers, woodworkers, tilers, carpenters, masons, waggoners, muleteers, porters, barbers, bakers, cobblers, greengrocers, butchers, poultry dealers, fishmongers, as well as lawyers and students, innkeepers, ball players, chequer-board players and many others.

Trade associations served several purposes. The imperial government was intensely nervous of any kind of corporation, especially in cities, and especially in the East; for when town workers were permitted to meet and discuss, riot and disturbance might be feared. The danger was greater in the older cities of the East, whose tradesmen and labourers inherited a long tradition of political and social struggle from the centuries before the Roman conquest; but in the western cities, founded and trained by Roman discipline, urban workers had never had the opportunity to challenge the authority of their Roman masters, and had no experience of defiance. That experience could be averted by the proper control of licensed associations, and such associations were safe. They avoided the main causes of discontent and forestalled danger. The regulations of mining towns forbade unlicensed trade and laid down the fees that licensed contractors might charge for their services. Authority was able to ensure that there were enough barbers, laundrymen, or cobblers to meet public demand, but not so many that each was short of a livelihood, nor so few that services in short supply might tempt the tradesman to inflate his charges. In London, similar responsibility fell upon the associations; the pressure of established members was able to oppose excessive licensing, but the authority of the patron was strong enough to curb excessive restriction and protect the public.

The operation of the trade associations was a principal control of one inborn problem of large Roman cities, chronic underemployment. It is starkly outlined in a tale told of the emperor Vespasian. When an ingenious engineer invented a simple mechanical crane to lighten the labour of rebuilding the Capitol in Rome, perhaps a crane worked by cog-wheels rather than the conventional treadwheel worked by hundreds of human feet, Vespasian rewarded the inventor but suppressed the invention; his duty, he said, was to ensure that the poor earned enough to buy their food.[23] Overabundance of cheap urban labour was the chief reason why antiquity did not employ steam power, power reductions, mild steel and innumerable other devices whose principles its technologists worked out; it was also the most powerful underlying cause of discontent, the gravest threat to the quiet that all rulers strove to maintain.

Trade associations were designed to insulate their members from discontent, and to prevent them causing serious discontent among their customers. Through their patrons, they could bring to the notice of authority grievances that seemed justified by the accepted standards of the day. They were also rudimentary welfare societies; their funds provided for funeral expenses, probably also sometimes for some maintenance for widows and for retirement. But Roman society was more complicated than later economies, when simple class divisions operated on their own. The duties and responsibilities that society imposed upon master and slave, patron and client, constituted a web of controls and palliatives, in which the associations formed one element. Many men were slaves in law; and by law a slave was a chattel, an absolute possession to be bought and sold, without rights and property of his own, barely human. In the celebrated definition of the philosopher Aristotle, he was a 'vocal tool'. But though in legal theory the slave had no rights or property, an enormous volume of legislation defines and protects the rights and property of the slave.

The status and opportunities of the urban slave were greatly superior to those of the rural slave; though even in the country, landowners increasingly discovered that their lands were tilled more profitably by 'cottage slaves', *servi cassati*, equipped by their masters with their own house and basic tools, and delivering a substantial fixed rent or proportion of their crop in return. *Cassati* became a large and important rural category, that long outlived the Roman empire. In the towns, many slaves were similarly set up on their own, as *institores*, particularly if they were skilled men or capable organizers. In the economic jargon of antiquity, they 'leased their own labour power', their *opera*, from their masters. The profitable operation of a slave working on his own required that he should have a reasonable expectancy of security, and hope of betterment. The incentive was freedom. The industrious, skilled slave paid a high quit rent to his master; but he might also retain much more than he needed to maintain his family, and accumulate a *peculium*, his own property, which he could use to purchase his freedom. When freed, he became a freedman, a *libertus*; and if his master was a Roman citizen, his descendants also became Romans.

The career of Pertinax advertised the limitless possibilities open to the loyal and industrious slave; very many instances of modest advancement were present among his acquaintances in the personal experience of most urban slaves. But the freedman was a client of his patron. He owed respect and service in a general sense; and often his contract of freedom specified particular service, due by him and his heirs to his patron and his patron's heirs. The well-to-do commonly relied upon their freedmen doctors, musicians, and children's tutors, as well as upon their tailors, cobblers and carpenters. But in return, the patron was supposed to protect his client, the master his slave, to see that he was properly defended in a law court, fed when he hungered, housed somewhere and somehow, clothed, shod and educated. The legal obligations were minimal, the social obligations stronger. The writings of antiquity frequently pillory the mean patron and harsh master who failed to care for his dependants, and also condemn the slaves and freedmen who withheld due deference from their owners and patrons. But strong social pressures and practical experience taught dependants that their personal welfare was better protected by submission, and taught masters and patrons that they secured better service and earned the approval of their fellows by observing their obligations.

Slave and freedman were legal categories. In practice, there were immense social differences within these categories, and the differences increased through the early empire, so that economic and social status widely differed from classification by law. Many slaves, most of them labourers, were in fact bought and sold. But even the humblest slave had to be well enough fed, clothed and housed to keep him alive and fit for work; his master drew no profit from a corpse, or from an invalid who could not work, and the cost of maintaining slaves who could not profitably be employed was one of the principal factors that induced masters to sell freedom to their slaves. But there were also many poor free men who had difficulty in earning as much as a slave received from his master, and some of them voluntarily sold themselves into slavery to win a guaranteed maintenance. At the other end of the scale were wealthy slaves. Even before the time of the conquest of Britain, one imperial slave, Musicus, employed as a senior clerk in the provincial treasury at Lugdunum, was buried beneath a tombstone erected by fourteen of his own slaves, those who had accompanied him on a visit to Rome, where he died. They were named, and the functions of thirteen were set down. They included his business manager, his doctor, two chamberlains, two cooks and other attendants. The fourteenth, whose duties alone are not engraved upon the stone, was a woman.[24] Imperial slaves had greater opportunities than slaves of private persons, and occasionally ambitious, free-born provincials sold themselves as slaves to the emperor, in the hope of advancement in the civil service and eventual liberation as an imperial freedman, especially in the middle of the first century when imperial freedmen might rise to become the chief ministers of the government. Thereafter, knights were added as colleagues and superiors in the topmost appointments, and freedom came sooner; the second-century equivalents of Musicus commonly became freedmen long before they reached his wealth and eminence. But none the less, trusted slaves of wealthy private citizens, and their freedmen, might enjoy large incomes, a high standard of living, and personal security that was unlikely to be threatened unless they committed serious criminal offences.

Legal and social categories did not coincide. Seasonal labour cut across them. One profitable kind of business enterprise was the supply of labour. A labour contractor maintained a permanent labour force, and hired it when there was a demand – at the harvest of corn, vines and other crops at their due seasons, for building work, haulage or other jobs at other times. The legal status of the labourers was necessarily mixed. Some might be the contractor's own purchased or home-bred slaves, or slaves hired from their owner; others, particularly skilled and semi-skilled men, might be freedmen; others free men who sold their labour power in return for a guaranteed annual wage. To each of them, their legal classification mattered greatly; but to the employer who hired a labour force from the contractor, their classification mattered not at all.

Over and above the legal categories of slave and free, and the obligations of client and patron, the actual relationships were determined by their incomes and their standard of living. Even in modern society, where statistics are easily available, the measurement of the standard of living and the analysis of income and social class defies precise description; and the random figures for wages and prices in antiquity are too full of uncertainties to permit useful statistical analysis or comparison. Only one text offers clear information, valid only for one moment in time. In AD 301, the emperor Diocletian issued an edict fixing maximum prices and wages in great detail, that was publicly engraved on stone throughout the empire; fragments of more than a dozen of these inscriptions survive, and enable a large part of the text to be restored.[25] The government proclaimed itself 'protector of mankind' against profit, defined as a 'crime against the state', and fulminated against the avarice of the rich who exploited the poor, especially the soldier who protected them, whose spending power was provided by the taxpayer, so that taxation must increase if his expenditure grew greater.

The edict fixed maximum prices intended to be valid for the whole empire, without regard to local variations in the cost of transport, and fixed them in very general terms, pricing meat by the pound without regard to cut, fowls by the bird without regard to size. It quickly failed, for its immediate result was to starve the controlled markets of goods, and drive great quantities onto the black market. It is no guide to actual prices in its own day, or to relative prices at other periods; but it sets down precisely the relation between wages and salaries for different occupations and prices for many commodities that the government in 301 considered to be fair and normal. Though the absolute prices are an aim rather than a reality, the relative figures accurately express the differentials between different trades and the relation between wages and prices.

The wages and prices are expressed in denarii, and the value, meaning and physical coin there denoted are matters of argument. Most measurements are given by the Italian pound of about eleven English ounces, fractionally less than an English pound weight, or by the capacity measure of the *modius*, about two gallons, or else by the time spent on the piece-work done. The looseness of the evidence does not warrant attempts at closer precision. It is not possible to attempt an actual expression of the denarius in terms of modern currency, for both ancient and modern currencies changed their values by inflation, but there is a rough and ready consistency in the relation between some basic commodities. Pork was priced at 12 denarii a pound, beef at 8, light ale at 2 denarii a pint, strong beer at 4, a pair of trousers at 20, top quality stout boots for farmers or muledrivers at 120. These and other prices of essentials in denarii in 301 happen to be roughly similar to the scale of prices of the same commodities in English shillings at about the end of 1970. Since modern currency is expressed in larger units, of a pound sterling composed of shillings and pence, old or new, comparative prices are not easily grasped if they are expressed in large mathematical figures of thousands or millions of denarii, shillings or pence. For purposes of comparison, the Latin word 'denarius' is here rendered by the English word 'shilling', of 12 old pence or 5 new pence, and figures of 20 denarii or upwards are translated by pounds sterling, at 20 shillings to the pound. Such translation is designed only for ease of comparison.

The wages of labourers and tradesmen were reckoned by the day, the salaries of the professions by the month. Wages, but not salaries, were paid with maintenance added; the cash value of maintenance is not stated, but the commodities it involved, bread or porridge, salt, cheese, a pint of wine, a little meat or fish, cannot have amounted to less than 10 denarii, or shillings, a day on a rough average. Over and above maintenance, the lowest paid workers, such as shepherds, received 20 denarii or £1 a day, plus maintenance, a gross payment for six days, the modern week, of about 180 denarii or £9. Most of the humbler workers, the farm labourer, the donkey or mule driver, the sewage worker, received more, 25 denarii, translatable as about £11 or £12 in a six-day period. Carpenters, bakers, and river boatmen received twice as much, the seagoing sailor 60 denarii, of the order of £25 a week. The labourer's wage brought him his daily food, and also the cash equivalent of 3 lbs of beef, or of a gallon and a half of light ale, or of 3 pints of ordinary wine. Clothing was relatively cheap. A pair of trousers cost a labourer a day's pay or less, rough leggings one sixth of a day's pay; a first quality overcoat with hood cost 60 denarii, £3, or two and a half to three day's pay. Some foodstuffs were relatively expensive; butter cost 16 denarii or shillings a pound, chickens £1.50 each; a shave and a visit to the baths each cost 2 shillings.

Some prices were fixed in terms of Italy and the Mediterranean, and cannot have been valid for Britain and the Atlantic provinces. Olive oil, the universal Mediterranean equivalent of lighting fuel, of soap, and of cooking fat, was expensive; the cheapest quality cost 24 denarii a pint, a day's wage for the labourer. Since olives do not grow north of the Mediterranean coast lands, its transport to Britain was prohibitive; and in practice, oil lamps, common in the Mediterranean, were very rare in Britain, even in the richest houses. Lighting was evidently by tallow and candle. But in contrast, oysters cost a shilling each in the Mediterranean values of the edict; but in Britain oyster shells are discovered in large quantities even upon poor sites of the Roman period, and for many centuries thereafter, throughout and after the Middle Ages, for before the oyster beds of Britain were polluted in modern times, the oyster was an abundant poor man's food.

The basic foodstuff was cereals. Their price cannot be determined. In most cities, it varied greatly from year to year, according to the harvest, and variations in the price of corn and bread were a chief cause of riot. In Rome, and a few other great cities, perhaps including London, the government cut down the risk of riot by buying a year or more's supply cheaply in many markets, and issuing it at a controlled price, so that the actual price of a loaf of bread was decided by the government of the day, and often involved a subsidy. The edict fixed bulk grain prices, at £40 a hundredweight for wheat, £24 for barley, which might well have given an economic price of 4s. or 5s. for a 1 lb loaf of bread; but too many unknowns intervene between the price of corn and the price of a loaf for the edict's maximum to indicate the actual cost of bread. Figures for rent are also not available. What evidence there is is negative. Numerous incidents report discontent and disturbance over the cost of commodities at various times and places in the empire; corn prices are the commonest cause of trouble, but meat, oil, wine and other articles are also listed. Yet rents are rarely named as a cause of protest. The silence of the sources suggests that in general rents were not a major problem, and were therefore probably relatively a smaller item in the cost of living than food.

The prices in the edict indicate what the government thought a labourer's daily wage ought to be able to buy, and imply that their purchasing power had been roughly equivalent to the provisions of the edict in the recent past. That purchasing power formally demonstrates that at least the urban labourer at the end of the third century had achieved a somewhat higher standard of living than urban workers in many other societies; it had evidently been achieved by continuing effort and pressure, for it argues a somewhat higher standard than is indicated by the less precise, haphazard information available for the early empire; and it follows after a long history of recorded discontent and disturbance, the outward and visible signs of a mounting pressure for improved conditions, whose gains necessarily resulted more often from concessions granted to avert trouble than from the outcome of particular riots. When the policy of the empire grouped men into large cities, and made the cities the basis of their political society, they gave urban workers the power to win better standards than they could achieve in many other states at other times. In general, it is probable that the larger cities were able to obtain the greatest concessions, and likely that the purchasing power of the London worker increased significantly during the second and third centuries.

The edict observes sharp differentials between different social classes. Skilled craftsmen in general earned about double the labourer's daily wage. The professions were substantially better off. Teachers were paid so much a month for each pupil. The elementary school teacher who taught 40 children received about £100 a month, at 20 denarii to the pound; in higher education, the teacher with 30 pupils earned about £300. The skilled calligrapher, who could copy books for a publisher, received 25 denarii, a labourer's wage, for each hundred lines, and an experienced writer could produce several hundred lines a day; the lower grade of penmanship, suitable for business correspondence, earned slightly less, 20 denarii, and the lawyer, the notary or scrivener, earned 10 denarii a hundred lines for a legal document. The barrister's brief was fixed at 1,000 denarii, £50, the jurisconsult's fee at a quarter of that sum.

The professions were better paid than manual workers, but an enormous gulf separated both from the nobility. Salaries and incomes of senators and knights are not recorded in the edict, but the figures reported of the early empire mark the differential. Then, the value of the coin termed denarius was vastly greater than in Diocletian's time. In the second century the legionary soldier received 300 denarii a year,[26] and his pay was probably roughly equivalent to a labourer's. The second-century wage was about one twentieth of the number of denarii earned in Diocletian's time, and at the rate of 20 denarii to the pound, amounted to no more than £15 in a year. But the annual salaries of second-century equestrian procurators ranged from 15,000 to 75,000 denarii, £750 to £3,750 at the later values: the highest salary of a senator, as proconsul of Asia or Africa, was £12,500.[27] Inflation was twentyfold; it was not matched by increasing the nominal salary in coin values, but salaries were supplemented by fees, allowances, and valuable privileges and exemptions on a proportionate scale. In the early empire, the highest-paid senatorial governor had received about 800 times the annual salary of the private soldier or labourer. The scale of great men's incomes was maintained in the late empire; the annual income of a rich senator was reckoned at 4,000 lbs of gold, the equivalent, at Diocletian's price of gold in denarii, of over £10 million a year, more than 15,000 times the labourer's annual earnings. No senator of such outstanding wealth is likely to have lived in London; but some of the great houses and splendid mosaics of London were evidently the property of more modest millionaires. Far below were the professions, the skilled workers and the labourers, each of whom had achieved a standard of living that was worth maintaining, and needed defence against rising living costs.

Chapter 11

Learning and Belief

AN IMPORTANT ELEMENT in urban living standards was the provision of amenities, education and health, books and paintings, religion, sport and entertainment, and travel. Cities needed literacy, and government legislation compelled them to maintain elementary schools, even in quite small towns, with provision for higher education, the equivalent of the university, in larger cities. In the early empire the most highly-paid professors in Rome earned the same salary as the higher equestrian officers in provincial departments, about eighty times a labourer's wage. In Diocletian's time, the normal run of teachers in higher education earned about ten times as much as labourers. In London, they were numerous. By the late empire it was normal practice for the sons of good families to be sent away to boarding school at the age of sixteen or upward, where they were taught in classes, seeking promotion to higher forms. Much is recorded of Roman education in general, and the evidence has been well summarized in modern times;[1] the extensive publications of the greatest of the Roman educationalists, Quintilian, who wrote in the 90s, when the public services of London were in process of establishment, have not lost their pungency or relevance. The basic scheme passed through three main stages: the mastery of the grammar and syntax of both languages, Latin and Greek, beginning with Greek in the west, since the children learnt Latin at home from their parents, thereafter the study of literature and history, and, in the third stage, training in fluency of expression, equally in writing and in speaking. The central theme of Quintilian's method was to arouse and maintain the pupil's interest, and to keep his education geared to changing modern life. The greatest evil was a boring teacher, and he ridiculed the aridity of teachers in his own day who tried to train their pupils to write like Cicero, for Cicero had been dead for a century and a half, and usage had changed in the meanwhile, for 'grammar is the servant of custom'. Not all Quintilian's precepts were generally followed; he discountenanced the cane, as degrading to human dignity and inimical to learning, but many writers recall the fear of the cane that turned their affections away from schooling, and earned their contempt for masters too weak to maintain authority unarmed.

London is rich in signs of literacy. A number of inkwells and pens have been recovered, and some hundreds of *styli*. The *stylus* was the equivalent of the pencil, in an age when paper was not yet cheap, or of the slate in more recent centuries. It was used upon a writing tablet, two recessed pieces of wood hinged together, with wax in the recess; one end of the *stylus* was pointed for writing, the other end flattened for smoothing the wax and erasing previous writing for re-use. Some messages on tablets survive, written by economical persons who used the last thin coating of wax before buying a new tablet, and impressed their words upon the wood itself. Pieces of a dozen or so such tablets have survived in London, but only a few of them preserve enough legible letters to make even a fragmentary and uncertain reading of their message intelligible. One, whose interior is blank, was stamped on the outside 'Issued by the Procurators of the Province of Britain', and was found in the Walbrook.[2] The only dated letter is probably commercial;[3] its text reads:

[I swear] by Jupiter the Best and Greatest and by the divinity of the Emperor Domitian Caesar Augustus Germanicus and by the Gods of the Fatherland. . . .

The date lies between 84 and 96, but what was sworn has perished. Another is plainly commercial and legal:[4]

. . . which money Crescens, or whosoever the business concerns, shall pay to me, likewise according to the record of the claim.

A third, found with these two in Lothbury, by the crossing of the Walbrook between the fort and the basilica, preserves disjointed fragments of an important transaction:[5]

. . . to have sold the goods . . . from his office . . . for the construction of a ship, and to have authorized . . . the manufacture of a rudder.

One, probably also from Lothbury retains most of the address on the outside: '*Londinio, L. Vital. ad S. . . .*, London, to L. Vitalis, by the S. . . .' The text is the best preserved of all. It reads:

Rufus, son of Callisunus; greeting to Epillicus and all his Company. Let me assure you that I am quite well. If you have done the list, please send it. Take great care of the whole business. See that you turn that girl into cash. . . .[6]

The matter may have been the inheritance or purchase of an estate or a business, and it entailed the sale of at least one redundant slave girl.

These four tablets from the same area might have come from a single office, and might have been of much the same date as the one dated document. One other legible and informative letter was found west of the Walbrook, further to the south, in Queen Street.[7] Its tale is livelier, but some key words are missing, and make its meaning not quite certain. Its probable wording is:

That boy swiped the ordered goods from the waggon and ran away. But the next day I left London. This is to let you know that I am staying at Rochester, and the horses (?) ...

The letter concerns the misfortunes of a haulage contractor, or of one of his customers. As in the other letters, the handwriting, the grammar and the syntax compare favourably with those from elsewhere in the empire. The businessmen of London, from the late first century onwards, were literate enough to have no trouble with commercial correspondence, the keeping of invoices and inventories, the drafting of contracts. Literacy was not confined to employers. One tile in a London brickworks was scratched with a joke while the clay was wet:[8] 'Austalis has been going off by himself every day for these thirteen days.' At least, the craftsmen who earned his 50 denarii a day, or £15 odd a week, could write easily; and since Latin was the only written language, he could speak Latin as well as British. These are the products of the elementary and higher schools that developed from the late first century onward, the visible witness of the success of Agricola's intention to make fluent Latin a goal of the British.

The experience of contagious disease caused the government to care for public health. Many major cities were provided with main drainage; and one or two sections of sewers have been encountered in London. Most cities were also provided with an ample, fresh water supply carried by aqueducts. No signs of any London aqueducts have yet been observed, and it may be that they were not necessary; the Thames brought plenty of fresh water, as yet uncontaminated, and a large cluster of wells about the junction of Queen Street and Queen Victoria Street afforded a greater supply than is likely to have been needed by the houses in the immediate area; it may have served a wider public, either maintained by the city, or developed by private enterprise for sale. Doctors, like teachers, were maintained by cities, according to a statutory minimum, and wealthy persons kept their own doctors. Some temples in some cities provided free medical attention for the poor, and some doctors also worked without fee. In Bordeaux, Ausonius' father was a well-educated land-owner with an adequate income, brother to two university professors, one of whom was tutor to an emperor's son; he disliked city politics, and disliked idleness. He therefore graduated at the medical school and practised in his own city, but did not charge his patients, since his income was sufficient without addition.⁹ Such philanthropists were doubtless exceptional; but the Bordeaux doctor is unlikely to have been unique. Other medical practitioners commonly charged. One chance fashion has preserved many stamps used by chemists or opticians to mark eye salves; other ointments and medicines were not so stamped, and have left no record, but the use of a proprietary stamp indicates a charge for the medicine.

Men carried with them the physical consequences of their education. Books, and with them publishers, bookshops and libraries, are known in Britain from references in writers from the late first century onward; and were clearly easier to obtain in London than in the state capitals. There is plenty of evidence for expensive furniture in Britain and in London, and for the elaborate decoration of houses. Many fragments of decorated wall plaster remain, some large enough to show the prevailing taste. Both decoration and furniture most commonly affected a rococo taste, that was to be imitated by the elegance of the eighteenth century. The richest houses were adorned with elaborate floor mosaics (Plate 9), and some wall fragments (Plate 10), as in other Roman towns and houses, suggest fresco pictures as well as designs. The men who made them were well paid. The publisher's scribe earned a good professional salary in Diocletian's time; the house painter earned three times a labourer's wage, the artist painter six times, and mosaic workers were still better paid.

The skills of the craftsmen were also needed in the temples. Half a dozen or more are known in London, or inferred from inscriptions that are likely to have stood in temples. In addition to the temple of the emperor, probably in Cannon Street, others dedicated to the principal deities of the Roman pantheon were erected in all sizeable Roman towns. The worship they housed varied, and is not clearly recorded, for it was the every-day, familiar practice, known to everyone, that no one there-fore bothered to explain. Due sacrifice from time to time was a proper conventional observance, as it still is in many eastern lands, a ritual as respectable as formal attendance at church in nineteenth-century England. It marked conformity with the established order. Some massive and imposing temples were built with a small interior, that could admit only a priest and attendants with a single worshipper and a few friends to sacrifice on the altar; only the ground plans of most are known, but one, in Split in Jugoslavia, is preserved entire, exterior and interior roof and walls unaltered, save for the intrusion of a medieval bishop's tomb and crucifix, and a modern bronze statue. Not more than a dozen people could conveniently attend at one time.

Many temples were equipped with a forecourt big enough to contain a considerable number of people on festival occasions. Antiquity, like the Middle Ages, knew no regular secular holidays. But the calendar marked many holy days, free from work, in honour of important events and of particular gods, both those common to the whole Roman world, and to particular towns and regions. Some few festivals, such as the midwinter Saturnalia, the equivalent of Christmas, extended over many days, but most were confined to a single day, many attached to a particular deity and a particular temple. Men of wealth often paid for a sacrifice, or more often endowed a lasting festival in their wills. When an animal was sacrificed, only a small portion was burnt on the altar for the benefit of the god; the rest was distributed to the worshippers, and in the early empire was often the main or sole occasion on which the poor tasted meat.

The sacred days were marked in calendars in all cities. Most do not specify what sacrifice attended the festival, but the early third-century calendar of the military town of Dura Europos on the Euphrates gives details:[10]

January 3. Vows for the well-being of our lord the Emperor Severus Alexander and for the eternal empire of the Roman people. To Jupiter Best and Greatest, an ox; to Juno, a cow; to Minerva, a cow; to Jupiter Victor, an ox ... to Father Mars, a bull; to Mars Victor, a bull; to Victory, a cow ...

January 7. Discharge of veterans; pay day for the troops. To Jupiter Best and Greatest, an ox; to Juno a cow; to Minerva, a cow; to Salvation, a cow; to Father Mars, a bull. ...

January ... Birthday of L. Seius Caesar, father-in-law of the Emperor ...

January 24. Birthday of the late Emperor Hadrian, an ox.

January 28. The ... Parthian victories of the late Emperor Severus; and the accession of the late Emperor Trajan; to the Parthian victory, a cow; to the late Emperor Trajan, an ox.

All over the empire January opened with official congratulations to the emperor; its ample feasts followed upon the seven days of Saturnalia, December 17 to 23: February had but one festival; March, the old opening of the year in spring, had five; April five and the summer months eighteen, including:

August 1, Birthday of the late Emperor Claudius and the late Emperor Pertinax; to Claudius, an ox; to Pertinax, an ox.

September had five festivals, including Augustus' birthday; the autumn and early winter no more till the Saturnalia. In all, some forty days in the year were devoted to festivals. The military calendar of Dura differs in its selection of days and events from the calendars of civil towns, but the principle was common to both.

The costs were sometimes met by the city treasury, sometimes born by private citizens, voluntarily or by designation and selection. They were commonly authorized by the city council, and are elaborately and formally set forth in the early years of the empire, when the worship of the emperors was first established. Most of the decree establishing the annual worship in Narbonne, the chief town of Provence, is extant, dated 22 September, AD 11:[11]

Good fortune attend the Emperor Augustus, ... the Roman senate and people and the citizens and inhabitants of the colonia of Narbonne! The people of Narbonensis have placed an altar in the forum of Narbonne, at which, annually on 23 September, the day on which the felicity of our age brought Him forth as Ruler of the World, three Roman knights from the plebs and three freedmen shall sacrifice one victim each, and shall at their own expense provide the citizens and inhabitants with incense and wine to supplicate his divinity; and on 24 September they shall provide incense and wine for the citizens and inhabitants; also on 1 January ... and January 7, the day on which he was first invested with the sovereignty of the world, they shall supplicate with incense and wine and each sacrifice a victim, and provide incense and wine for the citizens and inhabitants; and on May 31, because on that day in AD 11 he attached the people's courts to the councillors, they shall each sacrifice a victim and provide the citizens and inhabitants with incense and wine for supplication. Of these three Roman knights and three freedmen, one ...

The lost continuation probably laid down how the knights and freedmen should be chosen. The stone also reports verbatim the formal opening address; the name of the speaker, probably the proconsul, and the immediately following words have been erased, presumably because he later incurred political disgrace.

The people of Narbonensis dedicated the altar to the divinity of Augustus. (consecrated it in the following words according to) the laws cited here below. ... When this day I grant and dedicate this altar, I grant and dedicate it according to those laws and directions which I shall this day publicly declare to be the fundamental basis of this altar and its inscriptions. If anyone desires to cleanse, decorate or repair the altar a benefaction, he may lawfully so do ... if any desires to augment this altar with a gift, he may do so, and the same law that governs this altar shall also govern that gift. All other laws and directions touching this altar shall be the same as those which govern the temple of Diana on the Aventine Hill (in Rome). By these laws and directions I hereby grant and dedicate this altar on behalf of the Emperor Augustus ... of the Roman senate and people, and of the citizens and inhabitants of the *colonia* of Narbonne.

At first, the costs of the provincial shrine were delegated by its Council to selected individuals. In Italy, public and private expenditure was already more readily offered. In AD 18, the Council of a Tuscan town resolved:

In the duumvirate of Cn. Acceius Rufus Lutatius and T. Petillius. Decree. The two victims which are always normally sacrificed for the birthday of Augustus on 24 September at the altar dedicated to the Spirit of Augustus shall be sacrificed on 23 and 24 September. Also, the councillors and people shall hereafter dine on the birthday of Tiberius Caesar, the which expense Q. Cascellius Labeo has undertaken to meet in perpetuity, that thanks may be delivered for his munificence; and on that birthday a calf shall be sacrificed annually.... We will undertake the construction of the altar of the Spirit of Augustus at our expense; we will provide six days' games from 13 August at our expense. On the birthday of the Empress we will distribute honey and cake to the women of the wards.[12]

The wording of the decree reads like the expression of a contract or agreement reached between Labeo and the Council. The need for a shrine of Augustus was accepted, but no one was anxious to meet the cost. These inscriptions record the inception of the new form of state religion, before it had taken hold upon convention. They also show something of the internal structure of city government. The Narbonese distinguish between citizens and inhabitants; many other towns have similar distinctions, and some contrast an intramural and extramural population. Not all were citizens entitled to vote; freedmen, perhaps sometimes also slaves, and immigrants from other towns ranked as inhabitants, residents without the vote, comparable with the *metics* of Greek cities, or with the Latins who lived in early Rome without Roman citizenship.

Their numbers and importance varied from town to town, and

occasional stories report the pressure of long-established non-citizen groups to win citizenship of the town in which they lived. In the time of Trajan, the orator Dio Chrysostom endorsed the demand of the linen-workers of Tarsus for citizenship, but condemned the tactics of the young people who supported them, and showed their contempt of established authority by making vulgar noises with their noses at them.[13] In London, the inhabitants or strangers are likely to have been numerous in the first and second centuries, for, though the city began with the settlement of many foreigners from overseas, its rapid growth necessarily involved the immigration of many British. When the grandchildren of the foreigners and the grandchildren of British immigrants were equally Londoners born, the distinction became an out-of-date anomaly, and the situation was doubtless eased when London was incorporated as a Roman city. The different scale of entertainment offered in many towns to citizens and inhabitants at the numerous festivals constituted one of the powerful irritants that pressed for the abolition of antiquated distinctions.

Other distinctions did not become out of date. Narbo delegated three knights and also three freedmen to meet the costs of the holidays. Throughout the west, the government found it expedient to give freedmen their own corporate organization, and to ensure that its direction was vested in safe and respectable hands. Like many other corporations, its formal purpose was religious, its centre a temple. The responsible freedmen were known as *Augustales*, and their directing priests were usually six, known as the *Sexviri Augustales*, necessarily men of wealth. None happen to be named among the scanty inscriptions, but chance has preserved an inscription of Bordeaux, set up in the early third century by a wine merchant who was a *Sexvir* of the colonies of York and Lincoln.[14] He clearly had plenty of unrecorded colleagues, predecessors and successors, and London vintners no less than those of York and Lincoln were of the wealth and standing to serve as *Augustales* and to trade with Bordeaux.

The endowment of festivals and public charities was at first accepted without enthusiasm. But as the lengthening Roman peace ended uncertainties and dangers, men prospered. Expanding cities demanded more consumer goods, most of their raw materials were agricultural, animal, vegetable or mineral; the demand for them enriched noble and gentle landowners, and also enriched freedmen, manufacturers and traders. Prosperity involved display, and men earned honour by charity. Benefactions were controlled, and commonly required the approval of the city council; and councils lightened their load by encouraging benefactions.

Some inscriptions preserved the wording of the legislation that authorized private expenditure for public and religious purposes, and illustrate
the workings of the council as of the temples. The language was modelled
on the procedure of the Roman Senate. One, from Tibur, near Rome, is
unusually explicit:[15]

C. Sextilius Ephebus, freedman of the Vestal Virgins of Tibur, Augustalis,
curator of the temple of Hercules (submitted a request). It is entered in the
minutes (of the council) that on 29 August L. Alfrenatius Priscus and M. Musius
Tiburtinus, being *quattuorviri*, proposed that Sextilius Ephebus be permitted
to attend for the hearing of his request, whose content was that he should be
authorized to install a marble pedestal, wholly at his own expense, below the
Treasury of the temple of Hercules and Augustus by the Esquiline Gate. The
authorization on this matter is recorded. The Council duly approved the
motion, signifying the Council's desire thereon. 'Since C. Sextilius Ephebus,
freeman of the Vestal Virgins, is today not for the first time a benefactor of
the public welfare, let him further embellish it by the installation of a marble
pedestal below the Treasury of Hercules by the Esquiline Gate. Let thanks be
rendered to Sextilius Ephebus, and let him also be permitted to engrave his
name upon the inscription, adding thereto this the resolution of our senate, that
others also may be more readily prompted to follow his example.' Motion
agreed, AD 127. In the committee for registering the decree were present ...
Attius (and others).

Ephebus was a local man who made a relatively modest benefaction.
Richer men gave more substantial endowments. One made a generation
earlier in southern Italy to a temple of Silvanus, the god of field sports
gives vivid detail:[16]

Shrine of Silvanus. In pursuance of a vow undertaken for the well-being of
our Emperor Domitian, L. Domitius Phaon has assigned for worship, guard-
ianship and sacrifices for all time to come to those who are today members of
the College of Silvanus, and to those who shall hereafter be admitted, his estates
named Junian, Lollian, Percennian and Statuleian, together with their villas and
their territories. He has also decreed that from the rents of these aforesaid
estates, on 1 January, and on 11 February, being the birthday of our Empress
Domitia, and 27 June, being the dedication of Silvanus, and on 20 June, being
Rose Day, and on 24 October, being the birthday of our Emperor Domitian,
worship shall be observed for the appropriate occasion. The members of the
College shall assemble and proceed to dine, under the Master of the College in
office for the year ... Furthermore the place, or portion of field and woodland
that constitutes the game park and fish ponds, that is marked out by boundary
stones placed about the temple of Silvanus, he yields to Silvanus; also the
approach road that leads to the temple of Silvanus through the Caesician estate

shall be open to the public. In addition, timber from the Gallican estate and water for sacrifice or the game park and fish ponds may be used without restriction. L. Domitius Phaon, lawful owner of the entire property, ordered and permitted all these things to be granted, performed and instituted, without fraud.

Such extensive donations are rarely described in such detail. But they continued, and long outlasted the Roman empire; similar grants and endowments were bestowed, when the old gods declined and were dethroned, by late Roman and medieval magnates upon Christian churches and monasteries, many of which took equal care to record in writing the names, boundaries and values of the estates granted, and the services owed. On a smaller scale, they were repeated in Britain. One equestrian officer dedicated a much smaller shrine on the Durham moors, at Stanhope:[17]

Shrine of the unconquered Silvanus. C. Tettius Veturius Micianus, prefect of the Sebosian cavalry squadron, for the taking of a boar of outstanding size, that many of his predecessors failed to subdue.

The moorland shrine is unlikely to have received rich endowments; but it was erected, and intended for public worship at the cost of Tettius in the same spirit.

At the beginning of the first century, urban expenditure on temples and festivals was encouraged, but was not yet offered with enthusiasm. By the end of the century, in Phaon's time, it had become acceptable at all levels, urban as well as rural. A hundred years later, rich men vied with each other in public expenditure. Its scale is most often instanced in the Mediterranean lands. Ostia was grateful to

P. Lucilius Gamala ... aedile, ... duumvir ... censor ... curator of the collection and allocation of public revenues. When he was allocated public funds for the games, he refused it and paid from his own funds. At his own cost he paved the street adjacent to the forum from arch to arch. He gave a banquet to 217 citizens, and twice gave a supper to the citizens of Ostia. At his own cost he founded the temple of Venus ... the temple of Fortune ... the temple of Ceres. Jointly with M. Turranius he established the market weighbridge at his own cost. At his own cost he founded the temple of Hope. He constructed a marble tribunal in the forum. A gilt statue was decreed to him from public funds, and a bronze statue from public funds was decreed by the quaestor's tribunal, because when the city was to sell off lands to meet its undertakings for the navy, he donated 15,200 sestertii (3,800 denarii) to the city. The Councillors decreed that he be accorded a public funeral.[18]

Gamala earned honour by building temples and feasting the citizens. Others contributed time and energy. Gamala's close relative and contemporary, Sentius Felix, was:

quaestor ... and duumvir of Ostia, quaestorum of the youth. He was the first man to be nominated duumvir in the year after he was admitted to the Council. He was curator of sea-going shipping, honorary member of the Association of Adriatic Shipowners and supervisor of the wine market; patron of the associations of wax tablet writers, of book-keepers, of municipal employees, of silversmiths, of city wine merchants, of the grain assessors at the temple of Ceres and Augustus, of the lightermen and of the boatmen of Lucullus ferry, of joiners, of shopkeepers and of weight makers, of freedmen and of public slaves, of oil dealers, of apprentice cartwrights, of veterans and of the imperial procurator's staff, and of fishermen retailers, curator of young people's sport. Cn. Sentius Lucilius Gamala Clodianus, to his understanding father.[19]

Gamala spent money. Felix was immersed in the day-to-day supervision of the many-sided business, commercial and manufacturing activities of the city, on whose Council he sat throughout his adult life.

Ostia was a large and important city, the ancient port of Rome. But it was smaller than London. By the time of Felix and Gamala, London was already approaching its full vigour. Its temples and its trade associations were no less than in Ostia. Its citizens, like those of all great western cities, had long been trained to the same notions of government. It did not lack city fathers as wealthy as those of Ostia, some of whom deemed it an honourable obligation to devote as much time and care and as much money on the ordering and adornment of the city. The temples and the festivals held within or beside their precincts were one essential foundation of the fair appearance of its streets, and of the good order of its population. They prolonged and perpetuated in a new age the attractions, the *dulcedo*, of the city that Agricola had remarked in its early years.

Numerous temples were an important inducement to social conformity. They expressed and realized the hard-headed dictum of much older Greek and Roman statesmen, that the function of religion was to keep the working population obedient to their betters. But the appeal of religion was not limited to such material influence. The structures of the temple buildings proclaimed that the state and the community prospered if the gods were duly honoured; but, as in many other ages, men needed to believe that individual divinities cared for the successful outcome of their own personal day-to-day worries. Their belief was expressed in two main forms, whose plentiful traces remain in inscriptions and in some texts. Men paid considerable sums to consult the oracles, to be warned, encouraged in their fears and ambitions, to learn whether a journey would prosper, an illness be healed, or a petition succeed. Reputable oracles long retained their fame and wealth. The greatest of them, the Oracle of Apollo at Delphi, was the central sanctuary of the wealthy ecclesiastical establishment that maintained Plutarch among its priests. In the provinces, many local oracles attained a short-lived fashion, some of them patent frauds; one was investigated in the middle of the second century by the satirist Lucian, who detected and exposed the ingenious tricks by which its mountebank proprietor deceived his clients. But the exposure was not published until after it had converted an eminent Spanish senator, who had commanded a legion in Britain while his father was legate of the province; and the illustrious convert gave it wide repute and wealthy customers. Lucian derided him as a superstitious old fool: 'if you anointed any old stone with holy oil, he would incontinently fall down and worship'.[20] Such high patronage furthered the sale of oracular advice in all great cities; London is unlikely to have been exempt.

More important than the oracle was the bargain with the god. The worshipper who wished to recover his health, to profit from a journey or a business deal, to win promotion in his career, made a vow to make a sacrifice to the god, or to present his temple with a statue or an ornament if his hopes were fulfilled. A few disgruntled inscriptions upbraid a god who let his worshipper down, but most repay hope fulfilled. There are a number of them in Britain; one of the most striking is a relief of the god Mithras slaying the bull, found near the Walbrook, paid for by a soldier from Orange in Gaul to discharge a vow, perhaps on receipt of a commission (Plate 11).[21] The ex-voto memorials also outlived the religion of Rome, and persist in many Mediterranean lands, especially where the Roman past lies heaviest. The walls of the modern church by the ruins of Roman Pompeii are covered with tributes, often bronze representations of limbs, set up by worshippers who vowed them to the patron saint of the church if a diseased limb were cured.

The temples of the Roman gods served the political state and the immediate material hopes of men. But religion bit more deeply than these mechanical conceptions. Men of sophisticated education embraced various philosophies, many of them mystical, that preached a fundamental divinity, whose godhead was expressed in manifold different aspects by the deities of the several nations and of the hierarchy of official gods. Among the urban poor, and among some sections of the wealthier classes, the rich ceremonials of eastern mystery religions found a ready response. Most innovations were at first obstructed by authority, but were later accepted, acclimatized and disciplined as soon as they had established a lasting hold. Their common features were privilege for their initiates, gorgeous, comforting ceremonies on earth and a promise of reward hereafter. Converts were initiated by some form of baptism or rebirth, usually bestowed by anointing with a liquid, the blood of an animal, or sometimes water. Splendidly organized carnival processions, gay with flowers, floats and images, accompanied by games and contests, feasts and drink, impressed the public with the majesty of the god; their tradition is continued by the religious pageants of the Spanish peninsula, of Latin America, of Mardi Gras in New Orleans. The god's favour was manifest to the faithful in the festival; and the festival foreshadowed the happiness of the afterlife, that was the reward of the initiates alone, denied to those outside their number.

Several of the most important of these cults have left their traces in London. The Egyptian goddess Isis became the symbol of the gentle faith of women, absorbing and embracing the cults of older Greek, Roman and Syrian goddesses, and the mother goddesses of the Celtic west. The moving beauty of the Isis festival is graphically described by the second-century African novelist, Apuleius, himself a priest of Isis. His best known work, *The Golden Ass*, is a religious allegory; the hero, Lucius, is magically transformed into an ass, and learns that he can only recover his human shape by eating rose petals. The burden of the story treats of his miserable mischances and ribald adventures, constantly searching to escape from his ugly animal nature and attain human dignity, repeatedly thwarted by the bestial meanness of men. At the end the goddess appears to him in a vision, and bids him approach her garlanded priest during her ceremony on the feast day, and eat a rose dedicated to her. He does so, and regains humanity. Later generations adapted much of the Isis tradition to the worship of the Virgin in Mediterranean lands. One object records the Isis worshippers of London. A wine jug found in Southwark is marked with the address of the innkeeper who owned it, *Londini ad fanum Isidis*, London, by the Temple of Isis. The location of the temple is not now known, but it was sufficiently well known in its day to serve as an easily recognizable address.[22] The oldest and most widespread of the mystery cults was the worship of Bacchus, the god of wine. When it first expanded in Roman territory, two hundred years before the conquest of Britain, it was proscribed and denounced by conservative opinion, outraged at the uninhibited orgies and uncontrolled drinking of its devotees; but long before London matured, it had been disciplined to a licence that released men's emotions, but kept their actions within acceptable limits. The cult is attested in London by one of the finest sculptures found in the northern provinces, a carving of Bacchus and his companions, inscribed with the cheerful wish 'Long life to wandering men!', that was found in the temple of Mithras in the Walbrook, together with sculptures of the Egyptian Serapis and other gods (Plate 12).[23]

The most influential of the mystery religions in the second and third centuries was the worship of the Mesopotamian deity Mithras. Its philosophy was alien to the central beliefs of Roman and Christian religion, though it deeply influenced both. It was the most important western manifestion of the the near-eastern concept that the supernatural powers of good and evil are locked in eternal, equal, conflict, whose outcome mankind watches with hope, but passively, without the possibility of intervention. The philosophy of dualism appealed to temperaments and interest unlike those served by the Roman and Christian belief that the powers of evil had been cast into the outer darkness in distant aeons of time, long before mankind walked the earth, so that in human experience evil was no separate supernatural power, but the simple negation of good. That philosophy enabled the actions of man to assist the purposes of benevolent divinity.

The cult of Mithras in the western provinces principally attracted army officers and warrant officers, government officials and businessmen in large cities. Its temples are virtually unknown outside army premises and the bigger towns. A small, but well-furnished Mithraic temple, excavated by the Walbrook crossing in London conforms to the normal pattern; an oblong building measuring 58 feet by 26 feet, with an apse at the western end, furnished with altars and with a square baptismal water tank, was divided into a nave and two narrow aisles. The aisles were fitted with timber seating, that cannot easily have accommodated a congregation of more than fifty or sixty persons.[24] The severe mysteries of the cult were administered by officers, named 'the Raven', or after other birds and animals, who wore headdresses representing the power and menace of the animal concerned. The numbers of each Mithraic lodge were small, and competition for admission was keen among the classes whom the cult attracted. Benefits of membership were substantial, for members owed each other personal loyalties and favour in all human activities no less binding than those which unite Freemasons in modern society; the favours were worth having, for many Mithraic brethren held high military or civil office, or controlled considerable commercial enterprises, and were able to help or hinder the careers of many men.

Derivative extensions of Mithraic belief were prominent in the fourth century. The extravagant taste of the very rich sought purification through washing in the blood of the bull, symbolically slain by the hand of Mithras. Great magnates, arrayed in ceremonial white robes, entered a deep, wide trench; a bull was tethered above it, so that when its throat was slit, its blood gushed over the person and the raiment of worship. Very many inscriptions of the heads of the greatest families in the aristocracy of Rome proudly proclaim their performance of this rite, termed the *taurobolium*. Earlier ceremonies of baptism in animal blood had been content to sprinkle the initiate with sacred blood; and at all times the bull was an expensive beast, within the reach only of wealthy worshippers; poorer men found initiation through the cheaper blood of a lamb or a cock.

The extravagance of the *taurobolium* developed only after the dominance of Christianity. Christianity was the religion nurtured and bred by subjects of the Roman empire; and is the only major religion that has been fashioned by poor men in conscious opposition to the rich. For nearly two centuries, it was confined to the Greek-speaking population of, and from, the eastern provinces, strongest in towns, especially in the largest towns and in those where Roman influence was greatest. Its founders were conscious that their religion was Roman. The establishment of the monarchy of Augustus made the world one, and sought a single religion to unite it; the hierarchy of the city gods of antiquity failed to bind men together, and philosophical attempts to argue that all gods were differing manifestations of a single supreme divinity were intellectual fancies that did not fire the imagination of large populations. The architect of the Christian Church, Paul of Tarsus, understood the trend of his times; a Hebrew to the Hebrews, a Greek to the Greeks, a Roman to the Romans, he held that God had made the world one in order that the faith of Christ might prevail, and other early Christian leaders observed the empirical truth that the new possibilities of safe travel throughout the empire, secured by the government of Augustus, made the spread of their religion possible.

Christianity inherited and adapted the externals of the mystery religions – initiation, ceremony and rewards hereafter. Baptism was by water, but the symbol of washing in the blood of the lamb was carried over into Christian idiom. But the content of the new religion was wholly different. It promised imminent release from the evils of the world, and practised its principles in the immediate present. The afterlife was not a distant Elysium where virtuous shades might idle in blissful eternity. It was to be a total transformation of the physical and spiritual substance of the present world, achieved by divine intervention, as soon as men had made the world ready for the second coming of Christ; and to St Paul the second coming was but a few years hence, to catch up 'those of us who are yet alive'. The visible promise was foreshadowed by the conduct of Christian communities. All other poor men's associations observed respect for rank; among the Christians alone the president, chairman or leader of a local association could be and often was a slave, presiding over free men. Early tracts denounced the danger of subservience to men of rank, forbade Christians to have dealings with wicked exploiters who earn their living by the sweat of other men, and explained why and how it was impossible for a rich man to be a true Christian or take his place in the Christian world, unless he renounce his riches. Christian leaders forbade resistance to established authority or piecemeal reform of existing society; their belief rested on the immediate advent of a wholly reformed world, where justice and human kindness altogether prevailed.

Christianity did not make a significant impression upon the west until the last years of the second century, when severe political disturbance overthrew the long serenity of Roman society. Until then, all known Christian leaders and bishops, even in Rome and in Gaul, were Greek speaking, and the hostility they aroused included a substantial element of dislike of the foreign, and of the Greek traders and moneylenders of the cities, among whom Christianity spread. The first Latin Christians are recorded in the same generation, in Africa and in Britain, though they doubtless had other unrecorded fellows in Spain, Gaul and Italy. The first African Christians are reported in a trial in 189; a few years later the first writings of the lawyer Tertullian of Carthage were published, the earliest Latin Christian writer, whose keen thinking fashioned the doctrine of the Trinity; and in the early 190s an African, Victor, was chosen as the first Latin-speaking bishop of Rome.

Christianity made converts quickly. Within twenty years of its earliest record in Africa, an African Christian Congress assembled some seventy bishops. In Rome, two political leaders, highly placed at court, were acknowledged Christians. Early western Christianity had none of the poor man's origins of the Greek congregations; its leaders from the beginning included professional men and government officials, and the earliest known Latin Christian martyr of the European provinces, Alban, tried and executed in 209, was a young man of good family in Verulamium, whose expectations should have led to public office and the city council if he had conformed to normal convention.[25] Latin Christianity long maintained its principal appeal to men of standing. In the middle of the third century Cyprian of Carthage protested that imperial procurators should not serve as bishops, since they had not the time to discharge the office. By the 270s some Italian cities had laid out Christian cemeteries, whose tombstones honour some men who were both Roman knights and Christian bishops.

The blend of eastern poor men's Christianity and the outlook of respectable Latin Romans gave the Christian religion its strength and flexibility; and helped to find a due position for men of substance in the Christian communities of the Greek lands. The adherence of many men of standing enabled Christianity to become the religion of the Roman government in the early fourth century; the legacy of its formative years prevented it from becoming only the religion of rulers, like the pagan religion it superseded. But for long it had little popular appeal in the Gallic provinces and Britain. It was everywhere a religion of the towns, and remained urban so long that the Latin word for countrymen, *pagani*, became synonymous with non-Christian. It won significant support in the third century in Provence, as in Italy; but in the civil provinces of the Three Gauls, north of the Massif Central and west of the Rhineland, not more than nine Christian communities are known to have existed before Christianity became the religion of government. Even in the provincial capital of Tours, there was no bishop till 340, no church until the 350s. In the Gauls, the strength of Christianity lay in the Rhineland, at Trier, where emperors frequently resided, and in other towns where government officials and military personnel were numerous.

A single Christian symbol, the chi-rho monogram, is at present the only archaeological witness of Christianity in Roman London. But in 314, two years after the Christian emperor Constantine had mastered Rome, the bishop of London, Restitutus, attended a church council at Arles, together with the bishops of York and Lincoln, and the representative of a fourth bishop, probably of Cirencester. They may well have been provincial metropolitans.[26] London was a major centre of government, larger than any Rhineland city except the imperial capital of Trier. The religious changes that worked upon the minds of men in comparable cities cannot have passed London by; and London must therefore be classed with Trier, Mainz and other administrative centres, among the few northern towns that contained in the third century a substantial

Christian community, large enough and rich enough to afford a church building.

The site of the church has not been discovered. One consideration hints at a possible location. In most major cities of Britain, where new cathedral churches were established in later centuries by the English, they were built in the centre of the town, upon and above the ruins of the principal administrative buildings of the Roman government, as at York and Lincoln. In Europe, when the principal church was not built in the Roman town centre, a frequent reason is that it is a reconstruction of a church built in Roman times; for when churches were founded while the Roman city was still in full vigour, the town centre was still in use, and churches must be built elsewhere. In London, St Paul's Cathedral is far from the Roman centre on Cornhill, across the Walbrook on Ludgate Hill. One possible explanation of its position is that it was built while the Roman basilica and forum were still frequented, upon the most suitable site that Christians of the third or fourth century could acquire. There is, however, an alternative possibility. St Paul's is said to have been founded by an English king about the year 600; such traditions normally record the first English foundation, for the English looked back to the rights and titles conferred by their own kings, and some sites said to have been founded by English kings are known to have been renewals and re-foundations of older churches, whose earlier history was unknown to the English and without interest to them. The first English church was located for the convenience of the English, and the probable earliest centre of English government was within the Cripplegate fort, whose early English church was dedicated to St Alban; but it may be that St Paul's also was first built by the English, upon a site where no church had stood before, for purely English reasons. Whether an earlier church stood there or not could only be determined if the foundations of the modern church were exposed and examined; but even if they were, it is more than likely that the builders of the medieval and the seventeenth centuries destroyed whatever traces of earlier buildings remained.

Whatever its location, the evidence for Christianity in London argues that a Christian building was added to the temples of older Roman religions in London during the third or fourth century. The discovery and excavation of its site would demonstrate its scale, and perhaps show something of the stages of its growth. But Christianity did not immediately abolish the old religions; they remained fully legal until the end of the fourth century, with periods of decline and revival in their use; and at least in the countryside, some temples lingered longer, for the legislation that banned the old gods took long to enforce in practice, and the central government of the empire ceased to rule Britain within twenty years of the enactment of the new laws, before they had had time to take full effect. Christianity expanded at an uneven pace over several centuries; in third-century London it was a new faith, still relatively unimportant, as yet no serious challenge to the many temples that met the personal, spiritual and public needs of Londoners.

Chapter 12

Sport and Leisure

RELIGION WAS ONE important preoccupation of the minds of men, when they were not concerned with earning their daily bread and caring for their families. Temple ceremonies were important occasions at festivals and public holidays. So was sport and public entertainment. Until the present, no human society has evinced such intense attachment to public sport as the Roman empire. The athletic contests of the Greeks chiefly catered for the interest of the leisured classes, but outstanding sportsmen were popular heroes to the poorest Romans; pictures and mementoes of named sportsmen were widely sold; the fortunes of celebrated teams excited passionate, partisan supporters in the cheapest taverns; enormous crowds watched and applauded, and pressed for more frequent and more splendid sporting occasions in each generation. The principal forms of organized public sport were the diverse presentations of the theatrical stage, the horse races, and numerous sports of the sanded arena, or amphitheatre. All were in principle paid for by newly elected city magistrates; but growing public interest tended to demand more than ambitious political leaders could afford to pay. The imperial government and city governments repeatedly strove to keep down the cost of sport; and city councils were frequently obliged to supplement the disbursements of individuals. The relevant regulations of one Spanish town survive; they prescribe that at the duumviral games, each duumvir shall spend 2,000 sestertii (500 denarii) and the city treasury shall provide a like amount, the city half as much.[1] The figures provided, 14,000 sestertii, were the equivalent of nearly 4,000 daily labourers' wages at second-century rates, and this, in a small town; they date to the time of Julius Caesar, and the expense of games much increased in succeeding centuries. The cost of the London magistrates' games is unlikely to have been much under the equivalent of 80,000 labourers' day wages, £100,000 on the scale of living indicated by the edict of Diocletian, and were supplemented by the much more costly entertainment provided at the annual meeting of the Provincial Assembly, probably in the first days of January, and by games in honour of the birthday of Augustus, of the reigning emperor, and on the anniversaries of various important events in the history of the empire, of the province of Britain and of the city of London.

The principal centres of entertainment were the theatre, the race-course, or stadium, and the amphitheatre. Their locations in London are not known. The two well-excavated theatres of Britain at Verulamium and Canterbury were large, and, as in other cities of the empire, were built near to the town centre. Since theatres were semi-circular in shape, their curve covering sometimes a little more, sometimes a little less than a mathematical half circle, the recognizable foundation that remains is commonly a curving wall. Only one substantial curved wall that might have been a theatre is yet known in London, in Friday Street, west of the Walbrook and not far from the river (Merrifield 99); but the radius that its probable curvature suggests would have made its extension unduly large, and the curved wall may have served other purposes.

In Rome itself the principal stadium, the Circus Maximus, was laid out on the edge of the earliest city, allegedly in the sixth century BC, and in the empire was rebuilt, its walls and turning points built of stone, still preserved and restored for the modern visitor to view. But elsewhere in Italy and in the provinces such structures, long thin oblongs with semi-circular ends, are very rare. The probable reason is that they were normally marked by timber fencing, and by timber stands and seating, as are modern racecourses. The long stadium, or circus, might have lain upon any of the areas within the walls where excavation has shown only undisturbed natural gravel, or in areas whose Roman structures are poorly reported; or it may have been placed much further out from the centre, beyond the area that was ultimately walled, and there may well have been more than one circus or stadium.

The nature and the function of Roman sport and of the stadium has often been misrepresented by loose quotation of the cheap and silly sneer of one reactionary Roman, Juvenal, who in the late first century grumbled that the Roman populace was corrupted by *panem et circenses*, often rendered as 'bread and circuses'. The sneer was cheap in its own day, for the grain of truth that underlies it is no more than one detailed aspect of the fundamental Roman conception that stable government must be government by consent, and that consent cannot be expected unless the community is tolerably fed and housed, and provided with normal civic amenities; the epigram consciously and deliberately ignored the massive achievement of the empire it attacked. Its silliness is emphasized by its modern mistranslation, for the proper context of the cheap bread that angered some conservative opinion is that which modern jargon terms a food subsidy, and the entertainment provided in the Roman Circus had nothing to do with the performances normal in a modern circus; nor is the alternative translation 'games', with overtones of hungry lions and dying gladiators, any less misleading. The proper translation of the Latin word *ludi* is sport rather than games.

The circus or stadium was the place where athletic contests were held; but as in other societies, athletics had somewhat less appeal than racing and team contests. Horse-racing was the most prominent popular sport in the Roman world, and the principal function of the circus, its proper translation, is a racecourse. The horses were not ridden, but driven, with the driver standing on a light car or chariot harnessed to four horses, little heavier than the trotting-car of more recent times. Riding races, with a light jockey mounted, at first on a point-to-point course, were a novel innovation of the sixth-century British, and originally most commonly the sport of gentlemen amateurs. But the professional racing drivers of the circus were among the most celebrated and highest-paid Romans. Their fame induced their supporters to erect elaborate memorials in their honour, usually on their retirement or death, recording their successes in minute detail; and a number of these memorials survive, or have been recorded.

Much of the technical detail is obscure, but enough is intelligible to depict the nature and scale of the races. For centuries four teams competed, named the Reds, the Whites, the Greens and the Blues. In the simplest races, one chariot from each team competed, in the most important, four, giving sixteen on the course together. Some inscriptions record the names and colours of the finest thoroughbreds, and several report the prize money earned. The figures are given in sestertii, the quarter denarius that was the currency of the early empire; and their value is set between the extremes of current incomes, that varied between the second-century labourers' wages of 1,000 to 1,200 sestertii and the salary of the highest-paid political appointment in the empire, the million a year earned by the consular proconsul of Asia or Africa. The highest prize money for an individual race was 50,000.

Drivers drove for one team only at any given period; but in the second-century most of the recorded drivers were transferred during their career from one team to another, and some rode for all four teams at different stages in their careers. Transfers developed as more and more money was poured into the racing teams; for the number of race meetings increased, rising astronomically in the middle years of the second century, as the Flavian and Antonine impetus to city amenities reached maturity. In the early first century Scirtus drove for the Whites for a little over twelve years, from AD 13 to 25, and drove for no other team. His memorial lists the races in each year in which he was placed among the first three, and proudly acclaims 7 wins, all in his first five years, and a total of 110 places. Half a century later, another driver recorded three times as many places, including 47 wins, together with 26 placings in pair-in-hand races. The portion of the stone that recorded the length of his career is missing, but the chief reason for the larger figures is plainly that there were more races in which he could compete, for later figures list their rising number.

Crescens also raced for one team alone, the Greens. He first drove on 8 November 115, at the age of thirteen, and his last race was on 1 August 124. In nine years he drove in 686 races, with 288 placings, including 47 wins. His victories averaged five a year, where Scirtus had averaged one win in each two years; though he may have been more successful, he was not ten times more successful. He earned more than a million and a half sestertii in prize money. Probably a few years later, P. Aelius Gutta Calpurnianus raced for all four teams, winning 1,127 races; the money earned from major races only, with prizes of 30,000 and upwards, totalled over a million for the Blues and Greens alone, and came from thirty of his victories. His other 1,100 odd prizes were each of smaller sums, but together plainly totalled many millions.

Gutta had won more than a thousand races, and public opinion granted special favour and a special name to the few drivers who equalled or surpassed him. They were known as the *milliarii*, the thousanders. Their numbers, like the frequency of races and the size of expenditure, increased quickly in the next few decades, under Hadrian and Pius. Most famous among them was C. Appuleius Diocles, a Lusitanian, from the region that is now Portugal. His triumphs were recorded, probably by his colleagues on his retirement, in a huge monument on the Vatican, whose inscription contained nearly a thousand words. He raced for twenty-four years, beginning at the age of eighteen, from 122 to 146, and ended as chief driver of the Reds, after racing earlier for the other teams in turn. He took part in 4,257 races and won 1,462 of them; and the latter part of the inscription quotes from a racing record book, listing more than a dozen other notable thousanders of the day, admitting that one of them had surpassed Diocles' record by five wins, but arguing that Diocles' victories were more valuable, and more skilled. Diocles' prize money amounted to the immense sum of nearly thirty-six millions.[2]

Diocles won his first race in the year that Crescens died. His career lasted twice as long, but he drove in six times as many races, and his prize money was more than twenty times as great. He averaged 177 races a year, and 61 wins a year; Crescens had made a boast of 77 races and 5 wins a year, and Scirtus, 120 years earlier, had been proud of one win every two years. Diocles' annual average prize money totalled about a million and a half sestertii, twenty times as much as Crescens' average, one and a half times the annual salary of the most highly paid state appointment in the empire; since he raced two years before he won a race, the prizes of his peak years were clearly far greater.

The prizes went to the teams, who maintained a large establishment of grooms, cartwrights and many other craftsmen and labourers. The percentage that went to the successful driver is not recorded, but the sums he received were plainly very large. Juvenal complained that in his day, half a century before the triumphs of Diocles, one Red driver had an income a hundred times greater than a barrister, and that was at a time when a lifetime's prize money was hardly more than five per cent of Diocles'. Diocles himself was honoured in his old age, or after his death, at a shrine dedicated to Fortune by his children at Praeneste, a fashionable and expensive commuting suburb twenty miles from Rome. Evidently he was able to purchase a house there on his retirement, and place his children among the well-to-do classes who could afford to finance public worship.

The teams had many drivers, and though Diocles earned record sums, he was but one among many drivers whose combined prize money clearly gave each team a total income of very many millions. Hundreds of thousands of persons were devoted supporters of each team, and their power made them a political force. On three or four occasions in six centuries, the rivalries of team supporters erupted into serious political riots, one of which all but dethroned a powerful emperor. At other times their pressures were less marked, but they tended to favour contrasting ideologies and party groupings. The Greens tended to attract radicals and dissenters, and almost all the emperors who were disliked by the aristocracy and popular among the urban plebs received Green support, and officially proclaimed themselves Green partisans. The practical effect of such alignments between sporting teams and differing ideologies is impossible to assess or explain in a vanished society, for even in a living society it is not easy to explain the actual impact upon the thought and action of men of such equations between sport and belief, as in Glasgow, where one of the principal football teams is traditionally

Catholic, the other traditionally Protestant. It is equally easy to assert that the consequences are negligible, or that they are considerable; but it is not easy to explain or describe them.[3]

The energies of the teams were centred in Rome, but their branches extended into the provinces, and a few objects attest their existence in Britain. In the nature of the excitements that racing involved, team support was proportionately strongest in the largest towns. The stadium of London and the appeal of the teams is likely to have been more important than in the state capitals. London was a tenth of the size of Rome, but the frequency of races and the size of the sums involved are likely to have been much less than a tenth of the figures recorded from Rome, their impact correspondingly less. But it is also probable that the racecourses of London and other provincial cities also shared in the sharp and sudden increase in organized public sport in the middle years of the second century. Such phenomena may be observed, but not explained. Even in our present society, where the number of football matches played and the sums expended annually have much increased in the last fifteen or twenty years, a dozen experts will offer a dozen different reasons for the increase.

The chief function of the arena was the display of startling spectacles of all kinds. The arena or amphitheatre was necessarily a large building; the most imposing of all, the Colosseum in Rome, had a seating capacity of at least 50,000. The architectural problems of providing large crowds with a clear view of a central space were considerable, and a series of disasters early taught that timber amphitheatres were dangerous. They were therefore almost always built of stone in the empire. Their size and material make them more easily recognizable than racecourses or theatres, and their shape made them harder for later ages to dismantle. They therefore remain in very large numbers, enough to warrant the inference that almost every town of any size possessed its arena. They have been located at many of the state capitals in Britain, but not yet at London. Because of the large space they required, they were commonly built well away from city centres, usually so far away that when towns were walled, the walls were sited between the town and the arena. No record of the ruins of the arena has been observed in accounts of medieval London, or in early maps; it may well, therefore, have lain in a district that was built upon early in the Middle Ages, not far from the north-eastern or the western walls.

The spectacles included blood sports, offensive to some men in all ages. Contests between animals and men are far older than the Romans, and have survived in Mediterranean lands, notably Spain, into the present; fights to the death between animal and animal lasted long even in the north, most commonly between bears and dogs in the Middle Ages, and more recently between cocks. The large spectacular animals normally available in Europe are the bull, and, until recent centuries, the bear; the Roman conquest of Africa and Egypt made exotic non-European animals readily available in the city of Rome as long as Roman power endured. Mostly such animals were paraded for display at festivals, and caged out of sight between, only occasionally kept in zoological gardens for continuing public view. The rarer varieties then disappeared; no hippopotamus was seen in Europe between the middle of the fourth century and the middle of the nineteenth. Some of these animals, notably lions and other great cats, provided suitable combat displays, occasionally against one another, more often against men. But it was very rare for non-European animals to be seen in western Europe except in or near Rome.

In the Roman empire, as in other societies, the combat of men and animals for sport aroused disgust, and also exerted a compelling fascination. Then as now, attitudes varied between extremes, on two different levels. The hunting of animals in their natural environment seemed proper to men of means who owned horses and rights over woodland and moor, though most of those who rode could only watch the actual encounter between the animal and the man or dog who killed it; but the Roman *venatio*, the artificial hunting of the arena, allowed a wide plebeian public to share the excitement. On another level, combats varied from those in which the animal had no chance of survival to those in which the man had no chance; halfway between lie the bull fights of modern Provence, where neither man nor animal is seriously hurt, where the men are amateurs and the veteran bull retires to an honoured old age in a meadow. More popular in Roman times and modern Spain is the combat where the animal is almost always killed, but the man runs an appreciable risk.

The striking Roman extension of the blood sport was the mortal combat of man and man. The private combat of the duel was tolerated into quite recent times, but the public fights of the professional gladiators were the peculiar sport of the Roman amphitheatre.[4] Successful gladiators were second to racing drivers in popular acclaim; and their prominence prevented the less brutal sport of boxing from attracting wide interest and huge investment. But the profession of the gladiator was differently regarded and differently rewarded from that of the racing driver. Relatively few were freemen, most were provincial *peregrini*, foreign barbarians or slaves. Their trade was dangerous, and many died young; at Verona, Glauco fell in his eighth fight, aged 23, Pardo in his eleventh, aged 27. But others lived on to retire. In Sicily the Syrian Flamma died at 30 after 34 fights; he won 21 of them, and emerged alive from the other 13. In Rome, Felix, a Tungrian from the low countries, died at 45, after receiving Roman citizenship from Trajan. Retirement was early, and very few are known to have fought after they were 30; but many retired gladiators served on as managers, trainers and inspectors, dying at 50 or 60, and one reached the age of 98. Nevertheless the risk of death in defeat was high, and many tombstones of gladiators who died young go out of their way to emphasize that they were not killed in combat. One was killed 'by destiny, not by a man', another 'by robbers', a third 'in (or by) medicine'.

The figures of the age of the gladiator and of the numbers of combats, indicate that the trained professional normally fought no more than two or three times a year at most, in contrast with the drivers, who raced hundreds of times in each year. The difference determined the financing of the sport and caused its offensive extensions. The principal guide to the costs and wages is the law of 177, limiting expenses.[5] Ordinary gladiators received a labourer's wage, of 1,000 to 2,000 sestertii; the great majority of specialized performers received between 3,000 and 5,000; a few of the most outstanding might receive 15,000. The men needed long periods of training, with daily exercise, for relatively rare appearances. In Rome, several thousand were maintained in the gladiators' barracks, but elsewhere companies much smaller in size commonly travelled from city to city; an advertisement painted on the walls of Pompeii gave notice of a display by thirty pairs.

The expense in wages, training staff and maintenance was high in relation to the appearance of each gladiator. On special occasions the public expected extravagant, spectacular display in all branches of sport; the managers of gladiatorial troops had no wish to lose the lives of trained men, but an ill-tempered crowd cost lives, for when a victor had his opponent at his mercy, the decision to kill him or spare his life commonly rested with the presiding officer of the day, and the shouts of the audience were the main pressure that determined his decision. The numbers of professional gladiators were therefore augmented by the practice of sentencing condemned criminals, and sometimes prisoners of war, to fight as gladiators; and the practice of sentencing criminals to fight men in the arena led to their condemnation to fight beasts, with feeble arms or none at all, since the sentence was execution.

These bloody extensions aroused nauseated protest, and also excited the twisted emotions that the suffering of animals and men arouse at all times. Controversy on blood sports persisted for centuries; in the first century BC Varro condemned the cruelty and barbarism of the slaughter; Cicero admitted the sincerity of such sentiments, and agreed that the bloodshed gave no pleasure to a man of refinement, but pleaded that the sight trained men's fortitude in the face of pain and death. In the middle of the first century AD Seneca treated the public executions as light entertainment, but in his old age condemned the inhumanity of killing men for sport; but at the end of the century the polished letters of Pliny echoed the conventional justification of Cicero. In the second century the philosophic emperor Marcus Aurelius found the spectacles tedious, but attended because the public expected his appearance. Repugnance was always there, but was curbed by the deep emotions aroused by centuries of custom. Opposition to the killing prevailed only as Christianity became all powerful, and even then with difficulty. The conflicting pulls upon men's minds are sharply illustrated in the experience of Saint Augustine at the end of the fourth century. When he was persuaded to visit the arena and see for himself its hideous brutality, he was at first nauseated, but immediately thereafter appalled to recognize in himself the mounting excitement of the blood lust, and therewith to understand the hold of the contests upon the spectators. But the changing attitudes that worked upon him were also spreading widely, so that before the end of the century Christian pressure succeeded in banning the performances of gladiators, as well as the execution of criminals in the arena, though the animal hunts long continued.

Gladiators were plentiful in the provinces, as in Rome. One inscription refers to their recruitment in Britain,[6] and in Britain they have left several traces; the names of a gladiator and a dancing girl were signed upon a cup at Leicester; a couple of elaborately decorated vases show gladiators, and one of them adds their names; several statuettes and mosaics represent them.[7] Travelling troupes toured the amphitheatres of Britain, and it is possible that a permanent school was maintained in London. There the arena displays necessarily also included animal hunts, doubtless normally of bears, boars and bulls, with perhaps the exhibition of a non-European animal on rare and special occasions. The greater displays are likely to have been augmented by the execution of criminals; and such occasions also commonly included colourful exhibitions in daylight, torchlight displays after dark, and other spectacles that involved no contest, together with such boxing, wrestling and athletic contests as were not held in the stadium.

The third main public entertainment was the theatre. Its costs were far less than those of the races and the arena, and its audience smaller; the three known theatres of imperial Rome between them accommodated a considerably smaller audience than the Colosseum, and the known theatres of Gaul and Britain had a smaller seating capacity than the amphitheatres. The Roman stage adapted and continued the theatrical traditions of the Greeks. Very few texts of plays survive, but many titles and themes are known. There was some performance of translations or Roman adaptations of Greek tragedy, but variations of the New Comedy of Menander were commoner; their manner and themes are best known through their continuation in Italy, where they provided the model for the English Elizabethan comedy. But the popular plays most often played were the bedroom farces termed *atellanae*. No regular censorship existed, and polite opinion stridently condemned the vulgarity and obscenity of the stage. State intervention occasionally banned performances when, for short periods, producers staged nude shows, sometimes involving public copulation on the stage; the profession of an actress was popularly supposed to entail a loose morality, and polite writers looked unkindly upon actresses who married wealthy patrons or lived with them.

The early Roman empire made one lasting addition to the repertoire of the stage, the musical dance, termed pantomime in antiquity, whose modern survivals are the ballet and the opera. Its innovators, in the time of Augustus, were Pylades, from Cilicia in Asia Minor, and the Egyptian Bathyllus; a succession of later artists took their names, and also the names of the most celebrated performers who developed their traditions, Paris in Nero's time, Apolaustus under Trajan, and others. Pylades elaborated tragic themes, Bathyllus comic themes, but Pylades' tragic tradition soon predominated. The earliest forms of the new art were the dances and gestures of a single silent performer, accompanied by one or more flautists and by a narrator. Later other dancers were added to the single star, and elaborate choreography evolved; the vocal accompaniment was extended from one singer to a chorus, sometimes with soloists, from a single speaker to two or three reading parts, and a full orchestra was added to the original flutes, sometimes dispensing with chorus or speakers. The themes were normally well-known mythological stories, and the interest of the audience concentrated upon the dancer's skill and the producer's design. Keenly critical audiences brought fame and fortune to the most pleasing performers, and condemned the unsuccessful to poverty and oblivion. The magic of the pantomime is brilliantly depicted in an essay of Lucian's, describing one awe-inspiring performance of a ballet of the madness of Ajax; the dancer so thoroughly threw himself into his part that he himself became frenzied, and Lucian describes the unease of the audience as they began to realize that the performance had passed from the acting of lunatic possession to its reality.[8]

Great dancers toured the provinces. One, honoured at Ostia, had performed at festivals in Syria, Arabia and Africa as well as in Italy.[9] Outstanding performers were more highly rewarded than the greatest of race drivers. They were not only enabled to retire to pleasant surburban towns about the city, but several of them were chosen as councillors and magistrates of important cities, despite their freedman origin. Their social distinction matched that accorded to distinguished athletes, for the long traditions of the Greek world regarded athletics as a proper occupation for men of breeding; but the wealth and honours of the great dancers far exceeded the pensions voted to athletes in the cities of the eastern provinces, and placed them above the humbler status of ordinary stage actors.

The famous performers are remembered because they performed in Rome, and received memorials in Italy, where inscriptions of all kinds are very numerous. There is almost no record of them in the western provinces, beyond the existence of large numbers of provincial theatres. Like the cities they served, they were modelled on the customs of Rome and Italy, and the performances played upon their stages were plainly also those that pleased the public in the capital. Neither stars nor lesser actors could expect the same scale of reward, even proportionately, as those who won success in Rome; but the orchestral dance, the classical drama and bawdy comedy were equally the mainstays of the provincial theatre, in London as in other cities.

Public entertainment comprehended the whole of the exhibitions of the racecourse, the arena and the theatre. The range of spectacles in a city of moderate size is outlined in the memorial of a duumvir of Pompeii, whose presentation included bulls, bull-fighters and bull-prickers, boars and bears, boxers and wrestlers, athletes and gladiators, arena hunts, comedies, and all varieties of mime, with a Pylades;[10] and that of a Sicilian magistrate, near to the exotic plants and animals of Africa, who provided 'the delights of the theatre and the laughs' and also 'a herbarium and numerous eastern animals'.[11] The scale of the Ostia magistrate's entertainment is close to that which a Roman public expected from a magistrate of London.

Organized public sport, and entertainment on public holidays, was more important in the life of the towns of the Roman empire than of almost any other known society. Gladiators, racing drivers and dancers were public heroes, their pictures sold and exhibited everywhere, the merits of individuals and teams debated and warmly championed in great men's houses and in taverns. But these were not the only opportunities for recreation and leisure. Other sports and other gatherings centred upon the baths. Roman convention also placed a higher value on cleanliness and physical fitness than most other societies. Men of all classes took the right to a daily bath for granted, and much else besides washing centred on the baths. The form of the bath is preserved by what is now known as a Turkish bath, for the Turks inherited and maintained the Roman custom when they mastered eastern Rome. After exercise, the bather entered a hot steam bath, smeared his body with oil, and an attendant scraped it off with a shaped tool termed a *strigil*, together with the dirt that adhered to it. Thereafter the bather was acclimatized, refreshed and restored through a warm room and a cold plunge. The modern bather is commonly surprised, if he proceeds from a normal modern warm bathtub to a Turkish bath, to observe the dirt that remains for the steam to remove; and is driven to acknowledge that by Roman standards modern men are dirty folk. They are also in poorer physical shape; for the regular exercise that Roman practice enforced upon entire populations is nowadays matched only by a few, and for most of them only at certain ages.

Baths were of two kinds, ordinary baths termed *balnea* and elaborate establishments called *thermae*, equipped with ample exercise halls, ball courts and gymnasia, and with lounges for drinking and for conversation. The large establishments were relatively few. Rome had some eight hundred *balnea* and a dozen *thermae*; the ruins of some of them, notably of the *thermae* of Caracalla and of Diocletian, are among the most impressive memorials of antiquity. The numbers of baths was necessarily related to the population of each city, and Londoners might therefore expect two or three *thermae* and some scores of *balnea*. Since the remains of bath buildings and the characteristic shape of the strigil are easily identified, the location of five probable or possible *balnea* (e.g. Merrifield 86, 182, 233, 314, 348) are recognizable, and of two *thermae*, at Huggin Hill and Cheapside (Merrifield 121 and 55) (Plate 13 and Map 10).[12]

The *balnea* consisted of little but a bath tank and hot room, with a simple yard for exercise, or opportunities to use adjoining premises. Often they occupied all or part of the ground floor of a residential building; Seneca complained of the discomfort of living, in his youth, in a flat above a bath house, where he was constantly distracted by the noise, the shouts and obscene language of the plebeian bathers, their grunts as they exercised, and the strident voice of the scorer who cried the points of the ball players.[13]

The *thermae* provided professional instructors in gymnastics, boxing, weight-lifting and other exercises. Ball games were played professionally at the *thermae*, and by amateurs at *thermae*, *balnea* and recognized courts, as well as in the streets, where players found themselves liable for damages caused in play not in a recognized court. The rules and nature of the ball games are not known. Two principal kinds of ball were used: a large padded ball, as large or larger than a football, that could be used as a punchball when suspended in a sling, or thrown, perhaps in a way allied to basketball, or over a net, and a small ball, the *pila*, apparently of approximately the size of a tennis ball or cricket ball. The small ball was commonest. It was played either by individuals or by teams; it was served, caught, thrown and returned, and sometimes 'expelled'. In some forms of the game, the players may have worn some kind of glove or extension to the arm. It is possible that the Basque game of pelota, the ancestor of English fives, itself descends from the Roman *pila*; in pelota the players wear a long basket-extension to the arm, catch a ball of about the size and hardness of a cricket ball as it bounces off a wall above a line, and slam it back from the basket with terrifying force, so that a ball that leaves the court can do considerable damage.

The technical language that refers to the game indicates that there were many different kinds of small ball games, and suggests that they are likely to have differed from each other as much as indoor and lawn tennis, or fives and squash, differ from each other today. They were games for gentlemen; and though professionals were proud of their achievement, they received little of the high rewards of the competitors in the main public sports. One of Hadrian's freedmen boasted of himself as 'the greatest of all ball players', and a contemporary, Ursus, in a verse inscription, claimed to be the first Roman citizen 'to play properly with glass balls with my players'. The meaning and use of 'glass balls' is not known; but he performed 'in the *thermae* of Trajan, of Agrippa and Titus, and often of Nero', receiving 'loud public applause', and the congratulations of other ball players. In old age he was 'a gay and laughing ball-player', whose successes had lasted since AD 126, which was evidently long before the inscription was erected.[14]

Some other games were played in more open spaces. A poorly executed clay relief-mould from the midlands of Britain shows a player holding what looks like a walking-stick, with the crook in the air, and two balls in his hand, with one more served into the air.[15] The game might be the common ancestor of golf, hockey and cricket. But there is no reference to an equivalent of football, though it is not easy to believe that at least the unorganized kicking of balls without set rules escaped the imagination of Roman boys.

For men of means, sport and exercise accompanied leisure at the *thermae*. There men and women met, talked and drank. Poorer men frequented taverns and eating houses. They were numerous and specialized. The word *taberna* meant a shop in general, but was often used peculiarly of shops that sold wine; the *caupona* sold drink alone, the *popina* was a cheap restaurant or café selling food, though no laws prevented the sale of drink anywhere at any time. In Italy and other sunny lands, the common drink of all classes was wine, and wine was both imported into Britain, and made in Britain from British vineyards. But, since the climate was not greatly different from the modern British climate, native wine cannot have rated highly; and, especially in the third and fourth centuries, the commonest drinking vessels are of pint or quart size, more fit for drinking beer than wine. It is therefore probable that most of the taverns of Roman London sold more beer and cider than wine. Their structure is not known; but the surviving taverns of Italy, at Ostia and elsewhere, are constructed on the general pattern of most past and present drinking houses, somewhat closer to the French *café* or *bistro* than the English public house, but similar to both. The principal feature is a long L-shaped bar or counter, with its closed end touching the party wall and facing the street. In Ostia, wine jars were placed in recesses cut into the top surface of the bar. In northern climates, barrels may have been more conveniently stowed under or behind the bar than lowered into it.

A principal pastime of the taverns, as of wealthy men at home or in the *thermae*, was gambling. The favourite form of gambling was dicing; something of the rules of Roman dicing are reported, and they were far more sophisticated than the simple modern custom of conceding victory to the highest throw. Dice were also used with various board games, that included a remote ancestor of backgammon, and other board games were played with skill alone, on the general pattern of draughts and chess. Some rough gaming pieces and boards of stone or tile remain, but they are makeshift imitations of proper wooden boards, and the exact rules and moves cannot be understood.

The business and leisure of Londoners, to and from workplace and office, to and from the baths and the inns and restaurants, involved continual movement in crowded streets. In Rome, heavy wheeled traffic was banned from the streets in day time, and many writers complain of the noisy rumble of commercial waggons at night. It is likely that similar restrictions applied to other large cities. In the streets, most men walked. But persons who could afford it were carried, in two main forms of vehicle. The *lectica* was a couch, where the passengers reclined upon cushions, and was often covered, either with loose hangings or with complete wooden coachwork; most were carried by two or four bearers, holding loose poles attached to thongs or iron rings, their ends sometimes fitted with bronze ornaments, some of which may be preserved in some of the unexplained metalwork in the London museums. Occasionally, heavy *lecticae* for two people were carried by six or eight bearers. The lighter and easier vehicle was the *sella portatoria*, portable chair. The rich kept their own; others plied for public hire.

The rich also kept carriages. Their shapes and names were as varied as those of nineteenth- and early twentieth-century Europe, before the invention of the motor car; as the meanings of the names of modern carriages have been quickly forgotten, and are to be learnt only from museums and reference books, so the construction of the Roman carriages is forgotten, and is not preserved in books and museums. Only random scraps of information survive in ancient writers; they are sufficient to indicate that one of the most popular carriages, small enough to be used on occasion in city streets, was the *essedum*, a two-wheeled car named after the light war chariots of the British that Caesar had made famous, whose reputation was perpetuated by the Flavian generals who met them in the north. Since the vehicle was British in origin, it is likely that it was the commonest passenger vehicle seen upon the streets of Roman London, as and when the laws permitted, or were ignored.

The buildings and the decorations of Roman London, the tools, ornaments, clothing and other objects recovered from its soil, are sufficient to indicate its size and scale, and to indicate the kind of city that it became in its most prosperous days. Enough is known of the life of cities that matched the scale and situation of London in the Roman empire to describe the life that was lived upon its mosaic floors, in its slums and its public buildings, and to illustrate the livelihood, the interests and the attitudes of its citizens of all classes. It was a city great and prosperous in its own day, notable among the great towns of Europe, in some respects unique. It was the home of government and the centre of trade and manufacture, its metropolitan attractions at least as invigorating as those of medieval London, of a size and energy not significantly surpassed until the time of the Tudors. In itself, it was a great city. Its impact and influence extended over the rest of Britain, and its contacts reached far into Roman Europe.

Chapter 13

Food and Work

The Feeding of London

CITIES CONSUME MANY different foodstuffs, and thrive or fail according to the ease with which thay may be obtained. The principal needs of ancient cities were corn, oil or its equivalent, and meat or fish; of these the corn supply was by far the most important, and normally the most difficult to guarantee. It presented two great difficulties. A large bulk must be sold cheaply, but it was heavy and costly to transport; and the yield of the lands upon which cities depended varied from year to year according to the harvest. Even when normal supply areas had been established, a poor crop created an immediate shortage; and at all times the fluctuating price, cheap after an abundant harvest, rising towards the next harvest, tempted corn dealers to hold back supplies until the price rose. An important officer of most cities was the *frumentarius* or his equivalent, responsible for ensuring that corn was available at the right price. Ample records emphasize his difficulties and his frequent failures; in most cities famine was an endemic evil, staggeringly expensive bread a frequent complaint, and a frequent source of disorders, since dealers often profited from famine, and the public always believed that they did.

Most great cities prospered because they had a double source of supply. They were situated in the centre of rich arable land, whose corn could be carried cheaply to the city because the distance was short; and they also lay upon the sea or a navigable river, so that corn might be carried cheaply by sea in time of need. Commonly, the availability of local corn set a positive limit to the size of the city; it could not grow beyond the capacity of its hinterland to feed it. A few exceptional cities depended almost wholly on imported corn; they included Rome, Athens and London.

London was well served by its waterways, the Thames and its tributaries; but it has no cornlands. The nearest soils that could grow corn cheaply and plentifully were the chalklands of the North Downs; in all other directions distance was prohibitive. Post towns were quickly established where the roads that radiated from Southwark first reached the chalk, at Ewell, Croydon and Crayford. In Kent the rivers Darenth and

Cray, leading to the Thames, made water transport possible; but no useful rivers flowed north from the Surrey Downs. Even these distances were considerable. Ewell and Croydon lay by the nearest edge of the chalk, and most of the easy farming land lay further still. The costs recommended in Diocletian's edict permitted 20 denarii per mile, just under a days wages, for a standard half-ton waggon load; a half ton of wheat or barley, approximately 60 modii, was retailed at 6,000 denarii, equivalent to the cost of transport over 300 miles. The freight charge even from Croydon or Ewell, 10 or 15 miles from the city, amounted to a thirtieth or a twentieth of the cost of the corn; and the actual charge from the farms that lay beyond them was much more. Government and military requirements might be met by compelling farmers to deliver corn at their own cost; and the standard economy of ancient cities endeavoured to impose money taxes upon the farmers in their territories, that the farmers might be forced to carry their produce to the city in order to earn the money to pay the taxes. But none of these expedients could come anywhere near meeting the needs of a city of the size of London.

Long experience of corn shortages and consequent political disturbance had taught the Roman government the way to forestall the danger. Nearly a hundred years before Caesar's time, Gaius Gracchus built in the city huge granaries, able to house more than a year's supply for the entire population. The government then bought corn cheap, often green, and transported it by sea. At first it was sold at an approximately economic price, equivalent to the cost of cheap purchase and sea transport; and the same price was maintained throughout the year, for the city was no longer dependent upon fluctuating harvests. But once the price of corn was determined by the calculations of government, it became the centre of political contention; radicals who sought plebeian support pressed for lower prices, and ultimately obtained a free issue of a stated amount, while conservatives sought to raise the price. Caesar and his successors closed controversy by limiting free corn to 200,000 persons.

A low, uneconomic price or a free issue, amounting to a significant food subsidy, was the outcome of the particular history of the city of Rome in the first century BC. But the principle of buying in a year's supply cheap, and carrying it by sea, was of wider application. Throughout the empire, the city of Rome depended on guaranteed corn supplies from Africa and Egypt, carried to Rome in large grain ships of 1,000 tons burthen or more. It is likely that the founders of London learnt and applied the the experience of Rome. The main waterways led to London from large and rich corn lands. The Thames and its tributaries joined Buckinghamshire and Oxfordshire, Wiltshire and the West Country, to the city; and the Lea and its tributaries had their source in the Chiltern chalks by the Icknield Way.

Though some corn could be secured by taxes imposed by the government and by the city, most had to be bought. Throughout Britain, farmers who had easy access to urban markets prospered early; they were able to afford to build rectangular stone-footed farm houses, the first villas, from the end of the first century, and to enlarge them in the ensuing centuries. Roman farming introduced one main new technique, the corn-drying flue or oven. The device is at first sight simple enough, and plainly appropriate to the uncertain climate of the Atlantic lands. But it was not normal. In the Roman empire it is, as far as is yet known, peculiar to Britain; and in lowland Britain it is peculiar to the Roman period. After the coming of the English, the corn kiln, somewhat differently constructed, persisted among independent British of the west, and was taught by them to the Irish, who remarked that it was then a peculiarity of 'the westerners, that is of the British and the Irish'. It was not imitated by the self-sufficient farming of the early English.

The precise place of the corn-drying flue in the economy of the farm cannot be determined, for the excavation of a flue does not explain what corn or how much was parched and for what purpose. But its peculiar development, in Britain during Roman rule alone, at the time when the countryside was first obliged to support a considerable urban population, argues that its purpose was to supply a commercial market. These ovens were first recognized fifty years ago, at the excavation of a large Roman country mansion at Hambledon, on the Thames, downriver from Henley, where the Thames is joined by the waters of the Fingest valley, that also supported half a dozen lesser villas.[1] The excavators then suggested that the large numbers of drying ovens at Hambledon were concerned with the feeding of London; the larger mansion was at the point where the produce of the valley reached the Thames, and might be processed and loaded onto barges for transport to the city.

Subsequent observations have confirmed the likelihood of their inference. The little river Ver flows down from Verulamium to join the Colne, a tributary of the Thames. At intervals of two miles downstream from Verulamium, prosperous Roman villas are located immediately on the banks of the river. The cause of their prosperity is evidently the same as at Hambledon. To have transported half a ton of wheat or barley from Verulamium to London down the Watling Street would have cost 400 denarii, the equivalent of the daily wages of 16 labourers. Half a ton is the weight of about 5 standard sacks of 16 stone for barley, 18 for wheat, by modern measurements. The Ver is shallow and narrow, and even in antiquity, before modern towns drained its springwaters, cannot have been much larger. It could take no barges; but among the river craft of the Roman period that have been recovered are a few dug-out canoes, hollowed from a tree trunk, sometimes with an added gunwale. Two or three such little craft could convey the corn of the Verulamium countryside to the mouth of the Colne, and thence by barge to London, by the labour of perhaps three men taking three days, rather less than the cost of land transport.

All that can be surveyed are the possibilities open to those who were responsible for ensuring the food supply of London. The evidence cannot determine what use they made of their opportunities. Yet Roman councillors and city officers are not known to have been markedly less intelligent than their successors in later ages; they were able to observe the opportunities afforded by the Thames and Lea, and they knew the manner in which the corn of Rome was organized. It is likely that they made sensible use of the means at their disposal, secured permanent options on the produce of estates served by the main rivers, possibly sometimes buying lands, and provided adequate grain warehouses in, or near to, the city.

Meat and the equivalents of oil, for washing, lighting and cooking, were considerably easier to secure than corn. Animal fat is the principal oil substitute of the north, so that meat and oil came from the same source. Demand grew, for both the army and the urban poor lived on relatively little meat in the early empire, but consumed more in the third and fourth centuries, wherever evidence is available. It has been remarked that the Roman army conquered the world upon a diet of porridge and lost it upon a diet of roast beef and pork; the truth behind the epigram is that the continuing pressure of soldier and civilian workman for better living standards in time earned a better diet, though change in diet is not a convincing explanation of the fall of Rome.

At all times, meat was easily transported by road. Cattle and sheep on the hoof could be driven to city markets wherever roads were open, and slaughtered on arrival. The wide roads that led from London were built for the benefit of government and used by traders of all sorts; they also served the needs of London's food supply. Post stations lay at convenient intervals of about eight to twelve miles along the roads: Crayford and

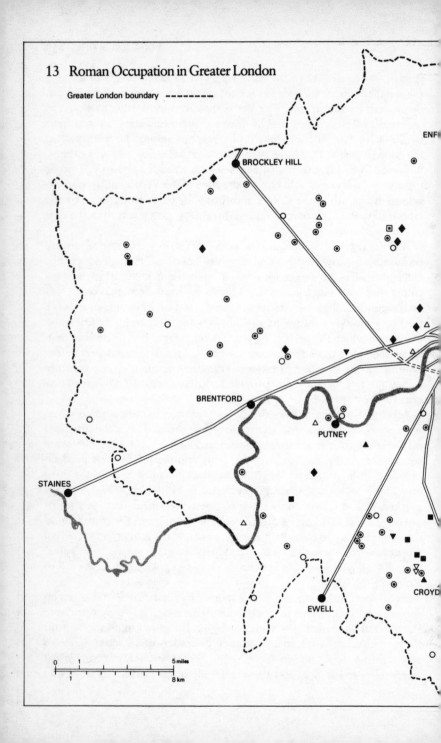

13 Roman Occupation in Greater London

Greater London boundary --------

ENFI

BROCKLEY HILL

BRENTFORD

PUTNEY

STAINES

EWELL

CROYD

0 1   5 miles
1   8 km

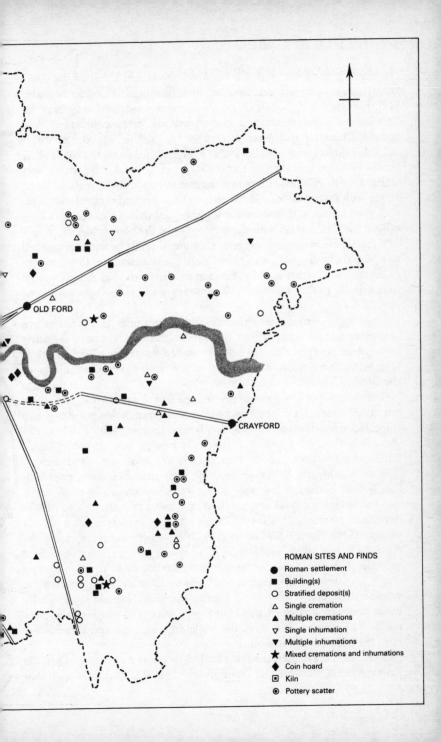

OLD FORD

CRAYFORD

ROMAN SITES AND FINDS

●	Roman settlement
■	Building(s)
○	Stratified deposit(s)
△	Single cremation
▲	Multiple cremations
▽	Single inhumation
▼	Multiple inhumations
★	Mixed cremations and inhumations
◆	Coin hoard
▣	Kiln
◉	Pottery scatter

Dartford on the Kent road; Croydon, Mitcham and Ewell on the south coast roads; Brentford on the road to Staines and the west; Brockley Hill, the Roman Sulloniacae, on the Chester road, half way between London and Verulamium; and on the north road to Lincoln and York at Enfield, Cheshunt and Ware. Across the Lea, similar sites are probable at Little London near Abridge and at Romford. All along the roads other stations were established at the same sort of interval. The wide three-tracked roads enabled competent herdsmen to use them without interfering with faster traffic, and the post stations assured them of overnight accommodation with enclosures for their animals. Distance was little object, for, in contrast with the economics of the corn trade, the wages of a couple of drovers in charge of substantial herds or flocks amounted to a very slight proportion of the value of the commodities they brought to market. The roads enabled London to buy cattle and sheep from all over Britain; all that was needed was money, and London was not a poor city.

London required much else besides its basic supplies, and the existence of a great market brought into cultivation land that had not previously been tilled. Wealthy country houses reached no nearer to the city than Orpington and Keston in Kent, Walthamstow in Essex. On the edge of the Downs, known farming sites were more numerous than in the days before Rome, but were virtually confined to the same areas, and were not much richer (see Maps 2 and 13). A small number of potsherds and coins and miscellaneous objects have been discovered beside or between the roads that led southward from the bridge, but no recognizable buildings have been encountered outside the relatively small area of Roman Southwark. Whoever used the pots and coins lived poorly in lightly-built houses. A few poor farming sites are known by the Wandle and the Beverley Brook, and north of the river a thin straggle of ribbon development reached to the old river crossing at Westminster. Many objects of the Roman and other periods have been recovered from the river itself, but on its banks there is otherwise no sign of habitation or cultivation between the city and Putney. Recent excavations suggest a small, but substantial village or small town at Putney, and upstream the volume of riverside settlement greatly increases, becoming especially dense between Brentford and Hampton Court, and south of the river beside and between the Wey, the Mole and the Hogsmill Brook, that joins the Thames at Kingston.

North of the Thames, the future Middlesex was empty land when the Romans came. Between the Brent and the Lea, it stayed empty; all that has been recorded in ten square miles is a little woodland industry and a couple of stray potsherds. There was doubtless a little more that has not been discovered, but the silence of the ground is not caused by accidents of modern discovery, for north and west of the Brent, chance has happened upon plentiful evidence. There, a score or more of sites, including the remains of a dozen small farm sites, have been reported, mostly to the west upon either side of the Watling Street. The Brent marks a frontier between cultivated and untilled land. The map explains the reason (Map 4, p. 76). The soil is similar on both sides of the little river, an uninviting heavy clay, in nature thickly wooded. But the course of the Brent is by a mass of boulder clay, several miles long, deposited to its east. Eastward, no streams drain the clay, for no waters can reach the Brent. But to the north and west the Dollis Brook and half a dozen other tiny watercourses drain the clay and offer water to the farmer.

This land was not farmed before London was founded. Thereafter, the forest was hacked down and the clay ploughed. London plainly made it profitable to bring marginal land into cultivation; and Roman farming could cope with heavy clays that had some natural drainage when a good market was available, but could not cope without drainage. The evidence indicates that the land was cultivated. It does not show what was grown. These farms might have grown some corn, for the Brent offered a cheap means of transport, and even by land the Watling Street crossing of the Brent, by the Welsh Harp on the Edgeware Road, still called Brent Bridge, is no more than seven miles from the city, and the nearby post town of Brockley Hill also required some of the local produce. But it is likely that land so situated found an easier profit in growing vegetables, perhaps also fruit, that a mule, a donkey or a barrow might transport to London in a few hours.

The city was immediately surrounded by uncultivated clays, naturally rich in oakwoods. In early agriculture, when timber was still cheap and plentiful, the most profitable use of oak forests was the pasturing, or pannage, of domesticated pigs, and herds of pigs were numerous when forests were nearby. It is likely that pork and bacon were cheaper and more often eaten in London than in most Roman towns, and that leather goods of pigskin were commoner, and were perhaps numerous enough to form an article of export. The roads also offered cheap and easy means of transporting eggs, fowl and a wide range of other light food-stuffs that it was worth a man's while to carry to market, or to load in the panniers of a beast of burden. The main food problem was the bulk and low price of corn. Once that problem had been solved, and the city's supply of cheap bread ensured, a large population created an eager market for very many lighter commodities and agricultural raw materials that could profitably be carried to the city from many miles around. Distance clearly varied with the margin of profit on each commodity. A man might comfortably walk 12 or 15 miles a day, and must allow as much for his return. If his wage were 20 of Diocletian's denarii a day, or their equivalent in goods, a four-day journey of 30 miles there and back, or 40 miles in five days, would repay the effort if it brought a gain of 80 or 100 denarii, reckoned as a profit margin, or as the sale of goods that would otherwise find no market. Such small-scale trade was clearly profitable in the many commodities whose price was high and weight was light, such as honey, listed at 40 denarii to the pint for good-quality honey. To many quite distant farms, with labour idle between the peak seasons of agriculture, bee-keeping for the London market and other incidental enterprises plainly offered a ready source of additional income.

The Produce of London

London was not only an exceptionally large city. It was also a large and busy port, probably handling considerably more tonnage each year than any other port in Roman Europe. Statistics are not available, and would not be of prime importance if they were, for ancient economic thought did not share the assumptions of the modern economist. The calculations of the cost accountant were unknown, and would not have been considered helpful or even desirable. Roman society was geared upon the interests of the consumer rather than the commercial producer. It was dominated by great landlowners, who annexed the larger share of available consumer goods; economists urged them to make profitable use of their land and its equipment, and not to waste their potential resources, but the purpose of earning more money was to spend it. Great estates, and large incomes earned from them, bought social and political honour and influence; but the goal was mastery of men and pre-eminence among them.

The manufacturer and the merchant were necessary agents in the creation and distribution of wealth, but the workings of the economy were not designed to serve their interest or augment their profit. It was deemed proper that their services should be adequately recompensed, and that the most successful among them should amass large fortunes, sufficient to invest in land and make gentlemen out of their children. But the pursuit of commercial profit gained no honour, and dealings in money more commonly brought dishonour. Financiers of all sorts were regarded as usurers, and their dealings incurred the same social stigma that medieval Christendom attached to usury.

Practice found many loopholes in the social code, and found specious justification for particular anomalies at different times. In the greedy chaos of the civil wars before Augustus' triumph, the honourable Brutus advanced money to Cypriots, hard pressed by Roman extortion, at an annual interest of forty-eight per cent, and Cicero condemned the excessive rate, but not the loan itself;[2] shortly after the conquest of Britain, the philosopher Seneca thrust forty millions upon unwilling British borrowers in the hope of high interest, and incurred censure because his avarice was regarded as a main cause of the wide and rapid support accorded to the rebellion of Boudicca.[3] City councils also sought high interest upon their surplus capital from reluctant borrowers, but in the settled security of the second-century empire, the government forbade compulsory loans, and ordered investors to be content with the prevailing interest rate of six per cent.

Throughout the empire, the prevailing sentiments of the aristocracy regarded financial investment as the mark of meaner men, and formally forbade senators to traffic in money. In the stable government of the Flavian and Antonine empire, their ethic was commonly accepted. But convention allowed one important exception, marine insurance, or bottomry. Pliny, the arbiter of acceptable public morality, was at pains to emphasize that his considerable wealth was tied up in land, and that what cash he had available was all invested in bottomry. The morality of the exception was not argued, but it served the security of Rome. The city depended upon import by the Mediterranean sea routes, especially from Egypt and the Levant; and repeated legislation offered rewards and privileges to freedmen and simple citizens who built and employed ships. But the employment of ships by men with small capital reserves was a risky undertaking, and at the same time a speculation with high hopes. A well-chosen cargo brought safely to harbour earned a large return; the seas were safe from pirates, the hazards of navigation well understood. But the medieval invention of the centralized sternpost rudder was not devised until the stresses of the Channel gales impressed its utility upon Flemish and English shipbuilders in the twelfth century. Ancient ships were manoeuvred by a large oar or rudder thrust over the right-hand side of the stern, whose ancient usage still names that side of a vessel its 'starboard', or steer board, or sometimes by oar rudders on both sides. Turning in an emergency was slower and more uncertain, especially with larger ships. All shipping was vulnerable to freak weather, and most sea trading was confined to the fair-weather months, and most captains stayed in port from late September to March.

Normal safety put a premium on gambles, for a cargo landed out of season fetched higher prices, and shipowners and captains were tempted to take chances with the weather. Some, like the captain who carried Saint Paul to Italy, met mischance, and lost their ships and cargoes. Even those who took no gambles might sometimes be upset by freak weather that forced unhandy vessels upon a lee shore; for most of the smaller vessels avoided the uncertainties of the open sea when they could, and preferred to hug well-charted coasts, that offered known havens when dirty weather threatened. The uncertainties of seafaring gave the merchant seamen a hope of large reward, and also a high risk of disaster. Men of substance were exposed to the dangers that closed upon Shakespeare's merchant of Venice, when the loss of one argosy might bring instant bankruptcy. The life-line of Rome was a mercantile marine run on a slender capital; it could only be maintained by a system of insurance, whose high premium could be set against the cost of cargo and freight, but whose guarantee ensured the continuing business of the shipper. The needs of the city sanctioned the investments of the wealthy landlords, who alone had the necessary capital, in a speculation necessary to the public well-being.

The physical and financial conditions of merchant shipping were chiefly determined by the needs of the port of Rome. They applied with equal or greater force to the port of London, situated in the stormier outer ocean, 'beyond the edge of the world'. But in London as in Rome, they served a consumer, and were not controlled by the advantage of the importer or investor. Earlier societies did not share the modern view that a 'favourable' balance of trade, an equality in money values between exports and imports, or an excess of exports, was a desirable goal or economically profitable. The economy of a nation was not treated on the principles that govern a housewife's budget. Pericles had praised Athens for the magnitude and variety of her imports, and Aelius Aristides of Smyrna in the second century AD equally gloried in the imports of Rome; when he praised the city as the 'workshop of the world' he did not have its exports in mind, but marvelled at the riches that the city craftsmen's use of imported materials brought to the city's consumers. Even in the spacious days of nineteenth-century English prosperity, the scale of import impressed public thinking, and industrial expansion at many periods flourished on an excess of import over export. In antiquity large imports were regarded as a sign of wealth, prosperity, and of a healthy economy, evidence of the affluence of those who consumed them; excessive export was the mark of a poor and backward economy in decline that could no longer pay its way. The source of wealth was the produce of the soil and the extraction of the minerals beneath it; their fit use was in the purchase of what was not available at home. When the elder Pliny, uncle of the letter writer, deplored the drain of gold to India and the east, wasted on the purchase of silks and spices, the reasoning that underlay his disapproval was not concerned with trade balances. He did not deplore an export of commodities; he regretted the expenditure upon trivial luxuries of money that would have been better employed upon the embellishment of the cities of the empire.

The motive of the London shipowner and merchant in the Roman empire was the profit that he might realize from his cargo; and one factor in his calculation was that his ships might be laden in both directions, avoiding voyages in ballast with empty holds whenever possible. But when high profit rewarded one way traffic, then it was acceptable. But the motive of the wealthy citizen or landowner who underwrote and financed his operations was to import and consume commodities that he could only obtain by sea; and additions to his income, from marine insurance or any other source, were welcome because they enabled him to import and consume more commodities. Attempts to judge the purposes or consequences of Roman trade by the assumptions of modern economic thought, or in the terminology of its costing, are irrelevant and misleading. Roman London and Roman Britain prospered by their imports; their exports were a means of increasing import and consumption.

The port of London was a threefold source of prosperity. It imported the city's own needs; it imported much that was re-exported to other destinations in Britain; and the export of the produce of its own craftsmen, together with the re-export of goods produced elsewhere in Britain, increased the sums available for further imports. Its traffic was also of three main kinds, riverborne, coastal and overseas.

The logistics of the corn trade, and the density of settlement on the banks of the Thames from Putney upstream, are the visible evidence of river trade. On the river frontage of the city, the piles and timbers of numerous wharves and quays have been detected, together with many more timbers that were probably or possibly concerned with the loading, unloading and transhipment of cargoes. One small coasting vessel that sank at Blackfriars, on the mud that is now flanked by the road and railway bridges, has been carefully and exactly excavated. It sank towards the end of the second century, and was then probably at least thirty to fifty years old, for when it was built a moderately worn coin of the late first century was placed beneath the stepping of its mast. It was a broad, shallow sailing vessel with a capacious hold, of a little under 100 tons burthen, over 50 feet in length, with a beam of 22 feet, built of massive beams and caulked planking upon a rib skeleton; it had carried a cargo of Kentish ragstone, the commonest of all London building materials, probably from the Medway. It had sailed above London bridge, and its mast, that is unlikely to have been hinged for lowering, probably reached to at least 20 feet above the water. It was therefore probably one of the larger vessels able to negotiate the bridge. The insertion of a drawbridge, to be lifted for the passage of tall ships, as in some modern imaginative artists' reconstructions of Roman London is theoretically possible, but Roman London, like medieval London, had no need of such a contrivance. The boat, sunk at the mouth of the Fleet, evidently carried stone for west-end building, or possibly for suburban building further up the Fleet. Another small vessel, somewhat longer and somewhat narrower, carvel-built in the Mediterranean fashion, was sunk higher up the river a century later, by County Hall, opposite Westminster (Plate 14), and fragments of another have been found below the bridge, in a creek south of the river in Bermondsey. These were all small vessels, and it is likely that all wharves above the bridge, and perhaps most of those within the city below the bridge, catered chiefly for barge and coastal traffic, or for smaller sea-going ships.[4]

Other discoveries suggest the accommodation of larger ships and of the main overseas docks and quays. The line of Newgate Street, continuing to the south-east, was provided with a gate on Tower Hill; the continuation reaches the Thames at Wapping, where it meets the continuation of the Ludgate Street early road. Their conjunction may have been the site of an early landing place, possibly in origin military, itself the cause of the direction of these early roads. It is also likely that another road ran due east from Tower Hill, skirting the northern loops of the Thames by Shadwell and the East India Dock, with a causeway or ford over the mouth of the Lea, for there is a considerable concentration of Roman finds in the Beckton area, between East and West Ham, as far south as the Albert Dock, immediately west of the outfall of the Barking Creek, where the Roding river flows into the Thames. The discoveries include a cemetery whose dated burials range from at least the middle of the second century to the middle of the fourth, perhaps later.[5] The occupation of a not inconsiderable, isolated population in these unlovely flats cannot have been agricultural. Their concern, as of the Albert Dock in the same situation in later times, was plainly with larger ships, that in the days of sail found the negotiation of the great bends of the Thames about the Greenwich Marshes and the Isle of Dogs a time-consuming operation, hazardous when large vessels manoeuvred only by an outboard oar must pick their way through crowded shipping against unkind winds, and against the current when winds were slight or still.

It is possible that the connecting road from Beckton to London ran up to the regular Lee crossings at Old Ford and Bow; but wherever the roads ran, the northern shore from Poplar to Barking is the likely berth of the larger sea-going vessels, that in Mediterranean shipping were of a thousand tons or more. Wide reaches, clear of river and estuary traffic, were also necessary for the laying up of a considerable tonnage in the winter season, when few sailed the open seas, and fair-weather vessels must lie in safe anchorage, and the projection of the Plumstead marshes offered that last secure protection against the North Sea easterlies that blow up the estuary in winter.

There is little direct record of commercial voyages to Britain in the Roman centuries; but many such voyages are reported in the fifth and sixth centuries, after the collapse of Roman power, when commerce was less, not more, than in the days of the empire's strength and security. The political conditions of the sixth century severely hampered the trade of London, though they did not altogether end it; and the volume of trade with any part of Britain was plainly less than in the past. But an Egyptian writer found nothing remarkable in the description of a direct voyage of a merchant vessel from Alexandria to Britain about the year 600, except the miracle wrought upon its cargo of tin, presumably loaded in or near Cornwall.[6] Centuries before the Roman conquest, Carthaginian vessels from the ports of Spain and North Africa sailed across Biscay to Britain, and Roman captains and Greeks from Marseilles followed them. The travellers' tales incorporated in Homer's *Odyssey* also include a voyage far beyond the Straits of Gibraltar to rocky Atlantic coasts; a late Roman writer identified them with British cliffs, and reported the existence of an inscription alleged to have been erected in Britain by Odysseus, and to have been seen and reported in Roman Britain.[7] The reports are quite possibly true, for the antiquarian conventions of the Romans of the empire would have found nothing amiss in setting up the inscription that Odysseus should have erected, and in treating it as a restoration or replacement of its supposed original.

These several stories of the centuries before Rome of the empire, and the centuries immediately thereafter, indicate that direct voyages from

Britain to the Mediterranean were neither particularly difficult, infrequent or exceptional. Trade with Bordeaux is evidenced by one inscription of a 'British merchant',[8] in the sense of a merchant engaged in the British trade, and of Lunaris, whose business in Britain was centred in Lincoln and York,[9] and whose landfall in Britain was therefore not in Cornwall or any west-country port. Though doubtless the greatest volume of the traffic of the port of London was with the harbours of the Rhine estuary and northern Gaul, some of it reached to south-western Gaul, and through the Straits of Gibraltar to the Mediterranean, to Italy and Egypt. It is probable that much of this long-distance trade was operated with larger vessels, that berthed or docked between Poplar and Barking rather than at the city wharves; many were doubtless foreign vessels that reached as far as London, especially in the city's early years. But it is not unlikely that the shipowners and shipyards of London learnt, by at least the later second century, to build and operate their own large sea-going ships. One of the few surviving business documents of London concerns the authorization of the building of a ship (above, p. 222); it does not indicate the size or purpose of the ship, or why or from whom authority was required, but it does formally demonstrate the obvious, that shipyards and a shipbuilding industry existed. It is not probable that that industry overlooked the opportunity to profit from long-distance trade.

No direct evidence, other than the inscriptions of the Bordeaux wine trade, indicates the cargoes carried by long-distance trading. Some of the Mediterranean commodities imported into Britain are known: some oil, and some Italian wines, particularly in the second and third centuries when Italian vineyards enjoyed government protection, Mediterranean sculptures and bronzes, some Italian marbles, substantial quantities of bronze jugs, dishes and elaborate candlesticks from Italy, Spanish sauces, and a few other commodities, almost all of them serving the personal requirements of the very rich, or the public works which they financed. The land transport of most of these commodities to the harbours of northern Gaul would have made their cost prohibitive, and their probable carriage was in long-distance ships. Some of the corresponding exports are also evidenced or indicated, and some of them plainly concerned London rather than other ports. British oysters were known in Rome in the early empire, and with them pearls. Within Britain, the oyster industry was organized on a massive scale; oyster shells are found in great quantities on Roman sites of all kinds, poor and rich, deep inland as often as near the coast. They were evidently very cheap, transported live in sea water in barrels. The most extensive oyster beds of Britain are those of the Thames estuary; British oysters reached Rome, and most of them originated in the neighbourhood of London. In Rome oysters were expensive; a dozen cost half a labourer's daily wage. Overland transport across Europe is unlikely, direct carriage by sea from the port of London to the port of Rome probable; and Rome was but one of the innumerable Mediterranean cities whose population liked oysters, and welcomed even the second-grade pearls of British oysters for their wives' necklaces.

Another essential product of the Thames estuary was salt. It also was expensive in antiquity, and heavy and bulky to carry. Its principal sources were inland mines or extraction by pans on the sea coast; more Roman salt pans are known in the province of Britain than anywhere else in the Roman world, and the largest concentration of them is on the Essex coast. The modius of salt, about 25 lb, cost 100 denarii in Diocla-tian's pricing; a half ton load of 50 modii cost 20 denarii a mile by road. Land transport for 250 miles equalled its retail price, and ruled out any question of conveying British salt to Italy and the Mediterranean by land, even if Rhine barges covered part of the distance. But the sea cost of a half ton load from Alexandria to Rome was 800 denarii; London is about twice as far from Rome by sea as Alexandria, and even if the freight was doubled for a double distance, its cost would amount to 1,600 denarii, about one third of the selling price of 5,000 denarii for 50 modii. It is likely that the freight over the double distance was not more than half as much again, and that the freightage of British salt to Rome was less than a quarter of its selling price.

Various other commodities reached the Mediterranean from Britain: bears, slaves from Scotland or Ireland, dogs, especially bulldogs and Irish wolfhounds, woollen goods, mined metals, especially silver and lead. Some, though not all, were most easily handled at London at the peak of its prosperity, from the later second to the mid fourth century. The road system of Roman Britain rested upon its four main estuaries, the Thames and Severn, Dee and Humber. Of these, the Humber was the least important for distant trade, and Chester dealt most easily with north-western and Welsh coastal trade, and with Ireland. The port of Bristol, located at Sea Mills, downstream from the modern city, was well sited to export the metals of the Midland and Mendip mines, though in the early Roman centuries, sufficient stamped lead pigs have been found along the lines of transit to argue that many of them were shipped from Southampton; some doubtless also used Plymouth, Poole and other southern Roman harbours. The western and southern harbours may also have handled a fair proportion of the trade with barbarian Ireland and the north. But London was, in and about the third century, a likely main centre of the textile and leather industries, for its size made it the largest importer of cattle and sheep.

Though long voyages were doubtless numerous and earned high returns, it is evident that cargoes to and from the nearer coasts of Europe formed the greater volume of London's overseas trade. Plutarch estimated the sailing time from the coasts by the Rhine estuary to Britain at about thirty-six hours. With plenty of time for turn-around, vessels of well-organized firms would manage at least three voyages a fortnight in the sailing season, fifty to seventy trips in a year. Passenger journeys were more conveniently made by the short sea crossings to Dover and Richborough, and thence by road. Though the port of Dover increased in importance, European writers continued to regard Richborough as the main port of entry into Britain up until at least the middle of the fourth century. At Diocletian's costings, the coach fare from the Channel ports to London was equivalent to somewhat over a journeyman's weekly wage, of the order of £10 in relation to the cost of essential foods. The fare was well within the reach of the professional and leisured classes who customarily travelled; the poor who needed to save the fare by a direct and longer sea voyage rarely travelled, and it is unlikely that London handled much overseas passenger traffic.

The articles imported were many and miscellaneous. Rhine and Moselle wines, querns of Andernach and Niedermendig lava, some clothing and raw materials, silks and light luxuries of all sorts, Rhineland glass and much else, were among them. Pottery is the principal index. Until the early third century, enormous quantities of continental fine wares were imported into Britain. Pottery is bulky, but relatively light, and careful packing can often compress much into a relatively small space, particularly with dishes and cups whose shape permits them to be stacked. In the first few years after the conquest, some quantities of Italian products reached Britain, brought in the baggage of officers and government officials, or by Gauls who had purchased them in Europe. For some decades thereafter, the bulk of the imports came from southern Gaul, and might have travelled all the way by sea from the Mediterranean coast, or with a relatively short land haul through the port of Bordeaux. But from the Flavian period onwards, most of the imported pottery came from central Gaul, and most that came from elsewhere was manufactured near the Rhine.

London was plainly not the only port of entry for these goods. Colchester and its harbours remained a convenient centre for distribution in East Anglia, conveniently linked with the eastern midlands. An enormous bulk of pottery was imported by the army, for use in forts and fortresses; and from the late first century onward the great majority of the troops were concentrated in the north. Their supply routes are not known; clearly individual officers and messengers in need of haste travelled from Europe by Richborough and London through the posting stations. Large bodies of men might march, but distances were long, and where evidence is available, they did not waste time and energy on the roads. In the early 120s, the Sixth Legion arrived in Britain to help in the construction of Hadrian's Wall; they dedicated an altar to the god of Ocean, that was recovered from the Tyne at Newcastle.[10] The plain inference is that the altar was erected in thanksgiving for a safe voyage, at the port where the men disembarked. It is likely that when reinforcements came to the northern frontier in the 150s, they reached it by the same direct route.[11] If troop transports could sail directly up the east coast from the Rhine to the Tyne, the cargo boats could do the same, and it is likely that the greater part of the army's import of pottery was carried across the North Sea, to the Humber and up the Ouse to York, and to the Tees, Wear and Tyne.

But civilians were more numerous than soldiers, and most of the markets for imported pottery were situated within easier reach of London than of any other east coast port. The south coast harbours were placed to serve some of the rich southern chalklands, but Wiltshire, northern Hampshire and the wealthy lands about the Thames were most cheaply supplied by the return voyage of the vessels that carried corn downstream to London; and the shape and nature of pottery also made it easily transportable by mule train or pack horse along the roads that radiated from London. London itself was the largest single market, and one plain trace remains of boats that brought central Gaulish ware up the Thames to London. Over many years dredgers have pulled up large quantities of middle second-century vessels from Pudding Pan rock, four miles from the coast off Herne Bay, north-west of Reculver. They were evidently the cargo of a ship which foundered on the rock while on its way to London.

London itself consumed a considerable part of its imports. Much else was re-exported to the rest of Britain, by coastal shipping, by river or by road, according to how the weight, bulk and value of each item determined its most profitable means of distribution. These re-exports were supplemented by the city's own manufactures, and the produce of its neighbourhood, some of which doubtless also went overseas. Much of Thamesside oyster and salt production necessarily passed through London, doubtless more directed to destinations in Britain than overseas. The size of London also enabled it to develop specialities that were beyond the reach of craftsmen in most smaller towns. The permanently wet condition of the Walbrook has preserved tools in immense quantity, of an extensive range.[12] There were specialized saws and other carpenters' tools of sophisticated design and limited purpose, whose modern equivalents could not be bought from an ordinary ironmonger, but must be ordered from particular firms, who still today manufacture only in London, or sometimes in some other single centre. It is probable that in Roman Britain a number of these specialized tools were manufactured only in London, and the London makers supplied the needs of craftsmen in other towns and in country villas who needed them.

Similar considerations apply to other tools and commodities not in everyday use; and in some cases it is likely that manufacture began in London, and was subsequently undertaken in some other centres, leaving London to supply a large part or the greater part of the market. Gear like the very large crane and shackle hooks, heavy chains and other outsize lifting equipment were clearly needed earliest, and always in the greatest quantities in London. Their forging was within the general capacity of smiths elsewhere, but few other smiths are likely to have had the experience to make them quickly and cheaply. Glass was manufactured in London,[13] and few other glassworks are recorded in Roman Britain. London and Colchester are the only places in Britain where potters made the standard red samian ware normally imported from central Gaul and the Rhineland;[14] but the London kilns do not seem to have lasted long, and the Colchester kilns were little more successful The probable reason is that the available local clays proved unsuitable.

Various light metal goods of high quality demanded similar experienced specializations. Rulers of various kinds are known from Britain and London, varying from a piece of bone, nicked in Roman inches, to a precisely fashioned folding rule, with a locking catch, measured on one side in Greek digits, on the other in Roman inches, as accurately as a modern ruler that gives centimetres and English inches. It might have been an import; but if it were made in Britain, it is likely to have been the product of a particular workshop, supplying all or most of Britain. Weighing scales and steelyards are common in Britain; some of the most delicate balances come from London, and also belong to the category of specialities. So also does some jewellery. Publishing is another profession that in most ages is concentrated in the largest cities; when books were written by hand by professional calligraphers, a publishing house could maintain profit only if the demand for new books was regular, and sufficient to maintain the writers in steady employment. Some private individuals owned calligrapher slaves or retained freedmen, and in some of the larger cities demand may have been sufficient to keep a publisher in business; but it is probable that most of the books read in Britain were made in London. Similarly, the production of stationery of all sorts required some specialist skills; *styli* might be cast by any bronze smith, ink wells cast by any potter, wooden writing tablets prepared by any carpenter, but the preparation of ink, the fitting of wax into a tablet of precisely the right density and consistency, the preparation of vellum, required experience that could be acquired only when the demand was large. In the same way, small metal tools like nail cleaners, scissors or toothpicks could be made by any local smith; but the precision needed for the surgical instruments found in several Roman towns in Britain could only be provided by a man who spent all or most of his time in making them. There cannot have been many towns in Britain where the surgeon's demand for new instruments was enough to keep a full-time craftsman busy.

These are random instances of the kind of skilled tools and ornaments that are unlikely to have been made in more than a very few places in Britain. It is probable that London was the only place in Britain where all such objects were made, and the only place where some particular kinds of tool were made; in other cases, London was doubtless one among a restricted number of towns where particular articles might be obtained. A few customers from other parts of the country might purchase goods by visiting London themselves, but the relatively efficient letter post, attested by the wax tablets found in London and elsewhere in Britain made such personal visits unnecessary, unless extreme haste were needed. As in modern and other commercial societies, letters enabled specialized goods to be ordered by post, for direct delivery to the customer, or to his local shop.

The imports, exports and re-exports of London required much movement of vehicles. Goods transhipped between river craft, coaster and sea-going ship could be handled in docks and wharves alone, and need not intrude upon the streets. Goods destined for London, or for further delivery by road, or goods made in London, had to be carried through the streets. If, as is probable, London followed the example of Rome, the city authorities imposed severe restriction upon the day-time use of heavy goods vehicles in the streets. Though it is clear that such restriction cannot have been absolute, and must, at times at least, have permitted the transfer of grain from quay to granary, and the movement of other necessary public service vehicles, it is not probable that long-distance vehicles travelled at will to every quay, or stopped at every workshop door to collect goods consigned. The needs of London trade required delivery points and loading bays, stations where goods might be transferred to road haulage vehicles.

The discoveries of one particular region suggest the possible location of one such main station. London grew to the size of the area walled in the third century, and any subsequent expansion was contained within the circuit of the walls. Outside the walls, some roadside development has been observed, but hardly any other expansion. In the land immediately outside the walls, very many burials have been observed in several large cemeteries, but hardly any houses, or signs of living activity. One area is exceptional. Beyond the north wall, in the district that was Moorfields, and is now Finsbury Circus, several hundreds of Roman objects have been recovered, many times more numerous than the total of all objects found near to the outside of the whole of the rest of the wall circuit, cemeteries excepted. The public reports of the building and sewage excavations there observed are vague and inadequate, and give little idea of the nature and extent of discovery; it is indicated by the quantity of objects that have found their way into the London museums from Finsbury Circus.

The collection of objects is not only large, but peculiar in character. The pottery includes an unusually large proportion of drinking vessels, and the metal objects include an unusually large number of the iron objects that archaeological jargon calls 'hipposandals', whose probable purpose was to restrict the movement of cattle and horses turned out to graze. The area lies immediately north of the industrial district enclosed by the northern arms of the Walbrook, and was sundered from it in the third century by the construction of the city wall. The quantity of objects, that point to grazing animals and drinking men, suggest a large waggon park, beside the north road at Bishopsgate. It may have had an additional exit, directly linking it with the roads to the west, for Moorgate was inserted into the wall, probably not before the Middle Ages, but earlier than the late fourteenth century, when a street not related to the main medieval city streets crossed the Roman wall, and was itself cut off by the medieval barbican extension. A gate was not inserted to the wall unless a road led from it at the time of its insertion; though no medieval road is known, at Moorgate, a pair of medieval streets led south-westward at a dead right-angle from Old Street, the Roman road from Stratford to the west, one of them called Golding, the other pointing directly at Moorgate. In the fourteenth century, it no longer preserved its alignment to Moorgate, for the Barbican extension cut off its course, and it veered southward to enter the city through Cripplegate. The likely inference is that it was laid out at right-angles to Roman Old Street in Roman times, leading straight to the Walbrook industrial area; though the Roman city wall cut off its course and gave it no gate, it still linked the Roman region of Finsbury Circus with Old Street, giving direct access to the west. Another medieval road, called Hog Lane, also disturbed by the Barbican extension, lay two hundred yards outside the city wall, and ran parallel to it, in the short section from Aldgate to Bishopsgate. If a Roman road lay beneath it, it gave the Finsbury Circus grounds direct connection with the main eastward road from the city centre.

Finsbury Circus is the possible location of a main roadhead station, placed on the main north road and linked with the main east and west roads, and it is the only area whence any relevant evidence has been reported. But whatever the location, Roman London needed a station or stations. The mechanics of transport required loading places, and authority needed to supervise them. Tolls and customs duties were an important item in the revenues of the city and the government. Practical convenience might admit, examine and tax men and animals on foot at the city gates in day time, or at appropriately sited road blocks before the wall and gates were built. But in any age the customs examination of heavily laden goods vehicles requires much time for the checking of individuals and of the small baggage carried by animals, or in light cars. For customs purposes alone, modern borders require separate waggon parks, off the main road, where vehicles may be parked for lengthy periods without interfering with traffic. Roman needs were greater. The government post service required sheds for its waggons and carriages, stables and grazing for its animals, storage sheds for their fodder. Privately owned commercial vehicles had the same needs. Checking involved not merely the examination and taxation of loads that passed on beyond the customs barrier; it needed supervision of offloading from a long-distance to a local vehicle.

Beyond these plain inferences, the working of the traffic controls cannot be learnt. Long-distance traffic north of the river did not need to pass through the city streets; but goods bound from north to south, or south to north, must cross the bridge. It is likely that a corresponding station existed on the Southwark shore; and any heavy loads that needed to cross London in transit might travel between Bishopsgate and the bridge at night. But it is not likely that transit traffic was large. Then as now, London stations were termini. Most freight was consigned to or from London, or for transhipment between sea and land transport. The probable essentials of the traffic system were that goods despatched from London were conveyed to the *statio* of the customs and the post through the city streets in handcarts, litters, or by pack animal; and were cleared for customs, invoiced and loaded in the station. Most goods imported could be as simply checked and offloaded in the same way, and it is entirely possible that enterprising persons ran carriage services between the city shops and the station. If the practice of Rome were followed, goods too heavy for offloading onto handcarts and animals must await nightfall. Such goods plainly involved the dock traffic, save for the cargoes discharged downriver from the city, that had no need to pass through the city, unless they were destined for delivery to the city itself. But, apart from waterfront cargoes, it is not likely that much of the freight involved was too bulky for carts and animals.

The trade of London entailed a great deal of invoicing, docketing and filing, and many offices in which to organize the records. It is probable that, as in most port towns, the offices of the most important merchants and shipowners were close to the waterfront; in Ostia their sites are marked by floor mosaics, where the names of African, Sicilian and other firms and corporations who used the port are written, lining the waterfront. Shorter-term records were kept on the wax tablets, more permanent registers on papyrus or animal membrane, recorded in ink. Sums were necessarily worked out in the cumbrous letter figures of Roman notation; and the difficulty of adding such figures by eye made an abacus an essential part of the equipment of any office; occasionally its perforated beads are recovered in excavation.

The records chiefly related to the exchange of goods and service for money. Most transactions were settled in coin, but they entailed a heavy and increasing dependence on bankers. Coins were valued not as tokens, but as metal of specified value; but the face value was not always reliable. Gold coins in particular were issued with declining metallic content by successive emperors, and silver coins also lost value; both might be clipped by former users, who hoarded the clipped metal. In the Mediterranean, several currencies were in circulation; Egypt retained its own coinage in Greek drachma, and many eastern cities retained the right of issuing their own bronze coinage throughout the early empire. In London the problems were less acute, for foreign coins were infrequent, and only the coinage of the imperial government was in normal use; but wise men accepting coin from strangers in quantity and of high value concluded their deal with the assistance of a professional banker, a *nummularius*, who verified the value of the coin.

The functions of the banker went further than changing and verifying coin. In large cities, where businesses were established and bound to their houses and property, businessmen commonly deposited surplus cash with bankers, and received interest thereon. Bankers who received the deposits loaned them to others to finance undertakings in which they had confidence, charging interest rates higher than those that they themselves paid. They faced some competition from wealthy corporations; well-endowed temples with idle cash, on which they paid no interest themselves, were often ready to lend it, and so were city corporations. Credit was developed as far as the businessman who needed it could offer security; its chief limitation was that most businessmen worked with so little reserve capital that they could offer little security. Credit chiefly depended on borrowing from a money lender whom the creditor knew personally; it was occasionally extended to a banker's draft, to be cashed elsewhere, where one banker knew another in a distant town. It is likely that several London bankers had sufficient acquaintance with bankers in several of the main ports that traded with London – Bordeaux, Boulogne and the Rhineland towns, and other main towns in Britain – to be able to issue letters of credit that their customers might cash elsewhere. But there is no sign that any regular and widespread banking organization developed in the Roman world; the principles of banking were known and practised, but they were limited to dealings between men who knew enough about each other to trust their faith and solvency.

Cash remained the main medium of exchange, and distress and disturbance followed shortages of cash. In Britain, expanding trade brought such difficulties in the early third century, when less money was minted at a time when more was needed. The problem was faced and overcome by the simple expedient of men making their own money. In several parts of the country coin moulds have been discovered, and sometimes irregular silver coins struck from a die. The latter were not forgeries, for their metallic content is not less than that of the government's coins; and often the obverse of one emperor's coin is matched by a reverse of a different emperor. There was no intention to deceive. The coins were made by men who had the metal, but lacked the coin. Their expedient is not dissimilar from that of late eighteenth-century English tradesmen, who suffered from a lack of government copper coins; their solution was to issue coins of the appearance of halfpennies or pennies, marked with the name of the grocer, the baker or the butcher who issued them. They were accepted by those who knew enough of the man who issued them, personally or by repute, to trust his issue. The homestruck coins of the early third century served a similar purpose; but they bore no maker's name, and served no local purpose. They were worth their metal content; and their existence demanded the expert service of the banker and money changer to assess their actual value.

The province of Britain and the city of London were both products of the uniform and unifying civilization of Rome. They adopted and developed the normal habits and enterprises of the empire. But within the complex organism of Roman Europe, their independent growth determined the pace, the scale and the peculiarities that were theirs alone. The formation of the province was rushed. It was first formed and heavily capitalized by the ambition of the emperor Claudius. Its teething troubles, its early revolt, and its acceptance of lasting Roman rule were all experienced and left behind in time for it to receive the full benefit of the Flavian impetus to polished urban manners. Other provinces had formed more slowly, and were already more set in their ways when that impetus reached them; the few provinces that were founded after Britain, south-western Germany and Dacia, modern Rumania, were too raw and underdeveloped to make full use of the second-century expansion of Roman urban security, and both succumbed early to the barbarians beyond their borders.

Britain differed from almost all other provinces in that its chief city was an entirely Roman foundation, with no native past at all. London began as a city of foreigners, and long continued as a government town, whose resident authority overawed native British custom. By the end of the second century, the contrast between native and foreigner was obliterated, earlier than in the rest of the province, and magnates of the city, wealthy in land and in the profits of commerce, stood on a level with the government officials who lived beside them. The accelerating growth of London slipped into top gear in the generation in which the civilization of the empire reached its peak, ceased to expand, and rested quietly in the 'old age of the world'. Londoners had not yet acquired any such sense of old age and lassitude. The greatness of their city was new, its vitality undimmed, its mastery and leadership of Britain recent. London continued to grow of its own momentum as the signs of decline and disorder became more and more obvious in the centre of the empire.

Part Three
The Survival of London

Chapter 14

Imperial London

THE SERENE STRENGTH of the empire was summarized in the dying word of the emperor Pius, 'Equanimity'. But equanimity died with Pius. Soon after, his successor, Marcus, fought and won a Mesopotamian campaign, and the victorious armies brought back a fearful plague, that struck down rich and poor in the Mediterranean lands on the same scale as the bubonic plagues of the 540s and of the 1340s. A small force of Langobardi from the lower Elbe attacked the Roman Danube; their name, more familiar in its shortened form of Lombard, looked to the darkening future. They were repelled, but a long German war followed. The Danube frontier broke, the Balkans were overrun and northern Italy was invaded. Marcus is said to have intended the annexation of two new provinces, in the lands that are now Czechoslovakia, but no new conquests were achieved. Soon after Marcus' death in 181, his son and successor Commodus signed a peace treaty, restoring the frontier on its ancient line of the Danube bank, that was not again seriously threatened for eighty years.

The long war transformed the government of the empire. Confidence was shaken. No enemies in arms had been seen in Italy for almost three hundred years, and Italy had been invaded. The barbarians discovered that Rome was not invincible, and began to learn how the empire might again be assaulted. A thin garrison, stretched along the northern rivers without reserves, had been able to hold the frontier for centuries because each small people attacked on its own, at differing times and places. The Germans learnt to combine in large federations, able to concentrate overwhelming force at particular points. The *Franci*, or free men, assembled the nations of the lower Rhine, the *Alamanni*, or All Men, those of the upper Rhine; the Goths, whose ancestors had migrated from Scandinavia to the lands that are now Poland, extended their authority to the Crimea, and bound the many small peoples of eastern Europe into a formidable empire. The new combinations are first recorded in the earlier third century, and took long to exert their full strength. Their first efforts tested and selected weak points; one among them was the narrow sea that separates Britain from the Rhine mouth, where Rome could build no wall, and the Franks and their constituent peoples earned a reputation as daring seamen.

The sea lanes of the port of London were for the first time threatened. At first, the threat was slight. Small enemy flotillas faced fearful risks from the Roman navy, for the *classis Britannica*, the British fleet, based on Boulogne, Dover and Richborough and on the coasts of the low countries, was still powerful. The target of the enemy was not shipping, for their small vessels were not adapted to tow prizes home or to offload a captured cargo, even if the cargo was of value to them. Easier and richer plunder was to be had by raids upon the coasts of Gaul and Britain, in search of slaves, of gold and silver and other valuables. The attacks of the Franks were not yet a major danger, but they were an outrage and an irritant. The Thames estuary was fortified, and in the third century London itself was walled, probably early in the century.

The war ended in 181. Over the next three generations its aftermath slowly emboldened the enemy. Its impact within the empire was immediate and catastrophic. Seventeen years of unwelcome war had occasioned large-scale desertions, and bands of armed deserters stirred discontented slaves, peasants and urban poor, who had hitherto seen no means of resisting omnipotent authority. In the 180s an organized force of deserters and runaway slaves seized many of the larger towns of southern Gaul, whose gates were opened by sympathizers within. They were not suppressed until the government despatched an army of two legions; and then the bolder among them melted away, and gathered in Rome, plotting an ambitious coup whose aim was to dethrone the emperor and replace him with the deserters' leader Maternus. The plot was betrayed and the conspiracy defeated. But the rebellion of Maternus opened a new dimension in the history of Europe, the conscious struggle of the poorer classes in a large, territorial state against the rich, and against the government. The struggle continued. Thenceforth the government had frequent and increasing need to pursue outlaw bands, whom it denounced as bandits, criminals and terrorists, but who flourished because they received sufficient popular support. The forests and the maquis of Gaul sheltered peasant rebel bands, termed *bacaudae*, from the beginning of the third century to the middle of the fifth, repeatedly suppressed by government expeditions, and repeatedly renewing their rebellion.

The extent and strength of the rebel movement is impossible to assess save on the infrequent occasions when it was strong enough to provoke major campaigns of repression. Its importance was that it existed. In the past, the protests of the poor had been confined to the agitation of urban poor, acting within the framework of city constitutions and asserting the political rights of the assembly of citizens against council and magistrates, or else rioting in protest at the price of bread. Struggle was confined to each individual town, acting in isolation, and to townsmen who had little sympathy with rustics. The urban policy of Rome had learnt long since to contain such movements, and the only serious opposition that Rome had encountered had been national; in turn the Gauls, the Pannonians, the Asians, the Jews, and the British, had been combined in national movements to resist Roman conquest. National antagonism had long since been effaced by making Romans of the leaders of each nation, and subsequently by extending citizenship to all. The enduring rebel movement that Maternus initiated was for the first time a movement of social class on a world scale, an alliance of the poor against the rich, not based upon national sentiment and not confined within separate towns, uniting peasant and urban labourer, slave and poor citizen, soldier and civilian. Hitherto government had ruled by consent because its omnipotence was taken for granted; now men could envisage the possibility of resistance. The record of the third century is too poor to show how often men resisted, how consciously and with what success; but it may be that one of the reasons for the repair of old towns walls and the erection of new ones was to guard the rulers against insurrection at home as well as against the danger of barbarian assault.

When they ruled by consent, the masters of the empire had achieved agreement among themselves. The outcome of the wars divided them. War cost more than static defence, and taxpayers resented the cost. The principle charge upon the revenues of the imperial government was the maintenance of the army. Careful management had ensured that cash disbursements were as few as possible; troops in garrison drew the bulk of their supplies from the region in which they were stationed, and owned their own estates, that provided them with grain and timber, meat, leather and much else. Armies on the move must be supplied by baggage trains; governments might compel individuals to supply some needs at their own cost, but most must be paid for, and the high cost of land transport astronomically increased the cost of warfare when armies campaigned beyond the frontiers, or were switched to reinforce another sector of the frontier. But the income of government rested upon fixed taxes and the rents of government estates. Even Augustus, at the height of his power, and Vespasian, at the close of the civil war, had found it impossible to secure more than slight additions to the revenue, beyond the customary payments that men of wealth accepted as proper. Defence cost inordinately more than in the past; taxpayers bitterly resisted additional levies, denouncing the avarice or extravagance of governments that demanded them. Before the death of Marcus, government and nobility had worked in fundamental accord; thenceforth the government's lasting need for more money than the nobility was willing to allow it engendered a growing antagonism between government and nobleman.

The antagonism of landowner and government fostered and sharpened regional differences. Many local antagonisms were embittered, but one major division sundered the empire. The languages of the provinces were many, but almost all Romans spoke either Latin or Greek as well as the native speech of their own province, and well-educated persons spoke both. The two languages divided the empire; Greek was the common speech of the eastern provinces, Latin of the west. The border between them is one of the most enduring in human history, running from north to south through the centre of the Balkans. The frontier that in the third and fourth centuries separated the Greek from the Latin provinces does not greatly differ from that which distinguishes Croatians from Serbians, long after Greek and Latin have disappeared from the Balkans; Croats and Serbs speak the same language, but write it in different characters, Croatian in an alphabet based on Latin characters, Serbs in one based on Greek characters.

The Greek provinces had never wholly forgotten their nostalgic mem-
ories of past independence or their resentment of Latin arrogance. Resentments had been stayed as citizen rights spread, and concord was advanced by Hadrian, whose enthusiasm for Greek culture not only extended citizenship, but admitted to the Senate and to a full share of the government of the empire a number of eminent Greeks from Asia Minor and Greece, and a couple of young Syrians of oustandingly ancient family, Claudius Pompeianus and Avidius Cassius. Pius and Marcus did not share his enthusiasm for living Greeks; no more Syrians entered the Senate for some sixty years; some of the Greeks whom Hadrian had ennobled held high office under his successors, but not many more were admitted, and few among them achieved political influence. Eastern opinion grumbled. The emperor Vespasian was depicted as a deceiver, who had been enthroned by the money and the good will of the eastern provinces, but had denied their aspirations and curtailed their privileges. Easterners deplored the expenditure of their taxes upon unprofitable German wars by a Latin government. Their distrust was reciprocated, although the two Syrian senators attained high office under

Marcus, embracing opposing policies. Pompeianus commanded the armies on the Danube, while Cassius was the principal commander in the east. When a rumour of Marcus' death reached the east, Cassius marched on Rome to seize the person of the young prince Commodus. The rumour was false. Cassius was killed by one of his own officers, and the rebellion immediately collapsed. But Marcus was obliged to suspend the war and devote eighteen months to the pacification of the east, while one of his Latin generals described the disturbance as *motus orientalis*, the rising of the east. A generation later, a powerful section of opinion proposed the division of the empire and the independence of the east; one emperor was to rule the west from Rome, assisted by the senators of the Latin provinces, while another was to be enthroned in Syrian Antioch with a Greek-speaking senate. The proposal was rejected, but its essence was realized at the end of the third century.

The stable structure of Roman government was split apart. Bolder barbarians had made the old static frontier line obsolete, no longer a sure protection, and much increased the cost of defence. Diverging interests separated government and nobility; the latent antagonism of Greek and Roman was revived, and regional differences preferred local needs above the welfare of the united empire. Divided rulers faced insurgents who had newly learned that rebellion was possible. These several causes of disorder were enflamed by the personality of the new emperor. He was the first sovereign whose father had ruled before him since the accession of Domitian, exactly a hundred years before. Like most other emperors who displeased the aristocracy, he had little personal interest in politics and government. Caligula's passion had been horse racing, Nero's drama and poetry; Commodus was devoted to the gladiators. He abandoned his father's wars, and the generals were outraged. Unsuccessful attempts at assassination embittered the young emperor, who turned to wealthy, eastern ministers, to the further fury of the Latin nobility. Many eminent nobles lost their lives. Baffling intrigues transferred power through a succession of unstable governments, and their frail authority was weakened by disasters in Britain. The northern wall was overrun, and the armies defeated, with enormous casualties, at about the time of Marcus' death. Though the frontier was quickly re-established the army of Britain remained mutinous and ungovernable; on one occasion 1,500 lancers rode from Britain to Rome, demanding the head of the chief minister of the day, and Commodus granted their request.[1] The circumstances that underly the dramatic incident are unknown, but the disorder of the British legions was an exaggerated manifestation of the sudden disharmony that rent the empire. Men who had been born in the comfortable security of the reigns of Marcus and Pius were appalled and knew not where to turn.

The excesses of Commodus enflamed the tensions and soon passed beyond tolerable decency to the verge of madness. On the last day of 192 he was murdered by the inner circle of court politicians, and the aged marshal Pertinax was enthroned, to enforce a curtailment of government expenditure. Within three months he was killed by a mutinous soldier. The commanders of the three main frontier armies, of Syria, the Danube, and of Britain, were simultaneously proclaimed emperor, and an ineffective civilian seized brief authority in Rome. Severus, the Danube commander, took Rome within a few weeks, made a bargain with Albinus in Britain, and spent three years subduing and pacifying the armies of the east, before turning upon Albinus, who took the army of Britain to Gaul in an unsuccessful effort to master the empire.

Severus attempted to restore the stable government of Marcus; but he had won power as a frontier commander whose armies had obeyed his command to march upon Rome. The example was ever present to future army commanders, thenceforth the instruments and the champions of opposing interests. In Severus' day the mutual hatreds of his two pugnacious sons gave a focus to rivalries of all kinds. The emperor tried to dampen their dispute and to stabilize the northern frontier by bringing them to Britain on campaign. A renewed attempt to subdue all Britain failed, and Severus died at York in 211. His elder son, Caracalla, gave the frontier its permanent shape, based on Hadrian's wall with outposts along the Cheviots, near to the modern border between England and Scotland. He returned to Rome, murdered his brother, and extended Roman citizenship to the whole empire. Five years later he was himself murdered.

For nearly half a century, a succession of short-lived emperors were enthroned by different frontier armies, most of them senatorial commanders. The nobility was still powerful; twice the empire was governed by senatorial regency councils, and twice civilian Italy repelled invasion by Danubian legions led by their emperor, in 238 and in 253. But none could cure the causes of crisis. Emperors were brought to power either by army officers who expected higher military expenditure, or by civilians who wished to halt the rising burden of taxation. None could satisfy either demand, and none could repair the damaged frontiers, more heavily pressed from without and cracked by repeated civil war within. In the years about 260, the whole of the continental frontiers suddenly collapsed. The eastern armies were destroyed and the emperor Valerian captured by the reinvigorated Persian monarchy; Syria and its capital, Antioch, were overrun, and Persian columns are said to have reached the Dardanelles. In Europe, the Goths swept across the Danube into the Balkans and Greece, and their fleet burst through the Dardenelles into the Aegean. The Alamanni plundered northern Italy, and they and the Franks overwhelmed Gaul, German raiders reaching across the Pyrenees into northern Spain. Sudanese and Saharan nomads invaded Egypt and Roman Africa, and the Moors entered southern Spain. Only Britain and peninsular Italy escaped barbarian invasion.

The fabric of the empire was violently shaken, but it was still tough enough to recover. The enemy were still raiders, in search of booty to carry home, not yet migrants seeking to settle within the empire. Each region saw to its own safety. Valerian's son Gallienus recovered Italy, Africa and the western Balkans; the princes of Palmyra, in the Syrian desert, drove back the Persians; and western emperors, obeyed by Spain, Gaul and Britain, recovered the Rhine. South-western Germany beyond the Rhine, and Dacia beyond the lower Danube were lost for ever. The central government reformed its institutions, and reunited the empire. Senators were forbidden to command armies and legions, for experience had shown that senatorial noblemen, whose rank placed them near to the throne, were easily induced to rebel; and the new strains of war recommended that troops in action were better directed by experienced career officers than by gentlemen amateurs. A mobile reserve was enlisted, that in the next few generations grew large. A staggering inflation knocked the bottom out of the old taxation system, and government was driven to impose emergency levies in kind and in services. The regional emperors were subdued, but it was soon discovered that career officers were as easily proclaimed emperor and as easily deposed as the senators they had replaced. Stability was not attained until the accession of Diocletian in 284; he too faced rivals and rebels, but experience had shown that even successful rebels lacked the authority to govern. Sufficient sentiment inclined men to prefer the existing government to civil war and the promises of rebels, so that Diocletian, unlike his predessors, prevailed over all rivals, and held power for more than twenty years.

At first, these calamities touched Britain lightly and London not at all. Detailed information is scrappy and disjointed. The third century is the dark age of Roman history, for the sources that describe earlier and later centuries whisper faintly. No adequate history survives, and the archaeological evidence is either dateless, or not yet dated by modern students.

In Britain and Gaul, first-century events and buildings are closely dated, for texts report when Claudius landed, when Boudicca burnt towns, when the armies first advanced to the northern forts, and so provide dates for the pottery found in them. The evidence of the second century is less precise, for texts give few relevant dates; but great quantities of imported samian vessels from Gaul, many stamped by their makers, are repeatedly found with quantities of coins, and may be approximately dated. In turn they show the changing fashions of the plentiful coarse wares.

The third-century disasters silenced the archaeological evidence. From Severus' time, the kilns of Gaul ceased to produce for export, and no more of their wares reached Britain. From the time of Commodus, little small change was issued until the inflation of the late 260s; men must use what coins were then in circulation, supplemented by small amounts of more recent issues. The basis of dating disappeared, and has caused confusion in modern studies. Until quite recently it was commonly assumed that British-made pottery, of forms comparable to those found with late second-century coins and imported samian, commonly termed 'late Antonine', was used and broken no later than the end of the second century. Recognizable new forms were not known in quantity before the 270s; and though early third-century forms are now observed in increasing quantity, they are still relatively few. The older assumptions monotonously reported buildings that ceased to be inhabited at the end of the second century, and were reoccupied or rebuilt three generations later, and these reports prompted a belief in a 'recession' or 'slump' in early third-century Britain. More exact observation has removed some misapprehension; analysis of the burials in the large cemeteries of Colchester has shown that if these assumptions about dates were valid, then the death rate quadrupled at the end of the second century, and thereafter hardly anybody died for three generations. Similar scrutinies elsewhere reveal similar anomalies, and the common-sense conclusion is that a large part of the pottery and sites termed 'late Antonine' in fact date to the first half or first three quarters of the third century.[2]

Even the alleged signs of slump have not been reported from London, and some of the elegant and expensive rebuilding of rich men's houses may have been undertaken in the earlier third century. The city and the fertile lowlands of Britain received benefits as well as harm from the troubles of the empire, for shortages created by disaster elsewhere created greater demand for the produce and crafts of undamaged Britain. At the end of the third century skilled masons from Britain were imported to aid the reconstruction of cities in Gaul,[3] and unmistakeable signs of great wealth are numerous in the British countryside. The processes that then culminated in affluence are likely to have begun much earlier, for Britain, and London in particular, was still expanding in the generations when disaster first hit the rest of the Roman world.

The province of Britain was not wholly immune. The northern frontier held, but the Irish grew bold as European barbarians showed that Rome might be raided with impunity. Numerous inscriptions of the west coast record the repair and reconditioning of old forts in Wales and Lancashire; some villas close to the shore of the Severn estuary were destroyed or damaged, and the number of hoards of coins buried and not recovered sharply increased. The Irish raided; they did not yet settle. The coin hoards also suggest that Britain suffered one major raid. Suddenly and dramatically, the hoards buried in or about the year 270 exceed the normal annual average ten or twentyfold, and, unlike earlier and later periods, are widespread all over the fertile lowlands. No text explains the occasion; though individual hoards might be lost and not claimed for a variety of reasons, the sudden increase argues a major crisis, that cost many men their lives and prevented them or their heirs from regaining their property. The cause might have been barbarian raids, by the Franks and the Irish in concert, or a general rising of the disaffected, equivalents of the *bacaudae* of Gaul, or a combination of raids and rebellions. It is probable that Frankish raiders were at least in part responsible, for very soon afterwards the east coast was protected by the massive forts later known as the Saxon Shore defences, from the Wash to Southampton Water, and the coin hoards of the following decades disappear as dramatically as they had appeared. It is likely that the great fortifications were built because a particular raid had shown the need, and that for a considerable time they served their purpose. It is also probable that the towns which received stone walls in the second half of the third century took precautions against the same danger.

Unsafe seas plainly affected London's trade, altering its character, but not necessarily lessening its volume. Increased demand from Europe is likely to have meant more rather than less cross-channel traffic, for the raiding vessels were not adapted for sea fighting. The coastal trade is more likely to have been damaged, both because coastal vessels were more exposed to danger than ships on the high seas, and because demand lessened, or did not increase with demand elsewhere. The pattern of rural development in different parts of Britain shows uneven changes. Men ceased or curtailed investment by the south-eastern and Severn coasts. In most of the fertile lowlands in the late third century and the fourth, country houses were enlarged and more elegantly furnished, in some districts on a dramatic scale. But in the fertile strip of the Sussex coast by Chichester, below the South Downs, most of the numerous country houses of the early empire ended before the close of the third century. Poorer farms remained, and the population of the small coastal villages at Worthing, Brighton and elsewhere was not diminished; nor was the life of Chichester within its walls. The phenomenon was local, for the great country mansion at Bignor, on top of the Downs, was rebuilt in imposing splendour. But men ceased to invest in fine houses within a few miles of the coast. The probable reason is that wealth within easy reach of the sea was unsafe. Similar evidence comes from the Thames estuary. The rich lands of east Kent and of East Anglia had supported a proportionate share of the villas of the early empire. Several of them remained into the fourth century, but neither region participated in the expanding wealth of the early fourth century. Further inland and nearer London, soils no richer supported great wealth; the country mansions of the Darenth valley matched those of the interior, but little such investment was undertaken in east Kent or East Anglia.

These consequences suggest the overall success of the coastal defences and also their limitations. The forts were placed near to the sea, sited so that they could use ships, but also had infantry or cavalry garrisons. When the alarm was given, they were able to despatch troops to the beach where the raiders had landed, and to send warships to intercept their return. Since the forts were far apart, it required a good many hours to reach an enemy who beached half way between forts. The defences were designed to limit the enemy to hit-and-run coastal raids, and to prevent deep penetration inland. They could not protect property near the coast. Their siting and garrisons translated into terms of the British coastal defence the principles of protection devised for land frontiers in the face of third-century assaults in Europe, Asia and Africa. The government decreed that all inhabited places must be defended, and be furnished at all times with adequate provisions for a siege, a year's supply in large towns, a fortnight's in small blockhouses. The army could no longer attempt to keep the enemy out altogether. An invader must either sit down to a large number of sieges, or leave garrisons unreduced in his rear. If he did, the Roman army had time to assemble, to catch him on his way home, and to deter him from further raids.

The new strategy brought important political consequences, dramatically realized in Britain. When raiders were intercepted after raiding, the army recovered booty taken from civilian homes. Not all of it found its way back to its rightful owners. Several senior commanders were arraigned by the government for annexing recaptured civilian property, or for permitting their troops to retain it, and on at least two occasions a commander ordered to restore property rebelled, doubtless because it was more than his life was worth to attempt restitution, even if he so desired. One of these was Carausius, commanding officer of the British fleet, who rebelled against Diocletian in or about 287. The rebellion was formidable, and occasioned a radical alteration in the government of the empire. Diocletian had already observed that when an emperor was long absent on eastern campaign, the western armies were tempted to proclaim their own emperor, and likewise the eastern armies when an emperor spent long in the west. He had forestalled the danger by appointing a loyal colleague, Maximian, as joint Augustus in command of the west while he himself took personal command in the east. The long war with Carausius gave Maximian more enemies than he could master single handed, for he also faced heavy attacks on the Rhine, and a serious rising of the *bacaudae* in his rear. He was therefore provided with a junior colleague, Constantius, and Diocletian took a similar colleague, Galerius, in the east. The two colleagues received the title of Caesar, that had long been accorded to acknowledged heirs to the throne, but were denied the rank of Augustus, reserved for sovereigns. The innovation also served in theory to guarantee the succession; when an Augustus died, his Caesar should theoretically succeed, and appoint a new Caesar, so that disputed succession need occasion no future civil wars.

The war against Carausius was entrusted to the Caesar Constantius. Eccentric chance has preserved one text that provides a patch of brilliant light in the midst of the obscurity that envelops most of third-century Roman history. A fourth-century Gaulish publisher produced a collection of public speeches made in honour of emperors and important government officials, doubtless for use in higher schools, or for the benefit of others called upon to make such speeches. Several of the speeches were delivered in the late third century, and one refers in flowery language to the Caesar's recent triumphs in Britain.[4] He recovered Boulogne, and for some time hostilities were suspended. Carausius was himself overthrown, and replaced by his chief minister, Allectus. In 297 Constantius undertook the invasion in two divisions. A fleet assembled in the mouth of the Seine, and made for Southampton Water, under the command of the prefect Asclepiodotus; another fleet from the Rhine under Constantius himself made for the Thames. They sailed in rain, against unfavourable winds, and ran into fog in British waters.

In Southampton Water, Allectus scuttled his fleet and stood to battle on land. Asclepiodotus defeated him and he fell back on London. The citizens feared destruction at the hands of immense numbers of Franks and other barbarians whom Allectus had enlisted, but were saved by the timely arrival of men from Constantius' division, fogbound in the Thames. The citizens had the double pleasure of being saved by the destruction of the Franks, and of watching the spectacle of the slaughter from the safety of their walls. One probable material survival of that engagement is the small ship discovered at County Hall (above, p. 276); it contained coins of Allectus, and was probably sunk at about this time; and it appears to have been sunk deliberately, by artillery fire, stones thrown from small catapults. Its position suggests that it was attempting to guard the river crossing by Westminster, but not enough is known of the engagement to suggest which side used it and which attacked it.

The recovery of Britain was proudly celebrated; the island was

immensely fertile, happy in its wide pastures, flowing with streams of precious metals, yielding great sums in taxes, its immense circuit girdled with harbours.[5]

Constantius celebrated its recovery by striking a gold medal, that gives the earliest picture of the city, though wholly stylised (Plate 15). The Caesar rides to the city, accompanied by a warship, and is greeted by a woman kneeling outside the walls, respresenting the spirit of the city, with the letters LON written beneath her; the medal is inscribed with the legend *Redditor Lucis Aeternae*, Restorer of Eternal Light.[6]

Constantius retained the government of Britain. York and London also became imperial capitals. During his rule, Diocletian and his colleagues, collectively known as the Tetrarchy, the Power of Four, reorganized the administration of the empire. The old set taxes and the main weight of the extraordinary levies of the years of inflation were swept away, and a novel financial principle was introduced. The income of all previous governments and most later ones until recent times, had been limited to the yield of fixed taxes and the income from government property; expenditure was restricted to the available income. Diocletian devised the expedient now termed a budget. The government worked out in advance its anticipated expenditure, and collected the taxation necessary to meet it. To ease assessment and collection, the wealth of the empire was surveyed in a new census, and tabulated in simple form, reduced to multiples or fractions of two kinds of unit, a yoke and a head, *iugum* and *caput*. The methods of reckoning differed from province to province, but in principle a *iugum* was so many acres of average arable land, twice as many of poor land, half as many of exceptionally fertile land, and a *caput* was an able-bodied working man, women, children and animals being reckoned at fractions or multiples. When the *census* was complete, each city province and region in the empire was valued at so many millions of *iuga* and *capita*, The sum required was divided by their number, and the resulting figure was the rate per *iugum* and *caput*.

The new system came into force on 1 September 297, and in theory the census was to be revised every fifteen years. In practice, the neat arrangement operated rarely and imperfectly, but the census period of fifteen years, termed the indiction, remained for six or seven centuries as a main means of dating years. More important than the form of the scheme was the principle; henceforth governments might raise the taxation they needed; all that hindered them was the actual capacity of the taxpayer.

The chief purpose of the new revenues was the payment of the armies. It symbolized the essential difference between the old order and the new. The early empire had been governed by landed gentlemen who maintained an army as a necessary evil at the minimum cost. The later empire was ruled by army officers, contemptuous of tight-fisted, wealthy civilians too mean to pay the army that protected their wealth and estates; and the landowners feared and resented the arbitrary power of ill-educated soldiers, arrogant and licentious. Their resentment was accentuated by the workings of the new system. At all levels, the command of troops and civilian appointments were separated, but civil servants were placed under military discipline and given military titles, for their essential job was to serve as an extended army pay corps. Taxation yields were secured by compelling each man to pay the taxes that his father had paid; a shipowner's son might set himself up as a jeweller, but he was liable for a shipowner's tax as well as a jeweller's. Among poorer people, the new rules froze men's trades; a soldier's son must serve in the army, and a peasant must not leave his land, for unless he worked it, he could not meet its tax.

The new system entailed the legal obligation to perform many of the services that in the second century had been voluntarily undertaken by wealthy citizens, and many others beside. An immense volume of rules obliged individuals to do certain things at certain times and places, and forbade them to do others. Their principal purpose was fiscal, but they caused great inconvenience, and were often impossible of fulfilment. Protests established complex empirical rights of exemption. An increasing clerical staff was required to issue men with certificates exempting them from unwelcome obligations, permitting them to do what they desired, certifying that this or that duty had been performed. The staff were underpaid; appropriate certificates were hard to obtain unless fees were paid to the office responsible. The numbers of bureaucrats rose rapidly, and public dislike for the government and its officers grew in proportion. Their maintenance swallowed up large sums that should have reached the treasury. The government became top heavy. Men ignored or defied its demands when they could, grumbled when they could not. Men of wealth and influence could withstand demands more easily, and the heavier burden of taxation passed to poorer men. Many men of modest means gave up the struggle, and became clients or tenants of the great. During the fourth century, landed property concentrated in fewer and fewer hands, so that the wealthiest noblemen owned hundreds of estates in dozens of different provinces. Their tenants might be in law free or servile, but the power of the landlord and his bailiff, allied with the laws that forbade men to leave their lands, reduced the bulk of the agricultural population to a common resentful servility.

In separating military and civil administration, Diocletian divided the provinces, in principle separating frontier provinces filled with troops from their civilian hinterland. The number of provinces was in practice about doubled. Britain had been divided into two provinces by Severus, and was now divided into four; later in the fourth century a fifth was established. The great number of provinces required grouping into administrative units. Under Diocletian's successors the office of the Praetorian Prefect, formerly the chief minister of government, was divided into four territorial prefectures, the westernmost comprising Gaul, Spain and Britain. Within each prefecture provinces were grouped under vice-prefects, soon known as *vicarii*, whose section of the prefecture was termed a diocese. The terminology was perpetuated by the Christian church, but with different connotations. In the fourth century the provinces of Britain formed one diocese. London was the capital of one province, and also the seat of the vicar of the diocese. The devolution was carried further in the 340s when the *magister militum*, master of the soldiers, formerly a deputy of the prefect gained a status equivalent to the prefect's; and *magistri* also commanded in several regions of the same size as the prefectures.

The tidy hierarchy of four permanent prefectures and independent marshals did not settle to its lasting form until forty years after Diocletian's time; but the fundamental changes were introduced in his early years, while Constantius was recovering Britain. They were accompanied by a mounting pressure for religious uniformity. Almost all beliefs and philosophies were prepared to accept incorporation under the loose umbrella of the Roman religion, except the Christians; and in 303 the pressure of the Caesar Galerius persuaded Diocletian to authorize the proscription, arrest, imprisonment or execution of Christians who withheld loyal and proper respect from tutelary deities of the state. Persecution was ferocious, and failed. Christians boasted that every martyr made ten converts, for millions admired men whose faith was strong enough to matter more than their lives, in an age when no other belief or observance bit deeper than routine observance or self interest. The disasters of a century had robbed the government and old beliefs of the respect they had once commanded, and men yearned for something worth respecting.

The persecution did not extend to Britain. Constantius had married a Balkan girl, Helena, who was herself Christian, before he was promoted Caesar. Churches were closed and books confiscated, to conform officially with the policy of the other Tetrarchs; but, in the words of admiring contemporaries, 'the true temple of God, Man' was left unharmed. After three years, it was clear that the persecution had failed; the Christians were not broken. At the same time, Diocletian celebrated the twentieth anniversary of his accession, and determined to bring the new succession scheme into operation while he yet lived. He abdicated, and compelled his fellow Augustus, Maximian, to do the same. The two Caesars were elevated to the rank of Augusti, and new Caesars were appointed. But the choice proved fatal. Both Maximian and Constantius had adult sons, and both were overlooked. They and their fathers were infuriated, and public opinion sympathized with them. Its strength was first revealed in Britain. Constantius contracted a fatal illness; Constantine secured reluctant permission to visit his dying father, and reached Britain. When his father died in the summer of 306, he was proclaimed Augustus at York. He led his army south to master the rest of the Roman world, and plainly secured the immediate support of London. He was himself a Christian born, brought up in his mother's faith. London and York became the first capitals of a Christian emperor, though Christians were still few in Britain outside the capitals.

After six years Constantine secured Rome and the west, though for a dozen years more another emperor ruled the east. As soon as he had conquered the east, in 324, he set about the foundation of a new capital, Christian from the outset, the second Rome, that bore his name, Constantinople, later called Istanbul by the Turks. Religion was not the sole or principal purpose of the new capital. A century of enemy attacks had obliged emperors to spend most of their time on the frontiers, so that men looked with nostalgia on days of past serenity, when rulers might live at ease in Rome while generals obeyed orders sent by messengers, and had the time to wait for their arrival. The empire could no longer be ruled from a single centre, and Rome was poorly sited to co-ordinate the frontiers. Constantinople, an impregnable fortress in its immediate environment, was well placed to supervise the Danube and also the eastern frontier, whose capital and nerve centre was Antioch of Syria. Only the Rhine was inaccessible, and the foundation of Constantinople made Trier on the Moselle the effective capital of the west. It was the centre of imperial administration and of military command, but it was not a trading town. The west had become in practice self sufficient, its economy increasingly geared upon the maintenance of the Rhine armies. London became its chief commercial centre, and after London Lugdunum.

The altered circumstances of the empire brought enormous local benefit to the diocese of Britain. Damage in the wars had been far less than in Europe, and had been relatively easily contained by defences that limited danger to a few coastal regions. But the economy of eastern and north eastern Gaul had been irreparably damaged, and remained permanently exposed to the same risk of frontier raids that threatened the coasts of Britain. The evidence for the rural wealth of the Rhineland and the modern territory of France has not yet been assembled and analysed; but a brief examination of the territory that is now Belgium has catalogued some four hundred villas of the early empire, and has failed to find evidence of fourth-century occupation in more than four of them.[7] The lands that had formerly fed the Rhine were wasted in the great invasion of the middle of the third century, and never recovered their former prosperity. Texts from the fourth-century report that important military expeditions were compelled to delay their start until the 'usual supplies' from Britain and Aquitania arrived;[8] though Aquitania was as fertile as Britain or more so, the long land haul, cutting across the main routes of the past at right-angles, made the transport costs prohibitive. One text emphasizes the difficulties; one of the addresses preserved in the Gallic collection of public speeches includes a request to the government to construct more serviceable roads,[9] for in some parts all that was available was a *via militaris*, a military road laid out for marching troops, with gradients so steep that is was barely possible to haul an empty vehicle to the top, let alone a laden waggon. Similar military gradients are not uncommon even in the gentler hills of Roman Britain, and were replaced; the Roman road at Bishop's Stortford climbs westward from the river at an impossible angle, but the town is built upon a loop with manageable slopes, laid out in short, straight stretches, and the distribution of the homes and pottery of the Roman town argues that the by-pass was also Roman.

The opulence of rural Britain in the forth century is in total and dramatic contrast to the poverty of north-eastern Gaul. Throughout the fertile lowlands, most known country houses were somewhat larger and somewhat better built than in the past, and even poorer dwellings prospered. In some districts small farms were replaced by villages, some of them quite large; some poor men's timber cottages were equipped with window glass and door keys, evidence of property worth stealing. Sometimes a small two-roomed cottage could afford a tiled floor, roughly patterned, and a simple central-heating system. But the splendour of the age lay in the west country and the south midlands, in the Cotswolds, Oxfordshire and Hampshire, Wiltshire and Dorset, with a few extensions elsewhere. Upwards of a hundred vast country mansions are known, and more plainly remain undiscovered. Many have twenty or thirty rooms on the ground floor, some more than seventy, many of them adorned with rich mosaics. They were built about a central courtyard, very similar to each other in plan.[10] Their size and scale compares with the mansions of Tudor, Stuart and Hanoverian England. Longleat, residence of the Marquess of Bath, contains about forty ground-floor rooms. The central courtyard of the Roman mansion at Brading in the Isle of Wight covers a larger area than the whole of Longleat, or of Hatfield House, the home of the Marquess of Salisbury. At North Leigh in Oxfordshire, if the fourth-century extensions revealed in air photography on the western side were matched by similar extensions on the east, the house would be larger than Blenheim Palace, the mansion of the Dukes of Marlborough, the largest private residence ever built in Britain.

The style of living revealed by these great houses was matched in many towns. Cirencester, the second city of Roman Britain, is rich in mosaics and grew to be two-thirds of the size of London. Urban mosaics have not yet been fully investigated, but it is already plain that several of the finest London mosaics are also of the fourth century. The city shared the prosperity of the west country. No text sets forth its cause, but the fundamental reasons are plain. Britain grew rich by exporting the produce of its countryside to regions that had once been supplied by northern and eastern Gaul, to the Rhine armies above all. Though much could be exacted in taxes, and by compulsory government purchase at low prices, much else had to be paid for in cash and kind. There is no evidence for what was exported.

One possible new industry was timber. The armies of the Rhine needed much wood for the construction of artillery, for maintenance of the fleet, for fuel and for many other purposes. When the power of Rome was strong, the forests on the barbarian bank of the river might be exploited to supplement those in Roman territory, for those whose timber might easily be transported by water were not inexhaustible. Thick oakwoods were abundant immediately around the city, between the Thames and Lea and the Brent, and their timber might reach the forts of the Rhine with no more than three or four miles land haul at most. These forests were not cleared and settled at any time in the Roman centuries, but the later history of Middlesex suggests that they have been thinned in the later Roman period, as far as the northern heights by Hampstead, Highgate and Hornsey, and as far as Tottenham by the Lea; for thus far the names that the early English gave to their first homes in Middlesex include many of those that were most commonly used in the seventh century, and hardly any that describe woodland, but further north the names that describe woodland and woodland clearings greatly outnumber all other forms. Elsewhere, early English clearance of densely forested clays is not common, save occasionally under the enterprise of monasteries, and the probable explanation of the names is that when the English came, much of the natural woodland had already been removed. Since it was not removed to make way for Roman homes and farms, like the clays beyond the Brent, the trees were probably cut down for timber, in a process begun in the later Roman period, and maintained with less intensity by the needs of London in the years between; for when oaks are felled, it is long before new trees regain the density of natural forests.

Many of the older London exports were still available, perhaps in even greater quantity, though not all that was consigned to Europe necessarily passed through London. Western corn was doubtless shipped through the nearer harbours of Poole and Southampton, though the Thames waterway provided cheap transport from Oxfordshire and the northern estates of the west country through London. But corn by itself is rarely the foundation of great landed wealth, and in later ages sheep and cattle made the west wealthy. London remained the principal port for the transhipment of animals that might be driven, and as the terminus of the drove roads, it was fitted to be the centre of the leather and textile

industry. In the earlier fourth century, it might have contained a government clothing factory. Its mint, opened by Carausius, remained a principal western mint until the foundation of Constantinople and the firm
establishment of an imperial capital at Trier. Its treasury, one of half a
dozen in the western provinces, was kept in being until the end of the
empire, evidently to receive the silver of the Mendips and other British
mines. Two very long walls in Knightrider Street (Map 10, No. 1, p.
156), on an alignment that was probably not laid out until the late
empire, may have enclosed the compounds of some of these buildings.

Constantine was the last emperor to rule the whole empire for any
length of time; it was to be briefly reunited only twice again, for a little
over eighteen months in 361, and for four months at the end of 394. Two
of Constantine's sons survived a brief succession struggle, and from 340
Constans ruled the west from Trier and Rome, Constantius II from
Constantinople and Antioch of Syria. Constans was a light-headed and
unpopular prince, and was removed in 350 by a conspiracy that enthroned Magnentius, a capable army officer said to have been of British
birth, and also son of a German settled in the empire by Constantine. He
was well received by the aristocracy of Rome, and married a noble
heiress, but Constantius assembled the armies of the east, and inherited
the loyalties due to the son of Constantine. Magnentius was defeated in
a bloody Balkan battle, whose casualties are said to have numbered
about one-tenth of the fighting force of the Roman army. Civil disaster
in Gaul was greater still, for Constantius instigated the Franks and
Alamanni to attack the Rhine and bring down Magnentius' forces. They
succeeded, and stormed almost all the main towns of the Roman Rhineland.

The chief preoccupation of Constantius was religion. Like his father,
and previous pagan emperors, he believed that conformity in religion
earned the favour of heaven towards the Roman state. Constantine
sought unity in worship of the Christian God, and was pained to discover
that Christians were not in accord. Division took two main forms. Many
veteran Christians were dismayed at the numbers and the views of new
converts who embraced the emperor's religion, and distrusted the emperor's intervention in the affairs of the church, expressed by his claim
to be 'bishop of the church in external affairs'. Donatus of Africa met
Constantine's delegates with the memorable question 'What has the
state to do with the church'. Their dispute was resolved upon class lines;
African Donatism became chiefly the religion of upland peasants, catholic orthodoxy the faith of the cities of the plain, and its sentiments were

echoed by some other movements in some other provinces. Much more important were sharp differences of ideology. Orthodox catholic teaching held that Christ who endured human suffering was of the same divine being as God the Father. The symbol of the crucifixion, of the God who was executed as a human criminal, had long aroused the deepest emotions among the urban poor who had constituted the bulk of the early Christian communities, but it had proved the chief stumbling block to men of birth and breeding, who found excessive emphasis on the killing of the God a vulgar and offensive supersition. They, and educated Christians who sought accord with them, preferred to dwell upon the Godhead of the divine *Logos*, the Word that moved the world. Arius of Alexandria revived old heresies in a new form, arguing that God the Father was not of the same, but of a similar being, by definition superior. Constantine and Constantius sought concord, and found the Arian more pliant than the orthodox leader, Athanasius, and Constantius determined to enforce conformity with the Arian creed. It appealed especially to rulers and men in government service, for the sovereignty of one God within the Trinity, attended by archangels and angels, mirrored the earthly hierarchy of government.

When one creed was enforced by government order, its bishops appeared to the public as creatures of the government, and those who defied them attracted the sympathies of all who disliked or despised the government. In the west, the main heat of the controversy ended with the Congress of Rimini in 359, when a mixture of clever conference management and intimidation coerced and cajoled a decisive majority of catholic bishops into submission. An obstinate minority of fifteen probably included Augurius, bishop of London; and some of the British bishops proved themselves outstanding among their fellows in their contempt and defiance of government. But the prodigious effort of the government was vain. The world had watched the wrangle of Christians, still a minority among men, though championed by those in power; the spectacle of an emperor whose energies were spent in endeavours to win a favourable vote from delegates of small conventicles of plebeian subjects amazed those who recalled the authoritarian majesty of past emperors. Amazement turned to wonder at the sequel, for within a year Constantius lost control of the west; Christian congregations disowned the bishops who had submitted, and Arian support was quickly extinguished in the west. Men learnt not only that the children of Christians who had withstood a pagan government were themselves prepared to defy a Christian government that violated their consciences. They saw that defiance prevailed and overcame the power of the emperors. As men's confidence in government wilted, they saw the emergence of a new force, strong enough to rally and comfort ordinary subjects, to protect and defend them in the name of an all powerful divinity.[11]

Constantius' religion offended the west. His secular government savaged the nobles of Britain. As soon as Magnentius was defeated, Constantius arraigned his supporters at his temporary headquarters at Arles. Men of wealth were summoned before the courts, tortured, imprisoned, exiled, executed, their property confiscated. Britain proved to be a nest of the conspirators, and a special inquisitor, the secretary Paul was despatched to Britain to ferret out the ramifications of the conspiracy. In the words of a contemporary[12]

This viper ... was sent to Britain. ... Arbitrarily extending his commision, he flooded over the fortunes of many men, ... framing accusations in contempt of truth.

Arrest meant ruin, for

It is not easy to remember an occasion under Constantius when a man was acquitted, even though the accusation were but a whisper.

The danger provoked resistance:

Martinus, then Vicar of the Britains ... repeatedly requested the release of the innocent. ... When ... Paul ... threatened to arrest him and his staff ... Martinus, in alarm, drew his own sword on Paul ... but failed to kill him, and therefore drove it into his own side. By that disgraceful death died a most just ruler.

The site of the tragedy was doubtless in London.

A substantial number of coin hoards that end with coins of Magnentius, most of them in the fertile lowlands, in the regions of wealthy villas, are the probable relics of men hauled to prison by the secretary Paul. The properties of those condemned were forfeit to the crown, and many such estates were then or later granted to men who earned the favour of the government. Few of them are likely to have removed to Britain to live in the mansions they acquired, or even to have visited the diocese; their interest was in the receipt of the rents of their estates. Confiscations reinforced the general trend of the fourth century towards the ownership of more and more land by fewer and fewer people; by the early fifth century the imbalance of wealth had produced a closer concentration of the productive forces in the hands of a few than any society has known until the middle of the twentieth century. Concentration meant absentee

landlords, and absentees meant that though peasant cultivation continued, many mansions were abandoned to the ruin of the weather, or were
occasionally turned to industrial use. Their abandonment is no indication of any general decline in population or in Roman civilization, but
only of a changing social structure; the strength of the economy of
Britain is witnessed by the many other mansions that remained in the
occupation of the wealthy, or of men of modest means, into the fifth
century.

Absentee property plainly included some town houses, in London and
other cities. But the profit of town houses, unlike that of country mansions, lay in the rent or value of the house itself, not of attached land.
Fewer town houses show such signs of early abandonment, and their
continuance suggests that purchasers were still easily found by foreigners
who did not wish to live in them; a few indications hint at the possibility
that some London houses may have been turned to meaner uses, gentleman's residences let off as flats or workshops, or possibly even left
untenanted. But the evidence is slight; all else suggests that London's
prosperity was fully maintained at least until Magnentius' time.

Chapter 15

The End of Roman London

THE WEAK AND timid bigotry of Constantius soon brought disaster. When he returned to the east, he appointed his nephew Julian Caesar of the Gauls. Julian was brilliantly successful. He speedily recovered the ravaged Rhineland, routed the main German armies and wasted their homeland; and he also reformed the administration, greatly increasing the taxpayers' burden and at the same time augmenting the revenue by reducing the sequestration of funds at the many levels that intervened between the taxpayer and the treasury spending departments. His military success aroused his uncle's jealousy and suspicion, and his reforms infuriated the bureaucracy. Constantius ordered his best troops to the east. Their experience warned them that if they left the Rhine undefended, their families and relatives were exposed to enemy attack. They refused to go, and proclaimed the unwilling Julian emperor. Their mutiny is well documented, for the extant writings of Julian, including his correspondence with Constantius, greatly outnumber the surviving literary remains of all other emperors combined.

Julian sought accommodation, but Constantius refused. The armies of east and west advanced towards another bloody engagement, but the slaughter was averted by the timely death of Constantius, in 361. Julian disgusted by the squabbles of Christian factions, abjured Christianity and introduced an esoteric intellectual religion of his own. Rejection of Constantius' beliefs was welcomed both by his subjects and by many senior government officers; there are several signs in Britain of the reopening of old temples, and the dedication of new ones. But Julian's religion was short lived, and died with its founder, killed mysteriously on his return from a Persian expedition. The army council appointed his successor, and replaced him when he too died.

The new emperor, Valentinian was an experienced officer, an orthodox Christian who cared little for theology and left it to the churchmen. Unlike his predecessors, he chose the west as his own portion of the empire, and appointed his undistinguished brother Valens to rule in Constantinople. Julian's departure had occasioned another damaging German invasion across the Rhine, and Valentinian restored the frontiers, with massive fortifications, adding bastions to many town walls, probably including some in London. In the midst of his German campaigns came news of a disaster in Britain, in 367.

A barbarian alliance brought Britain to her knees. Nectaridus, Count of the Coastal Defence, was killed, the general Fullofaudes ambushed.... The Picts plundered at will, as did the warlike Atacotti and the Irish.... The Franks and their neighbours the Saxons raided the coast that faces Gaul, breaking in where they could.[1]

Barbarians had joined forces in Europe before but such an alliance was new in Britain; and Irish native tradition independently remembers a marriage alliance between their High King and a Saxon woman in about the 360s.[2] The ambushed general commanded the armies of the north, and ample archaeological evidence accounts for the damage done in the north by the Picts. The Irish attack, unlike theirs, passed beyond raiding; Irish colonists settled in numbers in parts of western Britain, and maintained their independence for several generations, some of them for more than 150 years.

The assault of the Franks and Saxons caused less damage. Valentinian sent an expeditionary force, under a Spanish commander, Count Theodosius, father of the future emperor Theodosius. He sailed from Boulogne to Richborough, and marched thence to 'London, an old town that later ages called Augusta', rounding up isolated bands of the enemy as he marched. He wintered in the city and next spring set out from 'Augusta, anciently called London' and restored order.[3] Damage in the lowlands was not severe; no large number of coin hoards, comparable with those of earlier and later disasters, indicates widespread disturbance at this date. Though excavators of innumerable villas have endeavoured to interpret their end as a consequence of the raid, they have been thwarted by some awkward items of evidence. In individual reports, concerned with one site alone, one or two later coins or other objects may often be explained away; but when special pleading is required for nine-tenths of the sites discussed, it cannot prevail. Only a few open-country sites can be shown to have ended in the 360s. Doubtless others also perished, where evidence is not available, and others were doubtless damaged and repaired. But the evidence is plain that Theodosius arrived in time to avert a general destruction. The historian gives much space to the raid and its defeat, far more than to earlier or later troubles; the reason is not that the raid was proportionately more serious, but that when Ammian wrote the reigning emperor was the son of Count Theodosius. Other incursions earned less notice because the generals who repressed them had less illustrious sons.

London retained its title Augusta until the last days of Roman rule, and is so styled in the *Notitia Dignitatum*, a document of the early fifth century. It was relatively recent when Ammian wrote. One possible explanation of its origin is that the city was renamed Caesarea when the Caesar Constantius recovered Britain, for two of the late provinces of Britain were termed Caesariensis, and imply the existence of a city named Caesarea; and that it received the higher title of Augusta either when Constantius became Augustus, or from Constantine in recompense for its loyalty during his accession and enthronement in Britain. But it is also possible that another town, perhaps York or Cirencester, received the appellation Caesarea at the same time as London was named Augusta.

The prosperity of Britain survived the great raid, and in some regions increased. It is most strikingly asserted by random evidence, that emphasizes the late date of fine building in some villas and some towns, but its full extent is masked by important changes in the working of the late Roman economy. The use and distribution of money took a different course, and one incidental consequence of the new trends was to disturb the pattern of the evidence that the modern student must interpret. In the late empire, coins are still the chief means of dating sites. In most regions it is still not possible to date much of the pottery more closely than to the fourth century in general. Some forms in most districts, and many forms in some districts, can be recognized as in normal use in the early or mid fourth century, or in the last generations of Roman Britain; but the majority of excavation reports base the dates they assign to the excavated buildings upon the latest coins found therein. The value of that evidence depends as much upon what is not found as upon what is found; if many coins of Constantine and his sons are found, minted no later than the 350s, and no coins at all of subsequent emperors, then it is a sensible inference that human activity ceased or declined, if later coins are normally found on comparable sites elsewhere. But if later coins are not normal, then their absence on one site says nothing of its later history; and there are many sites where pottery, structural evidence or other indications demonstrate that men were busy for generations, but left no coins behind them.

The evidence has not yet been thoroughly investigated. Ancient coins have always fascinated antiquarians and collectors; even among professional numismatists, whose occupation is the study of coins, more effort has gone into the study of individual coins, of their metallic content, of the legends stamped upon them, than into the study of their distribution;

and rare coins have excited disproportionate interest, for it is the use of the commonest coins that tells most about the men who used them. Adding up and analysing the millions of known Roman coins, estimating the length of time in which they remained in use, distinguishing the different histories of particular denominations at various periods, is a stupendous task that has not yet been tackled. In Britain, lists of coins from many sites are available, including London, but they have not yet been compared.[4] Only a few superficial and general inferences are therefore yet possible.

There is no average, typical site that may be taken as a standard, any more than there is an individual person who may be selected as the average man in the street, for each town, village, fort or country building had its individual history. But there are nevertheless certain overall proportions that vary with the quantities of particular kinds of coins minted at different periods, and the volume of money used at different kinds of site, though often the accidents of modern discovery vary the absolute totals, and sometimes the proportions within the totals. In London, many coins have been recovered from the Walbrook mud, and much of the central section of the Walbrook was partly enclosed in the middle of the second century, so that coins in circulation before then are disproportionately numerous.[5]

The significance of any list of coins is plainly clearer when the numbers are greatest; when all the necessary weightage due to known factors has been considered, the proportions of different issues in a total of ten thousand or more recorded coins from Cirencester are less distorted by the accident of discovery than in a total of a few hundred from Gloucester or London. Yet even within the smaller lists counted by the hundred, marked variations between different localities indicate something of their history.

In very crude overall generalities, the coins of the early empire, minted before the mid third-century inflation, found on sites in the fertile lowlands of Britain, constitute about one-third of the total, or a little more. Those of the inflationary years are somewhat fewer, amounting to about a quarter, though as the period in which they were minted was much less, the numbers minted in each year or decade are much greater. The issues of Constantine and his sons, ending in the 350s, make up two-thirds or three-quarters of all fourth century coins, and more than half of all later coins are those of Valentinian and his sons, mostly minted in the 360s and 370s. Ordinary bronze coins are almost unknown thereafter, and the coins of Theodosius and his sons, minted in the 380s and 390s, commonly run up to about 5 per cent of the total coins of Roman Britain. Their absence from a collection of less than one or two hundred coins may be without meaning; but when their proportion is much higher, as at Richborough, where they amount to 45 per cent of the total, or at Cirencester, where they total 12 or 15 per cent of a large collection, then these large percentages are due to particular causes. After about 402, the western mints issued very little small change, and hardly any of it reached Britain; its absence is without meaning, beyond the bare fact that it did not cross the Channel.

The striking feature of the distribution of late coinage is that it is uneven. Up until the middle of the fourth century, coins are common on sites of all kinds, though even the earlier fourth-century coins are proportionately rarer on poor rural sites than those of the early empire in many districts. But later coins, especially those of Theodosius and his sons, minted in the last decades of the fourth century, are concentrated on a limited number of sites, plentiful in some towns but not others, in some parts of towns but not others, in some temples, and in some country houses, but not in all. In the north, they are proportionately as numerous in the towns that served the army, Corbridge and Carlisle, as in the south, but they are very rare in forts.

So far the change in the circulation of money can only loosely be observed; it has therefore not been discussed or explained. Some of the most striking aberrations from the past prompt plain inferences. The high proportion of late issues at Richborough consists of the coins of only the last twenty years of Roman minting; the number of coins per year was fifteen or twenty times as great as in the past. The latest coins were necessarily employed as long as coins remained in normal use, perhaps for half a century more, for no more were available, but even so the volume of currency exchanged at Richborough was much greater in the last generations of Roman Britain than before. Richborough was still the principal port for the embarkation and disembarkation of passengers travelling to and from Boulogne and other Gallic ports, and also for the handling of light and valuable goods, cheaply transported by land. The pattern of Richborough is matched inland; the latest coins are not uncommon in the towns of east Kent on the London road as far as the Medway; west of the Medway they are rare, except at a temple site at Greenwich. There is no evidence that greatly more men or valuables landed at Richborough or were shipped thence; the plain inference is that there was more buying and selling at Richborough than before, that goods which had previously been carried through Richborough for sale elsewhere were now bought and sold at the port itself. The evidence of Richborough is matched, though not fully explained, by an enormous hoard of the latest currency discovered on the coast by the Rhinemouth, evidently concerned with Richborough traffic.

Similar indications point to local cash-trading centres elsewhere. Late money is unusually common not only in the city of Cirencester, but in many of the great Cotswold mansions, sometimes concentrated in some parts of the buildings. It is relatively plentiful in and around the great pottery centres of the Peterborough region, and also at many temples, and one of the functions of temples was to provide annual or periodic fairs. Clear conclusions cannot be reached until the evidence is properly examined. The implication of what can now be observed is that more buying and selling was concentrated in fewer centres. Men brought their produce to markets, and spent in those markets the money they received. It may be that the owners of great estates sold their produce in bulk, and that stewards bought in the market what the estate could not itself produce; within the estate commodities might be exchanged with less use of money, with estate carpenters servicing the tenants, and even perhaps pottery and other tools and utensils being bought by the estate and distributed by the bailiff in return for deliveries in kind by the peasant.

In the few towns whose excavation permits one part of the town to be compared with another, the same kind of conclusion emerges from limited evidence. In Verulamium, later coins are said to have been very numerous in the theatre, though the details of the coins found have not yet been examined and published.[6] They were probably dumped there with market rubbish, and they were apparently also plentiful in the shopping area of the town centre; but in the houses removed from the centre they were few. The overall tendency of the evidence suggests the concentration of cash dealings into local and regional centres; local and regional centralization also implies decentralization in Britain as a whole. Local centres gathered to themselves the money of their own region; but they had less intercourse with the main distribution centres that served all Britain.

The total number of coins recorded in detail from London is not great, but the proportions are emphatic. Coins of the early empire amount to more than two-thirds of the total, double the proportion of most of the country; though much of this excess is explained by the large number sealed by the Walbrook. But of the fourth-century coins recorded, which are not thereby affected, more than 90 per cent were minted before the accession of Valentinian in 364. The coinage of the next fifteen years accounts for 8 per cent; the Theodosian coins minted between about 380 and about 400 are less than 1½ per cent of the fourth-century coins. On present coin evidence, London was no longer a main centre of the trade of Britain. The implication of the London coins is emphasized by contrast with nearby sites. At the little towns of Brentford and Bow the use of money was entirely different. At Brentford more than two thirds of the total coins were fourth-century issues, exactly reversing the proportions of the city, and more than half the fourth-century coins were minted after 364, in contrast with less than 10 per cent of the city coins. Though the numbers of coins are not great, a little over forty in all, their weighting is plain. Small change was commoner than in the past in the small riverside towns near to London, much less frequent in the city itself.

The absolute figures would not imply that more money was used in the small towns; the evidence stresses only proportions and the tendencies of change. The function of these little towns is clear. Brentford is situated at the junction of the Brent with the Thames, the point of transhipment of the produce of the farms of the cultivated lands north and west of the stream, and is also at the end of the big bend of the middle reaches of the Thames, and the only point where the west road touches the river on its way to Staines. Bow is the nearest practicable point to the city on the Lea, that joined London to the Chiltern chalk, whence the road from Colchester runs direct to the city. These little towns whose cash dealings increased in the fourth century, and increased proportionately in the second half of the century, were not concerned with the long-distance trade of the city. Their business was the feeding of London. Supplies that had once been imported direct to the city's wharves, when vessels carried the manufactures of London and its imports from abroad in the opposite direction, were now purchased locally at the nearest riverside markets to the city. London lived less by its long-distance trade, and was more dependent on local food supplies.

The evidence of the coins is matched by what else is known of late Roman London. The distribution of small finds and pottery within the city has not yet been plotted in close detail, but two general changes in the late empire are immediately apparent. The total quantity of late objects found in London is a considerably smaller proportion of the total than in most towns of Roman Britain, even when many finds of the early empire from the Walbrook are disregarded. Though many areas, especially in the north and east of the city, are poorly recorded, in the areas where finds are plentiful, the late objects are relatively more numerous near to the river, and relatively fewer on and beyond Cornhill and Ludgate Hill. Whatever happened to the city's population in the late fourth century, it was relatively denser by the waterfront, relatively lighter further inshore than in the past.

The proportions cannot be explained by the accidents of modern discovery, by the removal of late levels by subsequent building, or the erosion of the hill-tops. Much was disturbed and destroyed, but no conditions obliged the men who dug medieval and later cellars and wall foundations to dig down to the levels of the mid fourth century, and there stop. Some later excavations removed all traces of the Roman city in their holes, others ceased at any level; the depth of their digging was determined by the needs of the building they constructed, not by Roman features.

The nature of the London finds cannot be explained by the topography of the city alone, for it is repeated in the countryside around. On the roads that radiate north and west of the city, late finds are even rarer than in the city. Along the Ermine Street towards Lincoln and York, many objects have been recovered from the small roadside post towns, at Enfield, at Cheshunt, less explored than the others, at Ware and at Braughing, thirty-five miles to the north. From all these sites, no single later fourth-century coin is known, though as soon as the headwaters of the Lea are passed, from Wimpole by Royston northward, late fourth-century coins are at least as numerous as elsewhere in Britain, and pottery or other objects that are, or might be, later than the 360s are very few. On the Verulamium road, Sulloniacae, at Brockley Hill by Elstree, is equally short of later fourth-century finds, and on the Staines road only Brentford has late coins and pottery. Not only London, but the communications of London were in decline.

Excavation can observe and report the signs of decline. It cannot by itself explain them. The decline of one great city, while the country that it governed still flourished, can rarely be explained by a single cause, and many of the developments of the late empire combined to lessen the trade of London. Some were political, some economic, some due to the workings of the elements. A main cause of the fourth-century prosperity of Britain was the need to feed the Rhine armies. London served that need so long as goods could be conveyed in safety by boat to the garrisons on the Roman bank of the Rhine. By the 350s, after Magnentius' rebellion and the storming of the Rhineland towns, safety could no longer be guaranteed. Julian was outraged when the Chamavi, Germans inhabiting the territory now called Gelderland, by the modern border between the Netherlands and Germany, about Arnhem, demanded payment for refraining from raiding the cargoes from Britain to the upriver forts. Julian refused payment and used force to ensure his supplies. Merchant vessels could still reach their destinations in convoy, escorted by warships. But repeated incursions in the next few decades weakened Roman control of the river, and not all Julian's successors shared his energy and resolution. The power of the Franks grew great by the estuary of the Rhine, and the Franks obeyed Roman generals only when they must; even away from the river, the roads that led to the forts towards the interior of Gaul were protected by newly-established garrison forts, many of them built by units transferred from the Danube for the purpose. Roman cargoes on the Rhine became less and less safe, and even armed troops sometimes found it safer to avoid the waterway; when Theodosius brought urgent reinforcements from the Rhine to Britain, they were not carried down by the river, whose current bore men more swiftly than they could walk, but were marched overland to Boulogne and there embarked.

The weakening of the Roman frontier in Europe much diminished the trade of London with the Rhine. When that passage was no longer open, and goods must be shipped to Boulogne and safer north-coast harbours, there were no longer advantages in routing the produce of the Cotswolds down the Thames, or in driving animals as far as London. The south-coast ports were nearer, and were better sited for the Boulogne trade. By the early fifth century, the only government clothing factory in Britain was located at Winchester, not London.[7] It implies the use of the port of Southampton for the shipment of animals; those destined to be eaten passed on by sea; fleeces of sheep left alive or of those consumed in Britain gave Winchester its raw material.

Economic change had shifted the wealth of Britain. Under the Belgic kings before the Romans, and under the early empire, prosperity was as marked in the south-east as in the west, but the great mansions of the late empire concentrate in the west country. Though buildings were somewhat larger and better furnished in the states nearer to London, they did not match the sudden and staggering wealth of the west. London had long been the commercial centre of Britain, and old commercial habits die slowly, but in time the shift in agricultural output to the west lessened the proportions of its output that might conveniently be handled by the port of London, even apart from the dangers of enemy attacks on the Rhine.

The changes caused by man were aggravated by nature. All over the Roman world, coasts and low-lying lands were flooded in the late empire. Salt pans in the Levant were swamped; the floors of ancient temples on the coasts of southern Italy and Sicily were covered by a foot or two of water; in the low countries farmers were obliged to raise their cultivated lands above the swamps by piling up the mounds known to the Dutch as 'terps'. In Britain other islands of cultivation on the Somerset shore of the Severn were surrounded by marshes; on the east-coast Roman farms laid out upon hard soils were swamped by silt, which created the fenlands that were reclaimed centuries later, and by the peat whose later excavation created the Norfolk broads. In the London region, the floors of early Roman houses were covered by the Thames, whose level is now some fourteen feet higher than it was when they were built (above, p. 57).

The evidence has been observed, but its date and impact in different parts of Europe and the Mediterranean have not been closely compared, and only random indications of date have been noted. At one Norfolk fenland site, the silt overlay early Roman building debris, and above it a late Roman hut was built.[8] Recent excavation in the Lea Valley river system indicates continuing flooding. At Braughing, houses and streets were covered in silt in or after the middle of the fourth century. The danger from the water was not then over; in the middle of the fifth century the British, harassed by Saxons, complained that sea was a threat as dangerous.[9] It is plain that the process extended over several centuries, at its worst in the fourth and fifth centuries. It is evident that any such natural process proceeded by fits and jerks, ebbs and flows, not by an even, annual rise in the river levels, but by sudden floods succeeding each other and receding, as individual waves advance and recede upon the coast as the tide comes in. The available evidence suggests that in the rivers of the London region the later fourth century was one period when the waters advanced sharply. One main additional damage that the rising rivers inflicted upon the trade of London was clearly the flooding of the low-lying parts of the north road up the Lea Valley. The roadside posting towns decayed, but Bow prospered, where the river meets the eastern highway from the city. Their combined evidence suggests that the old north road was in poor shape, out of action as a through route, at least for the winter season.

London declined, but it survived. Its great days were past, but some trade remained, even after the end of Roman rule, and the city remained the seat of government. The importance of the political capital was also diminished. In the early empire, all Britain had been governed by legates directly responsible to a single government in Rome, the centre of civil administration and justice, and of government finance. The hierarchy of the late empire involved decentralization from the top and also regional centralization in political government as well as in the economy and the use of money. On the one hand, Britain was responsible not directly to Italy, but to the prefecture of the Gauls at Trier. On the other hand, the diocese was divided into five provinces, and much of the business that had formerly concentrated on Government House now devolved upon the provincial governors in their separate capitals. The fiscal needs of the government involved more day-to-day interference with cities and individuals, and increased the total volume of administration, though the larger number of provinces and the hierarchy meant less of it in each capital. The London government offices no longer had such full control over the whole of the administration of Britain, and the city's function as a capital was less; but it was still the seat of the vicar, where all the provinces were co-ordinated, and it was also the capital of one province. Though the status of the city was lessened, much political business remained, and the actual number of government employees may have been more rather than less. Government and the slow run down of trade kept the city in being; and there is no marked and obvious sign of physical decay. Slow and partial decline is recorded of many late Roman cities, different in manner and extent from one city to another, and its effect upon the population is not easy to assess. In Italy, St Jerome remarked that in the later fourth century Vercelli was 'empty and thinly peopled',[10] but its decay did not deter the governor from holding his assizes there as in the past, and the holding of assizes required a sufficient population to serve the needs of government, and also was normally attended by business fairs.

In the later fourth century, little is recorded of Britain and almost nothing of London. Troubles beset the whole empire. Valentinian died in 374, and almost at once a new and terrible enemy threatened Europe. The savage Huns migrated from the Asian steppes, in numbers as fearful as in the later migrations of Mongols and Tartars. They destroyed the Black Sea empire of the Goths, and the powerful nation of the Visigoths sought and obtained protection inside the shelter of the Roman Danube. But the refugees were abused and exploited by Roman officers, the undertakings made to them overridden. Starving Goths were driven to open rebellion when the Roman general attempted to assassinate their leaders, and in 379 the rebels destroyed the armies of the east, and killed the emperor Valens. His nephew Gratian, ruler of the west, did not attempt to take over the rule of the east as well, but installed as emperor Theodosius, son of the general who had rescued Britain in 367.

The victorious Goths were masters of the eastern Balkans and threatened Constantinople. Theodosius could restore Roman authority only by hiring individual Gothic forces to protect the government against their fellow Germans. His innovation was startling. Rome had always employed barbarians. At the beginning of the empire, the manpower of newly-conquered provincials was enrolled in auxiliary units, and many units raised in Britain had served on distant frontiers. But when the first recruits died or retired, they were normally replaced by natives of the provinces near to their station. They were from the beginning supplemented by many *nationes* or *numeri*, units of barbarians raised from beyond the frontiers, who did not receive Roman citizenship on discharge. In the late empire, such units continued to be raised, though when they were stationed within the empire, their first recruits also were commonly replaced by native Romans from the frontier regions. From the late third century, many barbarians were settled in the interior with their families, in the double capacity of local defence forces and of bond cultivators; Sarmatians and Franks were introduced into Italy and Gaul, and probably Saxons into Britain, but after the first generation, their descendants were for the most part born on Roman soil. They remained barbarian, in language and breeding, members of isolated communities within the empire; but were equally isolated from barbarians without, who thought poorly of their fellows who took service with Rome, whether voluntarily or by compulsion. Volunteers were plentiful, and in the fourth century many Germans rose to high rank as officers and generals within the Roman army, and a few served also in the ranks. On critical campaigns and in civil wars, generals and emperors enlisted barbarian allies on several occasions.

All these earlier barbarians had served in Roman units under Roman officers and Roman laws. Theodosius' new forces served under their own leaders and their own laws. They were termed *bucellarii*, because they took the military biscuit, *bucellum*, in token of engagement, or as *foederati*, allies by treaty. Such forces were not admitted into the west for another generation, and then in very different circumstances. But the innovation foreshadowed one of the main military principles of the medieval centuries to follow. A substantial part of the armed forces was no longer employed directly by the central government, but by their immediate commander, who owed personal allegiance to the emperor and swore to him an oath to serve as his subordinate ally. If he broke his oath, alliance or allegiance, he might expect his men to follow him in preference to his sovereign.

Theodosius' restoration of the east was interrupted by another rebellion in Britain. The virtuous and gentle Gratian was described by a contemporary as 'more pious than was good for the state',[11] and lost the respect of the western armies. Magnus Maximus, a Spaniard who had come to Britain with the elder Theodosius, was proclaimed in Britain, and ruled for a while in London and York before he crossed to Gaul. He too mastered Spain and Italy before he was defeated by Theodosius and the armies of the east in 388. No proscriptions followed, as after Magnentius' rebellion thirty-five years earlier. Theodosius was praised for his clemency. But the military strength of Britain was weakened. Later generations believed that the armies that Maximus had led to Europe never returned to Britain, but were settled in Armorica, north-western Gaul, to become the first of the British who gave the peninsula its future name of Brittany. Various indications suggest that the belief may well have been justified, and no evidence contradicts it.

Six years later Theodosius faced and reduced another western rebellion, in which the British are not reported to have been deeply involved. For months he ruled the Roman world alone, the last emperor to do so, till his death in January 395. He bequeathed the throne to his two considerably less able sons, Arcadius in Constantinople and Honorius in Rome. The Roman world accepted them, and thenceforth resolutely frowned upon rebels; the emperor in power, however feeble, was safer than the most competent rebel, whose rise to power must entail civil war, and whose newly-won authority tempted further rebellion. A powerful urge to formal loyalty constrained ambitious political leaders to gain their aims by intrigue and palace assassination, at cheaper cost than bloody civil war.

The western emperor was controlled by a strong minister, Stilicho, by birth a Vandal, who also claimed tutelage of Arcadius in the east. In the late 390s he is credited with two military successes, the suppression of a rebellious border chief who had been invested with the command of armies in Africa, and a successful defence of Britain against renewed combined attacks by the Irish, the Picts and the Saxons. His troubles multiplied after 400, and his ruin and the ruin of the city of Rome were intimately linked with the fortunes of Britain.

Stilicho was a Vandal, and in both capitals the power of the Germans was great. It divided Roman feeling. One party growled with patriotic nostalgia at the dominance of uncouth, loud-voiced Germans, whose dandy officers offended gentlemen by smarming their hair with rancid butter and whose arrogant rank and file abused the public. Another party pleaded realism; the employment of barbarians cost landowners less than the provision of native recruits, and man for man the warlike German was a better soldier than the oppressed Roman rustic, and neither rustic nor landowner retained respect for the failing government. Their viewpoint was strongly supported by an influential trend in Christian thinking. The Germans had come to stay, and could not be expelled except by bloody slaughter and a risk of failure; Rome had always absorbed and tamed barbarians, and the empire of Christ, embracing barbarians as well as Romans, must prove mightier than the vanishing empire of the sword.

Decisive conflict broke out first in the east. In 400 the Goths of Constantinople were slaughtered, the survivors expelled, and Roman power reasserted in city and country. Over the next century the Roman government was able to reduce its own landed nobility to obedience and to the payment of taxation, and thereby to equip native armies to fight invaders, or alternatively to pay invaders to go away. The east survived because it was rich and because enough of its magnates were prepared to maintain and back their own government against the enemy. But the rescue of the east proved the ruin of the west. The Visigoths, under their king Alaric, quitted the provinces of the east and entered Italy, and other Germans crossed the Alps. Stilicho stripped the frontiers to save Italy, and managed to transfer one British legion, probably the Twentieth, from Chester. He repelled the invaders, but immediately faced new and more dangerous invasion. A horde of Alans, Vandals and Suevi, pressed in their homeland by the Huns of central Europe, crossed the Rhine and overran Gaul, threatening the invasion of Britain. The government in Italy was powerless to help the countries beyond the Alps, and the British enthroned a native British emperor, Constantine III, to save Gaul, in 407.

Constantine cleared the enemy from Gaul, but the bulk of them withdrew over the Pyrenees, not the Rhine. The Suevi remained in Spain, but the Vandals crossed to Roman Africa, and a dozen years later established a Vandal kingdom that endured for more than a century. Constantine in Gaul was a rebel in the eyes of the imperial government. In Italy, Stilicho was assassinated in 408, and many German troops slaughtered, as in Constantinople eight years earlier. But the native Roman leaders of Italy lacked resolution, clarity of purpose, and the will to pay for the salvation of the empire. Constantine was besieged in Gaul by Goths employed by the Roman government, with the double purpose of subduing a rebel and ridding Italy of some Gothic bands. His own principal general, Gerontius, also a Briton, rebelled against him and seized Spain, and the remnants of the Rhine armies proclaimed their own emperors.

In the midst of these confusions, the states of Britain withdrew their allegiance from Constantine, whose final defeat was plainly inevitable. They did not at first proclaim another emperor, but returned their allegiance to Honorius, and asked for men and money to withstand renewed Saxon attacks. They were too late. Alaric was the military master of Italy, and demanded a ransom for refraining from occupying Rome. The sum he demanded was not greatly more than the annual income of the richest individual senators of the day, but it seemed inordinate in comparison with the accepted norms of western taxation. The Senate sought to win time by equivocal negotiation, until Alaric lost patience and captured Rome, in September 410.

Alaric did little damage. A couple of records offices were burnt, as probably by plebeian malcontents as by the Goths. Churches and lives were spared. The Goths left Rome within a fortnight, carrying with them great quantities of gold and silver, and some prisoners, including the emperor's sister, who was to prove a useful hostage. Material damage was slight, but the moral and emotional impact of the blow was mortal. When Rome, the mistress of the world, was herself enslaved, the power of Rome and a thousand years of continuing Greek and Roman supremacy over alien barbarians was ended for ever. The aged Jerome echoed the distress of the elder generation in crying that 'the world is beheaded':[12] Some of the younger generation accepted the end with equal finality, but different emotions; one young Briton observed that God had ended the world once before, in the Flood, but had kept men alive to build a better world thereafter.[13]

It was shortly after the capture of Rome that Honorius replied to the states of Britain. He was unable to send help, and authorized the British to look to their own defence. He thereby legalized whatever government and laws the British chose to establish. Contemporary opinion remarked that they succeeded beyond expectation. Enemy attacks upon their coasts were beaten back, and Britain enjoyed a long period of prosperity.

There was no 'Roman evacuation of Britain' in 410, no 'withdrawal of the legions' or of any troops or civilians. What happened was that the imperial government in Italy admitted its inability at the moment to govern and protect Britain. None clearly foresaw that the abandonment of Britain was to be permanent, and nothing changed save the method of choosing the government. There was no 'national' sentiment of the British that rejoiced in any 'liberation' from Rome, for all British were as Roman as the Romans of Italy. Dislike of the government sprang from distress at its inability to protect Rome and Britain; men wished the empire to continue and the rule of the central government to be maintained, for beyond the frontiers were only violent, uncivilized enemies who threatened rich and poor alike.

Neither the names nor the exploits of the first British emperors who ruled in the years immediately after 410 are recorded; all that is reported is that their reigns were brief, their power unstable. Their authority faced a built-in weakness. For nearly four hundred years the British had governed their own citizens; but they had been co-ordinated by governors appointed by emperors in Italy, and their armies had been commanded by generals similarly appointed. States that were each others' equals, noblemen of comparable ancestry and wealth, civilian magnates, the masters of the armies, had agreed through long convention to defer to single, central authority, even though in times of civil war men might dispute the individual in whom that authority was vested. But when once the protective power of the Mediterranean government was withdrawn, the states, the magnates and the senior officers of Britain were compelled to seek agreement upon obedience to one of their own number. Though agreement could be reached and was reached, it could not invest native emperors with the majesty of their predecessors who had ruled the whole empire, or the whole of the west. Many others knew that they or their friends were as fitted to rule; and as government measures aroused criticism, voices were ready to urge that one among the numerous practicable alternative rulers be enthroned. The disasters of the next two hundred years, and the rivalries that permitted the English to subdue Britain and name its largest portion, ensued directly from the failure of the British to agree upon a viable form of government.

Record is resumed after fifteen years.[14] A ruler was enthroned about 425, known to later ages as Vortigern. The word is a colloquial expression of a title rather than a personal name. In British, it means 'top ruler'. Echoes of old native tradition suggest that he came from Gloucester, and was perhaps named Vitalinus, and the name by which he is known suggests something of the political forces that brought him to power. He was known by a title in the British language, and two of his sons were also known by British names. The use of British does not indicate antagonism between a 'British' and a 'Roman' tradition in a national sense, but rather an emphasis of social class and popularity. In Gaul, Africa and the east many men used both native names and Roman names. Throughout the provinces, most men were bilingual, and in Gaul the native Gallic language was widely spoken by the nobility down to the middle of the fifth century, and was also the normal language of the cities, even of the imperial capital of Trier. But Latin was the only language that could be written or read. The incidence of language usage clearly varied; the wealthier and better educated used Latin more often, the poor spoke British more often, and used Latin to converse with others. Throughout the fifth and sixth centuries, both British and Latin personal names are frequently recorded, and emphasis changed only slowly. At the beginning of the fifth century, British names are relatively rare, but by the later sixth century they were prevalent, and the surviving Latin names were chiefly those that had been naturalized into the British language. In the context of the early fifth century, the use of native names by Vortigern and his sons emphasizes that he sought and earned popularity among those who more commonly and more gladly used British, the urban poor and the rural population.

Vortigern's first years were outstandingly successful. The land is said to have prospered and men grew rich. Its main external problems were permanently resolved. The greatest dangers of the past had come from the attacks of the Picts in the north and of the Irish. To meet the Irish threat, Vortigern first compelled the High King of the Irish to accept a treaty, and to permit British missionaries to preach the Christian religion of Rome without hindrance in Ireland; then native forces were employed to reduce the Irish colonists in Britain without interference from Ireland itself. The greater danger from the Picts was averted as decisively. Both the records of the British and the late traditions of the Picts themselves report that the Pictish king, emboldened by the collapse of Rome, threatened not merely renewed raids, but full-scale invasion, intending the conquest and settlement of the British lowlands. The threat was real, for though the land frontier of the north still held, the Picts were seamen, and had learnt to turn its flank, sailing down the east coast to land at will. Against the threat of seaborne invasion Vortigern enlisted sufficient forces of the most experienced seafaring nation of the day, the peoples whom Romans and later British call Saxons, who themselves took the national name of English. Their homes lay about the mouth of the Elbe, between what are now Denmark and the Netherlands. At first, limited forces were brought to Britain, stationed along the east coast, with rear protection down the Icknield Way to the Oxford region, and in the neighbourhood of London. But their heaviest concentrations were placed by rivers near to the sea, strongest by the Wash. They performed the task for which they were invited. Whether they repelled a Pictish landing, or sailed out to destroy the vessels at sea, or whether their arrival was in itself sufficient to deter the invaders, the Picts did not prevail and no armed invasion from beyond the Forth and Clyde ever again threatened the fertile lowlands until the eighteenth century.

Vortigern's success was overturned by civil war. The same political divisions obtained in Britain as in Europe, between those who urged that Germanic settlers be accommodated, baptized and civilized, and those who demanded their expulsion. Those of the nobility who refused to continue paying for the German forces secured a majority in the council of the states of Britain; but Vortigern's armed strength depended on the Germans. To withstand the council, he brought over more Germans, and in or about 437 fought a major battle in Hampshire against the armies of Ambrosius, probably a former emperor whom Vortigern had dethroned and exiled. No text reports who won the battle, but its outcome was the triumph of the Saxons. In or about 441, they rebelled. The unarmed and unprepared civilians were caught unawares, and the economy of Roman Britain was irreparably damaged. Some cities and many forts long survived, but the revolt began a long-drawn-out war, whose issue was not decided for more than half a century. Though the British ultimately won the war, victory came too late. The economy had no chance to recover from the initial raid, and lasting fighting made the open country unsafe for trade or for commercial farming; when peace came, it was too late to restore the past. The civilization of Roman Britain came to a sudden end in the early 440s. It ended with a bang and an explosion, with no slow decay.

There is no direct reference to London in the last generations of Roman Britain. But it was clearly the centre of important events. Constantine III was clearly acclaimed, or confirmed, in London, for he had ousted a short-lived predecessor, named Gratian the Civilian. Nothing is known of him but his name, and the short duration of his power, no more than a few weeks. His civilian status argues a political force based on cities, whose chief centre was necessarily London, still the largest and most important of Roman towns, still the centre of government in spite of its decline. London was also the probable meeting place of the council of the states that rejected Constantine and sought help from Honorius; and was also the necessary centre of the administration of the emperors enthroned after the political break with Rome. Though emperors plainly moved, like their predecessors in Europe, and spent much of their time with the troops, nevertheless cost and convenience fixed a limit to the number of officials they could take with them. As in Europe, the larger part of the administrative officials of government necessarily remained in the capitals where their offices were located. At least the routine business of government remained in London, as in Europe it remained in Trier, in Rome or in Constantinople, wherever the emperor and his entourage might be.

Long before the destruction of Roman Britain, London was living on its past. Much of its ancient trade was gone, and the government it still housed was at a discount. In Britain as in Europe, Roman government was ended because men withheld obedience. It failed because the magnates of the empire ignored its commands when they chose, and denied it the revenues without which it could not govern. The western empire of Rome died because its subjects, great and small, no longer cared to preserve it; their affections were withdrawn after repeated failures, caused by the interaction of attacks from without and divisions within. As barbarians attacked more strongly, the cost of defence rose; civilians in discord refused to meet the added cost, or disputed about who should pay it; and each internal civil war weakened the frontiers, further emboldened the barbarians, and further increased the cost of defence and the needs of the government for greater revenues. None halted the cycle of spiralling disaster, though many delayed its momentum. Britain and London at first survived in better heart than much of Europe; when in the end they succumbed to the common ruin, its impact was the more sudden and severe.

One new turn salvaged something of the wreckage of Rome. The Christian church had appeared as an alternative federation of men, fit to replace the failing government. The sordid disarray of the Arian controversy was sorted out by a generation of outstanding reformers in the late fourth century. Pope Damascus gave visible might and splendour to the church of Rome, respected as the senior among the churches of the empire. Ambrose of Milan blended episcopal authority with a simple austerity that won men's hearts. Martin of Tours, who died in or about 397, pioneered dedicated monks, drawn from all walks of life, in conscious opposition to urban bishops who owed their office to their high social standing, and also initiated the preaching of Christianity to peasants. Thereby he enabled reformed Christianity to become the unifying faith of all classes within the former Roman west. His ideas were championed by bishop Victricius of Rouen who, in or about 396, visited Britain, and in a stormy synod claimed to have won decisive majority support from the British church. Traces of his thought and practice are evident in various parts of Britain in the next few years; and the probable place of the synod that won the British to the cause of Martin was London.

Christianity was to matter greatly to the London and the Britain of the future. Throughout the Gallic provinces, Christianity emerged from a religion confined to rulers and towns to a mass faith in the last days of the empire; it was in Martin's generation that 'the whole world became Christian'. British Christianity acquired a specific island character. The shocks of the Mediterranean brought to prominence the harsh discipline of Augustine of Hippo, in North Africa. In teaching that all men were damned by the sin of Adam unless released by the grace of God, that in practice was bestowed by a consecrated priest, ordained in a well-organized hierarchy, Augustine preserved the church from the fragmentation that overtook civilian government as the empire fell. But his apparent denial of human effort to attain goodness deeply offended the older humane traditions of Roman Christianity, who found their champion in Pelagius, the most polished scholar of early fifth-century Rome, who was himself British. At first, Augustine's views did not easily prevail; but they won the sympathy of the government and the clergy in the years after 410, and in 418 Pelagius and his views were banned. He disappeared from Europe, but not from Britain; for in 418 the writ of Rome no longer obtained in Britain. The outlook of British Pelagians lay far closer to the ideal of the monk than Augustine's sacerdotal discipline; and in time was to engender a powerful monastic movement in Britain, whose ultimate impact shaped the church of the English and transformed the Christianity of western Europe. Its distant impact was far from London. But in the formative years of the early fifth century, the bishop of London, the chief city of the diocese, was necessarily the metropolitan, the head of British Christianity, the first spokesman of the church that maintained older tenets.[15]

When Rome fell, London carried with it the ghost of the past. Trade failed; government and the church remained. The city was still huge, for its walls endured. They made it a fortress, of decisive importance in the wars of contending kingdoms for centuries to come. The status that it inherited from Claudius, from Agricola, Marcellus and its other Roman founders, developed in later centuries by its own momentum, made it a city too strong to be smashed when the empire fell, able to survive until another age again needed such a city as London had been in its early prime.

Chapter 16

After the Romans: The Age of Arthur[1]

THE LOSS OF Britain was one incident in the fall of Rome. The fabric of the empire survived in the west for two generations after the capture of the city, but it was mortally wounded in 410. Honorius was succeeded by his sister's son, Valentinian III, who lived until 455, while his cousin, Theodosius II, reigned in Constantinople. So long as the sons and grandsons of the great Theodosius survived, attachment to the dynasty held the empire together, and the officials who acted in their names commanded considerable authority in Gaul and Spain. Their power was circumscribed, for new, independent nations were hatching within the weakening empire. In 418 the Visigoths secured what the German nations had long demanded, the right to settle in fertile Roman lands under their own kings and their own laws, as federate allies. In law, they were Roman troops billeted upon landowners, who must assign to them a third of their lands and houses. In practice, they constituted a self-standing state, whose king owed allegiance to the emperor. The Burgundians in eastern Gaul soon achieved the same status, and the Franks permanently settled in the north-east.

When Valentinian was murdered, power soon passed to German generals in Italy, who made and unmade emperors with disastrous frequency, but in the western provinces, each region decided for itself whether or not it would recognize these insubstantial sovereigns. In northern Gaul, the last legitimately appointed Roman commander-in-chief, Aegidius, did not. In law, he was an army commander; in practice he was styled 'king of the Romans', his borders threatened by the Frankish and Burgundian kingdoms on the east, by the Visigoths and by regions that still recognized the Italian emperor on the south; and for a time he was accepted as king by the Franks, when their native king displeased his nobles and was exiled to central Germany. When Aegidius died in 464, his son Syagrius inherited his kingdom, with its capital at Soissons, but the Visigoths pressed upon his southern borders, and the Franks seized Paris. The remnant of imperial authority soon vanished. In 476, the appointment of nominal emperors in Italy was discontinued, and in law the empire was reunited under the single sovereignty of the emperor in Constantinople; but in practice the general Odovacer ruled as king in Italy for a dozen years.

Within a generation the new kingdoms took shape. In 486 the new king of the Franks, Clovis, overthrew Syagrius and annexed his kingdom. Ten years later he subdued the Alamanni, and mastered Europe to the Elbe; in 500 he conquered the Burgundians, and in 507 he defeated the Visigoths and drove their kings into Spain. The victories of the Franks gave Gaul its future name, France, and the monarchy of the first Clovis, or Louis, was prolonged into the nineteenth century; the Gothic monarchy of Spain survived into the twentieth. In Italy and Provence, Theodoric the Ostrogoth founded a strong kingdom in the same years in which Clovis mastered the north, and deterred the Vandal kings of Africa from intervention in the northern Mediterranean. By the beginning of the sixth century the western empire was partitioned between four great German kingdoms.

The transformation of Europe powerfully influenced the struggles of the newcomers and the natives in Britain; and for the first time the historical evolution of Britain diverged sharply from the society of Europe. In all four of the European kingdoms, the political supremacy of the Germans was accepted without serious resistance. The imperial authority was allowed to perish, because men of influence no longer valued it; but the principal institutions of civil society continued. Landed estates retained their identity and the control of their peasantry, though some few estates passed from Roman to German owners. The civil administration and the bishoprics continued. The Germans accepted Christianity, and west of the Rhine they and the native Gauls both abandoned their ancient languages in favour of various derivatives of late Latin, the language of the church, that became the French, the Spanish, the Italian and other related languages of today. German and Roman fused, and within little more than a century their separate identities merged.

In Britain alone, the natives of a western Roman province long withstood the Germanic peoples in their country, and in the fifth century they prevailed in arms. The ultimate victory of the barbarians, the Saxons or English, was postponed for more than a century, and was never completed. The conflict ended in partition; the greater part of Roman Britain, the lowlands and the north, in the end became English, but the west remained independent. In contrast with Europe, there was little fusion. The Latin language, that in Europe first became the normal speech of all classes during the fifth century, disappeared from Britain. In Britain alone, both the newcomers and the natives retained the languages that their ancestors had spoken during and before the rule of Rome; for English has evolved from old German, and Welsh derives from the language of the British. The long and bitter wars altogether snapped the continuity of land tenures, of political and social authority, that in Europe endured; but the survival of the languages maintained a continuity of peasant custom and tradition that the change of language buried in Europe.

The separate development of the British Isles also brought a new unity. Agricola, Severus and other Roman commanders had failed to subdue northern Britain; Agricola had considered and postponed the conquest of Ireland, and none had revived the project. The Roman walls in the north and the Irish Sea divided the sophisticated civilization of the Roman province from alien barbarians beyond, as hostile to the British as the English of Germany, or any other savage enemies. But the complex struggles of the fifth and sixth centuries broke down these barriers. From the seventh century onward, the English and the Welsh, the Irish and the peoples of the future Scotland, were united by a common religion and a common culture, organized in comparable political states. When the political Roman state disintegrated, the Christian religion of Rome absorbed the peoples whom Rome had failed to subdue; the descendants of the citizens of Roman Britain, of the barbarians beyond their borders, and of the invaders from Germany were combined in the common polity of the British Isles.

These profound changes in Europe and in Britain were the setting in which London survived; for London remained the principal link between Britain and Europe, between the old world and the new. Very little is remembered of the city for two centuries after the break with Rome; but its existence, its persistent links with Europe, and the stout barrier of its walls made it the pivot of political and military contention. The material evidence that the archaeologist has recovered is negligible, no more than bare evidence that men lived on. Some cakes of lead found at Battersea are stamped with the name of Syagrius; their use and purpose is uncertain, but they may be evidence that trade of some sort persisted with Gaul in the twenty years of Syagrius' dominion, between 464 and 486;[2] recent excavation in the ruins of the baths of a late Roman house in Lower Thames Street (Map 10, No. 6) discovered a Saxon brooch of the fifth century (Plate 16), and a sherd of a Mediterranean amphora, probably imported in the fifth century, was found in the ashes of a hypocaust furnace.[3] Subsequent museum research identified a number of other sherds from London of about the same and later date, evidence of some continuing Mediterranean trade, direct or indirect.

The evidence is slight in London because all material evidence of the age is slight throughout Britain. The destruction of the civilization of Roman Britain ended Roman technology; craftsmen ceased to manufacture, because the wars closed their markets. Enemy raids and marching armies altogether prevented the profitable exploitation of peasant farming; country mansions were no longer safe to inhabit; no man dared travel the roads with his wares, and could find none to buy them if he did. Roman life endured longer in many towns, but the incomes that had maintained the towns in their former style had gone. The potteries closed, the skills of the builder faded, and when the fighting stilled after half a century, none was left alive to teach forgotten skills. Men worked with perishable materials, or improvised objects that the modern excavator cannot yet date with any useful precision; for the circulation of money entirely ceased, and without coins the last practicable means of learning the dates of the few identifiable British ornaments, manufactures and buildings of the fifth and sixth centuries is lost.

The weak evidence of the British is overbalanced by relics of the English. Unlike the natives, they buried their dead with a rich assortment of jewellery, weapons and other grave goods; an immense number of objects has been recovered from tens of thousands of graves, and many among them can be dated to within a generation of thirty or forty years. Recent excavation has begun to detect in some quantity their homes and houses, hitherto little known. The evidence of the English is plentiful enough for its absence to be eloquent, where no traces are discovered on sites that are rich in relics of other periods, and are comparable with sites elsewhere where English evidence is prominent. The absence of the English does not automatically witness the presence of the British, for in theory it could indicate a deserted area; but where other evidence demonstrates or implies the presence of men, it argues that those men were British, if no evidence of the English can be found.

The weakness of the archaeological evidence is made good by a great quantity of documentation, describing or alluding to the events of these centuries. Most of it is utterly unlike the factual narrative of Roman, and of later English, record. It was chiefly written to edify and entertain later ages, by men who had little understanding of the memories they reported, and no wish to understand; they viewed the past in the light of their own day, and imposed upon it their habits and assumptions, as unconcernedly as theatrical tradition that dresses Romans, Greeks or medieval kings in Elizabethan doublets, or sometimes in modern dress. These misconceptions reach far deeper than the superficialities of dress, and intrude upon the purpose and the consequence, the circumstances and the date of the events related; stories are selected to point a moral, and twisted to that end. The vast majority of the statements made are neither true nor untrue, reliable nor unreliable; they are half truths to be assessed by examining the motive of the writer, removing his interpretation and embellishments, and restoring the original context.

Several main guidelines serve as pilots through this difficult evidence. Chief among them is Gildas, a priest who in about 540 denounced the evils of his day and inspired a momentous reform. His manifesto, *The Ruin of Britain*, brilliantly illumines the society of his own day, and is prefixed by a summary of the history of the previous century.[4] His narrative is supplemented and extended by a collection of historical documents brought together in the eighth century under the name of Nennius.[5] Much detail and circumstance is added to their outline history by numerous annals, saints' lives, inscriptions and other texts; and just sufficient contemporary continental witness records the precise or approximate date of critical events to make clear the main sequence of events.

The principal criterion by which any of these texts must be judged is the knowledge that the author shared with his readers. No writer, however tendentious, can altogether falsify the main events of his own lifetime, though he may malign the motives behind them and misrepresent their significance; and the living memory of men, that incorporates something of what their fathers have told them in childhood, sets limits to the distortions possible within the previous century. But when the threshold of living memory is crossed, the restraints upon error are removed. A modern illiterate audience, wholly ignorant of history, might readily accept confusion between Marlborough and Cromwell, or Queen Anne and Queen Mary, but would not believe an author who maintained that peace prevailed unbroken in their own lifetimes. The same audience would contain old men who knew that Gladstone and Disraeli had lived in their fathers' time, not in the time of Napoleon or George Washington. So, when Gildas reported the security and external peace of his own day, since the wars that had ended some forty years or more before he wrote, he set down what his readers knew to be true; and those who were fifty or sixty years old or more had some recollection of the main events of the wars that he described.

The substance of Gildas' narrative is that after the first fury of the wars against the Saxon rebels, the government of Roman Britain collapsed, and a large body of emigrants, including educated men who took with them books that he could no longer consult, crossed to Gaul. Thereafter, a partisan resistance movement fought back, and after a long war achieved ultimate victory, at Badon Hill, more than a generation before his own time. The war ended with a 'melancholy partition' of the island between the British and the Saxons, and thereafter the good, sound, strong government of the men who won the war lasted until comparatively recently. But in the last ten years civil wars between military commanders had altogether overshadowed the authority of civilian governors and their staffs. The graves of the English indicate the regions partitioned, and contemporary continental evidence dates the outbreak of the Saxon rebellion to 441 or 442, the migration of the British to Gaul to the time of Aegidius, in or shortly before 460. Gildas' own narrative, reinforced by a little other evidence, dates Badon to the 490s, a few years on either side of 495.[6]

One of Nennius' texts, termed the Kentish Chronicle, gives details of the early stages of the war, unknown to Gildas; and the bare outline of the same campaign is independently remembered in the tradition of the English. The captain-general of all the early fifth-century English, or Saxon, settlers was Hengest, himself a Danish adventurer whom chance had placed in command of a group of Jutes from Jutland, settled in Frisia. His first force had been garrisoned in east Kent, in Thanet, and Vortigern had soon after ceded Kent, or at least the territories east of the Medway. Hengest was established in Canterbury, master of a Roman city and territory taken over in full working order, without damage or violence. The evidence of the cemeteries discloses the location of the principal other forces that he recruited in the twelve or fifteen years between his arrival and the outbreak of the rebellion. The heaviest concentration was in Norfolk, extending down the Ouse to the Cambridge region; substantial but lighter forces across the Wash held the Lincolnshire coast, and a small concentration halfway between the Humber and York protected the East Riding.

Forty shiploads, a few thousand men, were despatched to the districts about, and beyond, the northern wall, and established permanent homes in a small coastal tract about Bamburgh and Lindisfarne. In the south, reserve garrisons guarded the intersections of the Icknield Way, about Luton and Dunstable, and on the Berkshire bank of the Thames in the Oxford regions. Either then, or soon after the revolt, others in Leicester and in Nottinghamshire held the line of the Trent, perhaps posted there as the civil war developed, to deter the Roman army of the north from intervention in the south. London itself was surrounded at a distance; substantial settlements were located at the foot of the Downs, by Mitcham and Croydon, and on the upper reaches of the Thames from Richmond to Shepperton and Hanwell, and soon after, if not at first, extended to the Darenth valley in west Kent, and in smaller numbers to the tributaries of the Lea, at Royston, Stevenage and Hertford.

Four major battles are recorded in the Kentish and Saxon Chronicles by the road from London to Richborough in the first eighteen years of the war, three of them in the first ten years, at Aylesford near Maidstone, at Crayford, when 'the British abandoned Kent and fled to London in terror', and at Richborough, where English tradition reported the slaughter of a dozen British commanders, but claimed no victory, while the British record claims a decisive victory, and the temporary expulsion of the English. The narrative reveals the essential strategy of the two armies, and emplicitly emphasizes a part of it. During these campaigns the British forces were commanded by Vortigern's sons; one of them, Vortimer, recovered Richborough, and soon after died. His dying injunction was remembered, that Richborough must be retained, and so long as it was held, British supremacy would endure, whatever other ports the enemy might secure. Richborough was the lifeline that linked Britain with the empire, and at the date assigned to his victory, about 451, the western empire was still in being. Valentinian III still ruled in Italy, and Roman commanders were still masters of Gaul. They might or might not be able to spare troops to help the British, but even if they would, reinforcements from Gaul could not safely be conveyed to Britain unless Richborough and the channel ports were secured, the enemy denied their use, the British provided with bases to protect the narrow seas.

At the other end of the battle zone, after the earlier English victory, the British fell back on London; but the English did not claim to have been able to pursue them, or to besiege or capture the city. Yet the success of Hengest's English depended upon whether he could unite his two largest forces, in Kent and in East Anglia; and their junction could be effected only by the capture of London. The narrative reports only the campaigns in Kent, fought by Vortigern's sons. It says nothing of Vortigern, and nothing of the East Angles. But the strategy required by the London end of the battle zone is as plain as that required at the Richborough end. If Britain were to be held, and Richborough rendered useful, London must be held, and the two main enemy armies must be prevented from joining forces. London alone kept them apart. Though its population was doubtless much shrunken, it was a fortress beyond the reach of the enemy, unless all resistance were first crushed. The simple weapons of the Saxons were limited to sword and spear; though they might assault a poorly defended town by scaling ladders, they had neither the training nor the equipment to undertake a siege, or batter walls. The obligation that the war thrust upon Vortigern was to hold London, and to beat off or buy off the East Angles while his sons endeavoured to confine Hengest to Kent. His principal immediate risk lay in the loyalty of the nearer Saxon contingents, on the Downs and upriver. They were far too few to defy British armies based on London that were still able to meet and rebuff the full strength of English Kent, and the evidence of their graves is decisive. They escaped destruction. Their earliest burials are as early as any in Britain, and burials continued uninterrupted. They can only have continued with the consent and tolerance of British London. Their ornament betrays their allegiance. Up to the end of the sixth century, it has much in common with the ornament of the Thames valley, upriver from London, but received nothing of the characteristic ornament of Kent, neither of its early fifth century brooches, nor of its later splendid ornament; even the characteristic Jutish pottery of early Kent and other regions is rare. Throughout the pagan period a harsh frontier between the Darenth and the Medway sundered the Saxons of the London region from the men of Kent. They were throughout dependent upon London; in Europe Theodosius had relied upon Gothic forces hired by the Roman government to restrain Gothic enemies, and throughout the troubled history of the fifth century it was normal for some Roman forces to ally with some barbarians against others, rare for all barbarians to fight on one side, all Romans on the other. So in Britain it is evident that the political and military power of London was still strong enough to enforce the allegiance of the nearby Saxons, at least so long as Kentish armies were kept at bay, and East Anglian armies were prevented from crossing the Thames.

The first ten years of the fighting is reported to have ended with British victory. Richborough was recovered, and evidently Canterbury with it. Hengest was expelled from Kent. But Britain was too divided to profit from the victory. The revolt had followed close upon a civil war, wherein a large section of the nobility had sought to dethrone Vortigern. They had not wholly succeeded, for he survived, and the shock of the revolt forced both parties into alliance against the common enemy. The alliance did not long endure when the enemy was contained. Evidently to face renewed pressure at home, Vortigern invited Hengest to return. After a further battle, all parties agreed to a peace, recognizing the status quo. For the formal ratification of the peace treaty, three hundred of the 'seniors' of Britain undertook to meet an equal number of the English, both sides unarmed. The 'seniors' were evidently the political leaders of the several states, the greatest landowners of Britain, delegates to the council. Hengest tricked them. He ordered his men to conceal their knives in the soles of their shoes, and at a given signal they massacred the whole of the British delegation, keeping Vortigern alone alive. The date indicated by the English record is about 459. In Europe, the legitimate dynasty of the empire had recently perished; northern Gaul was still Roman, ruled by Aegidius, but no longer obeyed the Italian emperors.

The disaster was total. The political leadership and government of all Britain was wiped out. The English everywhere were enabled to rise, plunder and destroy, without meeting organized resistance. A large part of the surviving nobility, accompanied by their dependents, emigrated to Gaul. Continental contemporaries indicate the date, about 460, and place the numbers of the fighting force of the immigrants at about 12,000. With women, children and non-combatants the total numbers cannot have been less than 50,000, and were more probably greater. The old ruler Vortigern was broken, and died a wanderer, 'hated and despised' by men of all degree.

There is no record of the immediate fate of London. It may be that it was entered and pillaged, or that the citizens were able to hold out within their walls, or to reach an accommodation with the enemy. Three or four dated brooches indicate that at some time in the fifth century some Saxons visited the city or dwelt within it; but they may as easily have been individuals from the nearby villages authorized to enter before the disaster or in later years, and there is no evident sign of destruction or substantial immigration. The one strong indication is the negative evidence. The English did not then establish permanent settlement within London. Wherever considerable numbers dwelt in or close to Roman towns, they left abundant traces, too numerous and too characteristic for the ploughmen, building workers and the pipe-layers of later centuries to overlook. Pot-sherds and miscellaneous small finds are often disregarded, coins are often surreptitiously removed in the hope, usually mistaken, of securing a greater reward by private sale. Even stone walls are often dug through without report, but skeletons rarely escape comment, and cremated bones in pots excite almost as much interest.

Commonly, the chance discovery of human bones is reported first to the police, and passed on the archaeologist only when the police are satisfied that the bones are not their business. Ancient cemeteries are therefore more often noticed and recorded than any other kind of site.

By Roman towns, pagan English burial grounds are almost without exception sited like Roman cemeteries, just outside the walls, and often adjoin or overlap their Roman predecessors for, wherever possible, the pagan English preferred to inter their dead in ground already dedicated to burial, and in the countryside they sought out prehistoric barrows when more recent consecrated ground was not available. Such cemeteries have been observed outside the majority of the Roman towns in the districts where the early English settled, most of them in places much less heavily disturbed in modern times than London. The repeated reconstruction of the buildings, and the laying of pipes and cables, has exposed many thousands of burials in and around London. All are Roman or medieval, or later; they include a few burials of the last years of the pagan English, in the early seventh century, but so far no English burial of the fifth or sixth century has been recorded. Since the reported discoveries include half a dozen or more major Roman cemeteries, none of them with pagan Saxon burials in or near them, the chances that any such pagan cemetery existed and has escaped detection are slight. It is therefore exceedingly unlikely that there was any significant English population in London until the practice of burying grave goods with the dead declined, towards the end of the sixth century.

London survived the crisis of 460, but its future was lean. The wars lasted longer, and when peace came there was no longer a· society or economy that had need of London. The resistance of the 460s was initiated by Ambrosius Aurelianus, described as a 'gentleman, last of the Roman nation', son of a former British emperor, possibly Vortigern's predecessor, the Ambrosius who had fought against him in the 430s. The war was fought by unusual forces, matched on a smaller scale in contemporary Gaul, by the combat of mounted troops without significant support on one side against infantry without cavalry on the other. The horse was the one weapon that gave immediate and unassailable advantage to the Roman provincials of the fifth century. It was familiar, and easily bred in the west, still relatively undamaged; it was wholly unknown to the pagan English, rare even among the Goths and Franks of Gaul. Even quite small forces, well officered, had the ability to set an immediate limit upon English raiders. The cavalryman could watch the march of an English force, assemble his own men speedily, and attack only when his numbers were enough, on ground of his own choosing, avoiding battle whenever the enemy seemed superior. Small raiding parties could be quickly destroyed, the English compelled to issue forth only in large contingents. But cavalry also prevented the easy assembly of large forces; for if most of them were withdrawn from a village, it was exposed to attack by British cavalry as soon as the men were gone. The existence of mounted British partisans compelled the English to leave large garrisons at home, and also to fight only in sizeable detachments. Their mobility and striking power was quickly reduced.

The war lasted for more than thirty years. Little is known of its detail. The faint indications of its course suggest that the heaviest fighting occurred between the heartlands of the British in the Cotswolds, and the strongest English, in East Anglia. Some signs hint at considerable garrisons placed in eastern Essex, suitably located to protect London from Norfolk, and direct statements report campaigns in the south. Before the destruction of the magnates, Vortigern had ceded Sussex and Essex to the English. They have left few fifth-century traces in Essex, save at its western end, and in an isolated group of villages near Tilbury; but in Sussex, though they failed to take Chichester, they established a small kingdom in the Lewes area, where the estuaries of the Ouse and Cuckmere offered safe and easy havens for their ships. Their kingdom survived attacks, and one place name suggests a treaty that fixed a formal boundary between the English and the British, probably upon the Arun. But about 470, further fighting ended with the capture of the Roman coastal fortress of Pevensey by the English. It lay beyond the Downs, outside English territory, and its capture was not followed by English settlement. It was not attacked in order to annex more land; the evident reason was that it threatened the English, for it was a base whence British vessels might assault the English estuaries, and British cavalry attack their homes.

The growing power of the Franks had altered the strategic needs of the British. The low countries and the north-eastern coasts of Gaul were now in Frankish hands. The Roman kingdom of Syagrius controlled Normandy and the mouth of the Seine, and there dwelt many British exiles, many of whom might be recalled to strengthen the reviving hopes of their countrymen, if control of the seas could be secured. But control of the south-coast harbours gave a new dimension to the power of the English. In these years, and these years alone, fear of the audacious Saxons, 'masters of the seas', are widely reported; they obliged the Visigoths to maintain a fleet and active naval patrols in the Bay of Biscay;

they raided the channel coasts of Gaul, plundered Brittany, and attacked Ireland.

The British failed to recover the south coast until too late; and the southern military situation deteriorated before it improved. At some time in or about the 470s, Ambrosius died, or retired from active leadership, or was overthrown. He was replaced by Arthur. His name, a version of the Roman family name, Artorius, and fragments of early Welsh tradition, suggest that his origin and background were similar to Ambrosius' own, set among the families of great Roman landlords; and he is specifically described as emperor. But he faced immediate trouble. His earliest reported engagement was an unsuccessful attempt to subdue a British rebel. Cerdic, British by name, ruled southern Hampshire, evidently as sovereign and leader of the Belgae, whose capital was Winchester. English forces, whose joint commanders bore the British name Maegla and the English name Bieda, reached Portsmouth harbour, where a Saxon force may already have been installed for some time in the Roman naval base of Portchester. Other English took control of the Isle of Wight, and were established at Winchester; their ornament proclaims that many among them came from the English kingdom in Sussex. Arthur attacked, with the help of the forces of British Dumnonia, whose name the later English corrupted to Devon. He was repulsed, and Gerontius of Dumnonia fell.

The rebellion of Winchester may or may not have been connected with the disappearance of Ambrosius and the enthronement of Arthur. His first reported action was a defeat, but thereafter the British prospered speedily under his leadership. The dates and the order of events are uncertain, but the East Angles were contained, and Lincoln was recovered, in an exceptionally memorable campaign; and the position of Lincoln implies that the midland English, later known as the Middle Angles, in Leicestershire and Nottinghamshire and Northamptonshire, were first subdued. These were campaigns north of the Thames. The English south of the Thames made a final effort; various items of evidence suggest that it was Oesc of Kent, successor of Hengest, Aella of the South Saxons, and Cerdic of Winchester, attended by his English federates, who led their armies deep into the British Cotswolds, to besiege Arthur on Badon Hill, near Bath. They were decisively defeated, and the war ended in a British victory.

The war ended with a military victory, but its outcome was a stalemate. The English infantry could not prevail; though in the later stages of the war they were reinforced by the migration of the whole of the remainder of the English nation from Schleswig, with the national monarchy, they had not the manpower to overrun the west, or to expand their existing territory behind defensible borders. The British cavalry checked their advance, but was equally unable to overwhelm and expel the English; for though cavalry on their own might destroy large infantry armies in the field, they could not overrun large defended territories, where men defended their homes and their families in their own villages. The weakness of cavalry at all times was revealed when men must dismount; between campaigns and at night, the horses needed protection against surprise attack. They found it in west-country prehistoric forts, whose grass-grown ramparts could easily be restored, and in the southeast in numerous walled Roman towns. But in battle, when once a charge was stopped, or a rider dismounted, the advantage of the horse was lost; and though an individual English village might be taken by assault on occasion, no cavalry force could hope to run down hundreds of stockaded villages, well defended, in lands where several Roman town walls were also available to the defenders.

The victorious British were therefore obliged to admit the continued presence of the English, in a number of defined reservations. Not all were of equal status. Kent and East Anglia, the South Saxons and the Deirans of the East Riding, were sufficiently sizeable and self-contained to exist as fully independent kingdoms under their own kings. The Middle Angles did not constitute a kingdom, and Lincoln may have been placed under British rule. Wide sweeps of territory, where no sixth-century English are recorded until the last years of the century, separated these territories from each other, and the separate English enclaves about Dunstable and Oxford, in southern Hampshire and the London region, were each too small to assert effective independence, though some of them may have been governed by their own kings.

London's opportunities were at their lowest during the war. Though some little intercourse with Europe remained, attested by the stamp of Syagrius, the Saxon mastery of the seas plainly prevented any extensive overseas trade, even if there were purchasers in Britain for foreign goods, or craftsmen able to produce for export. Continuing fighting in a ruined countryside precluded any significant internal trade, and the collapse of public authority left no Britain to govern. The functions that had created London and maintained it had ceased to be. The city remained a fortress, holding Kent and the East Angles apart; but there is nothing to show whether or not there were renewed attempts to unite their armies, or serious fighting for any other region in the London area during the war.

Something remained. Human activity endures so long as men live. On the Danube, where a little of the detail of day-to-day life in the ruin that followed Rome is reported, a few men still earned a feeble living on the remnants of trade; and on the eve of the final evacuation of one shrunken city, one trader incurred rebuke for clinging to his commercial hopes when all his world was gone. Other cities were worse hit than London, and recovered. A little later, in the middle of the sixth century, when Rome itself was battered by repeated sieges, men fled to safety, idle mouths were expelled, and the city's population dwindled to no more than five hundred. In Rome, the damage was permanent, for though the size of the city quickly recovered, the aqueducts were cut. The city centre became a swamp, and has remained a ruin, never yet rebuilt, preserved today as a melancholy tourist attraction. On higher ground several residential areas were abandoned when the water supplies failed, and are still open gardens and parks, romantically studded with the ruins of mansions deserted in the sixth century.

London is unlikely to have suffered severely from siege, for the Saxons were ill equipped to undertake it; and the Thames provided sufficient water. London is unlikely to have suffered as severely as Rome, but its former splendour clearly vanished. It had declined in the later generations of Roman rule, when its inhabitants left ampler traces nearer to the river than further inshore. The waterfront is likely to have remained the most populated region, particularly near to the bridgehead that gave the city its being. But Londoners no longer earned the fortunes that maintained the great houses. No one could afford their upkeep, even if men could be found to repair them. As in other dwindling towns, the weather ate at untenanted mansions; collapsed walls blocked streets that no one cared to clear, and it is unlikely that significant business maintained even the forum and the great basilica in good repair. In the nature of the evidence, no detail can be observed; but it is scarcely possible that London escaped the fate of other great towns whose roots were cut away.

It is probable that peace brought some short-lived relief and benefit to London. Arthur and his armies had fought for the preservation of Roman Britain and the restoration of its institutions. When the war was won, Arthur was emperor, the last Roman emperor in Britain, heir to the island emperors who had been enthroned since Honorius' decree in 410, and to their predecessors who had ruled more widely than in Britain alone. He had no choice but to restore the institutions of the past, at least in form. Gildas, who was born within a month of Badon, and grew to manhood under Arthur's government, reports the survival in his own day of *rectores*, provincial governors and their staffs, and of the *duces*, military commanders, whose arrogance overawed them, who had assumed in practice the status of kings, and ruled with the arbitrary authority of tyrants. The evil had arisen in very recent years; the offices themselves dated back to the days of good government by the victories of Badon. These named civilian and military posts imply others, at least a praetorian prefect and a *magister militum*, together with heads of the treasury. Some semblance of a Roman government was revived. One of the few possible places for its offices, for meetings of representatives of the provinces and the states, was London, dilapidated as the city doubtless was.

Arthur's empire set about the recovery of the whole of the former Roman diocese, to the farthest limits that Roman rule had ever reached. Various traditions report Arthur's highland wars; reasserting imperial power in the north, as far as the Clyde and over the nearer barbarians; in South Wales, where one campaign finally reduced the last independent Irish, and installed a Roman government over them; and in North Wales, where the revival of imperial authority was resented in the territory of Cardigan, but echoed by the Conway in the inscription of a man of means who proudly proclaimed his near relationship to a duly constituted magistrate.[7] Campaigning involved the feeding of armies and collection of taxes. The emperor's court was necessarily mobile, like the court of late Roman emperors in Europe, and tradition reports several favoured centres, Colchester, London, Carlisle and other major Roman towns. Though emperor in name, the ruler of a ruined economy cannot have collected the bulk of his revenue by centralized taxation in the ancient manner, and was obliged to live largely off the regions through which he progressed, as did Norman and Plantagenet kings in later centuries. Whatever central administration remained was probably supervised from offices in London; but it cannot have approached the scale on which past governments had operated.

Arthur's empire was brief, but it was the mould in which all future British government was formed. He was born at about the time when the first revolt of the Saxons ended the civilization of Roman Britain; the British power that his wars regained outlived him by half a century. That period, between the end of Roman Britain and the English conquest of Britain, extends for about one hundred and thirty years, four generations. Such decisive events mark off distinct historical epochs, not only in the tidy schemes of later historians but in the consciousness of men who lived through them. All men knew that the destruction of lowland Britain had violently and suddenly ended norms of personal and public conduct that had been universally observed for four hundred years; the outcome was dangerous, uncertain and unstable, but the British did not accept defeat until the irreversible English victories of the 570s. Then also all men knew that another age was ended, and that the future belonged to aliens of a different tongue who owed little to the past.

A period of such length, so sharply defined, is as firmly distinguished from what went before and what came after as the age of the Tudors or the Stuarts, or any of the periods which men are accustomed to recognize in their past. Such periods are commonly named in order that they may be understood; for the name relates the manifold aspects of each period with another, as Tudor denotes not only Henry VIII and Elizabeth but also Shakespeare and madrigals, colonization of North America and the development of the musket, and much else. Periods are commonly named from their principal rulers, and the age that extended from Arthur's birth to the ruin of the political society he created properly bears his name. Little is known of the man or the age, save essential outlines; yet these outlines were all important for the future. Arthur left a misty memory, that the imagination of the future elevated to the status of a golden age, when justice and fair government prevailed; and his successors were to fashion a Christian reform that changed the thinking of all Europe. But the real or imagined achievements of rulers and ruled were overshadowed by the stupendous importance of what actually happened. Arthur was the heir of Roman Britain; to the future he bequeathed England and Wales, and under his aegis the first Scottish kings were settled in Scotland. Later ages took these nationalities for granted, and looked not upon their origin, for they were not free to change them. But previously they did not exist, and no foreordained historical laws decreed that they must come to be. Choices were open, as never before or since; if men in power had made wiser or more foolish decisions, if humbler men had fought and striven with more resolution or less, the outcome would have been unimaginably different. What happened was their achievement. The victory and defeat of Arthur created the modern nations of Britain, though no man intended or foresaw the outcome.

The restoration of past forms could not take root. They fitted the urban society and the landed wealth of Rome. Both were gone. Cities were in Gildas' day 'not peopled as they used to be', and the nexus of the rural economy was gone. More than sixty years had elapsed since the outbreak of the revolt, and none but the very old had any personal memory of the Roman past. It was not possible for the grandson of a former landlord to compel the grandson of a former tenant to resume a rent that had lapsed for two generations. In much of the west, the old social structure was less damaged, and some towns continued to farm the lands around them elsewhere; but in the greater part of the fertile lowlands, the source of the wealth that had maintained Roman Britain, the basis for a Roman government, was gone for ever.

The personal prestige of the victor of Badon kept Arthur's empire in being for some twenty years thereafter. A bald notice in an annal is all that is reported of its fall: 'at the battle of Camlann Arthur and Medraut fell'.[8] Neither the place, the persons, nor the cause are known; the main later tradition made Medraut a faithless rebel subject and relative, enemy to Arthur, though a differing version makes him Arthur's ally. But though the occasion is unknown, the underlying causes are plain, and form the burden of Gildas' complaint. The British could not unite. When Arthur fell, none succeeded him. His empire died with him, for no man could command sufficient authority among his fellows to exact their submission and obedience. Effective power devolved upon the military leaders of large regions. Like the successors of Alexander of Macedonia eight centuries before, the generals fought each other when the enemy was altogether defeated, and the founder of the empire left no heir. Like Alexander's generals, the major wars were not immediate, for Gildas protests that the evil had grown to terrifying proportions in only the ten years or so before he wrote, a dozen or more years after Arthur's death.

The new military states recognizably emerged from the states of Roman Britain, and foreshadowed the future kingdoms of the English. Wales was partitioned among the heirs of the generals who had subdued the Irish colonists. The Cornovii of Wroxeter retained most of their ancient territory, in Shropshire and Staffordshire, with their borders on the Avon and the Wye, but on their east the lands of the Coritani of Lincoln and Leicester were thickly populated with English. On their south, the cities of Gloucester, Cirencester and Bath mastered the territories of the Dobunni. Their southern border was marked by the enormous earthwork of the Wansdyke. It protected three Roman states, the Dumnonii, the Durotriges of Dorset, and the Belgae of Hampshire and Wiltshire, and implies that when it was constructed they obeyed a single ruler. It may well be that Arthur's most prominent ally and companion,

Cato of Dumnonia, was rewarded by the acquisition of the disloyal Belgae. In the south-east, the town of Silchester endured, and was also protected by dykes; and north of the Thames tradition grouped most of the south-midland regions that had once been the *civitas* of the Catuvellauni into an important kingdom whose centre was believed to have been at Dunstable and Northampton. North of the Trent, later rulers whose most powerful armies were based on York, claimed descent from an early fifth-century ruler termed Coel the Old, whom medieval fancy turned to Old King Cole; he is likely to have been the last Roman commander at York, and to have turned his command into a hereditary kingdom, as Aegidius in Gaul turned this command into a kingdom that he bequeathed to his son. The city of London stood by itself, its southern boundaries indicated by the Saxon villages outside its territory, its northern limits the Lea and the unpeopled clays.

The states not only fought each other. Once the principle was established that the effective ruler was a military commander, and that his authority passed to his sons, the workings of the customary inheritance laws of the Welsh, and of Rome operated. Welsh law required equal division of a father's property among his sons, and Roman law expected a man to make decent provision for all his children. Where details of their history are preserved, several of the sixth-century British states experienced savage conflicts between heirs; some of the most vivid stories were reported by the sixth-century historian Gregory of Tours, who observed the disputes of the British of Armorica in his own day. Later accounts preserve similar stories about rulers in mainland Britain, and Gildas attacks the fratricide of the rulers of his own day. The wars were not only demoralizing and costly in themselves; they prevented the possibility of secure government, for each ruler of a powerful state was obliged to splinter his dominion, that could only be reconstituted by one among his heirs who devoted his life to butchering his brothers and uncles. The same succession law operated among the Franks; Gregory of Tours' mournful history of the brutal Merovingian kings of the Frankish heirs of Clovis explains the rapid degeneration of the monarchy and the distress of their subjects, and the unrecorded history of the sixth-century British lowland rulers is unlikely to have been calmer; for in the north, the heirs of Coel also brought each other down.

The new kings ruled arbitrarily, their military companions buttressing them against opposition and criticism; they overrode established law, intimidated magistrates, corrupted judges, and sold bishoprics to venal clergy. Gildas' protest coincided with a novel example in Italy. There, a nobleman of ancient family, Benedict of Nursia, withdrew to a cave as a hermit, and in later years, as he attracted disciples, to a monastery on the summit of Monte Cassino. Some years before Gildas wrote, some Irish Christians, returning from Italy, brought news of the new forms of monasticism to the pupils of a school in South Wales, founded by a British nobleman named Illtud, heir to a mansion on the Cotswold scale, the largest Roman country house yet known in Wales, at the place that bears his name, Llanilltud, or Llantwit Major, between Cardiff and Swansea. Like many Roman nobles before him, Illtud had taken a personal vow of monastic austerity. He and his pupils were already familiar with the monastic ideals of Martin and Victricius, and several of them sought to imitate Martin and Benedict. The best known was the rugged Samson, of south-eastern Wales, and Paul Aurelian, son of a Dumnonian landowner who had taken service with a minor military captain in Wales.

For some years Samson, Paul and their fellows were a freak minority, admired but little imitated. But in the years immediately after the publication of Gildas' manifesto, tens of thousands adhered to them. Enormous numbers of individuals established hermit's cells, usually in places previously uninhabited, commonly termed *llan*, the Welsh word for *claustra*, or monastic enclosure, the English cloister. Many rulers were hostile, for they lost manpower, both taxpayers and potential recruits for their armies; but the strength of public opinion forced them to grant lands to hermits, and to grant them exemptions from royal dues. Though the motive of the hermit was not to reform the world, but to escape from it, seeking personal communion with God without the intermediary of a priest, their numbers compelled them to form communities. The only model for such large-scale monasticism lay in the example of Egypt two centuries before, and the British monks eagerly absorbed the literature of Egypt, quoting its leaders and sometimes adopting their names.

The monks attracted all men who detested the upstart kings; but deserts were relatively rare in Britain. A main area of migration lay to hand across the sea, and very large numbers reinforced earlier British settlers in Armorica. The monks were accompanied by laymen, eager to escape the authority of arbitrary kings, and the numbers of immigrants were large enough to overlay the previous population of Armorica, and to give the land its permanent name of *Britannia Minor*, Lesser Britain, or Brittany. By the later sixth century the new name was in common use.

The monastic movement was carried to Ireland by British monks, and by Irishmen who visited Britain. In Ireland it aroused an equally massive response, for the Irish also suffered from the relatively recent rise of bloodthirsty and oppressive local dynasts, who had proliferated since Vortigern ended armed migration to Britain in the early fifth century. The vigour of the movement soon waned in Britain, but in Ireland it renewed itself in successive generations for many centuries, and was to become a principal influence in the shaping of the church of the English, to transform the Christianity of Gaul, and to be a chief agent in the conversion of the Germans and other central-European peoples to Christianity.

The monastic movement was born in south-western Britain. It made some little headway in the lowlands and the north, but there is no sign that it had touched London before the second revolt of the English overthrew British rule. The British power had retained its force, for the English remembered their defeat, and long had little stomach to renew the war. Most were men whose fathers and grandfathers had been born in the lands they now tilled; in many areas their population exceeded the lands allotted to them, and drove many to emigrate. Few were able to move to new homes in Britain, but very many migrated to Europe, to the several portions of the wide Frankish dominions. There they found men who spoke a language closely akin to theirs. For the irony of Arthur's victory had been that it came too late; when London and the channel coasts were recovered, the Roman powers in Europe had succumbed to the Franks, and the Gallic language, that had enabled the British to converse easily with Europeans, had given way to Latin speech, while spoken Latin was rapidly disappearing in Britain.

The English gained strength and confidence from contact with their fellow Germans in Europe. The British were isolated from the heirs of Rome. They maintained some trade with the Mediterranean and the Biscay ports, most of it by the western routes to the coasts of Cornwall, Wales and Ireland, a little probably through the port of London. That contact brought its own disaster. One of the worst known outbreaks of the bubonic plague swept the Mediterranean in the 540s. It attacked southern France, but spared the Rhineland; and it wasted Ireland and the western British, without harming the English whose foreign contacts were with the Franks of north-eastern Europe. It also depressed the last hopes of the revival of Roman power in Europe. In the 530s, the emperor Justinian launched a massive expedition from Constantinople, aimed at the recovery of Italy and the former western provinces. Its initial success was brilliant. Vandal Africa was quickly recovered, and from North Africa the Roman armies swept across Sicily, into southern Italy, and recovered Rome; even a substantial stretch of the southern coast of Spain was recovered. Success soon turned sour for many reasons: renewed eastern wars against the Persians required large armies; the finances of the empire were overstrained; and then the plague devastated the armies and the civilian taxpayers. The army in Italy was starved of supplies, and intrigue set its generals at loggerheads. The Goths recovered and counter-attacked, and though they were finally expelled from Italy, the cost was fearful, worst of all in the city of Rome. In the end, victory was vain, for in 568, soon after Justinian's death, a new northern enemy, Lombards, swept across the unguarded Alps, and seized and permanently named northern Italy. Their armies wasted the whole peninsula, destroyed Benedict's monastery on Monte Cassino, and established numerous small Lombard principalities.

The Lombard forces had included a large contingent of Saxons. Continuing German success in Europe encouraged the English in Britain, and the plague enfeebled the British, whose rotting governments inspired increasing hatred and contempt among their own subjects. The first stirrings came in the south. In 550 the English of Winchester seized Salisbury. They may well have fought as federates of a British ruler, but their armies made them effective masters. Their efforts to advance northwards over the Berkshire Downs were halted, but another English rebellion soon opened new possibilities. In 568 the young king of Kent, Aethelbert, newly married to the daughter of the Frankish king of Paris, broke out of his borders and attacked towards London. He was repelled by the combined efforts of Ceawlin, leader of the English of Winchester and Salisbury, and of Cuthwulf, whose territory was probably a small area south-west of Cambridge. London was saved by English armies. There is no sign that the city was yet peopled by English colonists, but the victory of the allies made them military masters of the London region. They did not yet hold the city, for they had other concerns. They turned westward. In 571 Cuthwulf defeated the midland British near Bedford, and marched down the Icknield Way to the Oxford region, and in 577 Ceawlin and Cuthwulf's successor destroyed the western British of the Dobunnic region, and captured Bath, Cirencester and Gloucester. Badon was avenged. All southern Britain was at the mercy of English armies. Ceawlin was honoured as 'ruler of Britain' and retained his supremacy for fifteen years more, though he was heavily defeated in an attempt to penetrate Wales. Throughout the midlands and the east, the

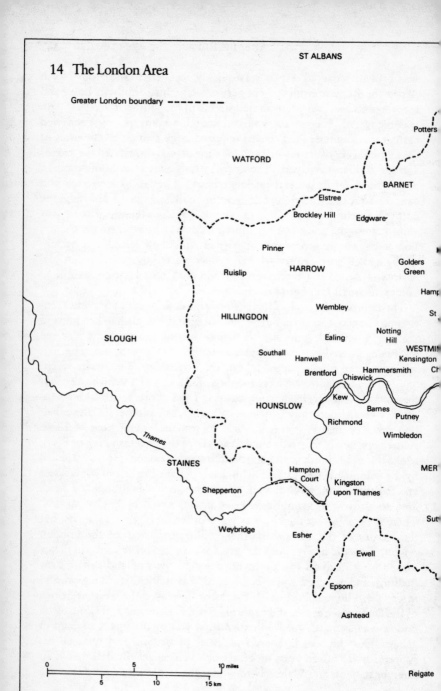

14 The London Area

Greater London boundary ‑ ‑ ‑ ‑ ‑

ST ALBANS

Potters

WATFORD

BARNET

Elstree

Brockley Hill

Edgware

Pinner

Golders
Green

Ruislip

HARROW

Hamp

Wembley

St

HILLINGDON

Notting
Hill

Ealing

WESTMI

SLOUGH

Southall

Kensington

Hanwell

Hammersmith

Ch

Brentford

Chiswick

Kew

HOUNSLOW

Barnes

Putney

Richmond

Wimbledon

Thames

Hampton
Court

STAINES

MER

Shepperton

Kingston
upon Thames

Sut

Weybridge

Esher

Ewell

Epsom

Ashtead

Reigate

0		5		10 miles
5	10		15 km	

separate English peoples proclaimed their independence. London passed under the control of the kings of the East Saxons, and when Ceawlin was ousted in 592, supremacy over the southern English passed to Aethelbert of Kent. English London begins with dominion of Aethelbert and the establishment of the East Saxon Kingdom.

Notes to the Maps

Map 1. As Morris 1973, p. 7.

Map 2. Based on map in Sheldon and Schaaf 1978, opposite p. 60. Findspots of single coins are plotted from the gazetteers in Allen 1961 and Haselgrove 1978, but note that the majority are plotted from four-figure grid references only.

Map 3. *Civitas* boundaries after Frere 1978, p. 13.

Map 4. Drawn by L. Schaaf of the Southwark and Lambeth Archaeological Excavation Committee, published in Sheldon and Schaaf 1978, map opposite p. 60, and reproduced here by permission of the SLAEC and the Museum of London.

Map 5. Based on map in Margary 1973, p. 55, and Grimes *et al.* 1976, Roman Period map. Roads in the Southwark area can now be plotted with some certainty as a result of recent excavations, and those shown here are based on the plan in Sheldon 1978, vol. 1, fig. 2, p. 16.

Map 6. After Wheeler 1928, plate 64 opposite p. 180.

Map 7. Boudiccan period map after Marsden 1980, p. 30. The cemetery to the immediate east of the later forum was not known to Dr Morris (see Chapter 5, note 11).

Map 8. Based on the O.S. *Map of Roman Britain*, 4th ed. (1978).

Map 9. As Grant 1974, p. 70-71.

Map 10. Based on maps in Merrifield 1965 and Marsden 1980. The forum buildings follow Marsden's reconstructions. Some features have been included which were not known to Dr Morris at the time of writing. These are: the riverside defensive wall (Chapter 8, note 18); the north-south road leading from the forum to the bridge (Chapter 5, note 4); buildings at St Mildred's Church, Bread Street (Marsden, Dyson and Rhodes 1975) and Watling Court (*Britannia* 10 (1979), p. 313); a north-south street just to the east of the Watling Court building (*Britannia* 11 (1980), p. 381); and a building containing a polychrome mosaic at Milk Street, to the north-west of the Cheapside Baths (Roskams 1978), but only the mosaic is shown on the map, as the plan of the building itself has not been published. The positioning of the bastions follows the scheme put forward by J. Maloney, *Britannia* 11 (1980), p. 380, and forthcoming.

Map 11. After Marsden 1980, p. 106.

Map 13. Based on Sheldon and Schaaf 1978, map opposite p. 60.

Notes

Abbreviations

ARS: V A.C. Johnson, P.R. Coleman-Norton and F.C. Bourne, *Ancient Roman Statutes*, Vol. II of *The Corpus of Roman Law (Corpus Iuris Romani)*, ed. C. Pharr (Austin, Texas, 1961).

CIL: *Corpus Inscriptionum Latinarum*, ed. T. Mommsen *et al.* (Berlin, 1863–).

Espérandieu: E. Espérandieu, *Receuil général des bas-reliefs, statues et bustes de la Gaule romaine* (Paris, 1907–).

ILS: *Inscriptiones Latinae Selectae*, ed. H. Dessau (Berlin, 1892–)

JRS: *Journal of Roman Studies*

LAMAS: London and Middlesex Archaeological Society

RCHM: Royal Commission for Historical Monuments

RIB: R.G. Collingwood and R.P. Wright, *The Roman Inscriptions of Britain* Vol. I (Oxford, 1965)

Merrifield: Merrifield 1965

PG: *Patrologia Graeca*, ed. J. Migne (Paris, 1857–)

PL: *Patrologia Latina*, ed. J. Migne (Paris, 1844–)

SLAEC: Southwark and Lambeth Archaeological Excavation Committee

Chapter 1

1 Or perhaps votive offerings, Merrifield 1969, p. 18.
2 For the distribution of sites from the palaeolithic to the medieval periods in the London area see now Grimes *et al.* 1976; Davison *et al.* 1976.
3 Wheeler and Wheeler 1936, pp. 16–22.
4 Caesar, *De Bello Gallico* v.12, refers to the use of bronze coins in Britain.
5 Caesar, *De Bello Gallico* v.19.

Chapter 2

1 Solon, *Elegies* Fr. 5.5–6. Diehl.

Chapter 3

1 In the Gallic revolt of 52 BC under Vercingetorix.
2 CIL xiii, 3026; Espérandieu iv, 3132–5.
3 On Julius Indus and his regiment, the *Ala Indiana*, see below, pp. 56 and 113.
4 In AD 68 under Vindex.
5 Frontinus, *Strategems* ii.13.11.
6 On Belgic coins and their distribution, Allen 1944, 1961, 1962; and for a recent summary, Cunliffe 1978, chapter 5.
7 Gallo-Belgic E coins.
8 On the distribution of Roman barrows in Britain and on the Continent see Dunning and Jessup 1936.

9 In the *Res Gestae Divi Augusti* Augustus names Tincommius of the Atrebates and Dubnovellaunus of the Kentish tribes among the kings who took refuge with him: *CIL* iii, pp. 769–799.

10 Allen 1971.

11 Strabo, iv.199.

12 Smith 1912.

13 Laver 1927.

14 Cogidubnus, see below, pp. 60 ff.

15 Tacitus, *Annals* vi.30.

16 P. Helvius Pertinax, see below, pp. 207 f.

Chapter 4

1 Suetonius, *Divus Claudius* xvii.

2 Suetonius, *C. Caligula* xlvi.

3 Tacitus, *Annals* xi.23–4; *ILS* 212; *ARS*, p. 145.

4 Dio, *Roman History* lx.19–23.

5 Above, p. 36, note 9.

6 Clifford 1961.

7 Bushe-Fox 1949; Cunliffe 1968.

8 Wheeler 1929.

9 Suetonius, *Divus Claudius* xvii.

10 *ILS* 216.

11 Suetonius, *Divus Vespasianus* iv.

12 Wheeler 1943.

13 On the possibility that the Ninth Legion was not established at Lincoln until the 50s, see now Frere and St Joseph 1974, pp. 38–9 and Frere 1978, pp. 86–7.

14 Hawkes and Hull 1947, p. 335; Webster 1958, pp. 75–8; and for the recent discovery of the Roman fortress which preceded the *colonia*, Crummy 1977.

15 Tacitus, *Agricola* xiv.

16 *RIB* 91. However, the traditional reading of the inscription has recently been disproved: Bogaers 1979. The title *legatus Augusti* apparently does not occur on the original inscription, although the title *rex* (king), possibly *magnus rex* (great king), does. On the basis of the earlier reading Dr Morris argued that Cogidubnus, as an imperial legate, had been co-opted into the Senate in AD 47/48, and may have been solely responsible for the administration of the whole province south of the Fosse Way, in the absence of the consular legate, who was engaged in subduing the tribes beyond this frontier; he would therefore have been one of the 'principal founding fathers of London'. In the light of the new reading, such references to Cogidubnus' special powers have been deleted.

17 Tacitus, *Annals* xii.31.

18 Cunliffe 1971a, 1971b.

19 *ILS* 6090, 6091.

20 *ILS* 6087; *ARS*, p. 97.

21 *ILS* 6090; *ARS*, p. 221.

22 Dio, *Roman History* lxii.2.

23 Frere 1972.

24 Nowadays perhaps in the region of £50,000 or £60,000.

25 e.g. Hardham, Alfoldean.

26 Nowadays simplified into counties, boroughs and districts.

27 *RIB* 707.

28 *RIB* 288.

29 *RIB* 311.

30 Tacitus, *Annals* xiv.33.

31 The diploma of M. Ulpius Novantico (*CIL* xvi, 160), a Coritanian auxiliary soldier, gives his *origo* as *Ratis*, not *Coritanus*, implying that Leicester had risen from the status of *civitas* to that of *munici-*

pium by AD 106. For the contrary view see Frere 1978, pp. 235–6.

32 *ILS* 6086.26–8.

33 Although *civitas Catuvellauni* appears in *RIB* 1962, and *natione Catuvellauna* in *RIB* 1065, showing that the title *civitas Catuvellaunorum* was still in use two or three centuries after the elevation of Verulamium to municipal status.

34 *RIB* 70.

35 *CIL* xvi, 163.

36 Tacitus, *Annals* xii.32.

37 See Hull 1958, pp. 259–70, and for the theatre also Dunnett 1971. The site was probably a sanctuary in pre-Roman times, Hawkes and Hull 1947, pp. 10–11

38 Hull 1958, pp. 162 ff.

39 Tacitus, *Annals* xiv.31.

Chapter 5

1 Here Dr Morris suggested a specific location for Aulus Plautius' camp. He observed that the London–Chichester road (Stane Street) took two unexplained kinks, about the junction of Borough High Street with Long Lane, and near the Elephant and Castle. As Roman roads must have a reason to deviate from a straight course and 'so far no natural cause, a softer or deeper patch of marsh or the like, has yet been detected', the kinks in the road may have been near two corners of the rampart of Aulus Plautius' encampment. The rampart would have been still standing when the road was built, and the road would have had to go around it. Thus the north-west short side of the camp (about 700 yards or 649 metres long) lay near and roughly parallel to Newington Causeway and Borough High Street, while the north-eastern long side (about 1000 yards or 914 metres long) lay somewhere about Manciple and Rothesay Streets, with the central gate of the camp's south-eastern short side near the Old Kent Road, close to the Bricklayers Arms railway goods yard. This would give an encampment of about 120 or 150 acres. The siting of this camp would also help to explain the alignment of the north road (Ermine Street) down the Kingsland Road on a point, not at the future Roman London bridge, but just west of the Tower, as a road from the middle gate of the long north-eastern side of the camp, at right-angles to it, would meet the south bank of the Thames opposite this point. A pontoon bridge would have connected the two.

Dr Morris' suggestion was based on the absence of any apparent reason for the kinks in the road. In fact it now seems that the curve in the road can be explained by the existence to its east of an extensive area of soft alluvium and peat, up to –19m O.D. in depth, centred on Rockingham Street (Berry 1979, pp. 21f.: I am grateful to Brian Yule of the SLAEC for the reference and information). Apart from explaining the kink in the road by natural causes rather than the need to avoid a standing rampart, this anomaly would be situated directly beneath the western corner of Dr Morris' proposed encampment, references to which have therefore been deleted.

2 On the course of this and other Roman roads, see Margary 1973.

3 Although recent evidence (Sheldon 1978, i, pp. 25 ff.) suggests that the roads leading up to the bridge on the south bank may not have been built before c. AD 50, and there seems to be only slight evidence of occupation in Southwark prior to this date.

4 Recent evidence supports the siting of Roman London bridge at Fish Street Hill: two roads excavated in Southwark, one a continuation of Stane Street, the other from the Westminster crossing, meet in Southwark very close to the south bank, opposite Fish Street Hill (Merrifield and Sheldon 1974; Sheldon 1978, p. 24); on the north side a stretch of road underlying Gracechurch Street was found in 1977 pointing to Fish Street Hill, or very slightly to the east of it (Marsden 1980, p. 28) and very recently timbers which might have belonged to the bridge itself have been discovered at the expected location: *Guardian*, 11 Nov 1981, p. 1.

5 Wheeler 1928, pp. 179-86; Pryce and Oswald 1928, pp. 73-110. However, Marsh (1979) has recently cast doubt on the provenance of some of the Arretine finds, and suggests that they may have been brought to London by dealers in recent times.

6 Hull 1958, p. 153; Hull 1929.

7 As suggested by Haverfield 1911, p. 169.

8 Recent excavation has confirmed a Claudian date for the Roman road beneath Fenchurch Street (Philp 1977).

9 *Charter of Urso* lxxiii: *ILS* 6087; *ARS*, p. 97.

10 A recently excavated ditch lying parallel to and outside the Roman wall at Duke's Place may represent a boundary, but it cannot be dated before the second century with any certainty, and lies well outside the boundaries that Dr Morris envisaged for his early settlement: Maloney 1979.

11 On these cemeteries, Wheeler 1928, pp. 29 ff; Wheeler 1930, pp. 41-3; Merrifield 1965, pp. 94 f. Some cremation burials of first-century date, possibly representing a cemetery, are also known from a site at the junction of Billiter Street with Fenchurch Street, but their date within the first century is not known: Marsden 1980, p. 24 (and see Map 7).

12 On the extent of the fire, Dunning 1945; Merrifield 1965, pp. 37 f., 89 ff. see now Marsden 1978, pp. 94-6, fig. 2; Marsden 1980, Chapter 3.

13 Since the time of writing and the death of Dr Morris, a great deal more has become known about the sequence of building in the forum area. A large area in the south-east corner was excavated in 1968-69, but the findings have only recently been published in full (Philp 1977), and in 1977, during the digging of

a tunnel along the length of Gracechurch Street, the forum and basilica levels were extensively recorded (*Current Archaeology* 5 (1977), pp. 370-1; Marsden 1978, pp. 96 ff.; Marsden 1980, pp. 99 ff.). On the basis of this new evidence the date, plan and function of the buildings have been reassessed (Marsden 1978).

It now seems that while Dr Morris' three phases of building in the forum area (based on Merrifield 1965, pp. 132-40), the second on a different alignment from the first and the third, are still valid, the buildings of the first, pre-Boudiccan, phase were timber buildings, laid out in the southeast corner of the forum area on the same alignment as the buildings of Phase 3. To their west was an area of gravel, possibly representing a market place. The buildings dated from *c.* AD 50 and were destroyed in the Boudiccan fire (Philp 1977; Marsden 1978). The monumentalized Phase 1 forum envisaged by Dr Morris, with a stone-built basilica *c.* 240 feet long underlying part of the great basilica of Phase 3 (see Wheeler 1928, p. 40 and Merrifield 1965, pp. 133 f.), does not seem to have existed: some of the walls thought to belong to it can now be seen to belong to the great basilica-forum complex of Phase 3 (Marsden 1978, fig. 5; 1980, plan on p. 101), although the double wall on the south side of the basilica (eastern half) has still not been adequately explained. I have therefore deleted references

to the possible size and extent of a pre-Boudiccan stone-built basilica-forum complex.

Dr Morris' Phase 2 comprised the buildings, including a temple, which underlay the great forum of Phase 3 (see Map 10, No. 5). He saw these as official forum buildings, the oblong east-west building (Merrifield 1965, no. 229) probably serving as a basilica, and this view has recently been advanced by Marsden (1978), who calls these buildings 'the first forum'. Dr Morris' Phase 3 buildings were those of the great basilica and forum completed in the Hadrianic period, which Marsden (1978) calls 'the second forum'.

14 The buildings of Phase 2 (the 'first forum') are now thought to date nearer AD 80 than 60, as a coin of AD 71 was found in a pit underlying the south wall of the 'basilica', and some pottery beneath a north-south street flanking, and probably contemporary with, the buildings, is dated *c.* 75-85 (Marsden 1980, p. 45).

15 The great basilica-forum complex (the 'second forum') was dated by Philp (1977) to *c.* 90/100, in the absence of any coins or pottery that need be dated later than 100. However, beneath a floor overlying the remains of the Phase 2 buildings and presumed to belong to this phase, some pottery dating to *c.* 125-150 was found, and a coin deposited during the construction of the great forum dates to 117-38 (Marsden 1978, p. 102; 1980, p. 103). It seems, therefore,

that the great forum was not completed until the Hadrianic period, although it was probably begun earlier.

16 Wheeler 1928, pp. 43 and 139; Wheeler 1930, p. 51.
17 Tacitus, *Annals* xiv.33.
18 Tacitus, *Annals* xiv.27.
19 Tacitus, *Annals* xiv.42-5.
20 Tacitus, *Annals* xiv.32.
21 Tacitus, *Annals* xiv.31-8.
22 Dio, *Roman History* lxii.1-12.
23 Oswald 1941.
24 On the skulls, Wheeler 1928, pp. 15-16.

Chapter 6

1 Tacitus, *Annals* xiv.38.
2 loc. cit.
3 *Aeneid* vi.8.53.
4 Tacitus, *Annals* xiv.39.
5 *RIB* 12; Brailsford 1964, p. 60, fig. 29, 5; Merrifield 1965, pls. 4-6.
6 Tacitus, *Annals* xv.48-71.
7 *ILS* 935.
8 Suetonius, *Nero* xlix.
9 Tacitus, *Agricola* xvi.
10 Statius, *Silvae* v.2.142.

Chapter 7

1 Into the provinces of *Britannia Inferior* (north) and *Superior* (south) shortly after AD 197 (Herodian iii.8.2).
2 Their careers are given in *ILS* 1011 and 1015.
3 Suetonius, *Nero* xviii.
4 Tacitus, *Agricola* xx.
5 *Minor Latin Poets*, ed. Duff and Duff (Loeb Classical Library), pp. 427 and 425.
6 Pliny, *Epistulae Morales* ix.5.
7 *ILS* 6870; *ARS*, p. 265.
8 Dio, *Roman History* lii.14.5.

9 Aelius Aristides, *To Rome*. See Oliver 1953 for translation and commentary.
10 *Scriptores Historiae Augustae*, *Pius* iv.8.
11 ibid., xii.6.
12 Tacitus, *Agricola* xix.
13 Tacitus, *Agricola* xxi.
14 Plutarch, *The Obsolescence of Oracles* 2 and 18.
15 Martial xi.3.
16 Martial xi.53.
17 Juvenal xii.46.
18 *JRS* 46 (1956), pp. 146-7, pl. xix.
19 *RIB* 288.
20 See chapter 5, p. 99 and note 15.

Chapter 8

1 Until the work undertaken in the 1960s and 1970s by Brian Philp and by the Department of Urban Archaeology: see chapter 5, note 13.
2 This number, and those used below, refers to sites numbered by Ralph Merrifield in *The Roman City of London* (1965).
3 The buildings are now thought to be a basilica-forum complex, considerably smaller and different in type to the great basilica-forum which succeeded it, but which can nevertheless be paralleled elsewhere: Marsden 1978; 1980, pp. 39-46. See chapter 5, notes 13-15, and Map 10, No. 5.
4 The major centres of production located close to London in this period were in the Brockley Hill, Highgate and Alice Holt/Farnham areas.
5 Tacitus, *Histories* i.2.
6 Frontinus, *de Aquis Urbis Romae*.
7 *ILS* 1032.

8 Grimes 1968, pp. 15-40.

9 *RIB* 19; Wheeler 1928, p. 173, no. 14, pl. 61.

10 Marsden 1975; 1980, pp. 88-93.

11 On the great forum, see Philp 1977; Marsden 1978; Marsden 1980, pp. 98-103. See also chapter 5, p. 99 and note 15.

12 Wheeler 1928, p. 155.

13 On the extent of the Hadrianic fire see Dunning 1945; Merrifield 1965, p. 91 f., fig. 10, based on a reassessment by Brian Hartley; and recently Marsden 1980, map on p. 106, reproduced in Map 11.

14 Wheeler and Laver 1919, pp. 141-4.

15 Wheeler and Wheeler 1936.

16 Frere 1949, p. 160. It is now known that they were not built before the later third century: Wacher 1974, p. 188.

17 On the Saxon Shore forts see Johnson 1976.

18 On the city wall, Grimes 1968, pp. 47-91. The existence of a defensive riverside wall has only recently been confirmed by the discovery of a length at Baynard's Castle, Upper Thames Street, dated by dendrochronology and carbon 14 to post AD 330. Another length at the Tower of London is dated on coin evidence to the 390s. See Hill, Millett and Blagg 1980 and Parnell 1977.

Chapter 9

1 Smith 1969.

2 See Marsden 1980, map on p. 118, showing the polychrome mosaics of possible third-century, or uncertain, date in London.

3 *ILS* 38; *ARS*, p. 74.

4 Cicero, II *Verrines* ii.32-34.

5 *Digest* xxxiii.7.12.43.

6 Pliny, *Epistulae Morales* viii.24.

7 *ILS* 5163, *ARS*, p. 216.

8 Tacitus, *Annals* xv.20-22.

9 *CIL* xiii.3162.

10 *Letter to Julius Africanus* 14: *PG* 11, cols 82-3.

11 *RIB* 21.

Chapter 10

1 *RIB* 2

2 Charter of Salpensa, AD 82-84: *ILS* 6088; *ARS*, p. 153. Charter of Malaga, AD 82-84: *ILS* 6089; *ARS*, p. 155.

3 Section 9, 11. 26-28: *ILS* 6086; *ARS*, p. 64.

4 See note 2.

5 *ILS* 6408.

6 *CIL* iv, 7273.

7 *ILS* 6411a.

8 *ILS* 6428b.

9 *CIL* iv, 4999.

10 *ILS* 6405.

11 *ILS* 6418d and f.

12 Ausonius, *Epicedion in patrem*.

13 *Acts* 19.23 ff.

14 *Digest* l.4.18.

15 *ILS* 6891; *ARS*, p. 163.

16 *Precepts of Statecraft*.

17 Cicero, *De Officiis* i.151.

18 Helen 1975.

19 *Digest* l.2.12.

20 *RIB* 202.

21 On Lullingstone, see Meates 1955.

22 *RIB* 91.

23 Suetonius, *Divus Vespasianus* xviii.

24 *ILS* 1514.

25 See Frank 1940, vol. 5, pp. 305-421 for text and translation; also *ARS*, p. 235.

26 On soldiers' pay, Watson 1969, pp.
   89 ff.

27 Frank 1940, pp. 5 note 5 and 71.

Chapter 11

1 e.g. Liversidge 1968, pp. 305-15;
   Stevens 1933, pp. 3-18.

2 Brailsford 1964, p. 48, fig. 22, 5

3 Wheeler 1930, p. 54-5; JRS 21
   (1931), p. 247. On this tablet and
   the four below, see now Chapman
   1974.

4 Wheeler 1930, pp. 54-5.

5 Wheeler 1930, pp. 54-5.

6 JRS 44 (1954), p. 108; Richmond
   1953.

7 Turner and Skutch 1960.

8 Wheeler 1928, p. 176, no. 58, fig.
   87, pl. 63.

9 Ausonius, Epicedion in Patrem.

10 Fink 1971, p. 442; Fink et al. 1940.

11 ILS 112.

12 ILS 154.

13 Dio Chrysostom, Oration xxiv,
   pp. 419-420 M.

14 Courteault 1921; L'Année Epi-
   graphique 1922, no. 116.

15 ILS 6245.

16 ILS 3546.

17 RIB 1041; ILS 3562.

18 ILS 6147.

19 ILS 6146.

20 Lucian, Alexander the False Pro-
   phet 30.

21 RIB 3; Wheeler 1928, pp. 43 and
   170, pl. 10; Wheeler 1930, p. 45, pl.
   xvii A.

22 For the jug, Wheeler 1928, p. 177,
   no. 104. New evidence for a temple
   of Isis in London has recently come
   to light in the form of a third-century altar recording the restoration
   of a temple of Isis after its collapse
   through old age by a previously
   unknown governor, M. Martian-
   nius Pulcher: Britannia 7 (1976), p.
   378, no. 2; Current Archaeology 5
   (1975-1976), p. 316; Hill, Millett
   and Blagg 1980, pp. 196-8, pl. 57.
   The altar had been re-used in the
   fourth-century riverside wall at
   Baynard's Castle, Upper Thames
   Street, and the temple would therefore have stood in the city rather
   than Southwark. Many other re-
   used stones of considerable interest were discovered at the same
   time, including blocks from a
   monumental arch and a monumental decorative screen of late
   second-, or, more probably, third-
   century date, perhaps deriving
   from a temple complex; an altar recording the rebuilding of a temple
   to Jupiter, and a votive relief of four
   'mother goddesses' (Hill, Millett
   and Blagg 1980). These finds point
   to extensive replanning and restoration in London in the third century,
   at least in the south-western area.

23 Grimes 1968, pp. 109-10, pl. 51.
   The sculpture was found lying on
   the final (fourth century) floor.

24 Grimes 1968, pp. 98-117.

25 Morris 1968.

26 See Mann 1961.

Chapter 12

1 Charter of Urso lxx-lxxi: ILS 6087;
   ARS, p. 97.

2 For the careers of Scirtus, Crescens, Diocles and Gutta, ILS 5283,
   5285, 5287 and 5288. 'Another
   driver', ILS 5284.

3 On circus factions see now
   Cameron 1976.

4 Single combat to the death between pairs of men was originally a funerary custom taken over by the Romans from the Etruscans, apparently first in 264 BC (Valerius Maximus ii.4.7). Its aim was presumably to provide an entourage for the deceased, and the 'winner' was the one who got killed. I am grateful to Professor Browning for this information.

5 *ILS* 5163; *ARS*, p. 216.

6 *ILS* 1396.

7 On the evidence for gladiators in Britain see Liversidge 1968 p. 373. More recently, finds have been made in Southwark of further fragments of a glass cup depicting gladiators (D. Harden in Sheldon 1978, pp. 605-7), and a lid in the shape of a gladiator's helmet (*Britannia* 11 (1980, p. 382).

8 *De Saltatione*, 83.

9 *ILS* 5233.

10 *ILS* 5053, 4.

11 *ILS* 5055.

12 Another bath building (Merrifield 1965, no. 353), at Billingsgate, Lower Thames Street, is now thought to be the small private bath-house of a large late-Roman building: see Marsden 1980, pp. 151-5 and 180-6. On the Huggin Hill and Cheapside baths, Marsden 1976.

13 Seneca, *Epistulae Morales* lvi.

14 *ILS* 5147, 5173.

15 Hawkes 1940, pp. 497-9, pl. 91.

Chapter 13

1 Cocks 1921.

2 Cicero, *Letters to Atticus* v.21,10-13; vi.1.3-7; vi.2.7-9.

3 Dio, *Roman History* lxxii.2; above, p. 66.

4 Blackfriars boat: Marsden 1967a; County Hall boat: Marsden 1967b; Bermondsey boat: Marsden 1967c. See also Marsden 1980, pp. 127-130, 157-60, and Merrifield 1969, pp. 33-40.

5 Museum of London Site No. 326.

6 Leontios of Neapolis, *Life of St John the Almsgiver* in *Analecta Bollandiana* 45 (1927), pp. 5-74. See Jones 1964, p. 869.

7 Solinus xxii.1.

8 *CIL* xiii, 634.

9 Chapter 11, p. 228.

10 *RIB* 1320.

11 See another inscription from Newcastle: *RIB* 1322.

12 For examples of these tools, and other items found in London and mentioned below, see Wheeler 1930.

13 Merrifield 1965, no. 288.

14 London: Simpson 1952: but it now seems that the potter may have worked in Sussex rather than London: Webster 1975. Colchester: Hull 1963.

Chapter 14

1 Dio, *Roman History* lxxiii.9.

2 On the question of a possible decline in the occupation of London from the later second to the mid third century, see Sheldon 1975 and ibid., p. 344, and Morris 1975.

3 *Panegyrici Latini* viii (v), *Constantio Caesari* 21.2.

4 *Panegyrici Latini* viii (v), *Constantio Caesari*.

5 *Panegyrici Latini* viii (v).11.1.

6 Wheeler 1928, p. 33 and 188, pl. 67; Merrifield 1965, pl. 13.

7 Maeyer 1940.

8 On corn supplies from Britain: Libanius, *Oratio* xviii.82-83; Ammian xviii.23; Zosimus iii.5. I am unable to trace the reference to Aquitania.

9 *Panegyrici Latini.*

10 On the villa in Roman Britain, Rivet 1964 and 1969, and recently Burke 1978.

11 See Morris 1973, pp. 13-14 on the Arian controversy.

12 Ammian xiv.5.

Chapter 15

1 Ammian xxvii.8.1.

2 Morris 1973, pp. 16 and 157.

3 Ammian xxvii.8.7, xxviii.3.1-2.

4 But see now Reece 1972, for a comparison of coin lists from 14 sites in Britain.

5 Merrifield 1962.

6 But see now Keay 1977.

7 *Notitia Dignitatum Occ.* xi.60.

8 Phillips 1951, p. 269; Phillips 1970, pp. 14 and 231.

9 Gildas 20.1.

10 *Epistulae* i.3.

11 Rufinus, *Historia Ecclesiastica* ii.13. *PL* 21, cols 522-3.

12 Jerome, *Commentary on Ezekial*, prologue and preface to Book 3.

13 Sicilian Briton, *Epistulae* i.1. *PL* Suppl. 1, cols 1687 ff. See Morris 1973, esp. pp. 23 and 340.

14 On the historical and archaeological evidence for events in Britain after 410 see Morris 1973, esp. chapter 3.

15 On Pelagius and the Pelagian tradition in Britain, Myres 1960; on Augustine and Pelagius, Brown 1967, chapters 29-31; see also Morris 1973, esp. pp. 79 f., 308 f.

Chapter 16

1 Dr Morris has covered this period in much greater detail in his book *The Age of Arthur* (London, 1973), to be used in conjunction with the 'Arthurian Period Sources' series. (Phillimore, general editor John Morris). The following books in the series have been published:
Vol. 7. M. Winterbottom, *Gildas. The ruin of Britain and other works* (London, 1978)
Vol. 8. J. Morris, *Nennius. British History and the Welsh Annals* (London, 1980)
Vol. 9. A.B.E. Hood, *St Patrick. His writings and Muirchu's life* (London, 1978)
See also Morris 1965, where he sets out the basis for his dating of the events described in this chapter.

2 Wheeler 1930, p. 25. Marsden 1980, chapter 9, note 24, points out that the stamps may refer to another Syagrius, perhaps of the fourth century.

3 On the Lower Thames Street (Billingsgate) house, see now Marsden 1980, esp. pp. 151-5 and 180-6. The amphora is now known to date to the 4th/early 5th century: Marsden 1980, p. 180 n. 28.

4 Winterbottom 1978.

5 Morris 1980.

6 See note 1.

7 Nash-Williams 1950, p. 92, no. 103.

8 The Cambrian Annals 516 and 537: Morris 1980, p. 45.

Bibliography

ALLEN 1944, D.F. Allen, 'The Belgic Dynasties of Britain and their Coins', *Archaeologia* 90 (1944), pp. 1–46.

ALLEN 1961, D.F. Allen 'The Origins of Coinage in Britain: A Reappraisal', in *Problems of the Iron Age in Southern Britain*, ed. S.S. Frere (London, 1961), pp. 97–308.

ALLEN 1962, D.F. Allen, 'Celtic Coins', in the Ordnance Survey *Map of Roman Britain in the Iron Age* (Chessington, 1962), pp. 19–32.

ALLEN 1971, D.F. Allen, 'British Potin Coins: A Review', in *The Iron Age and its Hillforts*, Papers presented to Sir Mortimer Wheeler, ed. M. Jesson and D. Hill (Southampton, 1971), pp. 127–54.

BERRY 1979, F.G. Berry, 'Late Quaternary Scour-Hollows and Related Features in Central London', *Quarterly Journal of Engineering Geology* 12 (1979), pp. 9–29.

BOGAERS 1979, J.E. Bogaers, 'King Cogidubnus in Chichester: Another Reading of *RIB* 91', *Britannia* 10 (1979), pp. 243–54.

BRAILSFORD 1964, J.W. Brailsford, *Guide to the Antiquities of Roman Britain*, British Museum Publications, 3rd ed. (London, 1964).

BROWN 1967, P. Brown, *Augustine of Hippo* (London, 1967).

BURKE 1978, J. Burke, *Life in the Villa in Roman Britain* (London, 1978).

BUSHE-FOX 1949, J.P. Bushe-Fox, *Fourth Report on the Excavations of the Roman Fort at Richborough, Kent*, Reports of the Research Committee of the Society of Antiquaries of London No. 16 (Oxford, 1949).

CAMERON 1976, A. Cameron, *Circus Factions: Blues and Greens at Rome and Byzantium* (Oxford, 1976).

CHAPMAN 1974, H. Chapman, 'Letters from Roman London', *London Archaeologist* 2 (1972–76), pp. 173–6.

CLIFFORD 1961, E.M. Clifford, *Bagendon: A Belgic Oppidum* (Cambridge, 1961).

COCKS 1921, A.H. Cocks, 'A Romano-British Homestead in the Hambledon Valley, Bucks.', *Archaeologia* 71 (1921), pp. 141–98.

COURTEAULT 1921, P. Courteault, 'An Inscription recently found at Bordeaux', *JRS* 11 (1921), pp. 101–7.

CRUMMY 1977, P. Crummy, 'Colchester: The Roman Fortress and the Development of the Colonia', *Britannia* 8 (1977), pp. 65–105.

CUNLIFFE 1968, B. Cunliffe, *Fifth Report on the Excavations of the Roman Fort at Richborough, Kent*, Reports of the Research Committee of the Society of Antiquaries of London No. 23 (Oxford, 1968).

CUNLIFFE 1971a, B. Cunliffe, *Excavations at Fishbourne 1961-1969*, Reports of the Research Committee of the Society of Antiquaries of London No. 26 (Leeds, 1971).

CUNLIFFE 1971b, B. Cunliffe, *Fishbourne. A Roman Palace and its Gardens* (Fakenham, 1971).

CUNLIFFE 1978, B. Cunliffe, *Iron Age Communities in Britain*, 2nd ed. (London, 1978).

DAVISON *et al.* 1976, B.K. Davison *et al.*, *The Archaeology of the London Area: Current Knowledge and Problems*, LAMAS Special Paper No. 1 (1976).

DUNNETT 1971, R. Dunnett, 'The Excavation of the Roman Theatre at Gosbecks', *Britannia* 2 (1971), pp. 27-47.

DUNNING 1945, G.C. Dunning, 'Two Fires of Roman London', *Antiquaries Journal* 25 (1945), pp. 48-77.

DUNNING AND JESSUP 1936, G.C. Dunning and R.F. Jessup, 'Roman Barrows', *Antiquity* 10 (1936), pp. 37-53.

FINK 1971, R.O. Fink, *Roman Military Records on Papyrus*, Philological Monographs of the American Philological Association No. 26 (1971).

FINK *et al.* 1940, R.O. Fink, A.S. Hoey and W.F. Snyder, 'The *Feriale Duranum*', *Yale Classical Studies* 7 (1940), pp. 1-222.

FRANK 1940, T. Frank (ed.), *An Economic Survey of Ancient Rome* Vol. 5: *Rome and Italy of the Empire* (Baltimore, 1940).

FRERE 1949, S.S. Frere, 'Canterbury Excavations, 1944-48', *Antiquity* 23 (1949), pp. 153-60.

FRERE 1972, S.S. Frere, *Verulamium Excavations* Vol. I, Reports of the Research Committee of the Society of Antiquaries of London No. 28 (Oxford, 1972).

FRERE 1978, S.S. Frere, *Britannia*, 2nd ed. (London, 1978).

FRERE AND ST JOSEPH 1974, S.S. Frere and J.K. St Joseph, 'The Roman Fortress at Longthorpe', *Britannia* 4 (1974), pp. 1-129.

GRANT 1974, M. Grant, *Ancient History Atlas. 1700 BC to AD 565*, revised ed. (London, 1974).

GRIMES 1968, W.F. Grimes, *The Excavation of Roman and Medieval London* (London, 1968).

GRIMES *et al.* 1976, W.F. Grimes *et al.*, *Time on Our Side? A Survey of the Archaeological Needs of Greater London*, Report of a joint working party of the Department of the Environment, the Greater London Council and the Museum of London (London, 1976).

HASELGROVE 1978, C. Haselgrove, *Supplementary Gazetteer of Find-Spots of Celtic Coins in Britain*, 1977, Institute of Archaeology Occasional Paper No. 11a (London, 1978).

HAVERFIELD 1911, F. Haverfield, 'Roman London', *JRS* 1 (1911), pp. 141-72.

HAWKES 1940, C.F.C. Hawkes, 'A Sporting or Mythological Relief-Mould from Roman Britain', *Antiquaries Journal* 20 (1940), pp. 497-9.

HAWKES AND HULL 1947, C.F.C. Hawkes and M.R. Hull, *Camulodunum. First*

Report on the Excavations at Colchester 1930-1939, Reports of the Research Committee of the Society of Antiquaries of London No. 14 (Oxford, 1947).

HELEN 1975, T. Helen, *The Organisation of Roman Brick Production in the First and Second Centuries AD: An Interpretation of the Roman Brick-Stamps* (Helsinki, 1975).

HILL, MILLETT AND BLAGG 1980, C. Hill, M. Millett and T. Blagg, *The Roman Riverside Wall and Monumental Arch in London*, LAMAS Special Paper No. 3 (1980).

HOOD 1978, A.B.E. Hood, *St Patrick. His writings and Muirchu's Life*, Arthurian Period Sources Vol. 9 (London, 1978).

HULL 1929, M.R. Hull, 'A Roman Pottery Shop in Colchester', *Trans. Essex Archaeological Society* 19 (1929), pp. 277-87.

HULL 1958, M.R. Hull, *Roman Colchester*, Reports of the Research Committee of the Society of Antiquaries of London No. 20 (Oxford, 1958).

HULL 1963, M.R. Hull, *The Roman Potter's Kilns of Colchester*, Reports of the Research Committee of the Society of Antiquaries of London No. 21 (Oxford, 1963).

JOHNSON 1976, S. Johnson, *The Roman Forts of the Saxon Shore* (London, 1976).

JONES 1964, A.H.M. Jones, *The Later Roman Empire, 284-602* (Oxford, 1964).

KEAY 1977, S. J. Keay, 'The Coins of Verulamium: A Quantitative Study', unpublished B.A. dissertation, Institute of Archaeology, University of London, 1977.

LAVER 1927, P.G. Laver, 'The Excavation of a Tumulus at Lexden, Colchester', *Archaeologia* 76 (1927), pp. 241-54.

LIVERSIDGE 1968, J. Liversidge, *Britain in the Roman Empire* (London, 1968).

MAEYER 1940, R. de Maeyer, *De Overblijfselen de Romeinsche Villa's in België* (Antwerp, 1940).

MALONEY 1979, J. Maloney, 'Excavations at Dukes Place: The Roman Defences', *London Archaeologist* 3 (1976-80), pp. 292-7.

MANN 1961, J.C. Mann, 'The Administration of Roman Britain', *Antiquity* 35 (1961), pp. 316-20.

MARGARY 1973, I.D. Margary, *Roman Roads in Britain*, 3rd ed. (London, 1973).

MARSDEN 1967a, P. Marsden, *A Roman Ship from Blackfriars*, Guildhall Museum Publications (1967).

MARSDEN 1967b, P. Marsden, 'The County Hall Ship', *Trans. LAMAS* 21 (1967), pp. 109-17.

MARSDEN 1967c, P. Marsden, 'A Boat of the Roman Period discovered on the Site of New Guy's House, Bermondsey, 1958', *Trans. LAMAS* 21 (1967), pp. 118-31.

MARSDEN 1975, P. Marsden, 'Excavation of a Roman Palace Site in London, 1961-1972', *Trans. LAMAS* 26 (1975), pp. 1-102.

MARSDEN 1976, P. Marsden, 'Two Roman Public Baths in London', *Trans. LAMAS* 27 (1976), pp. 1-70.

MARSDEN 1978, P. Marsden, 'The Discovery of the Civic Centre of Roman London', in *Collectanea Londiniensia*, Studies in London archaeology and history presented to Ralph Merrifield, LAMAS Special Paper No. 2, ed. J. Bird, H. Chapman and J. Clark (1978).

MARSDEN 1980, P. Marsden, *Roman London* (London, 1980).

MARSDEN, DYSON AND RHODES 1975, P. Marsden, T. Dyson and M. Rhodes, 'Excavations on the Site of St Mildred's Church, Bread Street, London 1973-74', *Trans. LAMAS* 26 (1975), pp. 171-208.

MARSH 1979, G. Marsh, 'Nineteenth and Twentieth Century Antiquities Dealers and Arretine Ware from London', *Trans. LAMAS* 30 (1979), pp. 125-9.

MEATES 1955, G.W. Meates, *Lullingstone Roman Villa* (London, 1955).

MERRIFIELD 1962, R. Merrifield, 'Coins from the Bed of the Walbrook, and their Significance', *Antiquaries Journal* 42 (1962), pp. 38-52.

MERRIFIELD 1965, R. Merrifield, *The Roman City of London* (London, 1965).

MERRIFIELD 1969, R. Merrifield, *Roman London* (London, 1969).

MERRIFIELD AND SHELDON 1974, R. Merrifield and H. Sheldon, 'Roman London Bridge: A View from Both Banks', *London Archaeologist* 2 (1972-76), pp. 183-91.

MORRIS 1965, J. Morris, 'Dark Age Dates' in *Britain and Rome*, Essays presented to Eric Birley on his sixtieth birthday, ed. M.G. Jarrett and B. Dobson (Kendal, 1965).

MORRIS 1968, J. Morris, 'The Date of St Alban', *Hertfordshire Archaeology* 1 (1968), pp. 1-8.

MORRIS 1973, J. Morris, *The Age of Arthur* (London, 1973).

MORRIS 1975, J. Morris, 'London's Decline AD 150-250', *London Archaeologist* 2 (1972-76), pp. 343-4.

MORRIS 1980, J. Morris, *Nennius. British History and the Welsh Annals*, Arthurian Period Sources Vol. 8 (London, 1980).

MYRES 1960, J.N.L. Myres, 'Pelagius and the End of Roman Rule in Britain', *JRS* 50 (1960), pp. 21-36.

NASH-WILLIAMS 1950, V.E. Nash-Williams, *The Early Christian Monuments of Wales* (Cardiff, 1950).

OLIVER 1953, J. H. Oliver, 'The Ruling Power. A Study of the Roman Empire in the Second Century after Christ through the Roman Oration of Aelius Aristides', *Trans. American Philosophical Society* 43 (1953), part 4.

OSWALD 1941, F. Oswald, 'Margidunum', *JRS* 31 (1941), pp. 32-62.

PARNELL 1977, G. Parnell, 'Excavations at the Tower of London 1976-77', *London Archaeologist* 3 (1976-80), pp. 97-9.

PHILLIPS 1951, C.W. Phillips, 'The Fenland Research Committee, its Past Achievements and Future Prospects', in *Aspects of Archaeology in Britain and Beyond*, Essays presented to O.G.S. Crawford, ed. W.F. Grimes (London, 1951), pp. 258–73.

PHILLIPS 1970, C.W. Phillips, *The Fenland in Roman Times* (London, 1970).

PHILP 1977, B.J. Philp, 'The Forum of Roman London: Excavations of 1968–69', *Britannia* 8 (1977), pp. 1–64.

PRYCE AND OSWALD 1928, T. Davies Pryce and F. Oswald, 'Roman London: Its Initial Occupation as Evidenced by Early Types of Terra-Sigillata', *Archaeologia* 78 (1928), pp. 73–110.

REECE 1972, R. Reece, 'A Short Survey of the Roman Coins Found on Fourteen Sites in Britain', *Britannia* 3 (1972), pp. 269–76.

RICHMOND 1953, I.A. Richmond, 'Three Roman Writing-Tablets from London', *Antiquaries Journal* 33 (1953), pp. 206–8.

RIVET 1964, A.L.F. Rivet, *Town and Country in Roman Britain*, 2nd ed. (London, 1964).

RIVET 1969, A.L.F. Rivet (ed.), *The Roman Villa in Britain* (London, 1969).

ROSKAMS 1978, S. Roskams, 'The Milk Street Excavations' and 'The Milk Street Excavation: Part 2', *London Archaeologist* 3 (1976–80), pp. 199–205, 227–34.

SHELDON 1975, H. Sheldon, 'A Decline in the London Settlement AD 150–250', *London Archaeologist* 2 (1972–76), pp. 278–84.

SHELDON 1978, SLAEC, *Southwark Excavations 1972–74*, Joint Publication No. 1, LAMAS and Surrey Archaeological Society (1978).

SHELDON AND SCHAAF 1978, H. Sheldon and L. Schaaf, 'A Survey of Roman Sites in Greater London', in *Collectanea Londiniensia*, Studies in London archaeology and history presented to Ralph Merrifield, LAMAS Special Paper No. 2, ed. J. Bird, H. Chapman and J. Clark (1978), pp. 59–88.

SIMPSON 1952, Grace Simpson, 'The Aldgate Potter: A Maker of Romano-British Samian Ware', *JRS* 52 (1952), pp. 68–71.

SMITH 1969, D.J. Smith, 'The Mosaic Pavements', in *The Roman Villa in Britain*, ed. A.L.F. Rivet (London, 1969), pp. 71–125.

SMITH 1912, R.A. Smith, 'On Late-Celtic Antiquities discovered at Welwyn, Herts.', *Archaeologia* 63 (1912), pp. 1–30.

STEVENS 1933, C.E. Stevens, *Sidonius Apollinaris and His Age* (Oxford, 1933).

TURNER AND SKUTCH 1960, E. Turner and O. Skutch, 'A Roman Writing-Tablet from London', *JRS* 50 (1960), pp. 108–111.

WACHER 1974, J.S. Wacher, *The Towns of Roman Britain* (London, 1974).

WATSON 1969, G.R. Watson, *The Roman Soldier* (Bristol, 1969).

WEBSTER 1958, G. Webster, 'The Roman Military Advance under Ostorius Scapula', *Archaeological Journal* 115 (1958), pp. 49–98.

WEBSTER 1975, P.V. Webster, 'More British Samian Ware by the Aldgate-Pulborough Potter', *Britannia* 6 (1975), pp. 163–70.

WHEELER 1928, R.E.M. Wheeler, RCHM (England): An Inventory of the Historical Monuments in London. Vol. III. *Roman London* (HMSO, 1928).

WHEELER 1929, R.E.M. Wheeler, ' "Old England", Brentford', *Antiquity* 3 (1929), pp. 20–32.

WHEELER 1930, R.E.M. Wheeler, *London in Roman Times*, London Museum Catalogues No. 3 (1930).

WHEELER 1943, R.E.M. Wheeler, *Maiden Castle, Dorset*, Reports of the Research Committee of the Society of Antiquaries of London No. 12 (Oxford, 1943).

WHEELER AND LAVER 1919, R.E.M. Wheeler and P. Laver, 'Roman Colchester', *JRS* 9 (1919), pp. 139–69.

WHEELER AND WHEELER 1936, R.E.M. and T.V. Wheeler, *Verulamium. A Belgic and Two Roman Cities*, Reports of the Research Committee of the Society of Antiquaries of London No. 11 (Oxford, 1936).

WINTERBOTTOM 1978, M. Winterbottom, *Gildas. The Ruin of Britain and Other Works*, Arthurian Period Sources Vol. 7 (London, 1978).

Index